Grace Joel

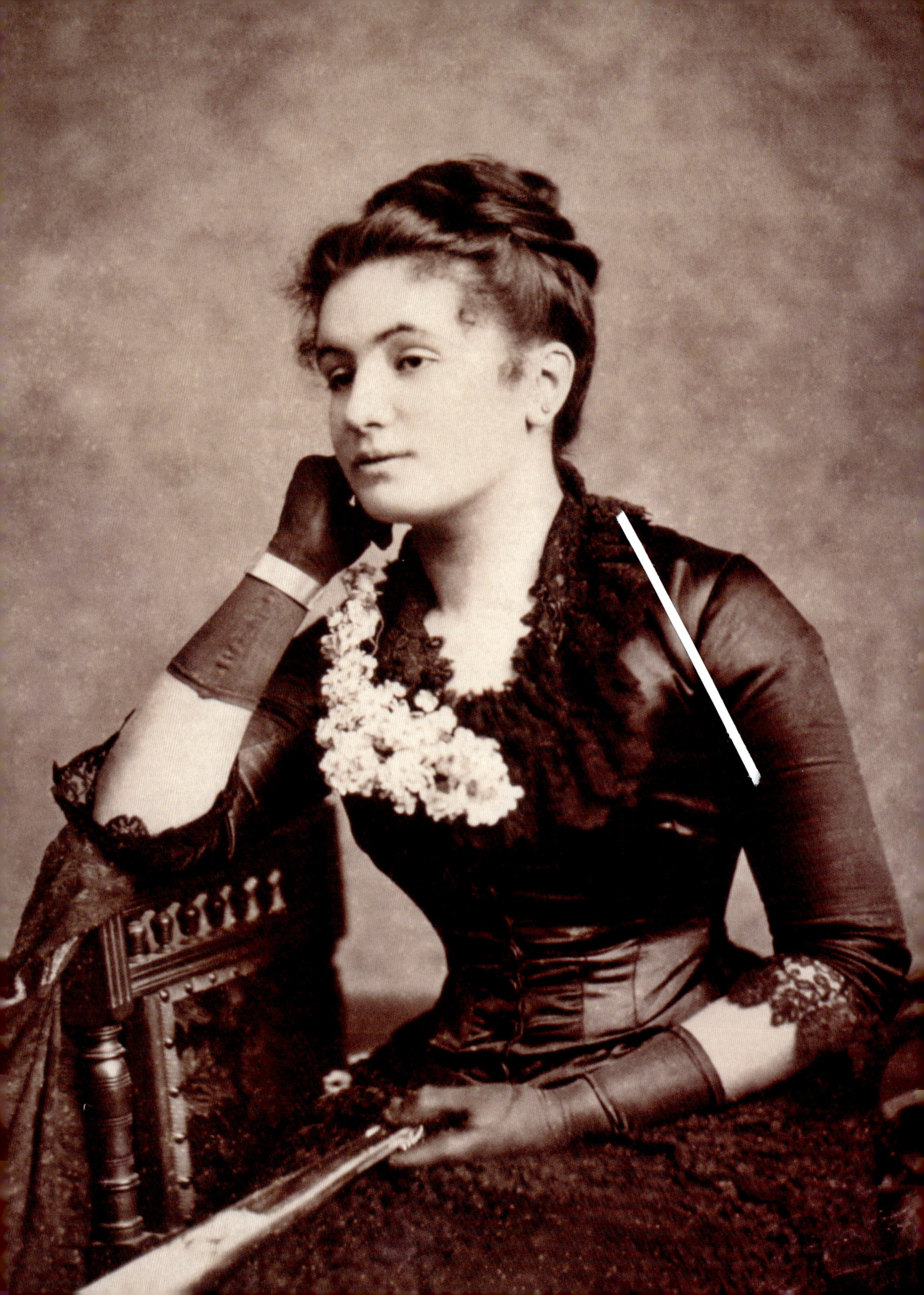

Grace Joel

An Impressionist Portrait

Joel L. Schiff

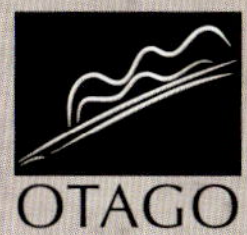

Published by Otago University Press
Level 1, 398 Cumberland Street
Dunedin, New Zealand
university.press@otago.ac.nz
www.otago.ac.nz/press

First published 2014

ISBN 978-1-877578-86-1

A catalogue record for this book is available from the National Library of New Zealand.

Publisher: Rachel Scott
Editor: Paula Wagemaker
Design/layout: Fiona Moffat
Index: Diane Lowther

Printed in China through Asia Pacific Offset Ltd

Front cover: *Nude with Fruit*, by Grace Joel, *c.* 1920, oil on canvas, 102 x 75 cm.
International Art Centre, Auckland.
Frontispiece: Photograph of the young Grace Joel, c. 1883.

Contents

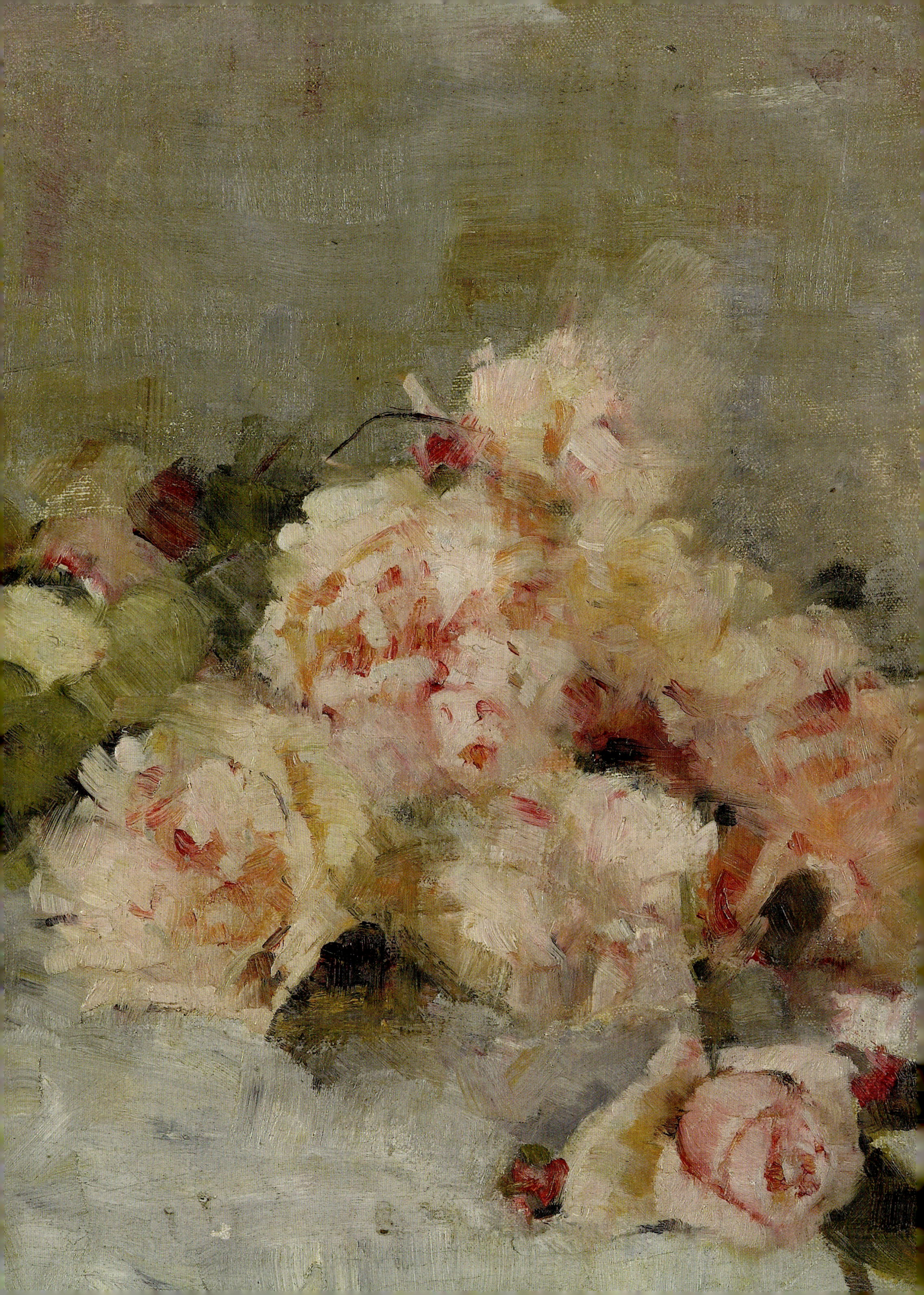

Preface

All art is a revolt against man's fate – André Malraux

One afternoon in 1981 I wandered into the Auckland City Art Gallery and came across an exhibition by an artist I had never heard of named Grace Joel. We coincidently happened to share a name, but it was her artwork that resonated. Here was an artist painting in an impressionistic manner, yet a manner of her own making. Her style seemed to vary according to subject matter: it could be very formal, as in a portrait of her mother, or joyously impressionistic, as with *A Rose 'midst Poppies*. The latter is one of those paintings that lodges itself in a corner of your mind just as *Soap Bubbles*, a painting by eighteenth-century artist Jean-Baptiste-Simeon Chardin, does.

Some time after the exhibition, wanting to find out more about Grace Joel, I visited Auckland University's Fine Arts Library. However, all I could find was the catalogue for the exhibition and a few other sources that mentioned her and various other artists. Yet, although scant, the information about her life in these sources intrigued me. She grew up in Dunedin, studied art in Melbourne for five years and went on to spend most of her artistic career in London, exhibiting both there and in Paris.

Despite learning so little about the artist, I created a folder with her name on it and placed the few items of information in it. Over the years, so the folder remained, occasionally picking up a new item or two, mostly through happenstance. I had a career as a mathematician, and it took precedence. Four decades later, in 2010, having at last put mathematics aside, I decided to pursue this largely unknown painter, Grace Joel, in earnest. Her talent was manifest but the recognition due her was not; not in the country of her birth, not in Australia, not in England.

This effort opened up a whole new world of Grace Joel relatives, some living in New Zealand, others in England and Australia. It also led to the fortuitous discovery of two Dunedin scholars, Roger Collins and Peter Entwisle, both with considerable knowledge about the woman of my quest.

As the life of this mysterious artist began to reveal itself, it did so in a fascinating way. Weaving their way through the fabric of the narrative were writers Mark Twain and Robert Louis Stevenson, artist Girolamo Pieri Ballati Nerli (the son of an Italian nobleman) and the brilliant but dissolute artistic associate of Oscar Wilde and Toulouse-Lautrec named Charles Conder, who died of syphilis at the age of 40.

There, too, was Sir Julius Vogel, a New Zealand premier and possible Grace Joel relative, along with one of New Zealand's most celebrated writers, Katherine Mansfield, the English suffragette, Sylvia Pankhurst, and a cast of stellar artists. The latter include Royal Academicians George Frederick Watts, Augustus John and George Clausen, the French giant of the nineteenth-century realism movement, William-Adolphe Bouguereau, the rebellious American-born, British-based James Abbott McNeill Whistler and the Dutch master, Jozef Israëls. Also making an appearance was a coterie of outstanding Australian artists, one of whom, and one of the best of whom, turned out to be Grace Joel's second cousin. And, tantalisingly, the name of Auguste Renoir.

My journey through Grace Joel's life has been a captivating one, taking me down unexpected alleys of inquiry. What made the journey particularly interesting for me, and hopefully will do likewise for the reader, is its traversal of the period known as La Belle Époque, which witnessed one of history's greatest outpourings of artistic endeavour. This was the period when Grace was at her most prodigious. Indeed, she often spent a *Midnight in Paris*, and it has been a very great pleasure to join her there.

Joel Schiff
AUCKLAND, 2014

Prelude

The mediator of the inexpressible is the work of art – Goethe

Letter from the Société des Artistes Français, Paris:[1]

> *15 February 1924*
>
> *Dear Miss Joel*
>
> *I received your kind letter and photograph of the picture you will send to the Salon. I have no doubt it will be as good as the one you sent last year with the same qualities of fine painting and I certainly hope you receive the fine reward you received from the last Salon.*
>
> *I much regret what you tell me about your health. Take good care of yourself so that you may recover quickly and devote yourself to your art, the only goal to which any artist can aspire to in this low base world and its only consolation. I'm surprised you didn't receive my New Year greetings – the post is entirely to blame. I renew them with my best wishes for your health.*
>
> *Yours affectionately*

Unfortunately, Monsieur's wish did not come true; Grace Joel died in London less than a month later on 6 March 1924, at the age of 58. However, the submitted painting, *La Première Séance*, was exhibited in May at the Paris Salon's annual artistic presentation to the world.

A few years earlier, in 1920, Grace Joel had bequeathed her portrait of New Zealand Prime Minister Richard John Seddon ('King Dick') to New Zealand's High Commissioner in London. She stipulated that the portrait should be hung in the city's New Zealand House.

> *PORTRAIT FOR HIGH COMMISSIONER'S OFFICE*
>
> *LONDON, November 5*
>
> *The late Miss Grace J. Joel, a well-known New Zealand artist, who spent many years in England and on the Continent, is a prolific painter, and she has left a great number of pictures. Among these is a picture of the late Richard J. Seddon. A clause of Miss Joel's will reads:*
>
> *'I give to the Dominion of New Zealand representative in London the portrait of the late Right Hon. Richard Seddon, to be hung in New Zealand House, in London.'*
>
> *Mrs Blanche Levi, sister of the late Miss Joel and an executor of her will, recently communicated with Sir James Allen and handed the painting over. This has been revarnished and suitably framed, and it now finds a place above the staircase in the High Commissioner's offices.*
>
> *The portrait is a life-size head and shoulders presentation, the sitter showing full face with the eyes looking sideways. More than one person who is in a position to judge, has expressed the opinion that it is a very true likeness. In addition, it is a good work of art, and is an acquisition to New Zealand House.*[2]

Seddon was Prime Minister of New Zealand from 1893 until his sudden death in 1906. Although he championed the 'common man', the same cannot be said of his attitude towards the 'common woman' – he vehemently opposed a bill on women's suffrage submitted to the House of Representatives by his own Liberal Party, for example. But despite his meddling opposition, the bill passed in 1893, making New Zealand the first self-governing nation in the world to give women the vote in a general election.[3]

Grace Joel's formal life-size portrait of Seddon (shown opposite) captures his enormous bulk and determination as a politician. He is turned away from the artist as if contemplating serious affairs of state. The background is insignificant: the man himself is the sole object of our attention. In his foreword to the catalogue notes for the 1968 Auckland Festival Exhibition, 'New Zealand Women Painters 1845–1969', John Stacpoole wrote this of the works on show: 'It is as representative as any other arbitrary selection would be, less concerned, perhaps, with the grandeurs than with the calmer aspects of life: people, children, even as with the Grace Joel Seddon portrait – with the quiddities of men.'

So who was this woman who painted portraits of prime ministers and who, according to Dunedin art scholar, Peter Entwisle, was the finest New Zealand portrait painter of the 1890s?[4] The limited information about her makes it difficult to answer this question. For example, unlike Grace Joel's Dunedin contemporary, Frances Hodgkins, who was a prolific letter writer with nearly 1000 letters surviving, only three letters from Grace's hand remain, and they are strictly business in nature. And whereas that other Kiwi expatriate of the time, Katherine Mansfield, had Middleton Murray to thrust her work into the public spotlight, Grace Joel had no such person. Moreover, because she never married, there is little in the way of family-based archival material, and because she trained as an artist in Australia and worked in Europe from the dawn of the twentieth century, many possible details about her during that time are difficult to source or lost to time.

What we must manage with then is information gleaned from what she herself left us – her art, the people in her artistic circle and the rapt attention of the Australasian media. We will never know her innermost thoughts on most matters, but we can still gain insight into the life of this gifted artist.

The portrait of Grace Joel that I paint here is therefore an impressionistic one. Some parts of the image are as sketchy as a Matisse; other parts have more detail, as in a Manet. But there are no regions as finely painted as a Bouguereau. Nevertheless, I trust that this portrait is well worth the price of admission.

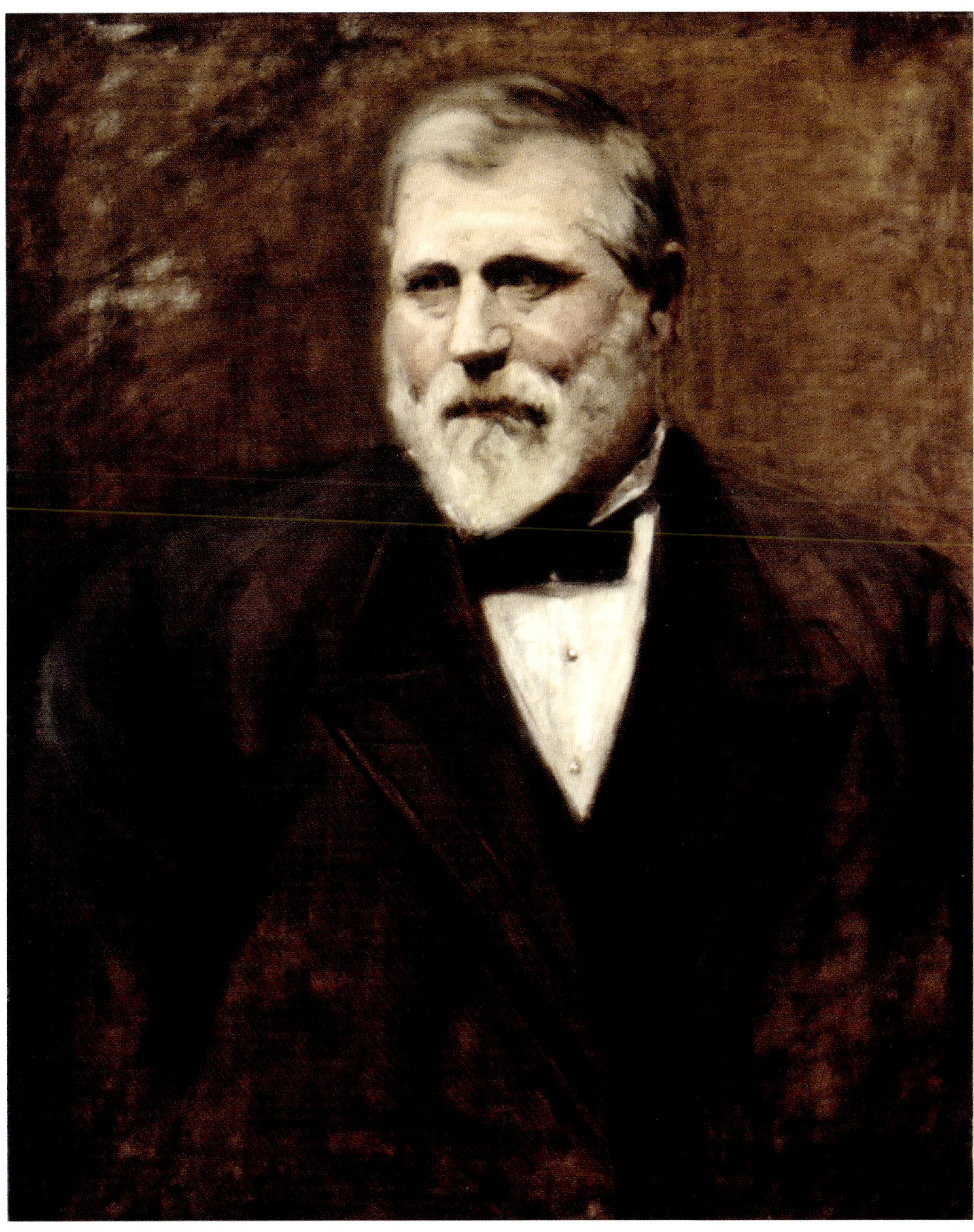

Richard John Seddon, a posthumous portrait by Grace Joel, oil on canvas, 92.5 x 71.8 cm, executed in 1906 when Grace was on a return visit to Dunedin, New Zealand, from London. Grace's niece's husband brought the painting back from London to New Zealand in 1967, where it was exhibited at the Auckland Festival Exhibition the following year. Ref: G-632, Alexander Turnbull Library, Wellington

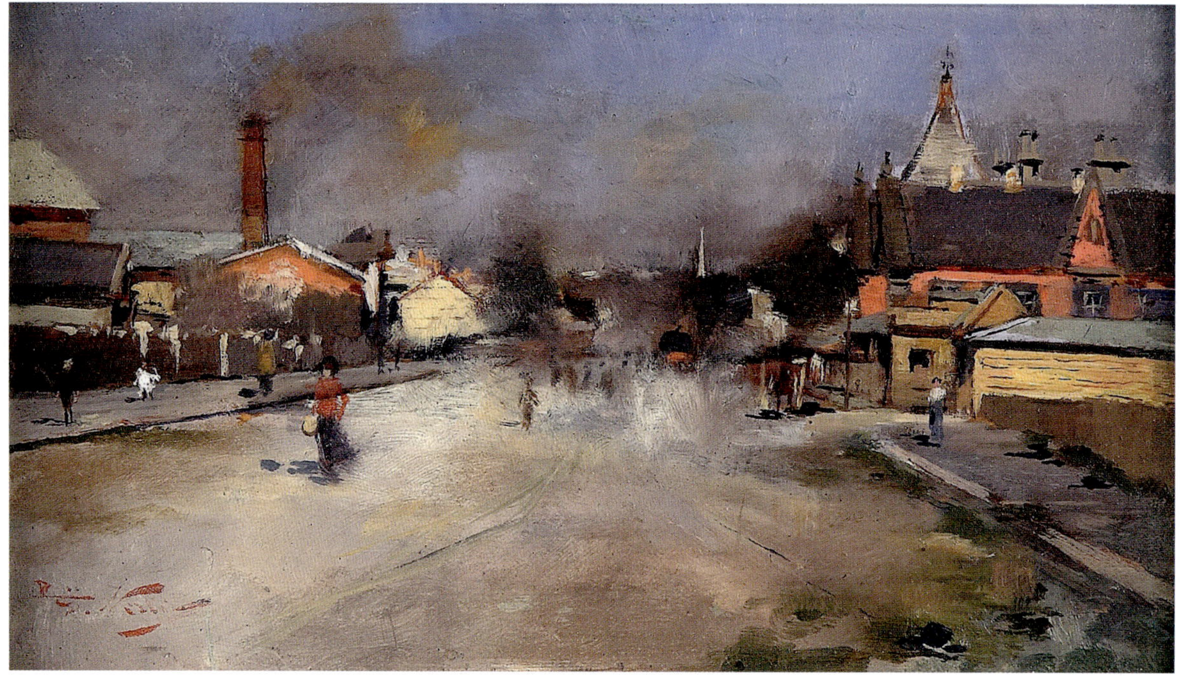

Image 1.1 (Right)

Advertisement from the *Otago Daily Times*, dated 8 January 1867.

Image 1.2 (Above)

Dunedin Street Scene by G.P. Nerli, c. 1894, 11 x 20 cm, showing the Red Lion Brewery with its smoking chimney on the left.

Image Jonathan Gooderham, Jonathan Grant Galleries Ltd & ARTIS Gallery, Auckland

Chapter 1

Early Life in Dunedin

Dunedin was more developed than most of the British provincial cities of the time. In this way it was not only an outpost of Empire, like Vladivostok or San Francisco, but an incongruously civilized one, like Melbourne, and perhaps nowhere else – Peter Entwisle, 1984

Grace's parents, Maurice and Catherine (née Woolf) Joel, married in Melbourne, Australia, in 1859. Maurice was born in Northumberland, England, in 1829 and Catherine, also known as Kate, in 1831 in the British seaside town of Brighton. Two years after marrying, the couple migrated to Dunedin, New Zealand, just as the Otago gold rush of the 1860s began transforming the town from a sleepy Scottish settlement into a bustling mercantile and cultural centre.

By 1869, Dunedin (now of city status) had founded the country's first university, Otago University, which opened in July 1871 and spawned the nation's first medical school in 1875. The city also hosted New Zealand's first government-funded art school (1870), first public school for girls (1871) and first public art gallery (1884). Given that the nation of New Zealand had only come into existence in 1840 with the signing of the Treaty of Waitangi between the British Crown and the indigenous Māori, these achievements were considerable. Of Dunedin's Scots settlers, Mark Twain wrote in his 1897 travelogue, *Following the Equator*: 'They stopped here on their way from home to heaven – thinking they had arrived.'[1]

Grace's parents were just two of the many settlers who assisted in Dunedin's development, with Maurice setting up a hardware and ship chandlery business upon their arrival. Trade over the next year was good enough to allow the couple to advertise locally for a 'Female Servant Girl. Liberal Wages.' Catherine's brother Joseph Woolf, who had also arrived from Melbourne, became the owner of the Red Lion Brewery (Image 1.2) in Dunedin, complete with four pigs on hand to dispatch spent grain. However, Joseph was soon in financial trouble, partly because of his weakness for gambling. A bill of sale gave legal title of the brewery to Maurice, but continuing financial decline resulted in Joseph ingesting strychnine in 1864. The well-respected Dr Thomas Morland Hocken, whose name was to become famously associated with Dunedin, attempted unsuccessfully to save his life.[2] As a consequence of Joseph's death, Maurice acquired the brewery after attempts to auction it off failed. He and Catherine were also left with the care of Joseph's two young children, whose mother (Joseph's wife, Julia) had died in Dunedin in 1863. For a few years

TO HOTEL KEEPERS AND OTHERS.

THE RED LION BREWERY continues to supply those MALT ALES AND BOTTLED STOUT For which it is so justly celebrated.

MAURICE JOEL, Proprietor.

Brewery, George and King streets.

Orders addressed to the Store, Princes street, will have prompt attention.

Maurice ran both businesses, but in 1867 he sold the hardware store in order to concentrate on the Red Lion.

The brewery, which provided the Joel family with a comfortable but not exorbitant income, had its ups and downs over the ensuing decades. The Dunedin Magistrate's Court records show numerous cases of the magistrate finding in favour of the plaintiff, Maurice Joel, against individuals for non-payment of ale supplied. In another instance, Maurice was one of the creditors of a local bankrupt. What Maurice needed was a son who could handle his father's many legal issues: Edward Joel became a barrister and solicitor in 1883 and so was able to do just that. Maurice also served on the Board of Directors of the Standard Insurance Company, represented the Chamber of Commerce on the Otago Harbour Board, became the owner of the Palace Hotel, donated to local causes and actively participated in various Jewish community affairs. In short, he became one of the pillars of Dunedin's burgeoning mercantile society.

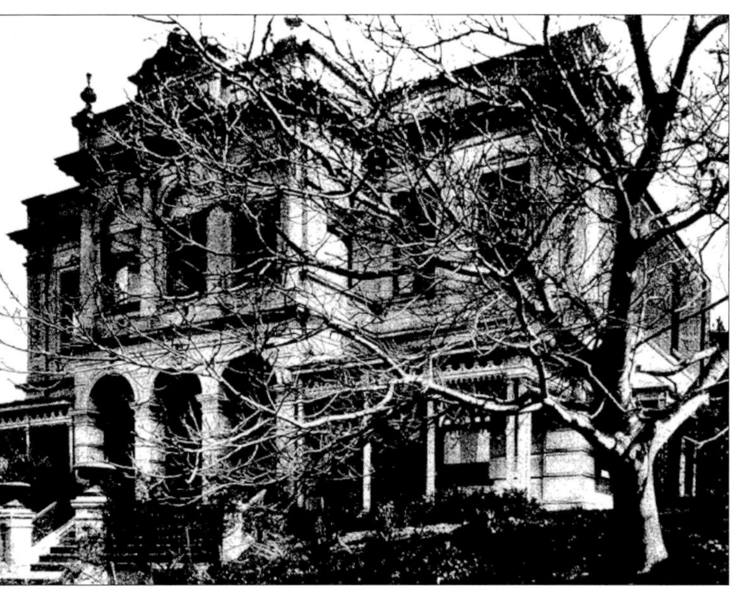

Image 1.3

The Joel family home for 38 years, Eden Bank, on Regent Road, Dunedin. Turned over to the government in 1905, it became the second of seven St Helen's maternity hospitals, dedicated to the training of midwives, nurses and medical students. The hospital saw in the birth of many babies until its closure in 1938. During this entire period, New Zealand's first female medical graduate, Dr Emily Siedeberg-McKinnon, was its superintendent.

Another major event for the Joel family, now seven in number, was their move in 1867 into a fashionable two-storey home, Eden Bank (Image 1.3), on the corner of Regent Road and Queen Street. A long drive extended from the house down to the city's main thoroughfare, George Street. Built in 1863, Eden Bank was originally the home of a Polish prince, Konstantine Drucki-Lubecki, whose British wife, Laura, used the premises as a school for 'young ladies', taking in boarders and day pupils.[3] Towards the end of his life, Maurice leased (and later sold) the house to the government for use as a maternity home, which was formally opened by the then Prime Minister of New Zealand, Richard J. Seddon, on 30 September 1905. The government of the day had recently passed (1904) the Midwives Act, which 'standardised midwifery training and enabled the setting up of a State maternity service through St Helens hospitals'. Regrettably, the Joel family home of nearly four decades was demolished; a block of flats now occupies the site.

The Joel family became part of a small but robust and active Jewish community whose members found their way to Dunedin during the mid-nineteenth century. Before 1861, only five Jewish families resided in the town. By 1880, when Maurice laid the cornerstone of a new synagogue in his role as President of the Dunedin Hebrew Congregation, the numbers of Jewish residents had swelled considerably. While some remnants of anti-Semitism no doubt persisted in the minds of some gentile immigrants, it was certainly not of the systemic nature found in Eastern Europe at the time. New Zealanders then, as now, tended to be relatively indifferent to a person's religion. Julius Vogel (1835–1899), of Jewish faith, was twice elected New Zealand Premier and received a knighthood in 1875.[4] This climate of tolerance enabled many families of Jewish origin to play a pivotal role in the nation building of New Zealand; some became household names over the next century.

Julius Vogel was also the man who, with associate William Cutten, launched the *Otago Daily Times* in 1861, New Zealand's first daily newspaper. It still thrives 150 years on, and its archives provide many historical facts about Grace Joel, although most pertain to her work as an artist. Years after retiring from politics, Vogel wrote an unusually visionary novel, *Anno Domini 2000 or Woman's Destiny*. Few men on Earth at this time (1889) would have had the foresight to write these words about the status of women at the beginning of the twenty-first century:

> *The barriers which man in his own interest set to the occupation of woman having once been broken down, the progress of woman in all pursuits requiring judgment and intellect has been continuous; and the sum of that progress is enormous. It has, in fact, come to be accepted that the bodily power is greater in man, and the mental power larger in woman. So to speak, woman has become the guiding, man the executive, force of the world.*[5]

As it happened, the year 2000 found New Zealand's top government offices of monarch, governor-general-designate, prime minister, leader of the opposition, speaker of the House of Representatives and chief justice occupied by women. Unfortunately, much of the rest of Vogel's narrative, such as total equality for women or a woman president of the United States, is yet to pass. But the 24-year-old Grace Joel would not have been immune to this liberal familial social atmosphere from which she had sprung. Keeping Vogel's vision alive, the University of Hawaii Press republished his book in 2002.

According to an account related by Maurice's grandson (also named Maurice Joel) to art historian Peter Entwisle, Julius Vogel and Maurice Joel were cousins. The younger Maurice based his account on the claim that the mothers of Julius and Maurice (Grace's father) were sisters. However, the historical record does not support this assertion. Julius Vogel's mother, Phoebe Vogel (née Isaac), was the first child born (in 1810) into a family of 19 children. Maurice Joel's mother was born in 1791, thus precluding any possibility of the mothers being sisters. Nevertheless, Vogel's and Maurice's mothers may have been related in some manner, but by the time this detail reached grandson Maurice Joel, the relationship had become something more than it actually was.

Over the years, Grace's father Maurice established himself as one of the cornerstones of the Dunedin Hebrew Congregation, being its president on five occasions and its treasurer on 10. The congregation ran a Hebrew school, which Grace possibly attended, and also formed the Jewish Philanthropic Society. The latter provided regional Jewish poor with financial assistance. Maurice Joel served as one of its presidents. The congregation not only supported Jews locally but provided 'for the assistance of starving Jews in Jerusalem and the

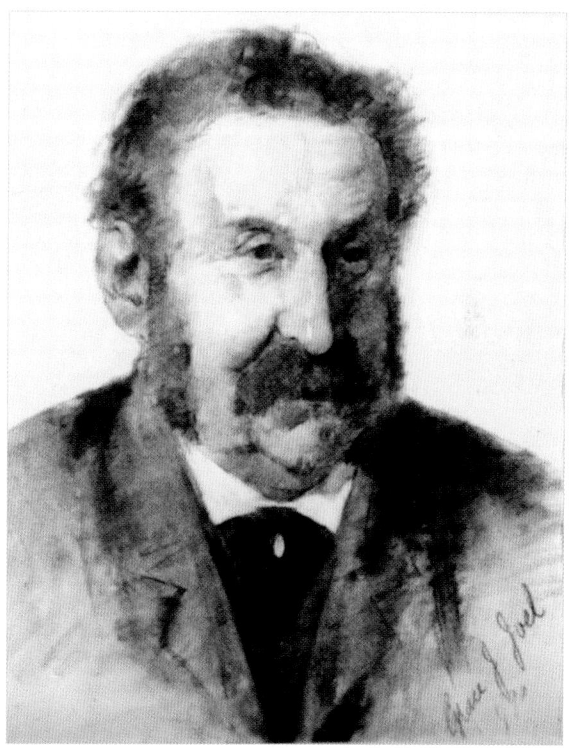

IMAGE 1.4

Charcoal sketch on laid paper by Grace Joel of her father, Maurice Joel, dated 1890, 40.5 x 33.5 cm. Grace completed this work after a course of study at the National Gallery School, Melbourne. Private collection

Sultan's dominions, as well as for persecuted Russian Jews'[6] – from Dunedin to Russia with love.

Another prominent member of the congregation was David Theomin, a thriving merchant who set up nationwide branches of the Dresden Piano Company. Like Maurice Joel, he held the congregation offices of president and treasurer numerous times. The Theomins built a stately home (1904–06), known as Olveston, that is presently one of the more genteel attractions in Dunedin. It, together with all of its contents, was bequeathed to the city by the Theomins' daughter, Dorothy, when she died in 1966. One of those possessions was Grace Joel's work *The Yellow Sunbonnet* (Image 2.11), proudly displayed on a dining-room wall.

Other Jewish families in the city, including those of Hallenstein, Nathan, Fels, Myers, Brasch and de Beers, became notable patrons of the arts and letters, supporting galleries, museums and Otago University. One of the Brasch progeny, Charles, in later years founded New Zealand's pre-eminent literary journal, *Landfall*.[7] Intermarriage among this group was not uncommon. The family tree of young Charles Brasch, for example, had branches labelled Hallenstein, Fels and de Beers.

Into this burgeoning Dunedin Jewish community was born, to Maurice and wife Kate, their fifth child and first daughter, Grace Jane Joel, on 26 May 1865 at their then home located in Cargill Street. The Register of Births inverts Grace's name as Jane Grace Joel, her grandmother's name on her father's side. Of the nine Joel children, one son (Trytle) died the same year he was born, and another (Theodore Julius) died before the age of six; such deaths were not atypical of the era. Two slightly older brothers, Alfred and Edward, did not live past 40. Grace subsequently acquired two sisters, Blanche (1869–1947) and Lily (1872–1959), both of whom survived her, as did a brother, Louis. Of the six male children, only Louis had progeny to carry on the Joel family name.

Grace attended Otago Girls' High School, one of the first state-supported schools in the world that

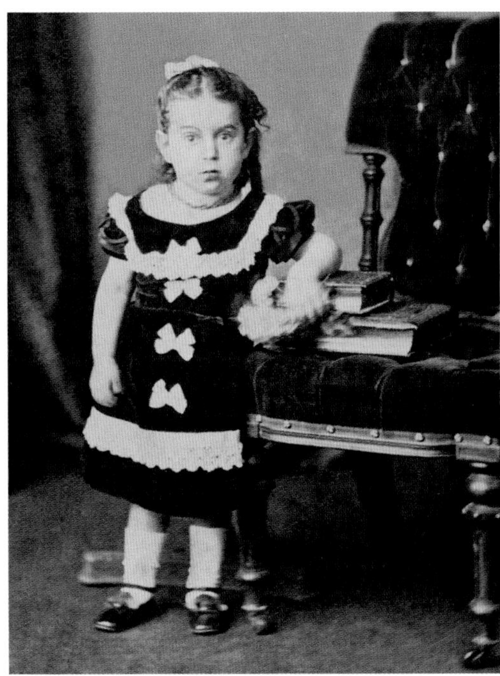

IMAGE 1.5

Grace Joel as a young child in Dunedin. Grace poses for the photographer with her arm resting gently on some books. In years hence, many a sitter will be the ones posing for Grace.

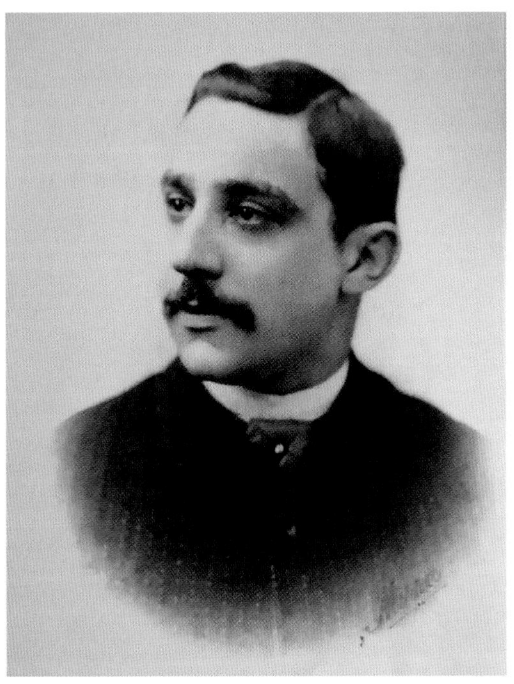

IMAGE 1.6

Grace's brother, Louis Joseph Joel (1863–1949).

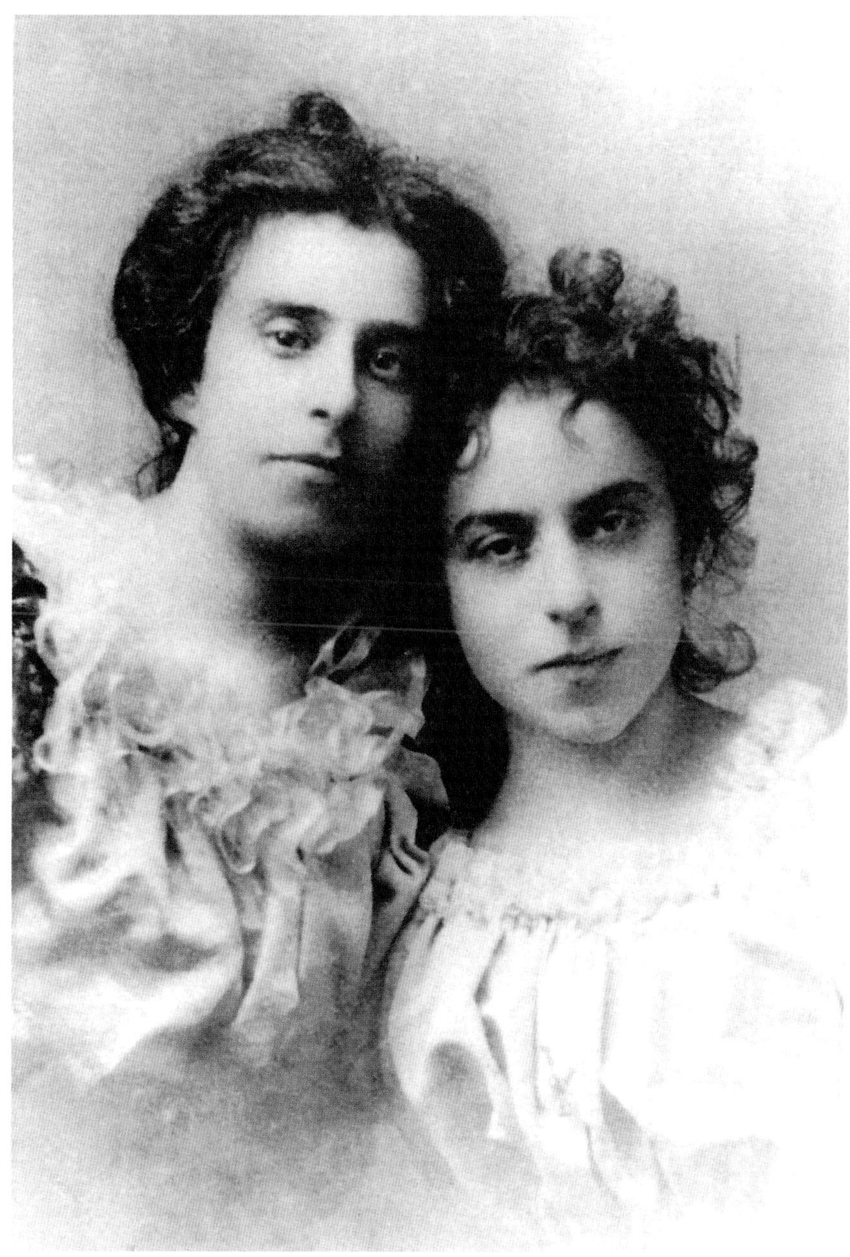

IMAGE 1.7

Grace (left) with either her sister Blanche (four years younger) or sister Lily (seven years younger).

was strictly for girls. Here, Grace won a handful of school prizes over the years, including a special one for 'fancy needlework' when she was 16. However, it was in her senior year (1882) that Grace really shone, winning Mr Towsey's senior prize in music, earning the title of senior German dux (Dr Bülau's prize) and, most significantly for her future, securing the Miss Holmes' prize for painting.[8] Especially proud must have been Form III student, Miss A. Park, who was awarded the 'Mr Dallas' prize for improvement in French pronunciation and ladylike behaviour in class'.

In the middle of the next year, Maurice, Kate and Grace, now nearly 18 years of age, embarked on a trip to London, Maurice having earlier expressed a wish to visit his childhood home in Northumberland, in a letter to his older brother, Edward, who was very much the English gentleman.

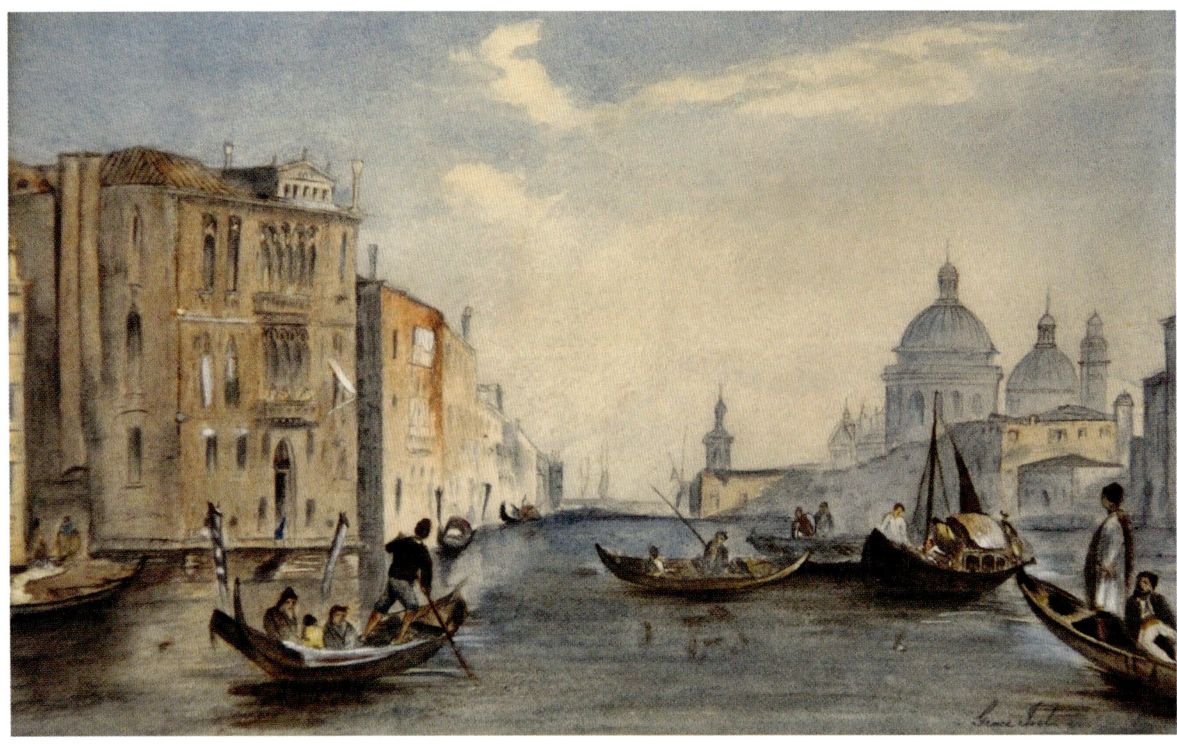

Image 1.8

One of two extant watercolours of Venetian canals, 1883, 24.3 x 39 cm, which Grace likely painted on an overseas trip that she took with her parents when she was 18 years old. Private collection

Edward lived a quiet life, employed two servants and spent his evenings at his club (Conservative) playing whist,[9] in sharp contrast to Maurice's days as a brewer and Jewish community leader in antipodean colonial Dunedin.

Grace and her parents left Dunedin on 19 May, travelling first to Melbourne aboard the SS *Rotomahana* in the company of their Dunedin friends Mr and Mrs de Beer and their five children, plus nurse.[10] In Melbourne, they boarded the P&O line Royal Mail SS *Carthage II* for the voyage to London via Colombo, Ceylon (now Sri Lanka) and the Suez Canal.[11] The family were away for six months and no doubt spent a pleasant time with relatives and friends in England. They returned to Melbourne on the P&O line's RMSS *Parramatta*, the passenger manifesto of which lists them as the Joels 'from Brindisi'.[12]

This mention places the family on the east coast of Italy at the end of 1883. At the time, P&O ran a regular hop-on hop-off ship service to various ports in the Mediterranean, including Venice and Brindisi. Did the Joels visit Venice? There is strong evidence that they did in the form of two extant rudimentary watercolours by Grace that are unmistakably of the Venetian canals. A verbal communication from Grace Joel's nephew, Maurice Joel, was that Grace painted the scene depicted in Image 1.8 when she was a teenager,[13] a timeframe that fits in with the trip abroad. Of course, it is always possible that these works were inspired by paintings Grace saw in galleries or magazines while in England or perhaps by postcards picked up in Brindisi. However, the likelihood of her copying only Venetian canal scenes while abroad makes this suggestion somewhat tenuous. In any event, these watercolours are the earliest known of her work, and more than the idle daubs of a bored young woman. They represent the first steps along her road to recognition as an internationally significant artist.

Several tentative sketches of family and acquaintances, undated, may have been done by Grace soon after the period abroad. Some, in pencil or charcoal on laid paper and unsigned, feature her mother. There are four different sketches on a single sheet of her father, and a faint one of a brother playing the violin. These are exactly what a budding young artist would be doing at this stage: a nascent talent needs to engage in careful study, a task to which Grace addressed herself somewhat later when she took up serious formal art studies.

In 1886, in keeping with their musical talents, Grace and her sister Blanche took part in a concert during which 22 young ladies simultaneously played 11 pianos. The concert, part of that year's Dunedin Jewish Bazaar,[14] must have been quite a spectacle and surely represents a singular moment in New Zealand's musical history. Six years later, in 1893, Blanche (Image 1.9), highly gifted as a pianist, violinist and vocalist, demonstrated her piano artistry when she played Chopin's *Grand Polonaise in A Flat* during a concert held at Dunedin's Garrison Hall: 'Miss Joel has every reason to be pleased with her performance last evening, it being in every respect an artistic one.'[15] Among the vocalists at the concert was brother Edward Alexander, who sang *Vienni la Mia Vendetta* as an encore to his 'stirring rendering' of *They All Love Jack*. Blanche also sang that evening. Two years later, the celebrated American writer, Mark Twain (Image 1.10), followed in Blanche's and Edward's footsteps by appearing at Garrison Hall as part of his speaking tour of New Zealand.

So here we have a picture of a cultured family very much a part of the social fabric of Victorian Dunedin. For the young women of the time, such as Grace and Blanche, there were certain expectations of etiquette to observe, including those associated

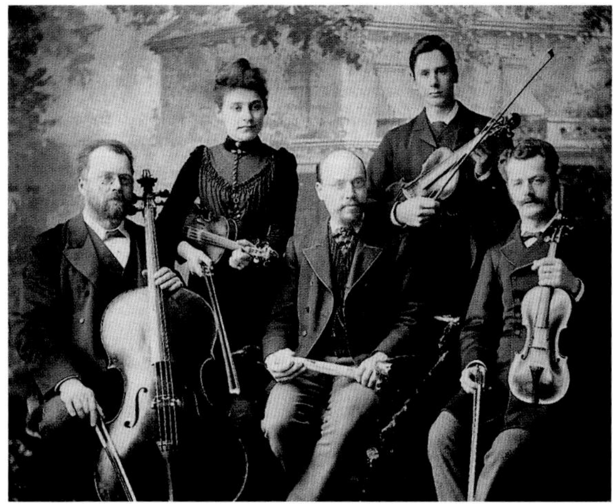

IMAGE 1.9

'One of the instrumental groups which contributed to the city's entertainment in the eighties – The Chamber Concert Company', c. 1890. This photograph shows Blanche Joel with her violin standing beside music teacher, Arthur J. Barth, centre.

Hocken Collections, Uare Taoka o Hākena, University of Otago, Dunedin

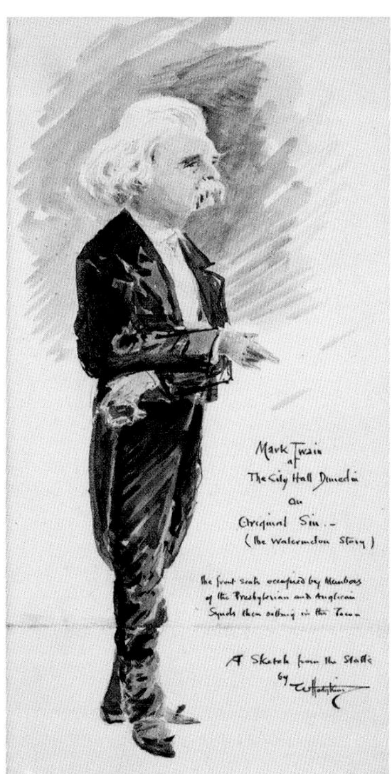

IMAGE 1.10

An ink portrayal of Mark Twain at the City Hall, Dunedin, by William Mathew Hodgkins, drawn during Twain's 1895 visit to Dunedin.

Ref: A-212-024, Alexander Turnbull Library, Wellington

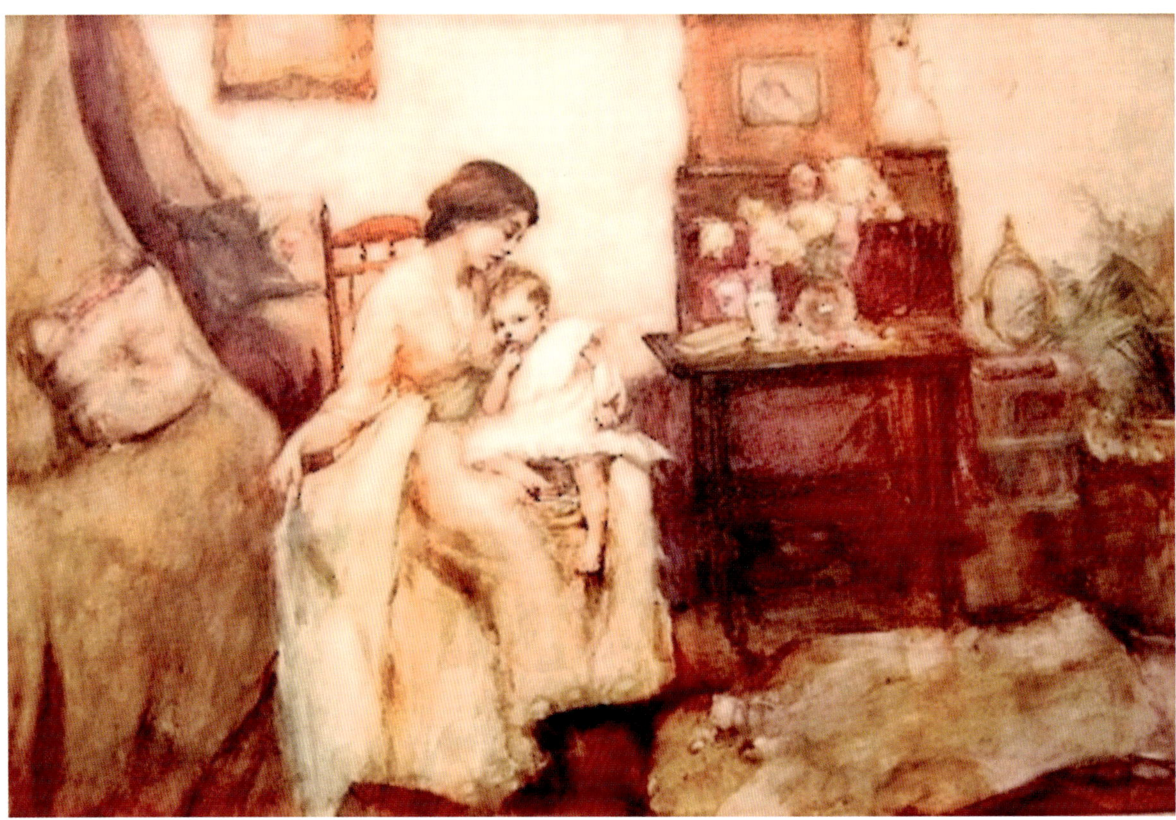

IMAGE 1.11

A watercolour by Grace Joel, c. 1890s, 43 x 65 cm. The mother and child theme was one that Grace Joel returned to time and again over the course of her life. Private collection

with the 'protracted round of extended visits to friends and relations interspersed with parties and picnics to while away the time between leaving school and making a suitable marriage. Playing the piano, singing and painting in watercolours were suitable occupations for a young lady at this stage of her life and joining an Art Society was often the outward sign of having adopted such a past-time.'[16] Grace Joel, exactly in this position by age 21, reflected in later years that 'she had the usual tussle that all girls must have whose parents are comfortably off and do not need the help of their children. Social gaiety and ease pulled one way, the delights of painting another.'[17]

Her art won the day. In 1886 Grace became a working member of the Otago Art Society, the second such society to be formed in New Zealand behind that of Auckland, established in 1875. One of the OAS's original six founders was William Mathew Hodgkins, who became its second president in 1880 and carried this title for the next 18 years until his death. He also formed the Art Club, whose select coterie of aspiring artists met in members' houses and took excursions so they could work *en plein air* (outdoors).

The ebullient Mr Hodgkins was a skilful amateur artist, 'ever willing with a word of kindly advice'.[18] He worked mainly in watercolours and became one of the most vigorous proponents of art in New Zealand. The theme of this art was predominantly landscapes, and Hodgkins was no exception in this regard, deriving his artistic inspiration from the works of J.M.W. Turner. He was the principal driving force behind the establishment of the Dunedin Public Art Gallery in 1884, where his innate tenacity won out over years of indifference from his contemporaries. The elder Hodgkins daughter, Isabel, showed artistic promise as an adolescent and joined her father in the Art Club, while daughter Frances, two years Isabel's junior, was becoming a proficient pianist. However, it was Frances Hodgkins (1869–1947) who was to become 'one of the most internationally significant New Zealand-born artists to date'.[19]

During her first year at the OAS, Grace Joel exhibited two portraits (not priced) at the society's annual exhibition. At the following year's exhibition, she exhibited eight paintings of various genres, three of which were for sale. The seed had begun to germinate but needed a little nurturing, which happened to arrive from Florence, Italy via Australia in the form of Signor Girolamo Pieri Nerli. Signor Nerli's reason for coming to Dunedin was to assist with the New Zealand and South Seas Exhibition, held in November 1889.

The exhibition, set up to celebrate 50 years of achievement in New Zealand under British colonial rule, was essentially a world's fair. It ran until April 1890 and featured a cornucopia of life and culture throughout New Zealand, Australia, the Pacific Island nations, several European countries, the United States and Canada. More than 600,000 people – about the same number of people in New Zealand at the time – visited the exhibition.

One member of the organising committee was Maurice Joel, Grace's father. The secretary of the fine arts committee was William Hodgkins. The latter managed to arrange for the purchase of some of the works for the Public Art Gallery collection. Hodgkins and his daughter Isabel exhibited some watercolours as did John Gully, the 'patriarch painter of New Zealand landscapes'. Other local painters exhibiting were J.D. Perrett, A.H. O'Keeffe and J. Wimperis, but Grace did not show a single painting, perhaps because she was studying in Melbourne at the time.

From Europe came dozens of dazzling works, including a Rubens, one that was purportedly a Rembrandt, and a portrait of Alfred Tennyson by the distinguished English painter, G.F. Watts, whom Grace Joel was to meet some years later in England. A depiction of the well-known biblical parable by Sir John E. Millais, *The Evil One Sowing Tares*, was valued at £3000. Watts and Sir Frederick Leighton (then President of the Royal Academy of Arts) also presented a collaborative painting of famed explorer Sir Richard Burton. The works submitted were certainly no mere castoffs for colonials.

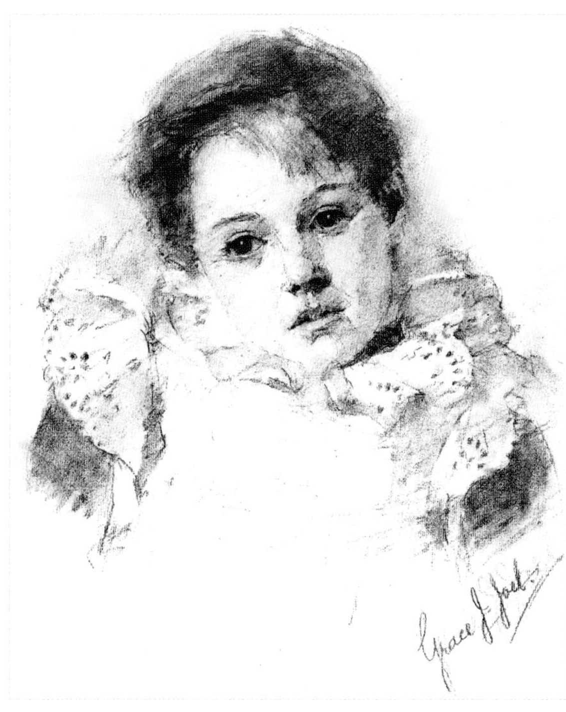

IMAGE 1.12

Study of a child, head and shoulders, full face, by Grace Joel, charcoal on laid paper, 45 x 35 cm. At the 1890 Otago Art Society annual exhibition, Grace exhibited *Study of a Child's Head*; conceivably, this is the same work. During this period, Grace executed a number of sketches of family members and friends.

Dunedin Public Art Gallery, Dunedin

Among all the cultural splendour listed in the exhibition's catalogue were numerous advertisements, including some from Grace's father. These ran across the tops of several pages and were variations on a theme: 'Joel's Ale Used by All', 'Joel's Ale took 4 Prizes Melbourne Exhibition 1889 Against World', to quote just two.

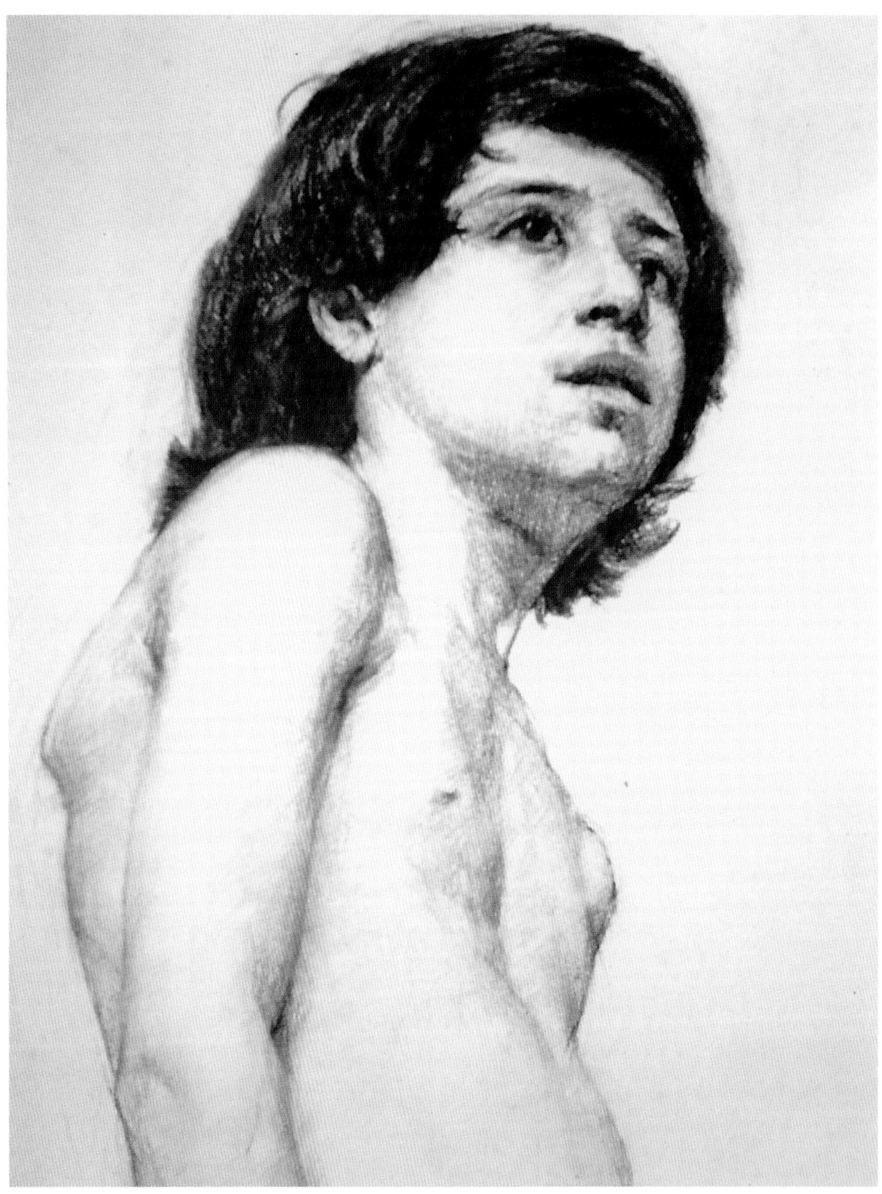

IMAGE 1.13

Study of a young girl, half-length, nude, by Grace Joel, charcoal, 60 x 41 cm. This early indication of working from a nude model could have been executed as a study in Melbourne, c. 1889. Private collection

The transcendent effects of the works of art on display at the exhibition were not lost on the locals of the new nation, as the *Otago Daily Times* observed: '[A] nation is nothing if not artistic. We are all agreed as to the desirability of fostering and cultivating fine art. It has a refining and elevating tendency, and the advantages to be derived from its early study in a young country like this can hardly be overestimated, so subtle and far-reaching must its influence be.'[20] These sentiments were echoed in the next century by Australian artist, Jane Price (1860–1948): 'Art is a matter of life and death for the building of a nation. Australia cannot do without it.'[21] The notion that art has a higher moral purpose was promulgated in the mid-nineteenth century by such cultural commentators as English art critic and social philosopher John Ruskin and also Oscar Wilde – flag bearer of the Aesthetic Movement. These lofty social ideals were soon to be challenged by the flamboyant James Abbott McNeill Whistler.

But let us not forget the peripatetic painter Girolamo Nerli, whose influence on Grace Joel cannot be excluded from any account about her. Signor Nerli's particular task at the New Zealand and South Seas Exhibition was to help set up the collection from New South Wales. Grace returned from studying in Melbourne in December 1889,[22] so she and Nerli might have met for the first time in early 1890, before the exhibition concluded. At the annual Otago Art Society exhibition, held at the end of 1890, Grace showed a painting titled *Under the Spell* (Image 1.15). It features a young woman looking very much like the young Grace herself, seated and pensive in mood. While we can never know the exact nature of the 'spell', it seems reasonable to suggest (not for the first time) that it was the heady new world of both Art and Nerli. Almost one century later, the painting's title informed the name of a 1987 exhibition held at the Hocken Library, Dunedin: 'Under the Spell: Frances Hodgkins, Nellie Hutton & Grace Joel: Three Women Artists Influenced in the 1890s by G.P. Nerli'.

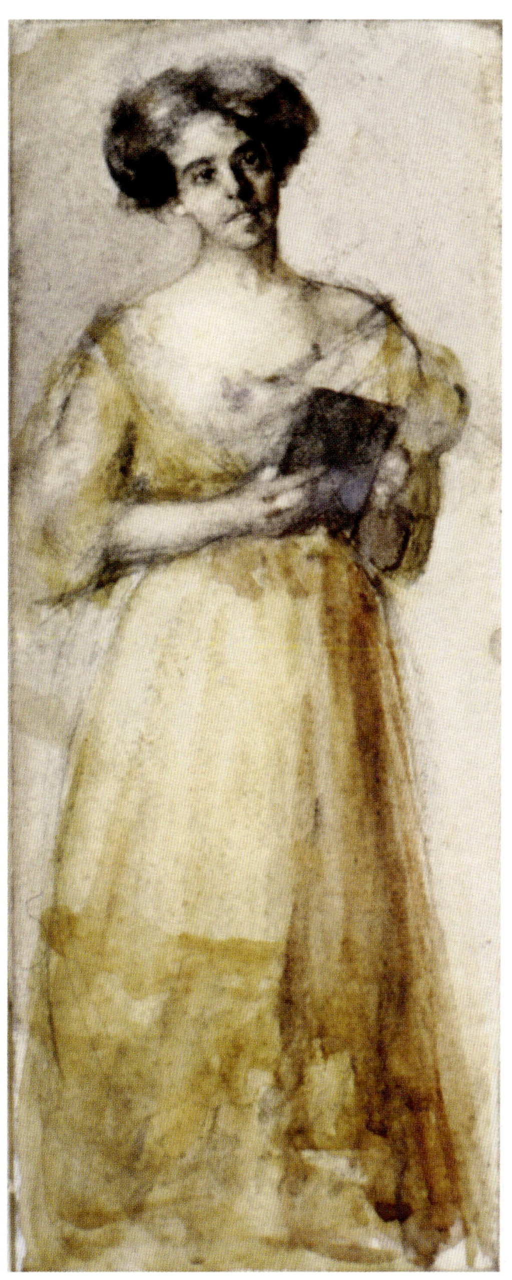

Image 1.14

***A Literary Aspirant (An Impression)*, exhibited at the 1890 annual exhibition of the Otago Art Society, watercolour, dated 1890, 18.8 x 7 cm. This is clearly a self-portrait of Grace, who was 25 years old at the time.**

Private collection

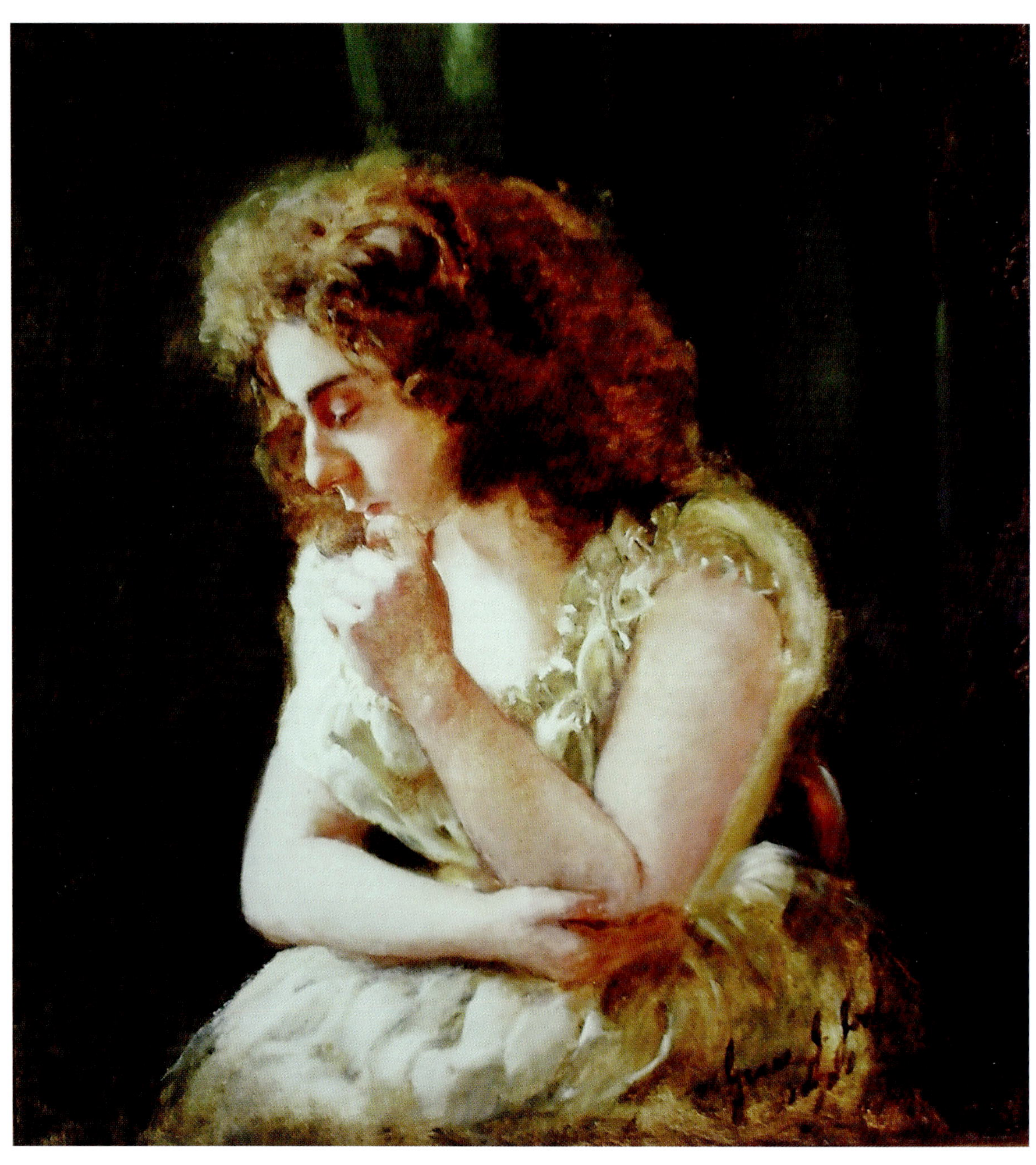

IMAGE 1.15

Under the Spell, by Grace Joel, dated 1890, oil on canvas, 61 x 51 cm. Private collection

Signor Girolamo Pieri Nerli

> *It is the aim of the true artist to bring new ideas into being, and Miss Joel deserves credit for trying along this thorny track instead of being content to simply produce a pretty picture* – Evening Star, 12 November 1896

Five years Grace's senior, Nerli was born into an aristocratic but impoverished family in 1860 Sienna. He received his art education in Florence, possibly as a student at the Accademia di Belle Arti.[23] In addition to his formal training, he would have been exposed to the influences of the Macchiaioli, the anti-academy Tuscan movement that portrayed scenes from everyday life and preceded French Impressionism. In order to capture the moment, the painters used blotches of colour known as macchia (meaning 'stain' or 'spot'). This pejorative term contributed to the work of the Macchiaioli being neither understood nor appreciated in its time.

Another artistic movement likely to have influenced Nerli was the Scapigliatura, whose rebellious adherents, known as the Scapigliati (dishevelled ones), advocated a bohemian approach to all art and life. A propensity for drugs and alcohol meant the latter was often short and tragic. In painting it meant soft contours, indistinctness between figure and background, strong contrasts and the use of colour to portray atmosphere – techniques not so different from those James Whistler was using in accordance with the Aesthetic Movement in England around the same time.

Nerli and his travelling companion, artist Ugo Catani, washed ashore in Melbourne in 1885, via Mauritius. Nerli spent time not only in Melbourne but also Sydney, and soon became ensconced in the Australian art scene. He befriended the group of Tom Roberts, Arthur Streeton and Charles Conder, all three of whom came to be influenced to some extent by the impressionistic style and European themes of the Italian visitor, and all three of whom achieved artistic distinction in their own right. They and their influence frequent the Grace Joel narrative.

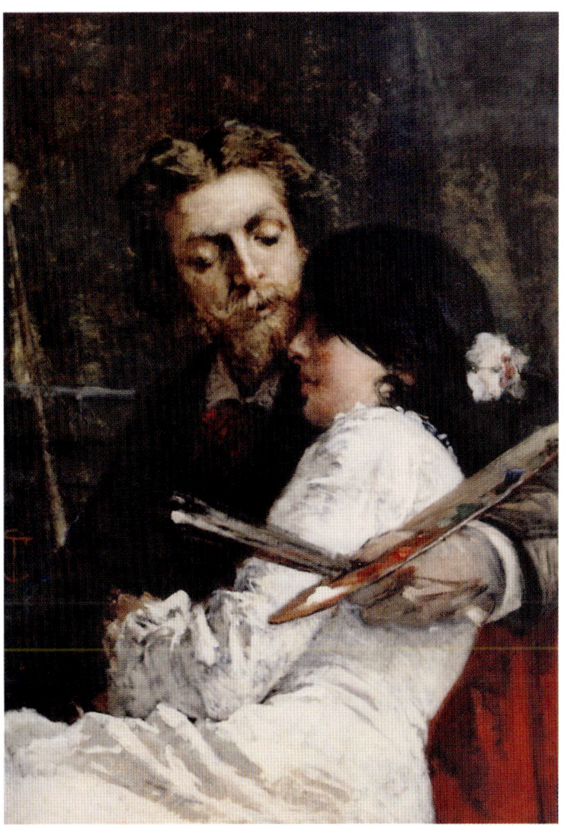

Image 1.16

***Il pittore e la modella*, by Scapigliati artist Tranquillo Cremona, 1870–72, oil on canvas, 91 x 63 cm.**

Private collection

Described by Peter Entwisle as 'Tall, Italian, good looking, single and rumoured to be an aristocrat, Signor Nerli displayed a benign contempt for social convention … [T]he most exhilarating thing of all was the fact that Nerli really could paint.'[24] Dunedin artist, A.H. O'Keeffe, who met Nerli during the New Zealand and South Seas Exhibition, referred to him as 'a true artist in every sense', as indeed he was.[25] The nine works that Nerli displayed at the exhibition included portraits and street scenes. His *Study of a Lady* earned a First Order of Merit. All relatively tame stuff.

Then there was the impressionistic scene *A Bacchanalian Orgy* (Image 1.17), one of several on the feast/orgy theme that Nerli painted. Previously exhibited in Australia, it was hung in the New South Wales Court. The *Otago Daily Times*, averring that the painting caused a stir in 'the sister colonies',

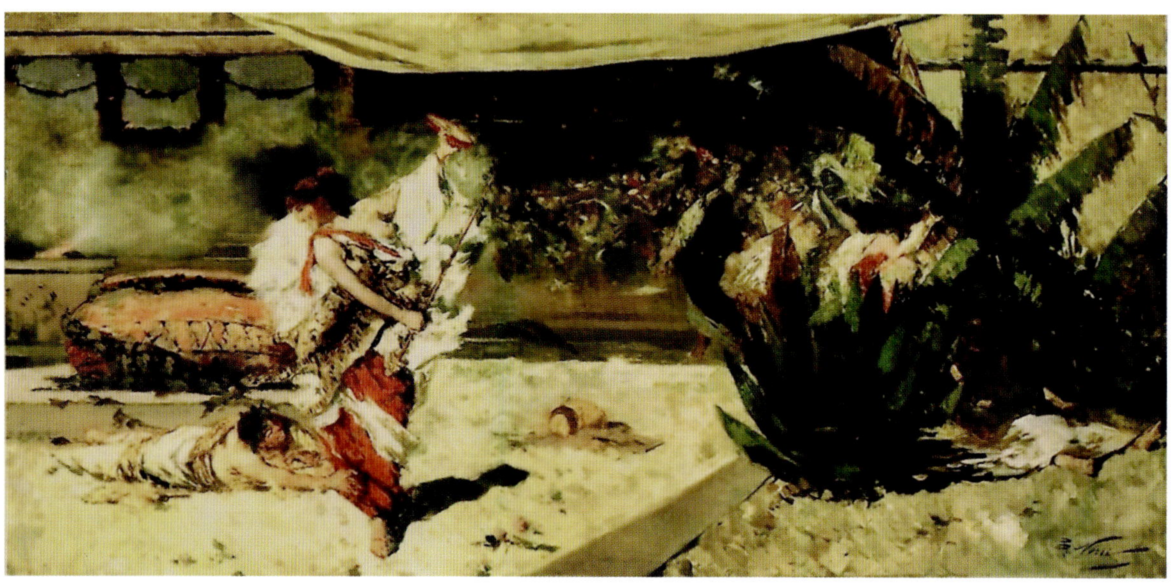

IMAGE 1.17

A Bacchanalian Orgy, **by Girolamo Nerli, 1888, oil on canvas on composition board, 64 x 130.3 cm. This work is from the Orgia series and could have been the one (or a variant thereof) exhibited at the New Zealand and South Seas Exhibition of 1889/90.** National Gallery of Australia, Canberra

nevertheless praised it: 'Taken as an impressionist picture it is undoubtedly a remarkably clever bit of work.'[26] The painting, in its suggestiveness, was much less indelicate than its title implied; its freely impressionistic rendering of the scene was perhaps the real shock for viewers. The painting also gives insight into the artistic repertoire that Signor Nerli drew upon.

Dora Meeson (1869–1955), from Christchurch but Melbourne born, also exhibited a few works, two of which were of Christchurch's Avon River. She was awarded a third prize for her floral painting *Gloire de Dijon Roses*. In 1889 the 20-year-old Dora and her family arrived in Christchurch, having come from Nelson and before that England. Dora studied at the Christchurch School of Art[27] and exhibited not only with the Canterbury Society of Arts but as far afield as Auckland.[28] After a brief sojourn at the Slade School in London, Dora returned to her family in Christchurch where she exhibited with the Palette Club in 1894 and presided over their April meeting the following year.[29] By then, the club had 85 members, one of whom was the exemplary floral painter, Margaret Stoddart. Dora received much praise – and many awards – for her work. The latter half of 1895 saw Dora leaving Christchurch to study at the National Gallery School in Melbourne.[30] From there she journeyed on once again to London's Slade School of Art and finally to the Académie Julian in Paris.

Before living in Christchurch, Dora's father, the barrister John Meeson, had gone into partnership with Dunedin solicitor Alexander Bathgate.[31] The firm of Bathgate & Meeson, which had its chambers in Dunedin's Dowling Street, provided legal services to the community from 1882 to 1885.[32] It seems likely that Grace Joel and Dora Meeson became acquainted during this period. John Meeson was a 'B.A. and Barrister-at-law of the Inner Temple', so Dora would have been part of the same social circle as Grace and was the same age as her sister, Blanche, to whom Grace was very close. The likelihood that Grace and Dora did become acquainted at this time is significant because the two women later met up in

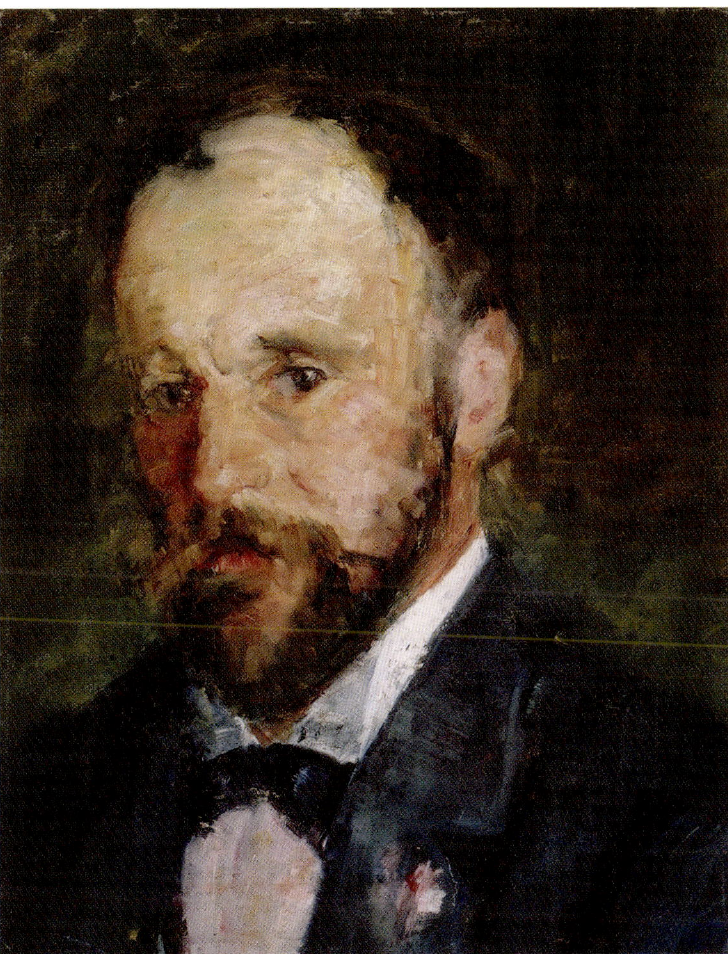

IMAGE 1.18

Portrait of G.P. Nerli, by Grace Joel, c. 1896, oil on canvas mounted on plywood, 47 x 36.5 cm. Although Nerli looks older here than mid-30s, a photograph of him and his wife Cecilia in 1905 that appears on page 16 of Dunn's biography of Nerli indicates he had put on weight by then and was clean shaven. Grace bequeathed this work to the Art Gallery of New South Wales.

Art Gallery of New South Wales, Sydney, Australia

fin de siècle Paris as if they were already old friends.

After the New Zealand and South Seas Exhibition, Nerli returned to Sydney, while Frances Hodgkins, perhaps inspired by the exhibition, took up the brush in earnest and joined the Otago Arts Society towards the end of 1890. Another artistic career was beginning to germinate in antipodean Dunedin.

Signor Nerli was not the only foreign artist of influence to arrive in New Zealand during this period. In 1890 we find two professional artists – Petrus van der Velden (1837–1913) from Holland and James McLachlan Nairn (1859–1904) from Scotland. Nairn settled, after a brief spell in Dunedin, in Wellington. His work brought to New Zealand the impressionistic style of the Glasgow School of Art's so-called Glasgow Boys, of whom Nairn was a member. Influenced by French Impressionism, these artists were particularly characterised by their preference to paint *en plein air*. According to art historian Eric McCormick, 'It is chiefly through Nairn that impressionism came to New Zealand.' While in Dunedin, Nairn joined the OAS. One of the works he exhibited with them in 1894, *Motif, Blue and Yellow*, probably had some influence on Grace Joel's *Harmony in Blue and Yellow*, shown a year later.[33]

***Painting**, n.: The art of protecting flat surfaces from the weather, and exposing them to the critic* – AMBROSE BIERCE (*THE DEVIL'S DICTIONARY*).

Impressionism during this period was a new and exciting form of artistic expression sweeping the Western world, but it was not met with universal

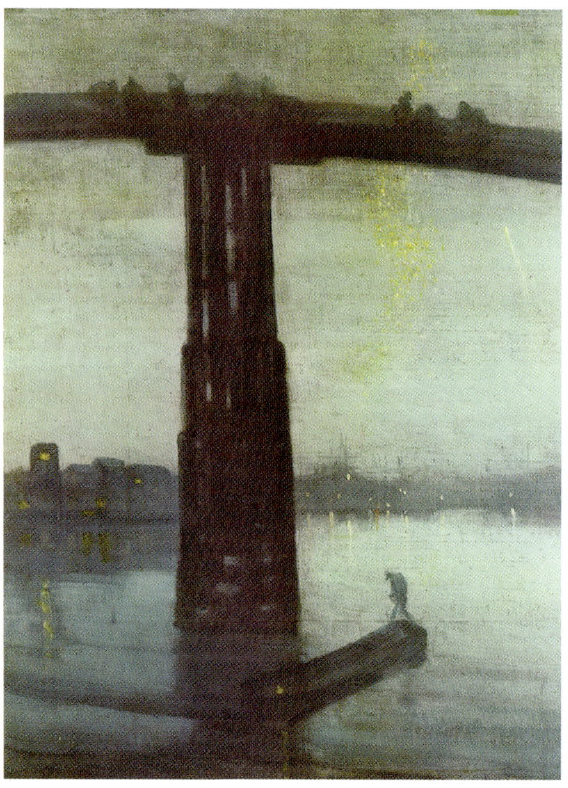

IMAGE 1.19

***Nocturne: Blue and Gold – Old Battersea Bridge*, by James Abbott McNeill Whistler, c. 1872–75, oil on canvas, 68.3 x 51.2 cm. Note that the bridge is not actually 'painted in'. Instead, the dark ground shows through, a device Whistler used to great effect. Another painting in the Nocturne series, depicting the fireworks seen here in the background, led to his famous court case against John Ruskin, the leading art critic of the Victorian era.**

acclaim; condemnation was more to the point among art critics such as William Powell Frith RA (1819–1909): 'Impressionism is a craze of such ephemeral character as to be unworthy of serious attention.'[34] Nevertheless, it was very popular with the general public, and so it remains to this day.

Contemporary neurological research suggests that the wiring of our brains makes us particularly emotionally responsive to impressionist images:

> *Impressionists used minimal detail in their paintings, yet their pieces evoke a strong sense of place and mood ... the inaccurate splashes of colour and hints of contour are often moving despite, or perhaps because of, discrepancies from a realistic portrayal. Why is this style so effective? Recent neuroscience studies of the connection between vision and the centres of emotion [in particular, the amygdala] suggest a possible reason ... Impressionist works may connect more directly to emotional centres than to conscious image-recognition areas because the unrealistic patchwork of brush strokes and mottled colouring distract conscious vision.*[35]

It seems that viewers experience the strong effect that impressionist works have on the amygdala as an emotional spike, stronger than that generated by realistic portrayals, which act more directly on the brain's image-recognition centres. So perhaps we can forgive Frith and others for their lack of understanding. Further research along these lines continues in the new field of neuroaesthetics.

Despite Dunedin's remoteness from the major centres of art, one Dunedin critic did 'get' it. Commenting on a work exhibited with the OAS by Grace Joel, *The Close of a Sultry Summer's Day, St. Clair*, he conceded:

> *Miss Joel has once more proclaimed herself to be a disciple of the school the aim of which is to show that what on a close inspection is seen to consist of confused slabs and streaks of pigment may be resolved at a distance of several paces into a harmonious perspective with defined objects – a method which, whatever exception may be taken to it, has the merit of producing broadly effective results.*[36]

In the more provincial town of Timaru, however, the art critic there, while admitting that Miss Joel 'evidently possesses talent', proclaimed that she regrettably 'has adopted the smudg [sic] and recklessness of colouring miscalled "impressionist"'.[37]

Another 'ism', Aestheticism, with its emphasis on composition of colour harmony and de-emphasis on the subject matter being portrayed, as advanced by Whistler, also influenced a number of Grace Joel's works. Some, such as *Flower Study of Roses* (Image 3.11) and (most especially) *Westminster, Early Winter's Evening* (Image 5.1), show that Grace fell in with Whistler's penchant for turning his subjects into

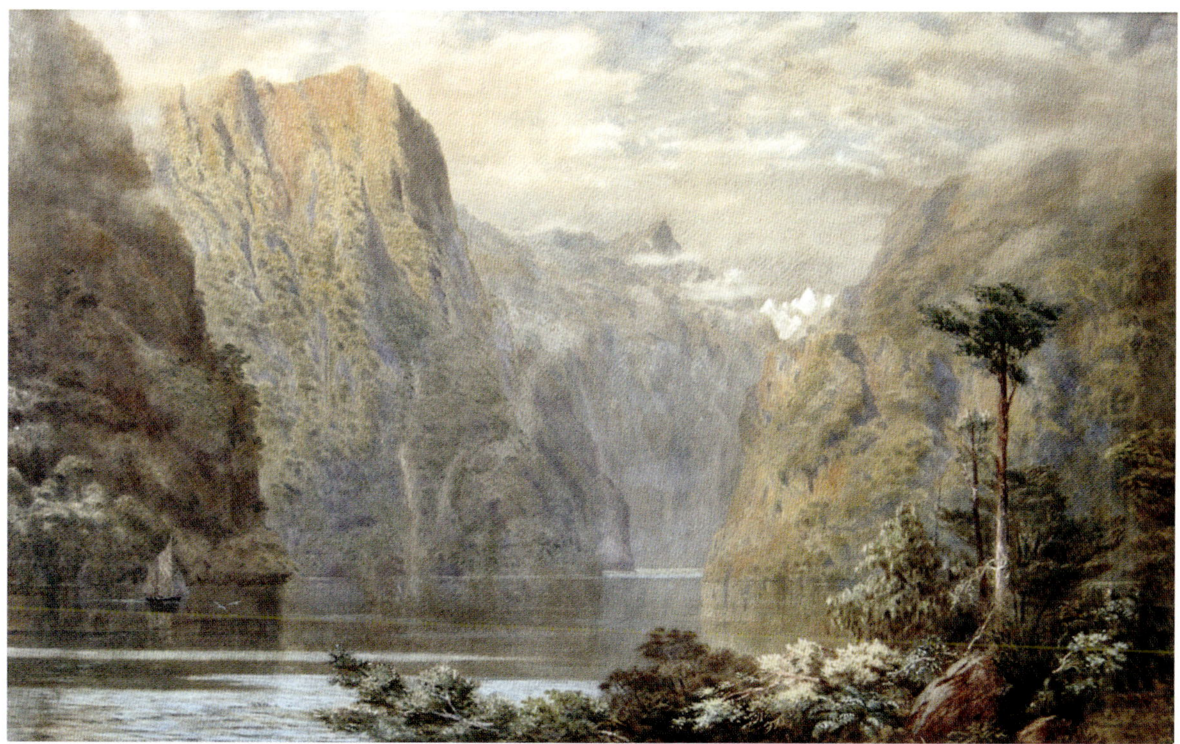

Image 1.20

***Mt Sheerdown, Milford Sound,* by the distinguished New Zealand landscape artist John Gully, 1883, watercolour, 57 x 88 cm.** International Art Centre, Auckland

apparitions. Not all of Whistler's audience were so beguiled: John Ruskin likened Whistler's *Nocturne in Black and Gold: The Falling Rocket* to 'flinging a pot of paint in the public's face'. Whistler sued for libel and won one farthing in damages, which he thereafter displayed on his watch chain. Although hollow, the victory was a symbolic one. The painting now resides protected and unperturbed at the Detroit Institute of Arts. In years to come, Grace Joel would do her own version of Battersea Bridge, as it was very close to where she lived on the banks of the River Thames.

In the faraway colonies of Australia and New Zealand, the ground was possibly far less hardened and so more receptive to the new forms of artistic expression than were England and Europe with their centuries of tradition and institutional guardians, such as the Royal Academy of Arts in London and the Paris Salon, which kept aesthetic matters in check. That said, Petrus van der Velden, having settled in Christchurch, continued to paint in a darker, sombre and more realistic manner, his palette seemingly not making the transition from Europe to the South Pacific. Once part of the circle of the esteemed Dutch artist, Jozef Israëls, van der Welden was apparently highly regarded by Vincent van Gogh as 'a real artist and I wish I knew him … I know for sure that I should learn from him.'[38] The *Otago Daily Times* hailed van der Welden's *Waterfall in the Otira Gorge*, exhibited by the OAS in 1892, as 'the great feature of this year's exhibition',[39] and William Hodgkins ensured its purchase by the OAS. Peter Entwisle regards Otira as 'probably the most important landscape painted in New Zealand last century'.[40]

A comment is in order regarding the New Zealand landscape that finds favour with artists to the present day. In a word, it is unique. Much of the vegetation is native to the country and unlike anything found in Europe or the Americas. The New Zealand forest that once covered much of the country is 'bush' whereas other countries have woods or forests. It has an enchantment and allure all of its own, and painters have been capturing it in its various manifestations since Captain James Cook first landed on these shores in 1769. Grace Joel was no exception, as two of her landscapes show (see Images 2.10 and 2.15).

In 1892 the intrepid Nerli arrived in Samoa to paint the portrait of the novelist Robert Louis Stevenson at the latter's estate at Vailima. Michael Dunn notes in his biography of Nerli that Stevenson's wife Fanny did not like the portrait (Image 1.21) and neither, it seems, did the sitter. Certainly, the 27 sittings for it, rendered in oil, pastel and charcoal, would have taxed the patience of the novelist. One of the oils (there were replicas made) was sold by fine art dealers, McGregor Wright & Co. of Wellington, for £40 to a Mrs J. Turnbull. It now hangs in the Scottish National Portrait Gallery, Edinburgh.

Nerli returned to Dunedin in May 1893, where he gave Frances Hodgkins private lessons. 'Nerli has been most awfully good to me and gives me an extra lesson on Saturdays at his studio.'[41] (Later, however, Hodgkins claimed that Nerli's advice was useless.[42]) Nerli became a working member of the Otago Arts Society at this time and established a studio in the town square, which is actually called the Octagon because of its shape. His election to the society's council that December strengthened his putting down of artistic roots.

In Dunedin, Nerli was surrounded by various young women of nearly his own age, including, of course, Grace Joel and Frances Hodgkins. Women were beginning to realise they too could make a career as an artist. It would be safe to assume that the young bachelor Nerli would not be oblivious to this confluence of good fortune. Dunn quotes Nerli remarking on the girls of Melbourne: 'By God they are dam fine.'[43]

The cultural and intellectual interests of the colony were now also being catered for and nurtured by a recently arrived Australian (Jewish) immigrant to Dunedin, Charles Nalder Baeyertz (1886–1943). Starting out as the music critic for the *Otago Daily Times*, he subsequently founded in April 1893 the monthly publication, *The Triad*, devoted to art, music and science. Baeyertz, a polymath, said to know 17 languages, had exactingly high standards. He sought to stamp out the cultural mediocrity he found in the colony by being a fearsome but tiresome critic. To some extent, his efforts to lift the cultural standards of a youthful nation succeeded. *The Triad* became a fixture of New Zealand's intellectual life, its circulation apparently reaching 10,000 by 1897 – a considerable number for a fledgling colonial nation at the bottom of the Earth.[44]

Baeyertz's artistic leanings were actually very conservative, and *The Triad* promulgated those views. Practitioners with a more modern outlook, such as on the trend towards Impressionism, might therefore have been inclined to seek a more liberal environment abroad. Nevertheless, what was most notable about *The Triad* was the high intellectual level it attained, even by modern standards.

Together with fellow Dunedin artists Lawrence W. Wilson and John D. Perrett, Nerli opened the Otago Art Academy in 1894, at premises in the Octagon. However, even the services of a 'Professional Lady Model' and the furtive attendance by W.M. Hodgkins and his friend Dr John Scott could not save it from closing by August of the following year. Hodgkins' daughter Frances wrote to her sister Isabel that 'For several evenings Father has gone out ostensibly on business but has always returned with a large portfolio which he instantly secreted in the most mysterious manner in the study.' Having entered his study to determine what Father was up to, she was shocked to find 'he is attending a *nude* class at Nerli's Studio' (emphasis hers).[45]

What this quaint little family episode illustrates is that William Hodgkins held the typical attitude towards nudity that many Victorians did, and that many people still do. But it also showed his acute

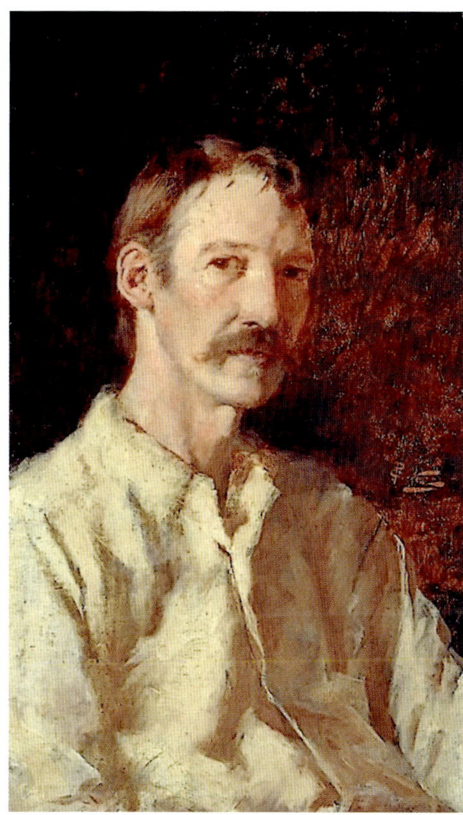

Image 1.21

***Portrait of Robert Louis Stevenson*, by Girolamo Nerli, 1892, oil on canvas, 61 x 35.5 cm.**

Bequeathed by Mrs J. Turnbull in 1915 to the Scottish National Portrait Gallery, Edinburgh, Scotland

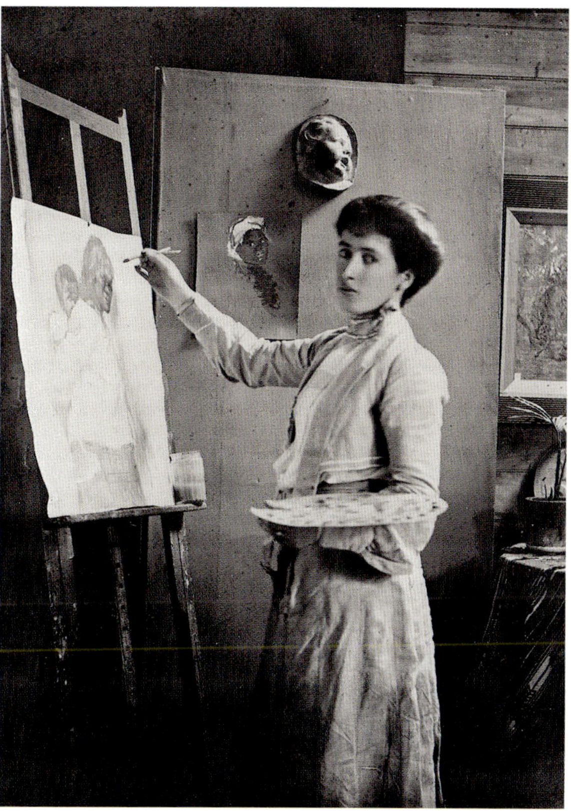

Image 1.22

Frances Hodgkins looking her fetching best, c. 1905, in a photograph likely intended to beguile her fiancé at the time. It was not enough, and she never married.

Ref: 1/2-010660, Alexander Turnbull Library, Wellington

awareness of the jurors' comments (being one of the jurors himself) published in the *Official Record of the New Zealand and South Seas Exhibition* to the effect that New Zealand art needed to give more attention to the figure and less to the landscape. Grace Joel was to do exactly that.

In 1895 David Con Hutton (1843–1910), the founding principal at the Otago School of Art and Design, appointed Nerli as a teacher of painting. Hutton was a neo-classicist whose teaching was based on drawing from an extensive collection of plaster casts of classical sculpture. Years later, Hutton's eldest son, David Edward, paid Grace Joel a noteworthy visit in London.

It seems that Nerli's heart was not in teaching. According to one published report, he told a friend who caught him slipping out to a local hotel: 'I open the student; then I come over here and rest. Then, by and by, I go back and shut the student up. Four hours a day I do that. It is too much work.'[46] Here we also have a sampling of Nerli's inimitable English.

There is no direct evidence that Grace Joel took lessons from Nerli; the five years she had spent studying in Melbourne would have made her more of a colleague than a pupil by this stage. However, as already indicated, she doubtless gained artistically from Nerli's years in Dunedin. His presence there would have been a source of inspiration and admiration for Grace and the other local artists. As Dunn points out, his 'exotic Italian manner, his accent and his approach to life would have been as influential as his method of painting.'[47] Nerli was

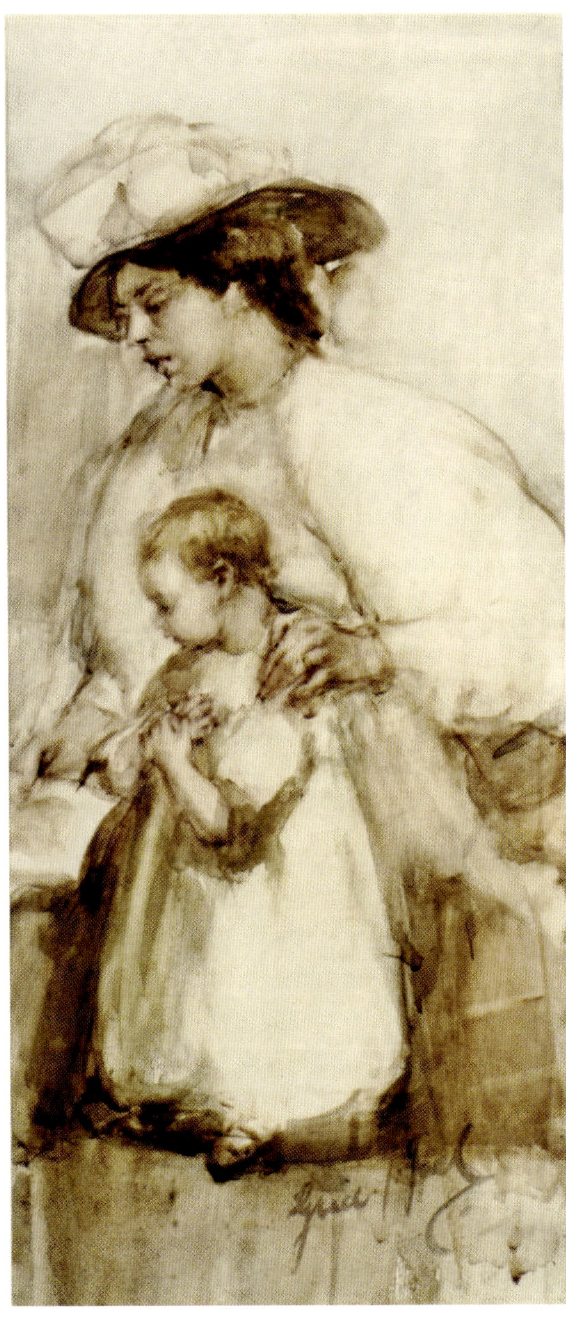

Image 1.23
***Mother and Child*, by Grace Joel, *c.* 1890s, sepia wash on paper, 42.4 x 18.3 cm, and possibly another rendering of the same pair as in Image 1.11.**
Hocken Collections, Uare Taoka o Hākena, University of Otago, Dunedin

the quintessential stranger who rides into town and changes it forever.

It was probably during this spell in Dunedin that Grace Joel painted Nerli's portrait (Image 1.18). Although she never exhibited the painting in her lifetime, she left it in her will to the Art Gallery of New South Wales, which had expressed an interest in purchasing one of her works. A reproduction appears as the frontispiece in Dunn's book, *Nerli: An Italian painter in the South Pacific*. Grace painted it in a style characterised by short brush strokes, giving it an impressionistic appearance, perhaps in homage to Nerli. It was one of the paintings featured at Australia's National Portrait Gallery's exhibition in 2011/2012 titled 'Impressions: Painting Light & Life'. Also included were works by E. Phillips Fox, Arthur Streeton, G.P. Nerli, Frederick McCubbin, Tom Roberts and other 'artists at the heart of Australian impressionism'.[48]

We will pick up the thread of Signor Nerli's life and how it weaves back into that of Grace Joel's after a detour to Melbourne where Grace now went to pursue her career.

Study in Melbourne

It was still maintained, in some quarters, that the greatest contribution to the world of art that could be made by any woman was to be the mother of a genius – Albert Ten Eyck Gardner, 1948

As well as being a picturesque ancient city in Germany, Heidelberg is a suburb of Melbourne, and it was here in the late 1880s and early 1890s that a loose association of painters who adopted the *plein-air* impressionist style came to be known as the Heidelberg School. Key figures in the movement were Tom Roberts and Frederick McCubbin. They were joined by others such as E. Phillips Fox, Tudor St George Tucker, Charles Conder and Arthur Streeton. As has been mentioned, Roberts, Conder and Streeton had previously met Nerli in Sydney and been exposed to his ideas.

Another feature of Melbourne's artistic landscape during the late nineteenth century was the National Gallery School, which was the leading centre of academic art tuition in Australia at this time. Some of the school's graduates became Australia's most distinguished artists. The school was very enlightened in that it allowed its women students to study the nude human body. Across the Tasman, the Dunedin School of Art offered similar classes for women,[49] yet Grace Joel chose the former over the latter to further her art studies.

There is speculation as to why Grace elected to study in Melbourne, and a variety of reasons can be advanced. Having on hand a host of relatives in Melbourne, as Grace did, surely made her decision easier. Her mother's sister, Hannah Woolf, had married Isaac Jacobs, and they lived in Melbourne. Although not all of their subsequent 12 progeny survived, worthy of mention is Deborah, born in 1870 and known as Daisy, who married Isaac Isaacs (a future attorney-general, chief justice, and governor-general of Australia) in 1888, the year Grace arrived. Grace completed a portrait of Daisy as a young woman possibly around this time or during a subsequent spell in Melbourne. It presently resides at the Mandelbaum House of the Australian Jewish Historical Society. In her will, Grace gave her cousin Daisy her diamond and sapphire snake ring; not that Daisy needed any more jewellery but Grace probably wanted her to have it as a family memento.

However, there was an even more interesting Melbourne connection for Grace, one that pertained to the Phillips-Fox family. Grace Joel's great grandparents (on her mother's side) were Phillip Phillips and Rosetta Moses. They were also the great grandparents (on the maternal side) of Emanuel Phillips Fox, who was born in the same year as Grace. This connection made Grace Joel and E. Phillips Fox ('the Australian Renoir') second cousins. If that were not enough, E.P. Fox's uncle on his mother's side, Simeon Phillips, married Rosetta Woolf, Kate Joel's niece, forming yet another bond between the Joel and Fox families. The Fox family

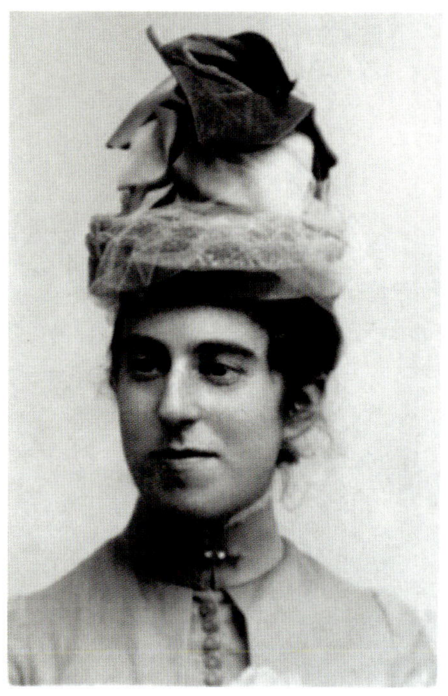

IMAGE 1.24

Photograph of Grace Joel taken from an album of season ticket-holders for the 1889/90 New Zealand and South Seas Exhibition, so probably from 1889 when Grace was 24. Toitū Otago Settlers Museum, Dunedin

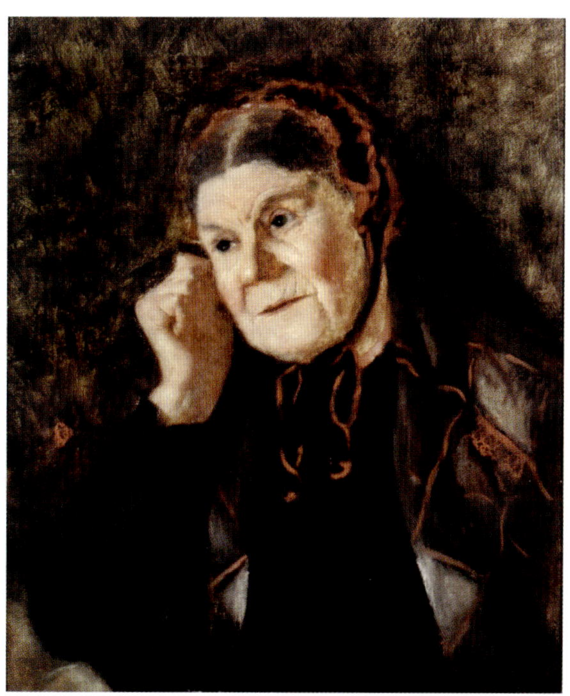

IMAGE 1.25

***The Nurse*, 1889, oil on canvas, 53.5 x 43.5 cm.** Private collection lived in Fitzroy, a suburb of Melbourne. Emanuel attended the National Gallery School from 1878 to 1886, and from there went on to study at the Académie Julian in Paris. Grace Joel did just the same – first the NGS in Melbourne and then the Académie Julian in Paris. We will witness further instances of Grace Joel following cousin Emanuel (Mannie) Fox's footsteps during her career.

The unpredictable nature of human existence, upon which all art depends, is nicely demonstrated in this charming vignette of how Mannie's parents, Alexander and Rosetta, came to marry:

> *In 1853 or 1854 Alexander Fox and his brother returned from the goldfields to Melbourne without any nuggets but wearing the 'gentleman digger's' outfit of red shirt, white breeches and revolver stuck in the back of a belt. When they visited some of the Phillips girls, Rosetta queried whether a revolver could be quickly drawn from such a position. Alexander said he would give a demonstration, and drew his revolver with such vigor that it accidently went off, wounding Rosetta in the leg. Full of remorse, Alexander was very considerate to her – and hence the marriage – and the artist E. Phillips Fox!*[50]

Whatever Grace's motivation for returning to Melbourne, by mid-1888 she was enrolled in the second term of tuition of the NGS's School of Design under Frederick McCubbin. Here she almost certainly met two fellow students – the future Australian war artist Arthur Streeton and the talented *bon vivant* painter Charles Conder. Streeton and Joel later became good friends in early twentieth-century London. In 1889 Grace continued her study at the School of Design over both terms. At the annual end-of-year exhibition (in November) of students' work, Grace won first-equal prize (£3.00) for first-year students' 'Best Charcoal Drawing'.

During 1888 and 1889, Grace would have been aware of and doubtless visited two exhibitions hosted by Melbourne. The first was the Centennial International Exhibition, set up to celebrate a century of Australian European colonial settlement. The exhibition ran from August 1888 to January 1889 and, as with the New Zealand and South Seas Exhibition, featured local, British and European art. Among the works on display were those by the illustrious William Mathew Hodgkins and daughter Isabel. To quench the great Australian thirst for beer, the Red Lion Brewery was represented as well.

The second – and more infamous – exhibition opened in 'Marvellous Melbourne' in August 1889. Organised by the Heidelberg School and titled the '9 by 5 Impression Exhibition', it showcased a panoply of paintings done mainly by Tom Roberts (62 works), Charles Conder (46) and Arthur Streeton (41). The works were painted on flat panels of wood, most of which were the size of cigar box lids – nine inches by five inches. The Heidelberg version of Impressionism was the order of the day, and the exhibition came to be recognised as a landmark event in the history of Australian painting. Although most of the works on display found no favour with Melbourne's chief art critic, James Smith ('a pain to the eye'), the exhibition struck a responsive chord with the public and about half the works sold.

By 1890, Grace was back in Dunedin, where she showed seven works at the Otago Art Society's annual exhibition. These included the charcoal drawing *Old Man's Head*, which won her the NGS prize in 1889, and the aforementioned *Under the Spell* (Image 1.15). Her penchant and talent for portraiture were starting to emerge, as noticed by the *Evening Star* of 12 November 1890: 'Miss G. Joel's contributions include a couple of portraits executed with marked fidelity and a considerable amount of technical skill, the young lady making a speciality of this branch of her profession. One of the two exhibits referred to is a particularly striking likeness.' A fortnight later, when the OAS held a promenade concert, Grace featured as one of its performers.

Having already spent a year and a half at the National Gallery School in Melbourne, Grace crossed the Tasman once again at the beginning of 1891 to resume her study of painting at the school. Here she remained for another three and a half years

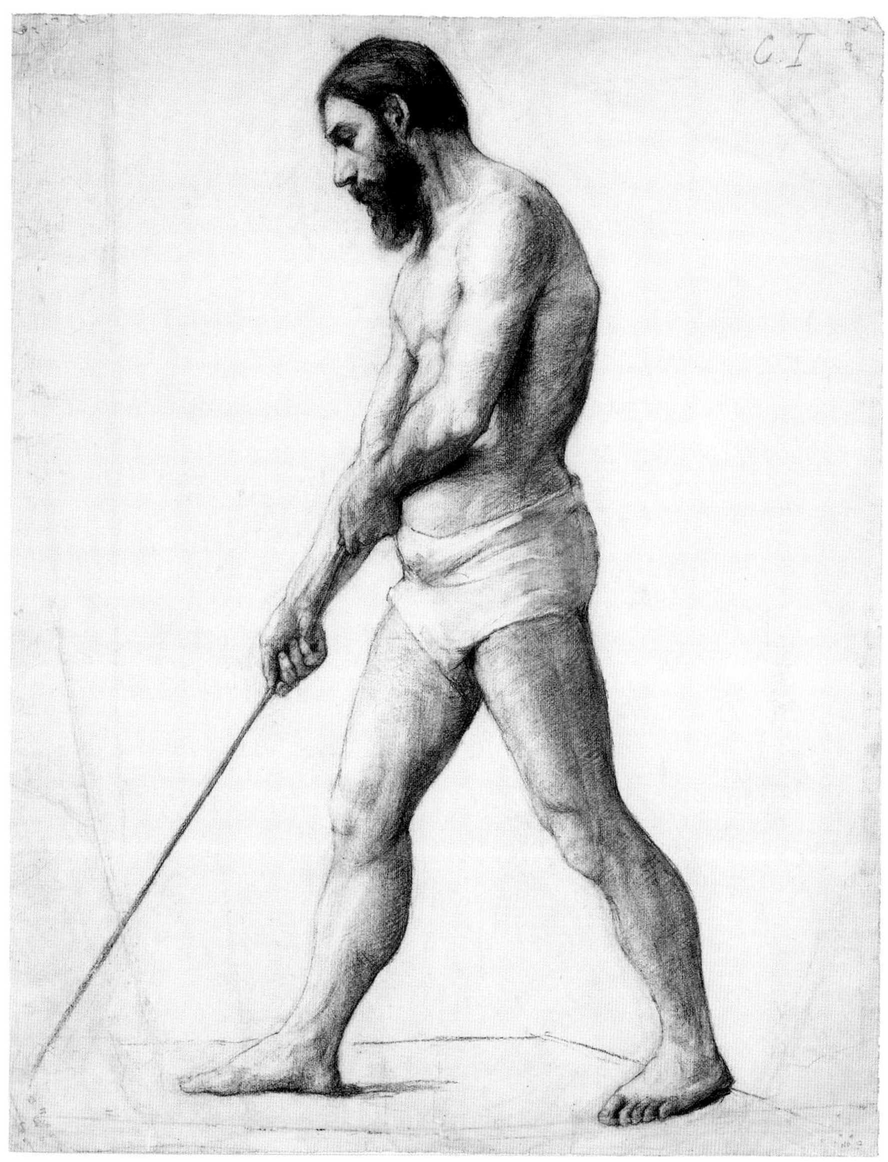

Image 1.26

Academic Male Nude, by Grace Joel, c. 1889, charcoal, 61 x 46 cm, completed while Grace was at the National Gallery School in Melbourne. This depiction of a powerfully built man, almost an iconic image – Grace Joel's *Vitruvian Man* – indicates the artist's acute eye for detail. However, a few years later, a critic from the *Star* (Christchurch), 16 April 1895, suggested that she 'bend her efforts to the close study of anatomy'. Dunedin Public Art Gallery, Dunedin

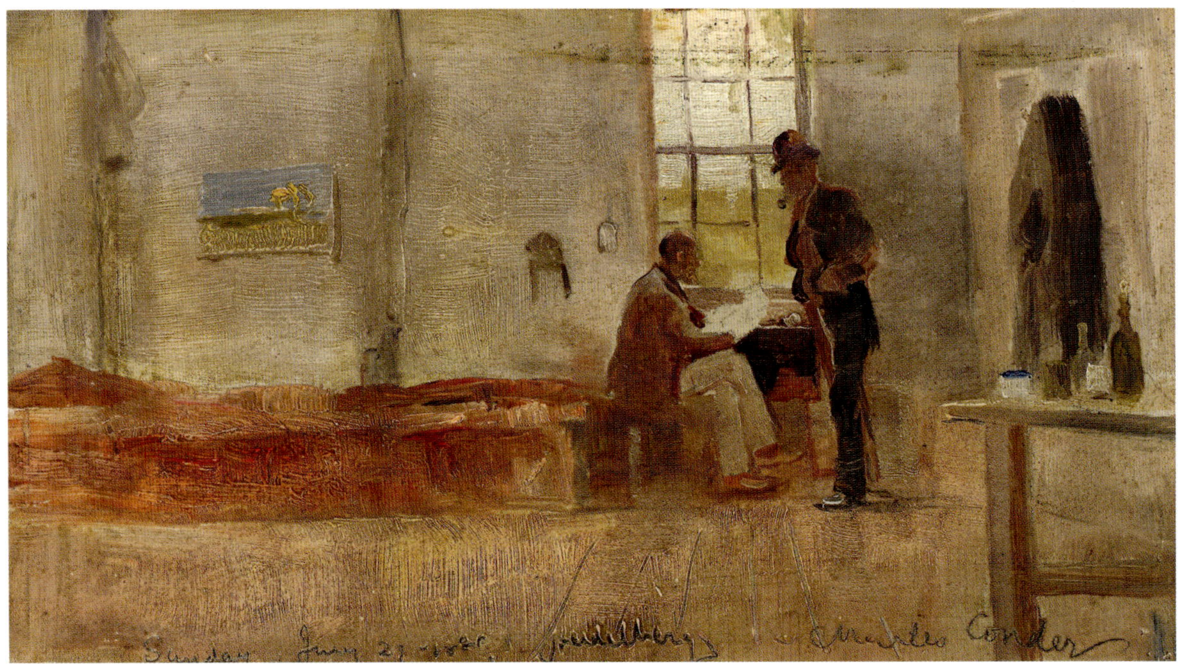

Image 1.27

***Impressionists' Camp*, by Charles Conder, 1889, oil sketch on paper on cardboard, 9.5 x 5.5 inches (24 x 14 cm) that appeared in the 1889 Melbourne '9 x 5 Impression Exhibition'. This, the 'home' of the Heidelbergers, depicts Tom Roberts (seated) and Arthur Streeton (standing). Here, the trio shared Streeton's derelict farmhouse accommodation (overlooking the Yarra Valley in Victoria, Australia), living and breathing impressionist painting for two idyllic summers.** National Gallery of Australia, Canberra

– until mid-1894. While at the NGS, Grace was elected a member of the Victorian Artists' Society in 1892.

The atmosphere between the men and women students at the NGS was particularly congenial, so much so that several couples married. One of these students was Dora Meeson, who attended in 1895/96, just missing Grace but nevertheless meeting future husband George Coates, both of whom appear in a NGS group photo taken in 1896.[51] (We will catch up with this liaison at the turn of the century in Paris.)

During her five years at the NGS, Grace built up a number of Australian acquaintances who would continue to feature in her artistic life abroad – and Australian art critics would continue to claim her as one of their own. Cousin E. Phillips Fox had just returned from studies in Paris, at the Académie Julian under William-Adolphe Bouguereau as well as at the École des Beaux-Arts under Jean-Léon Gérôme. Mannie walked off with first prizes at both institutions. However, it was Impressionism that really gripped his attention, not the establishment style of his teachers, no matter how sublime their work. His 1903 *Rêverie* resides in the collection of the Musée d'Orsay, Paris, the holy shrine of French Impressionism. Despite his Melbourne origins, Mannie Fox was a French Impressionist, and an excellent one at that (see Image 5.3).

On his return to Melbourne, Fox established the Melbourne Art School with friend and colleague Tudor St George Tucker. Fox and Tucker had studied together at the Julian as well as the École des Beaux-Arts. French Impression was most definitely on the new school's menu. The motivation to establish the school could have been thus: 'It was impossible to make a living as an artist in Melbourne in the 1890s but it was possible to make a bare living as an art teacher.'[52]

In a letter to the notable English painter, George Clausen RA, written many years later, Grace Joel related that she was a pupil of E. Phillips Fox and Frederick McCubbin.[53] She included with her letter to Clausen one from Fox in which he had presumably written something favourable on her behalf. That he did so indicates that Joel either enrolled as a student at the Melbourne Art School or received private tuition from Fox himself, or perhaps she just wanted to enhance her reputation abroad. She is not mentioned in a (not necessarily complete) list of students who attended the school in Moore's *Story of Australian Art*, although another New Zealand artist is – Ursula Foster. However, it would be safe to say that Grace's impressionist brush derived one way or another from E. Phillips Fox.

Tellingly, Fox's nephew and sometime biographer, Leonard Phillips (Len) Fox, quotes this passage from distinguished Australian art authority and critic, Daniel Thomas: 'The few examples from Melbourne at the same period [1890s] – Withers, Davies, Fox, Grace Joel – show quite a different technique of short, vibrant broken touches of rich crumbly textures. This is in fact the fully developed French impressionist technique, and must have been introduced by Phillips Fox.'[54] Thomas does draw a distinction between this latter group of Impressionists and the Heidelberg group of Roberts, Conder, Streeton and their adherents who 'share[d] a rather long brush stroke, and surprisingly thin paint'.[55] Grace's impressionist technique is evident in her works from a few years later, such as the portrait of Nerli (Image 1.18) and *A Rose 'midst Poppies* (Image 2.7).

Another crossover from the National Gallery School was Cristina Asquith Baker, who had a falling out with the newly appointed head of the NGS, Lindsay Bernhard Hall, and switched to the Melbourne Art School. There she became a star pupil and was the main figure in Fox's 1895 painting,

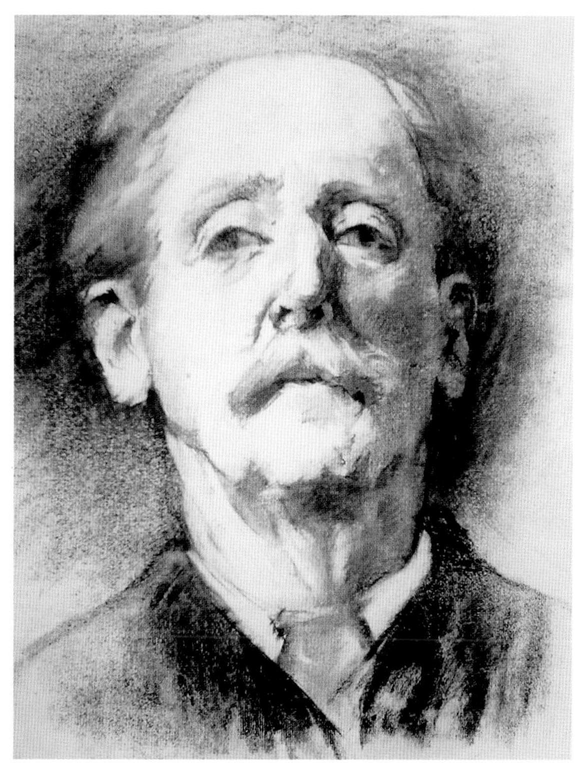

IMAGE 1.28

This could be the prize-winning charcoal sketch, *Old Man's Head*, which Grace executed at the National Gallery School, Melbourne, Australia, in 1889, 51.6 x 38.5 cm. Dunedin Public Art Gallery, Dunedin

Art Students (Image 1.29). Cristina and Grace would have known each other during their overlapping stints at the NGS. A book by William Morris Hunt, *Talks on Art*, belonging to Cristina and unearthed by Kirsten Fergusson during her Master of Arts study, has the inscription: 'To Dear Chrissie, From Grace'.[56] Could this be our Grace? Very likely.

During the first years of the new century, Cristina Asquith Baker shared a studio in Paris with another former Melbourne student, Ada May Plante. Next door in an adjoining studio was E. Phillips Fox; Grace Joel was in Paris too by then. *Plus ça change, plus c'est la même chose.* Grace and Ada probably met during the first term of 1894 at NGS, the last term for Grace but the first for Ada. Ten years later, in a letter to Cristina, Grace mentions not connecting with Ada during a trip to Holland.

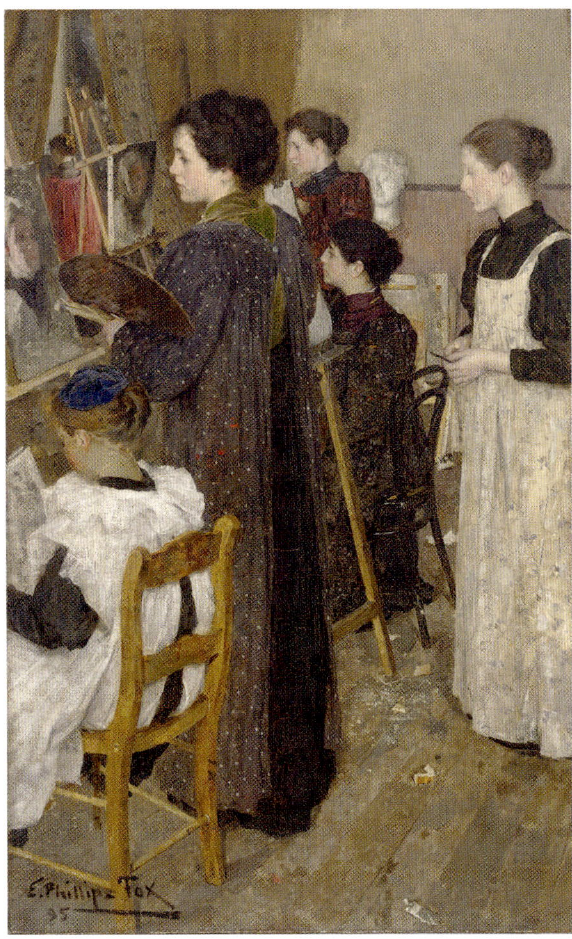

IMAGE 1.29

***Art Students*, by E. Phillips Fox, oil on canvas, 182.9 x 114.3 cm. Cristina Asquith Baker is the main figure in this 1895 scene from the Melbourne Art School. Cristina was also a contemporary of Grace Joel at the National Gallery School in Melbourne from 1888 to 1889. Fox's cousin, Etta Phillips, sits in the centre. Eminent Australian art critic Robert Hughes called this work 'the first truly Impressionist canvas painted in Australia'.** Art Gallery New South Wales, Sydney

IMAGE 1.30 (OPPOSITE)

***Nude*, the life-size study that won Grace Joel the 1893 Ramsay Prize for painting from the nude at the National Gallery School in Melbourne. Oil on canvas, 89.5 x 59 cm.** National Gallery School, Melbourne

In 1893 Grace won the Ramsay Prize for painting from the nude. The work, simply titled *Nude*, is still in the NGS's collection (Image 1.30). Grace was the first female student to win any major prize at the school, and the fact that she, a woman, had painted such a subject bordered on the scandalous given the school's repute among various members of Melbourne society. According to authors Victoria Hammond and Juliet Peers, 'Outraged citizens lobbied through the newspapers to close the life class or at least ban the public display of Gallery School work.'[57] Grace Joel's persistence in painting the nude human form would have continued to be considered very risqué, even salacious, and doubtless influenced how some individuals viewed her as a person.

Another fellow student, James Quinn (1869–1951), placed second. No need to feel sorry for Quinn, however, as that year he won a scholarship and duly headed off to Paris to further his artistic studies at both the Académie Julian and the École des Beaux-Arts. He subsequently became a successful portrait painter, exhibiting at the Royal Academy of Arts in London as well as the Old and New Salons in Paris. Grace later attributed winning first prize 'to the fact that artists were called in to judge the students' work instead of the matter being left to a body of trustees as heretofore'.[58] She visited Quinn years later in his Putney, London studio. Spotting a recent painting of a mother with her son on her lap teaching him to read, she gave it qualified praise: '… it had much more refinement, tenderness, and feeling than some of his work.'[59]

In July 1894 Grace again made the trip across the Tasman, returning to Dunedin where a photo of her *Nude* painting could be found displayed in the window of Messrs Begg and Co.'s music warehouse. She had opted not to compete for the National Gallery School's travelling scholarship of £120 per year that Quinn had won the previous year. For Grace Joel, her art was no mere pastime but a passion that would be life-long. For her, the pejorative expression – 'left on the shelf', was just that – left on the shelf.

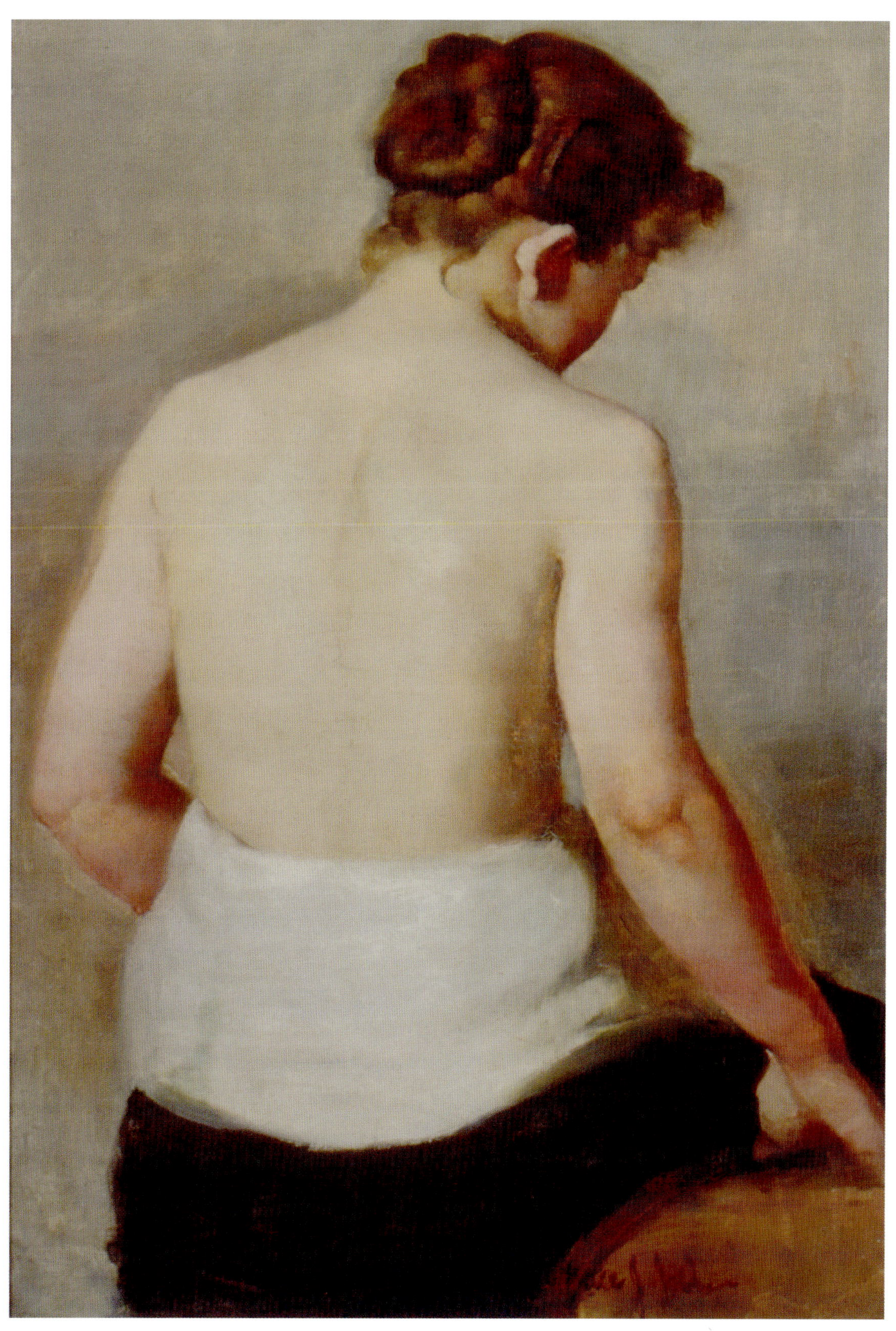

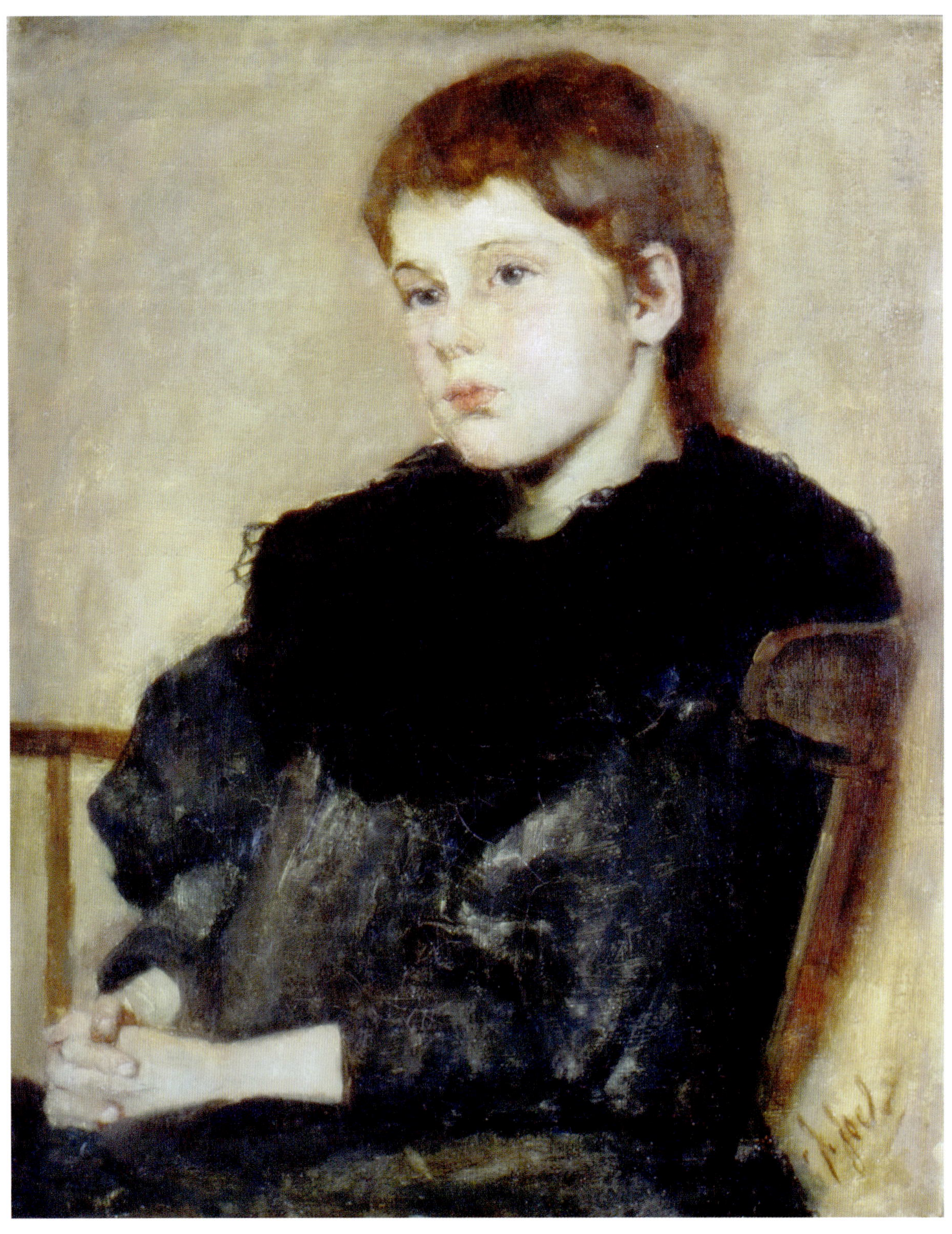

Image 2.1

Portrait of a Young Girl, by Grace Joel, c. 1894, oil on canvas, 65 x 50 cm. Grace almost certainly exhibited this work in 1894 in her studio at Occidental Chambers, Dunedin. Private collection

Chapter 2

Return of the Native

What woman was this who displayed such accuracy of touch, who so successfully treated the tonal qualities of her subject: who, setting her compatriots at defiance, worked out her own salvation, unaided and alone? – D.H. Souter, 1906

Back in Dunedin as of 1894 and full of artistic enthusiasm, Grace placed an advertisement in the *Otago Daily Times* advising of an exhibition of her work.[1]

ART EXHIBITION
Of
STUDIES FROM LIFE, &c.,
By
GRACE J. JOEL,
Occidental Chambers, High street.

All interested in Art invited. 11au

The exhibition, set up in her Occidental Chambers, High Street studio, ran for one week and featured a number of head and figure studies, some 30 paintings in oils and the photo of her prize-winning *Nude*, which remained with the National Gallery School in Melbourne. A reporter from the *Otago Daily Times*, having written of her 'praiseworthy specimens,' 'clever touch' and admirable flesh tints, concluded that 'Miss Joel's *forte* is figure-painting, and if she succeeds in bringing that branch of art, hitherto so much neglected, more prominently into notice in Dunedin, she will render great service.'[2] One of the works in the exhibition was probably Image 2.1, if the report in *The Triad* is correct.[3]

After the exhibition, Grace got into her stride as a working artist and placed further advertisements in the local newspapers stating that she was available to conduct painting and drawing classes.[4] She was also elected a working member of the Otago Art Society and on 14 December attended their annual general meeting, at which she was appointed to the society's council,[5] a coming of age acknowledgement by the Dunedin art establishment.

During this period, Grace's youngest sister, Lily, now in her early twenties, was engaged in all the activities required of a cultured young woman of her status. In keeping with family tradition, she played the piano and sang at various musical entertainments and concerts in the city, sometimes appearing on the same programme as sister Blanche and brother Edward. She joined dramatic clubs and no doubt looked very fetching in black velvet and white lace at the university ball. By age 27, she was giving lessons from the family home, Eden Bank, on Regent Road, in piano, singing, elocution and harmony.[6]

The years 1895 to 1899 were ones of great artistic fecundity for Grace. Once again living at Eden Bank, she continued giving classes in painting and drawing at her 'studio' there, of 'Life, Landscape, and Flowers; Term Commencing February 4.'[7] Even the language was moving upmarket!

Broadening her horizons, she exhibited six works at the Canterbury Society of Arts exhibition in April 1895 and three more at the seventh annual exhibition of the New Zealand Academy of Fine Arts, Wellington, in July. Throughout the year, she

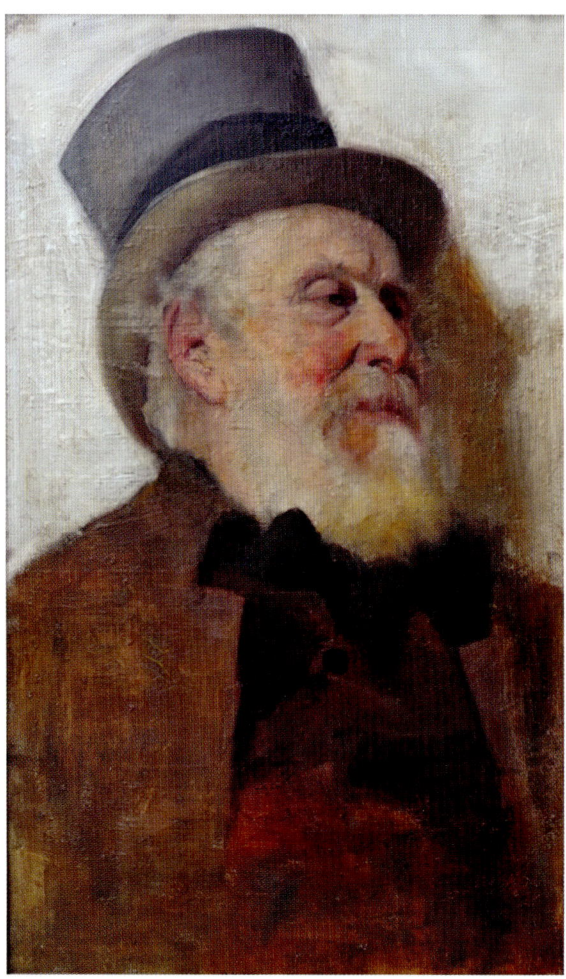

Image 2.2

***The Bon Vivant/Portrait of a Gentleman*, by Grace Joel, also known as *The Coachman* to the Joel family, c. 1895, oil on canvas, 59.8 x 34.5 cm. A Joel relative suggested Grace painted the portrait in Australia. Its unusual angle gives the gentleman a certain dignity and an aura of one who has seen a good deal of life. The angle is a challenging one to paint.** Private collection

also attended OAS council meetings. By this time, the society's membership had risen to nearly 200.

The Joel household was now a potpourri of artistic activity. Younger sister Blanche had placed an advertisement just above one of Grace's announcing her art classes. It declared her availability to give lessons at the family home in 'Pianoforte and Violin Playing, Singing and Harmony.'[8] Due credit must be given to the young women's parents, Maurice and Kate, who probably had no inkling until then that their home would become a private school for the arts owing to the activities of their multi-talented daughters.

In the middle of 1895, Grace took part in the formation of the Easel Club, becoming a founding member along with G.P. Nerli, A.H. O'Keeffe, L.W. Wilson, R. Hawcridge and Jane (Jenny) Wimperis. Frances Hodgkins, who had been one of Nerli's students, was absent from its membership, possibly in order to maintain her allegiance to her father's more conservative Otago Art Society, as this comment in a letter she wrote to her sister suggests: 'Mr O'Keeffe has returned from Paris and is shocking the proprieties by exhibiting a number of nude studies. Father won't let me go and see them! Boo hoo!'[9]

The Easel Club indeed had a life class in O'Keeffe's studio. The artist had only recently made his way back from his year at the Académie Julian in Paris. The club's first general meeting on 20 July attracted about 25 members, who agreed to hold meetings on the first Saturday of each month: 'The club will supply a long-felt want, as it is intended to arrange for a Saturday or Wednesday Life Class.'[10] It would not be correct to characterise this new group as bohemian relative to the more establishment-based OAS because several of its members, such as Nerli, Joel, O'Keeffe and Wilson, were common to both. However, it is fair to say that the Easel Club had broader horizons than the landscapes of the past.

We could assume that Grace Joel and Frances Hodgkins were by now close friends rather than mere acquaintances, as they were continually rubbing shoulders in the Dunedin art scene, but it seems they were not and never would be. Linda Gill, who edited Hodgkins' published letters, attributes this lack of closeness to the fact that the two women came from very different social backgrounds: Grace's a well-to-do Jewish cosmopolitan one and Frances's more middle-class provincial.[11] However, Hodgkins had a certain admiration for Joel's artistic talents. In a letter to her sister Isabel she complains: 'Aunt Bella is most snubby on the subject of my pictures and the only paper she has sent me is a very vulgar comic paper holding me up to great ridicule, but in the select company of Messrs Nairn, Nerli and Miss Joel.'[12]

However, 'Miss Joel' was not the only one to encounter the less than amiable side of Frances Hodgkins, who developed a loathing for little inoffensive Dunedin artist Jenny Wimperis (1844–1929). Years later, when Wimperis crossed paths with Hodgkins in Italy, Hodgkins wrote to her mother: 'She is now with me & a more depressing & tiresome little woman you can scarce imagine … There is nothing to do but to flee Italy.'[13] And flee she did! One must be understanding of Frances, though, as she had her own share of demons to grapple with, and the fear of turning into a Jenny Wimperis seems to have been one of them.[14] Perhaps with good reason, as Wimperis died essentially alone and unknown in 1929, age 85, in Epsom, Surrey.

A month after the Easel Club's first general meeting, Grace sent some paintings to Melbourne for exhibition that Baeyertz's *The Triad* reviewed before their departure: 'The magnum opus is the nude figure of a girl. The scheme of colour seems somewhat daring, but the effect is undoubtedly good. The girl lies on a pink coverlet, which forms no contrast to the flesh colour of the figure, but the figure is so cleverly lighted that an effect of gaiety, freshness, and light seems to pervade the air.'[15] When this painting was displayed the following year in Auckland by that city's Society of Arts, a reviewer expressed a similar view:

> *… to reproduce the naked body, to bring out every curve and muscle, not to falter in the sweep of a single line from head to feet, and to present the tender palpitating translucent flesh – there is a task … The picture is that of a young child lying naked on a pink-coloured couch. The general outline of the figure is very good, and the colour of the flesh, thanks in no small measure to the adoption of the pink foil, does not suggest unnaturalness … Her intention is to produce an impression, and she does it very well.*[16]

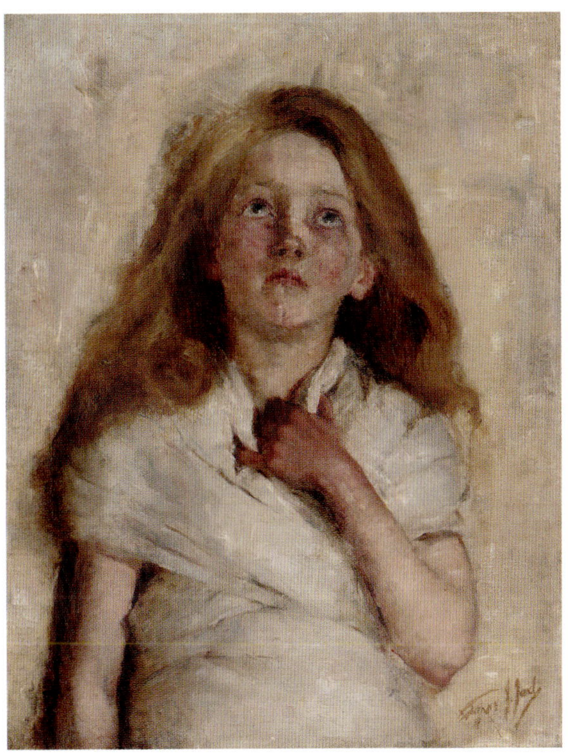

Image 2.3
A rather dirty looking *Little Nell*, the forlorn character in Dickens' *The Old Curiosity Shop*. Painted by Grace Joel, 1895, oil on canvas, 65.5 x 50 cm.
Te Papa Tongarewa Museum of New Zealand, Wellington

The work being praised here is the painting, *Youth*, initially exhibited by the Canterbury Society of Arts (1895) and then gaining exposure at the Auckland Society of Arts (1896), the Cliff Gallery in Sydney (1896) and the New Zealand Academy of Fine Arts, Wellington (1897). The subject of the young girl's nudity appeared to be (refreshingly) irrelevant. However, we shall let her momentarily bask in the enlightened vision of these two reviewers for she is yet to face a barrage of criticism on several counts.

Grace also exhibited another 11 works with the Otago Arts Society during 1895, including one titled *Little Nell* (Image 2.3) in reference to the Charles Dickens' character. The critic from the *Evening Star* praised it as one of Grace's 'most attractive contributions.'[17] The year found Miss

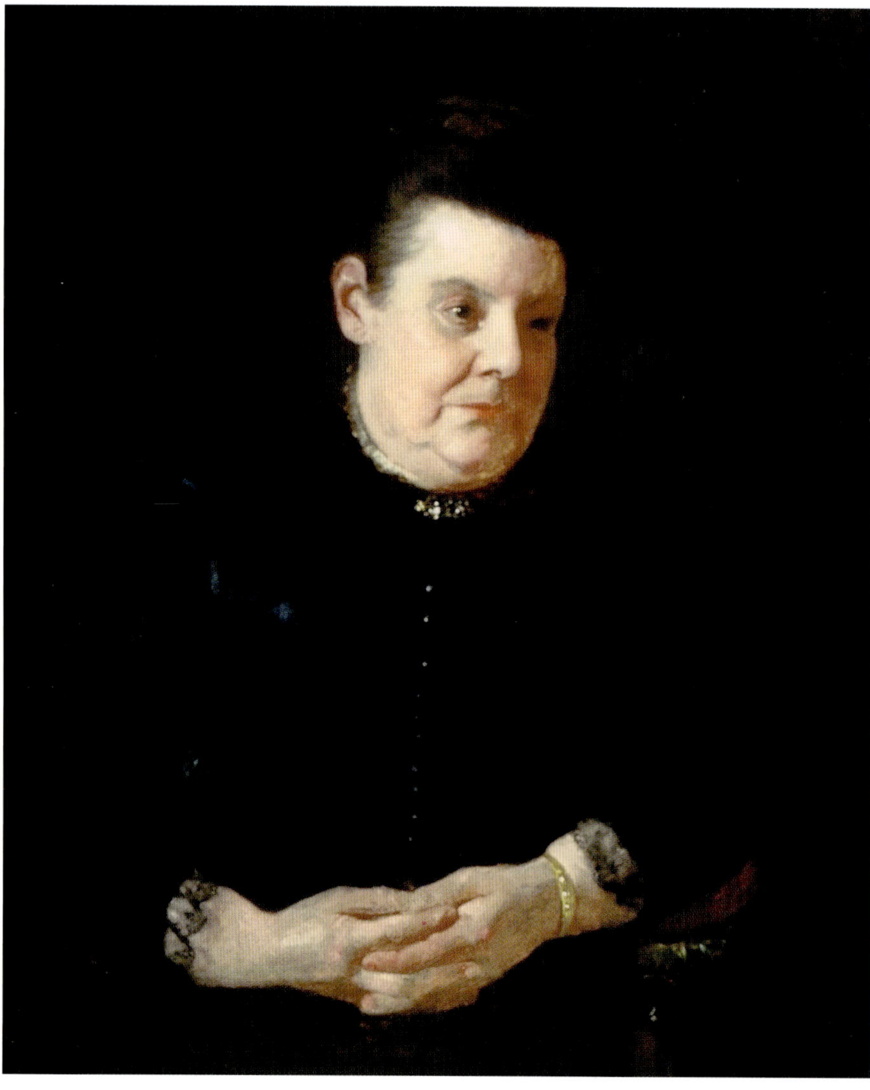

Image 2.4
***Portrait of Catherine Joel*, the artist's mother, c. 1895, oil on canvas, 75.4 x 60 cm. The tender feeling for the sitter is manifest.** Private collection

Joel again elected to the OAS council[18] and also appointed as a member of the selection and hanging committee for the forthcoming exhibition. She was furthermore given the responsibility, together with Mrs T.M. Hocken, of arranging concerts to be held during the exhibition, no doubt because of her musical background.[19]

Amid all the flurry of artistic activity, Grace's brother Philip Simeon died in October, age 29, at the Seacliff Lunatic Asylum, as the facility was then known. This institution, some 30 kilometres north of Dunedin, was noteworthy for being the largest building in the country. It was later to be the domicile of the (incorrectly diagnosed) New Zealand writer, Janet Frame, CBE, ONZ, winner of many literary prizes and holder of honorary doctorates.

Two other Grace Joel paintings from around this time merit closer attention. The first is a portrait of Grace's mother, Catherine (Kate) Joel (Image 2.4). Grace probably took this portrait with her to England because in 1903 *Mrs Maurice Joel* (NFS) was exhibited at the John Baillie Gallery in London. A portrait of Grace's father (Image 6.5) likely made the same journey as his wife's portrait. The second work, *The Bon Vivant* (Image 2.2), known in the Joel family as *The Coachman*, appeared in an Auckland exhibition in 1896 under the title of *Portrait of a Gentleman*. Decades later (in 1967), the Dunedin

Public Art Gallery included the portrait in its exhibition of New Zealand painters. The gentleman portrayed may have appeared elsewhere earlier in the century under another assumed name, but if not, why this work had to wait for more than 70 years to again be seen in public is just one of the many mysteries surrounding the life and works of Grace Joel. Her painting of Nerli (mentioned in Chapter 1) probably also originated from the 1895/96 period, before he left (fled?) Dunedin.

The year 1896 began on a festive note with the marriage of Grace's sister Blanche to optician Alfred Aaron Levi of Wellington (Image 2.5). The wedding took place at the Joel residence, Eden Bank, on 18 February 1896. The genial 'Alf' and Blanche in the ensuing years became luminaries on the Wellington musical scene. The marriage produced three children, but just four years later the 40-year-old Alf was 'chatting in his usual lively manner with friends on the Quay on Monday – dead on Thursday morning!'[20] His death was attributed to a blood infection caused by a boil. Blanche, pregnant at the time of Alf's death, named the child Alfred Aaron – his father's names.

After the wedding, Grace resumed her art classes at her Regent Road studio. In April she exhibited for the first time with the Auckland Society of Arts. One of the four paintings she showed was the aforementioned *Youth*. Among some favourable comments by the *New Zealand Herald* reviewer, we also find, 'and the artist would do well in the future to pay more attention to drawing and anatomy'.[21]

Grace's pupils displayed a number of studies in Mr David Scott's home décor shop in the Octagon. According to *The Triad*, the paintings had 'the distinct impress of Miss Joel's broad style'.[22] A reviewer for the *Otago Daily Times* discussed the work of four students, one being 'A still life study by Miss Arndt'.[23] Mina Arndt, of Jewish immigrant parents, is today recognised as a notable New Zealand artist. She and her family moved to Dunedin from Arrowtown after her father died in 1885. In 1907 Mina, her mother and two sisters

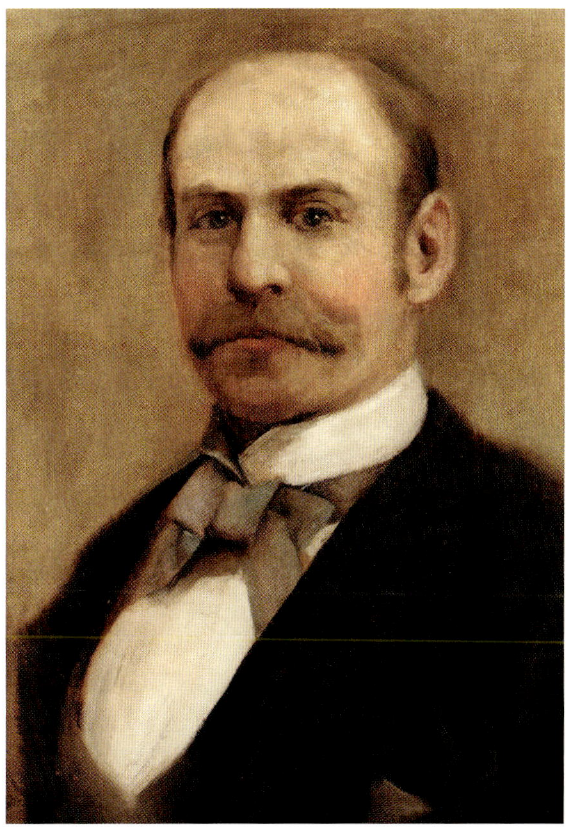

Image 2.5
***Alfred Levi*, a posthumous portrait painted by Grace Joel, c. 1912, oil on canvas, 55.5 x 40.5 cm.** Private collection

travelled to London where she studied for a time before moving to Berlin to take up further study. She exhibited in London, Paris and Berlin, returning at the outbreak of the Great War to New Zealand, where she continued to work as an artist until her death in 1926.

However, Mina Arndt was not quite 11 years of age by March 1896 and, according to the conventions of the day, the 'Miss Arndt' of the *Otago Daily Times* review would have been the eldest of her two unmarried sisters. So the student artist under scrutiny was not Mina Arndt after all. As to Grace Joel's teaching methods, again courtesy of the *Otago Daily Times* reporter, we have this precious glimpse: '... all the pupils study direct from nature, as Miss Joel strictly forbids the use of copies.'

On 12 May, in one of the very few letters that are extant from Grace's life, Joel wrote to a Mr Richardson of the Victorian Artists' Society to determine when the society's next exhibition would be held. She was thinking, she said, of becoming a member again – but in the event, she did not.

Grace exhibited several works at the Canterbury Society of Arts, one of which, *Study* (Image 2.6), 'a girl in an indigo-blue dress, is one of her best efforts. The pose is natural, and the expression of the face has been well caught.'[24] Senior curator at the Auckland Art Gallery, Ron Brownson, considers it 'one of the most innovative portraits made by a New Zealand female artist in the 19th century'.[25]

Little Nell also found her way to the Christchurch exhibition and may have been picked up by Mr G.H. Elliott, the Head of the Christchurch School of Art.[26] The *Evening Star* reported that Mr Elliott purchased a work of Grace Joel's to be hung at the Art School 'for educational purposes in the life class there'.[27] But it was highly unlikely to have been poor *Little Nell*, given her lack of suitability for a life class.

In a rare gesture for a New Zealand artist, but more common in England and some Australian colonies, Grace opened her studio to invited guests to preview works soon to be exhibited at the forthcoming Otago Art Society. 'They consist for the most part of figure studies, a branch of the profession which Miss Joel has cultivated with no little success.'[28]

Grace exhibited 11 works at the OAS opening on 6 November 1896, and also sang at the society's musical evening in the Choral Hall.[29] Her paintings included one of her most well known, the delightfully impressionistic *A Rose 'midst Poppies* (Image 2.7), which was praised by various critics. The 'best work by this artist ... is "A Rose 'midst Poppies" ... It is a very pleasing picture, and one that does Miss Joel great credit.'[30] She 'has succeeded admirably in her treatment of an admittedly difficult subject'.[31] The painting depicts 'a young girl smiling through a perfect bower of glowing poppies in sunlight ... One hand is pushing back the poppies as they impede her progress. The idea is original, and as in all her work the colour is rich and harmonious.'[32]

Another work had the highly suggestive title *The Dead, Dead Past is Gone, The Present* –: 'Miss Joel's large canvas ... attracts considerable attention, and deserves much praise. It represents a woman sitting in contemplative attitude. The line of poetry which forms the title makes obvious that Grace was comparing past and present, and one may reasonably conclude that her thoughts were painful and sad in character.'[33] The poem referred to is possibly *A Psalm of Life* by American poet Henry Wadsworth Longfellow (1807–1882), although the words, 'Let the dead bury their dead' traces back to Jesus (Matthew 8:22 and Luke 9:60). The pertinent stanzas of Longfellow read:

> *Trust no Future, howe'er pleasant!*
> *Let the dead Past bury its dead!*
> *Act, — act in the living Present!*
> *Heart within, and God o'erhead!*
>
> *Lives of great men all remind us*
> *We can make our lives sublime,*
> *And, departing, leave behind us*
> *Footprints on the sand of time;*

The woman in the painting 'who leans her head upon her hand'[34] ties the work stylistically to *Under the Spell* (Image 1.15). The significance of *The Dead, Dead Past* choice of a title (with its extra *Dead* added for emphasis), and the possible anguish it underscored in the life of 31-year-old Grace Joel, may (at a guess) be gleaned from the actions of Signor Nerli just before and after the exhibition.

Nerli attended his final Otago Art Society Council meeting on 26 October 1896 and by 11 November was no longer teaching at the School of Art, suggesting that he departed Dunedin, apparently without fanfare, within this brief interval.[35] Nevertheless, Nerli had three of his works on show at the November OAS exhibition. He headed north, eventually ending up in Auckland, where he became a member of the Auckland Society of Arts, exhibiting at its annual exhibition in April 1897.

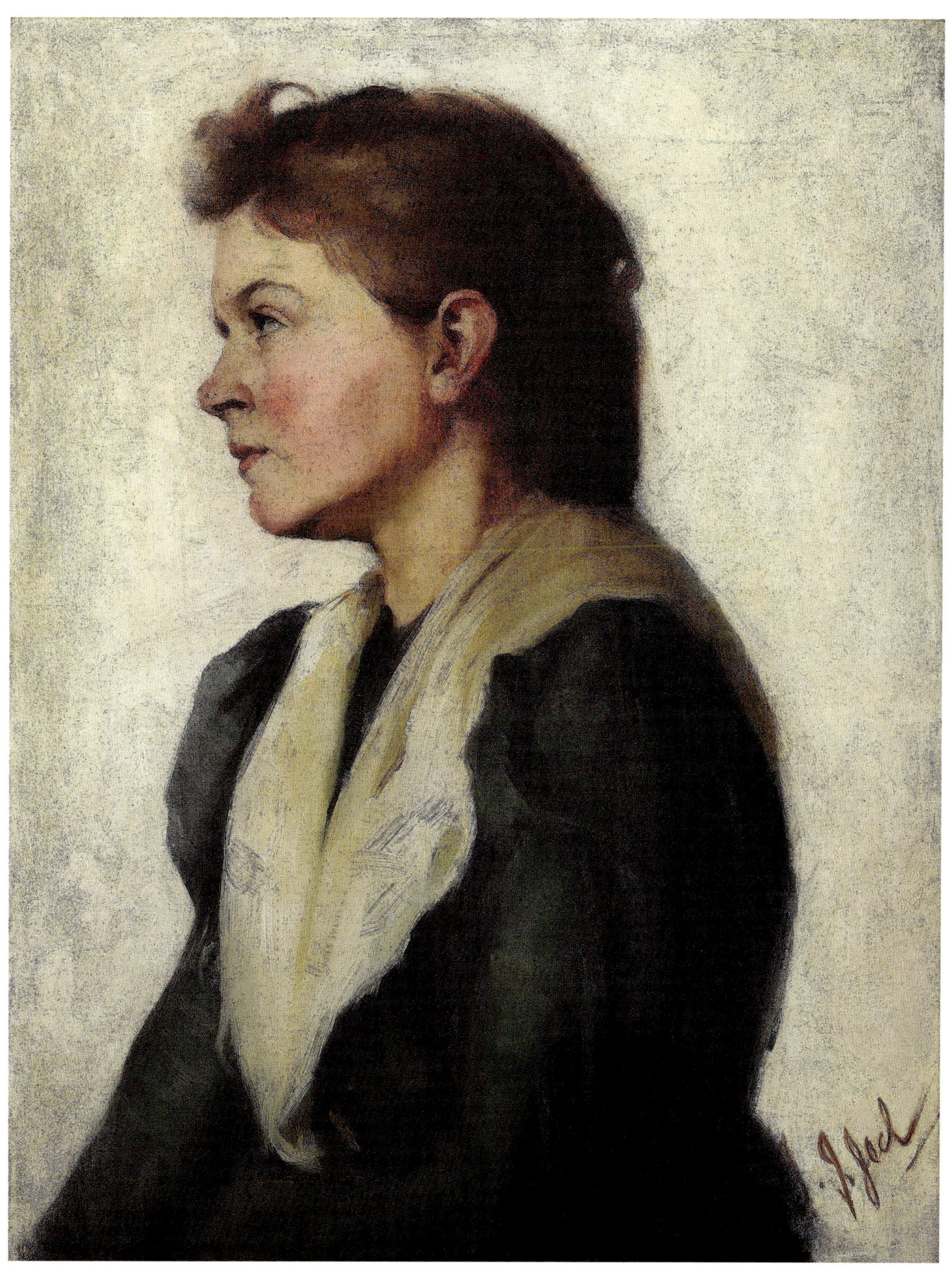

IMAGE 2.6

***Study* (now called *Girl with Scarf*), exhibited by Grace Joel at the Canterbury Society of Arts, 1896, oil on canvas, 69.8 x 52 cm.** Auckland Art Gallery Toi o Tāmaki, Auckland; purchased with funds from the Lyndsay Garland Trust, with generous assistance from Hartley Joel, 2010

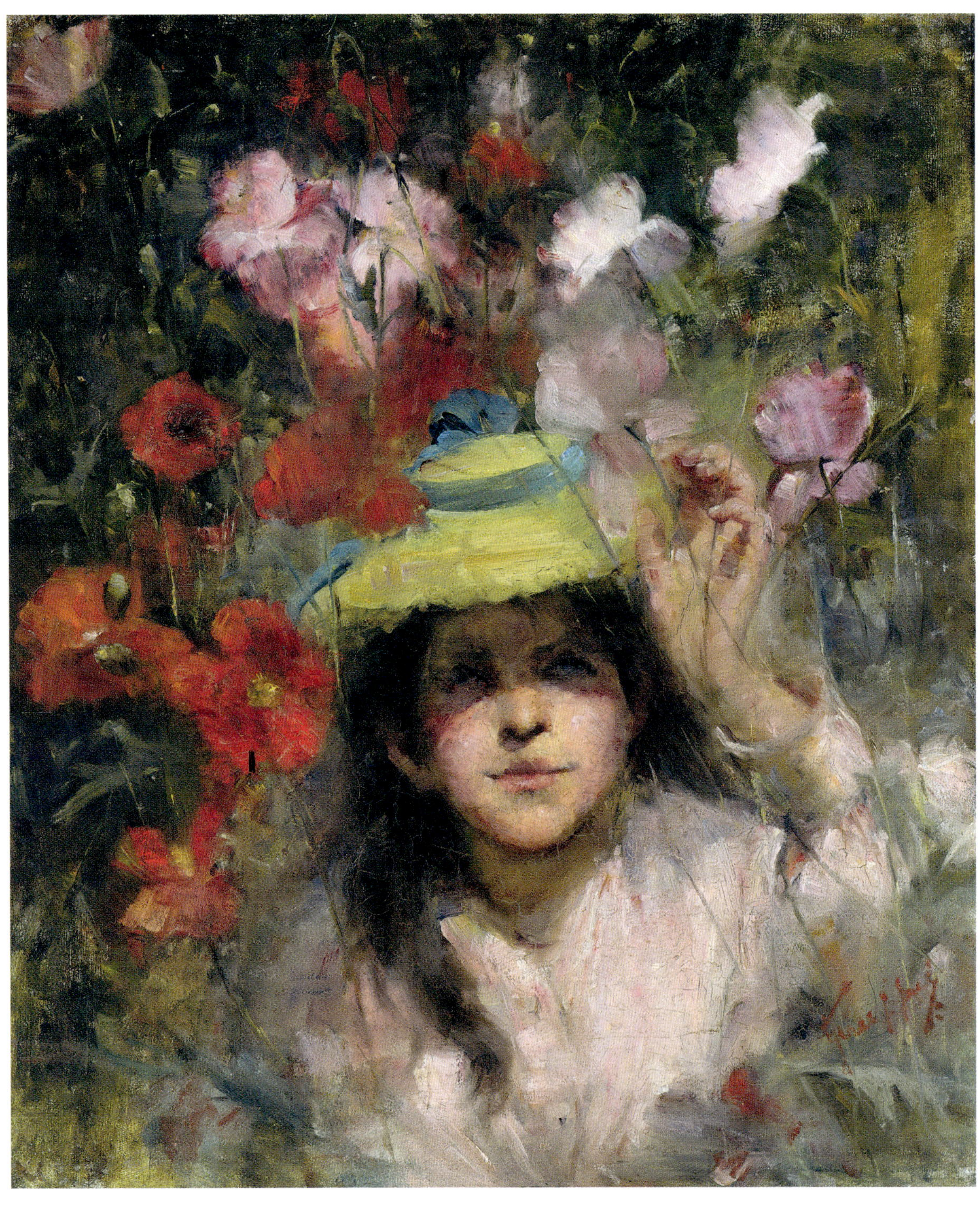

IMAGE 2.7

The impressionistic *A Rose 'midst Poppies,* by Grace Joel, 1896, oil on canvas, 60 x 49.6 cm. This is one of the best known of her works. A reproduction adorns a wall at the Grace Joel Retirement Village in Auckland.

Collection of the Christchurch Art Gallery Te Puna o Waiwhetu, Christchurch; purchased 1966

During his nearly year-long stay in Auckland, Nerli met Marie Cecilia Josephine Barron and married her on 5 March 1898 in Christchurch. She was 23, Nerli 37. They departed two days after the wedding for Australia, never to return to New Zealand.

Was there something untoward in Signor Nerli's behaviour that precipitated his sudden departure from Dunedin? Being somewhat indifferent to matters financial, perhaps he owed money about town.[36] However, it was very common in those days for creditors to file court claims for money owed them; businesspeople like Maurice Joel did this all the time. Yet Nerli seemed in no hurry to leave New Zealand or even simply disappear. His membership in the Auckland Society of Arts belies the actions of a man on the run from creditors. It was just Dunedin that he was apparently fleeing from.

Nerli's marriage to Cecilia and the couple's rapid departure from New Zealand offers the stronger clue as to his flight north from Dunedin. One does not have to be a Sigmund Freud (although this sort of historical psychoanalysis is always fraught) to suspect that between *Under the Spell*, in 1890, coinciding with the arrival of the exotic bohemian artist Girolamo Nerli, and *The Dead, Dead Past*, coinciding with his departure in 1896, some tectonic upheaval took place in Grace Joel's emotional life.

Indeed, *l'affaire* Nerli has gained literary currency, as this excerpt from *The Larnachs* by New Zealand author Owen Marshall illustrates:

> *At the recitations and musical evening held at Oaklands, when we were talking of the praise given to Frances Hodgkins in* The Triad *magazine, Bessie told me of the continuing gossip concerning Grace Joel, another very promising young painter whose father owned the Red Lion Brewery. 'She has given herself to Girolamo Nerli,' Bessie said. 'It's common knowledge and it will be the ruin of her career and acceptance in society.' Both of us were acquainted with Nerli, who established the Otago Art Academy. He is an unconventional, talented man not long among us from his own country, whom I could quite see taking advantage of a young woman, but I didn't say that ...*[37]

This very passage was broadcast to the nation by Radio New Zealand as part of the serialised reading of Marshall's book during May 2012.

The genteel sentiments of the Victorian expression 'She has given herself to ...' presume much more than meaningful looks across a crowded *atelier*. Peter Entwisle, having interviewed Maurice Joel, Grace's nephew, states that Maurice was absolutely certain that Grace and Nerli had an affair. And in the 1890s an affair was a serious matter for a woman – not the commonplace occurrence that it is today. Could Grace have become with child?

However, another conjecture might relate to the orthodox nature of the Joel family's religious beliefs. Did Grace's father refuse to entertain any thoughts of marriage to a bohemian Italian gentile? Was Nerli's hurried departure from Dunedin the result of Maurice Joel running him out of town? But let us abstain from further speculation upon this matter, as everyone is entitled to a degree of privacy in the conduct of their own affairs, even in posterity.

Another painting exhibited by Grace Joel at the annual OAS exhibition in 1896 is perhaps also telling of her emotional state at the time. It carried the poetic appellation: '*A vague unrest, / A nameless longing seiz'd her breast: / A wish, she hardly dared to own, / For something better than she had known*'. The poem from which Grace drew these words is *Maud Muller* by the American poet John Greenleaf Whittier (1807–1892). Was the young Grace unconsciously revealing a pictorial diary that traversed her emotional terrain from the wonderment depicted in *Under the Spell*, leading to her sense of despair in *The Dead, Dead Past* and then on to the contemplation of a brighter future in *A vague unrest?* The joy of the past is dead and buried; now it is time to move on in the present. Or, as Winston Churchill later put it, 'If you are going through hell, keep on going.'

Whatever the psychological undertones, the citation from the poem indicates that Joel had access to works by American poets such as Whittier

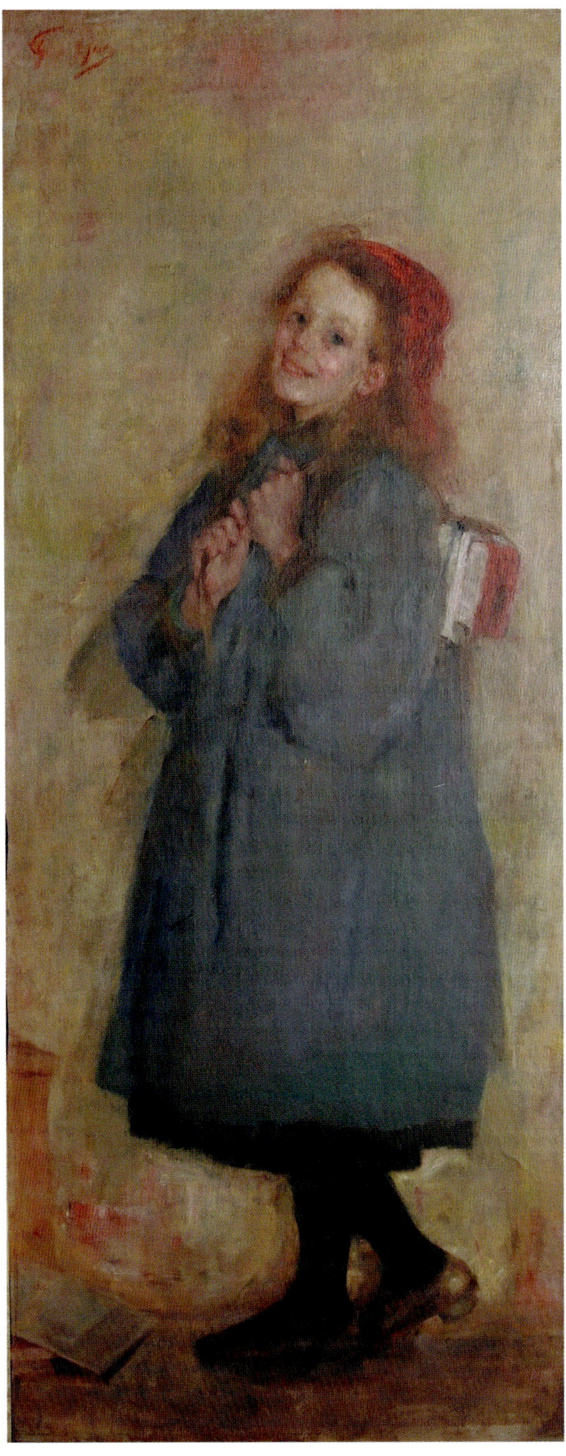

IMAGE 2.8

The School Girl (originally titled *Home for the Holidays*), by Grace Joel, oil on canvas, c. 1896, 152.5 x 60.5 cm. Grace exhibited the work at the 1896 annual exhibition of the Otago Art Society, Dunedin.

Collection of the Southland Museum & Art Gallery, Invercargill

and possibly Longfellow; contemporary poetry was capable of casting its spell as far away as the Antipodes. As to the painting itself: 'It is understood to be a portrait … The young lady represented is sitting back, her hands clasped, the attitude and the look of the eyes indicating that she is indulging in some sort of day-dream.'[38] Was this Grace, now contemplating a brighter future for herself? But then we also have the charming work from the same exhibition, *The School Girl* (Image 2.8),[39] whose lightness of mood contrasts sharply with *The Dead, Dead Past.* Thus we must be mindful not to over-psychoanalyse Grace's situation.

For Signor Nerli, life beyond New Zealand was relatively prosaic. After a restless few years painting portraits and figure subjects around Australia and a brief stint in London in 1904 (coincidently when Grace Joel was there), he went back to Italy. By 1909 he and Cecilia were settled in London where they continued to live until 1923. There he painted 'small landscapes of inner-city parks'.[40] Nerli's artistic star was no longer rising and his works were not exhibited in the prestigious salons, unlike those of his Australian counterparts who were actively making a name for themselves on both sides of the Channel. Grace, firmly ensconced in London by then, visited him over the intervening years. What did they talk about? Nerli visited Streeton in 1910. Grace visited Streeton. What did *they* talk about? Grace Joel died in 1924 and Nerli died penniless, as did many a Macchiaioli, two years later at Nervi, Italy, near Genoa.

Tellingly, Grace's portrait of Nerli was never exhibited in her lifetime and was never for sale, which is not the case for nearly all of her other works. Other such exceptions were the portraits of her mother and father. From the date of Nerli's hurried Dunedin departure, Grace Joel continued to leave these types of 'footprints on the sand of time' for the rest of her life.

To add insult to her possible emotional injury at the time Nerli left the city, a small clutch of Grace Joel works exhibited at the end of the year in the

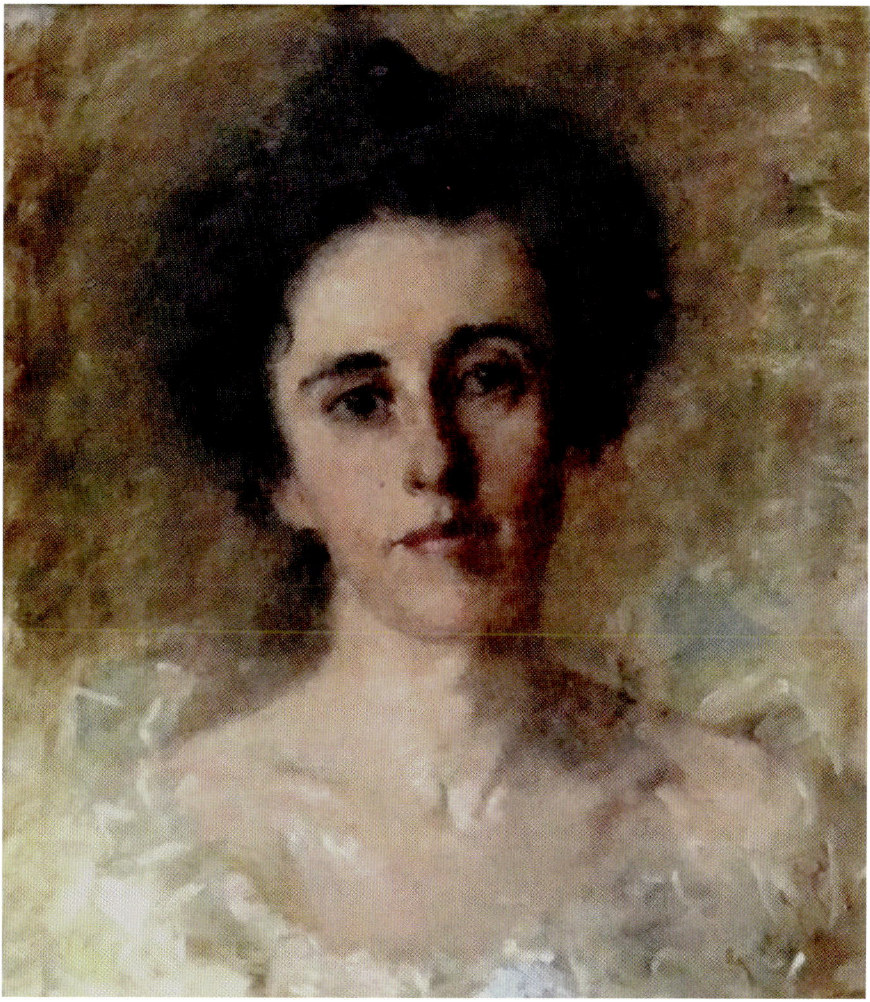

IMAGE 2.9

***Self-portrait*, oil on canvas, 44 x 38.5 cm. Grace Joel would have been 32 years old in 1897, which former director of the Dunedin Public Art Gallery Frank Dickinson suggests as the date for this work. The characteristic lilt of the head and portraiture style are found in other Grace Joel works of this period.** Private collection

town of Timaru north of Dunedin attracted the ire of the *Timaru Herald* art critic: '... cannot admire this lady's work; evidently possesses talent, but has adopted the smudg[e] and recklessness of colouring miscalled "impressionist".[41] The utterly charming *A Rose 'midst Poppies*, one of the seven works exhibited, no doubt elicited the same displeasure from the critic. As we shall come to witness in Chapter 6, these comments were tame fare compared to the vitriol that English critics later heaped on a Post-Impressionist exhibition held in 1910 in London.

The following year (1897), Grace exhibited three works, including *Dead, Dead Past*, at the Canterbury Society of Arts and dispatched three more oils to the annual exhibition of the Auckland Society of Arts. The three paintings, which again included *A Rose 'midst Poppies*, almost did not make it, having gone astray en route and ending up at the premises of a picture framer, Mr Leech, in Auckland's Shortland Street. Fortunately, they turned up and were hung (but not catalogued) only a day late at the exhibition, held in Choral Hall. Artists of the day found the

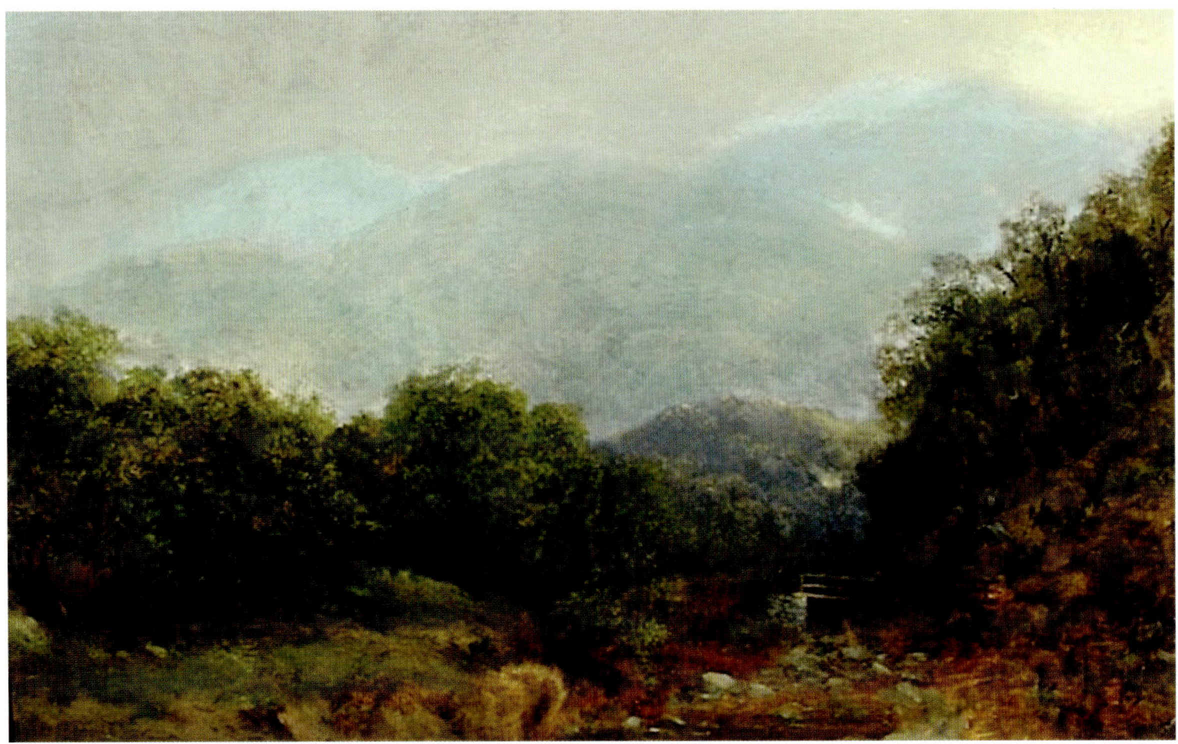

Image 2.10

***Waitati*, by Grace Joel, undated, oil on canvas, 29 x 44 cm. Waitati is a valley just north of Dunedin. The bridge over the stream draws the viewer into the enchanting world of the New Zealand 'bush'.** International Art Centre, Auckland

John Leech Gallery's shop window a favourable venue in which to exhibit their works. The gallery stayed in this location for many years, not moving to a more central city location until 1963.[42]

Coincidently, and presenting another little mystery, a painting by Nerli titled *Mr Leech*[43] obviously found its way into Grace Joel's possession, as it was one of the items she bequeathed in her will to the Melbourne National Gallery. However, the man in the portrait appears too old to be Mr Harold Leech, the picture framer of Shortland Street, and so it may be of another person altogether.[44] The National Gallery of New South Wales, now home to the work, titles it *Portrait of Mr Leach*, a change in spelling that racks up the mystery a notch further. But whoever the sitter may be, Grace held on to the painting for the remainder of her life.

Also dated to this period is *The Yellow Sunbonnet* (Image 2.11), which in due course became part of the Theomin collection at Olveston.[45] Nerli exhibited *The Blue Bonnet* with the Auckland Society of Arts in the same year. Both paintings depict young girls in sunbonnets in similar poses and were probably conceived before Nerli left Dunedin the year before. The delicate sensitivity of the facial features in *The Yellow Sunbonnet* compares with that of Nerli's *Portrait of a Girl* painted approximately two years earlier. However, Nerli's *The Blue Bonnet*, painted with variegated brush strokes *en plein air*, gives the work a distinct aura of French Impressionism.

The conjecture that Grace may have been painting her way out of emotional turmoil gains credence from the volume of work she produced and exhibited during this period. In September

1897 she exhibited four more works at the annual exhibition of the New Zealand Academy of Fine Arts, Wellington. One of these was *Youth*, a painting that had been doing the rounds of Australasian exhibitions. Depicting a nude girl 12 to 14 years of age reclining on a pink-coloured couch, the work got under the skin of critics on both sides of the Tasman. Except for the few positive comments mentioned previously, it was pelted with criticism.

First, the critics maligned the poor girl's feet: 'A study of big feet' was the dismissive comment of one New Zealand critic.[46] Grace demonstrated with her *Academic Male Nude* (Image 1.26) and other sketches that she could render the human form very skilfully, but exactness was not her primary interest. In her will of 1920 she explicitly stipulated the terms of her very generous scholarship allowing recipients to study painting of the nude at the National Gallery School: '... the principal qualities of this study of the nude shall be artistic feeling and beauty of colour and line and not technical exactness.' No doubt this attitude was one she applied to her own work, but the critics knew exactly what they wanted when it came to feet.

Then it was the flesh tones, with the *Sydney Mail* calling them 'rather muddy' and the Dunedin *Evening Star* decrying their 'want of cleanliness'. These were the same flesh-tints that the *New Zealand Herald* referred to as 'remarkably good'.[47] Most critics, though, had little tolerance for skin rendered in non-traditional colour: '... flesh looks rather like a skinned rabbit'.[48] *The Triad* declared that the painting should be renamed 'Unwashed Jelly-fish on Pink Coverlet'. Ironically, given the prevailing attitudes of the times with respect to the bare body, even in art, it was not the young girl's nudity that offended. No, not at all. It was her big feet and unnatural skin tones that were unacceptable. Perhaps her nudity was not even noticed as a consequence.

Another 'undraped youth' of Joel's (*Between Faith and Knowledge*) again had irritating flesh tones.[49] When the painting was shown at the Victorian Artists' Society annual exhibition in Melbourne in 1898, *The Argus* identified the figure's 'purple legs' and 'yellow stomach' as 'the chief defects of the flesh-painting'. This same critic would have been shocked to find that purple legs and yellow stomachs were perfectly acceptable, fashionable even, in certain quarters of Paris at the time. Grace Joel probably knew this. And soon she would be there to see it for herself.

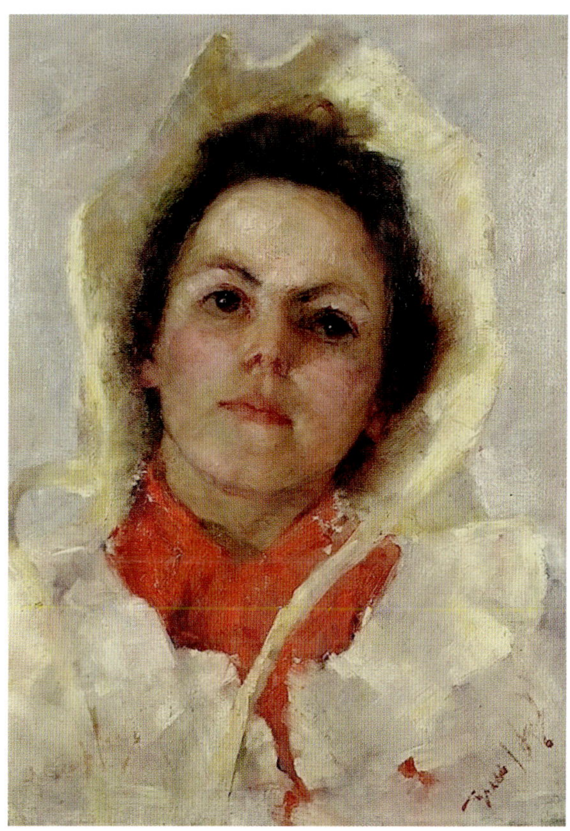

IMAGE 2.11

***The Yellow Sunbonnet*, by Grace Joel, c. 1897, oil on canvas, 54.3 x 39 cm. The painting hangs in the Theomin family's former stately home, Olveston, in Dunedin. Note again the slight tilt of the head, typical of many of Grace Joel's portraits. The Theomins' only daughter, Dorothy, was nine years old at the time Grace painted this work, so the sitter remains unknown. However, according to the *Evening Star*: '... we are assured on excellent authority that the artist has secured a good likeness of the young lady sitter.'**

Olveston Historic Home, Dunedin

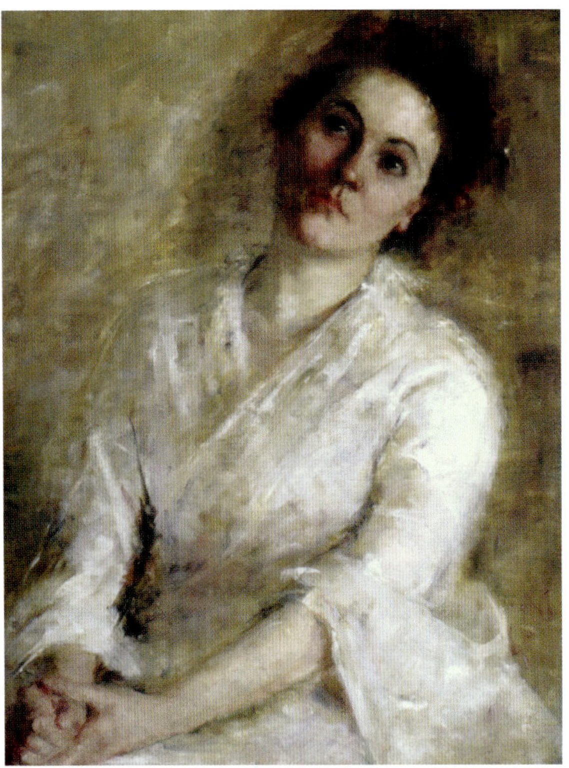

Image 2.12

Memories – Portrait of Kate Morrison, **by Grace Joel, c. 1897, oil on canvas, 75.5 x 56.3 cm. There are certain stylistic and colouration affinities between *Memories, Yellow Sunbonnet* (Image 2.11), the *Portrait of a Lady* (Image 2.13) and *Portrait of Vivien Oakden* (Image 2.14).** Dunedin Public Art Gallery, Dunedin

More of Grace's work appeared at the Society of Artists' spring (October) exhibition at Vickery's Chambers, Sydney: 'Miss Grace Joel has a very strong study of a woman of the people under the title, *A Dead, Dead Past is gone, a* [sic] *Present is*'.[50] If inclined to speculation, we might suppose that Grace, suspecting that Nerli had fled to Sydney, used this painting to send him a message.

Another of Grace's work receiving some praise in Sydney was the head of a man titled *An Old Colonist.* Two decades on, at an auction of the household contents of 79 Hawkestone St, Wellington, held on site, this same work emerged as one of the many items up for sale. A small sampling of the remnants of whoever's life was being auctioned off reveals a gramophone with 30 records, the contents of five bedrooms, including five duchesse chests and 20 pillows, an oak umbrella stand and a hospital bed.

When Grace later held a solo exhibition at Vickery's Chambers (in 1906), it prompted Australian art luminary D.H. Souter to exclaim: 'I remember [her] first contribution to the Society of Artists, and how we were impressed with its strong solidity and powerful virility of purpose. What woman was this who displayed such accuracy of touch, who so successfully treated the tonal qualities of her subject: who, setting her compatriots at defiance, worked out her own salvation, unaided and alone?'[51] Praise employing such phrases as 'powerful virility of purpose' needs to be juxtaposed with the prevailing attitudes towards women of the late Victorian era. Namely, a woman's place is in the home, bearing ever more children to raise and supporting her husband in his endeavours. Little else.

The Sydney-based Society of Artists' first president was Tom Roberts. Arthur Streeton was on its council, and membership was restricted to professionals only. During the formative years of Australian art, the various art societies created included lay artists and professionals alike. But the professionals often resented the amateurs and so formed their own organisations, which is why the Society of Artists split off from the Royal Art Society of Sydney. When, in 1895, the amateurs seized power of the RAS, 'There was a scene of utter disorder when all our men [the professionals] were not elected ... wild resolutions were passed; while above the din could be heard the voice of Fullwood who was denouncing the other side as a lot of "dingbats"'.[52] These folk took their art very seriously, and rightly so; many of them became world-class artists.

Another vignette exemplifying the art milieu in Australia can be found is this excerpt, also from William Moore: 'When Streeton and Roberts came over to Sydney during the nineties they were cordially greeted by the local group. "We are glad to see you chaps," said one of them. "But what are you poor devils going to do?" There were few buyers in those days and £20 was about the highest price for a picture. There was, however, the chance of a gallery purchase or a portrait commission.'[53]

Towards the end of 1897, Grace held another private viewing at her home studio on Regent Road prior to the Otago Art Society's annual exhibition: 'The *chef d'oeuvre* was a large painting, titled "There is no grief like the grief that cannot speak ..." There is a certain grandeur about the work which arrests attention at once.'[54] Despite the flurry of output, the subject of grief apparently was still not far from Grace's mind – nor, perhaps, its anguish.

Grace exhibited 12 works at the OAS exhibition, 'a number ... which exceeds the limit that the rules of the society impose upon the number that any member is entitled to exhibit.'[55] She showed *There is No Grief* under the title *Give Sorrow Words: The grief that does not speak: Whispers the o'er fraught heart and bids it break.* The lines, taken from Shakespeare's *Macbeth*, express sentiments perhaps befitting of how Grace felt as 1897 drew to a close.[56]

Among the other 11 of her paintings were *Youth*, *The Yellow Sunbonnet* and *Little Lily*, the latter perhaps being Grace's sister in years past, as she was age 25 at this stage. Another was *Mitherless Bairns*, a title and theme Grace took up again in a later work. In this instance the work was a modest oil sketch priced at £2.00, 'with a few apparently random touches of her brush she ... brings out very well the faces of the two little mites which have furnished the artist with her theme.'[57] Keeping the bereft *Mitherless Bairns* company at the exhibition was *Only We Two*, 'a couple of blue-eyed girls ... one of them having her arms circling the neck of the other and elder.'[58]

By early 1898 Grace had established a studio in Liverpool Street, central Dunedin, where she instructed students.[59] She also exhibited three works at the Victorian Artists' Society annual exhibition in Melbourne. At the end of February 1898, Grace held another exhibition of her pupils' work at her Liverpool Street studio. Her *Otago Daily Times*' announcement referred to the venue as 'Grace J.

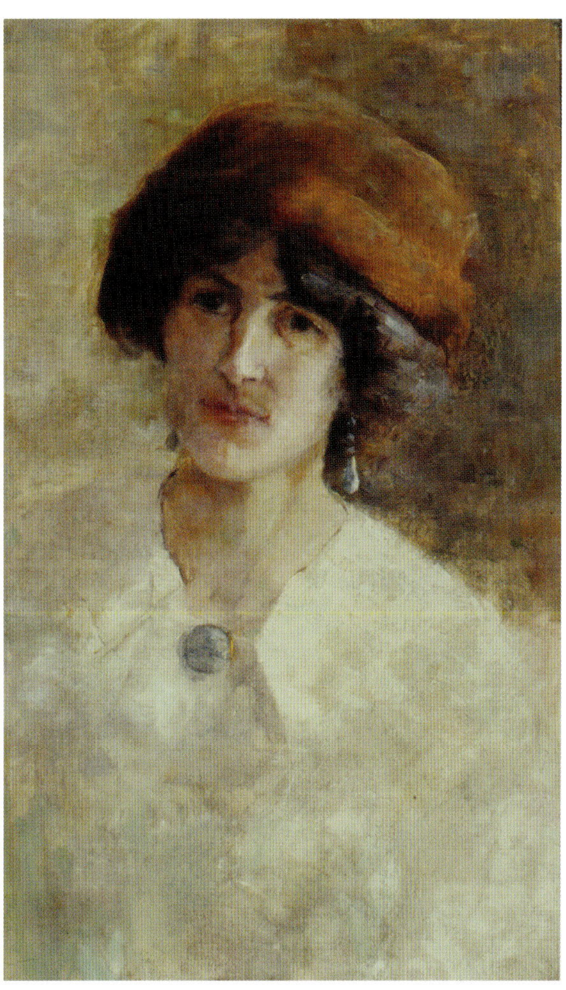

Image 2.13

***Portrait of a Lady*, by Grace Joel, late 1890s, oil on canvas, 59 x 34 cm. The sitter is thought to be the daughter of a farmer from Dunedin's nearby Taieri Plains.** Private collection

Joel's Art Academy'. A sense of pride underlies this epithet, with apparent good reason: 'The work is numerous, and the general quality of it may be described as excellent.'[60] One of the students was Jean Rollo Fisher who, in later years, exhibited with Grace at the venerable Paris Salon. The *Otago Daily Times* reviewed the work of six students, but it is possible that there were more presenting their work for scrutiny.[61]

Several of Grace's works appeared at the Otago Jubilee Industrial Exhibition, which showcased 50

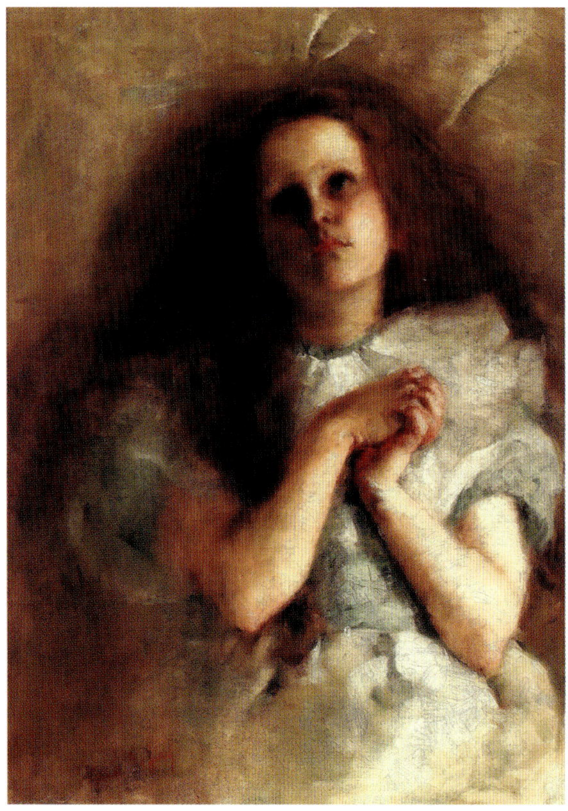

IMAGE 2.14

***Portrait of Vivien Oakden*, by Grace Joel, 1898, oil on canvas, 71.1 x 50.7 cm. The original is much more vibrant than any image can possibly convey.**

Hocken Collections, Uare Taoka o Hākena, University of Otago, Dunedin

years of the Province of Otago and was held between 22 March and 4 June. One of the paintings was a portrait of the Mayor of Dunedin, Mr E.B. Cargill ('manifestly a likeness'). Another was *The Yellow Sunbonnet*. Grace's *A Morning Idyll*, a nude study of a child, drew some welcome anatomical attention: 'Notice please, in this figure, the excellent drawing of the feet.'[62] Had Grace gone out of her way to render the feet just so in order to prove a point? Much of the rest of the Dunedin art contingent were represented as well. Two years later, a similar industrial Jubilee exhibition held in Christchurch featured *Little Nell*, no doubt on Grace's instruction, as it was lent by Mr G.H. Elliott (head of the Christchurch School of Art) when Grace was already abroad.

Another fine Joel portrait of 1898 is that of young Dunedin lass Vivien Oakden (Image 2.14). Vivien's angelic countenance is certainly consistent with her winning a Bible class prize at Anderson's Bay School the following year for reciting the Ten Commandments and two psalms.[63] This painting was the basis for the poster advertising the Hocken Library's 1986 exhibition, 'The Painted Portrait', drawn from works in the library's own collection. Miss Oakden's angle of repose is very similar to that of the sitter in *Portrait of an Actress* by G.P. Nerli (circa 1890).

The Joel family's fortunes must have been reasonably secure during these final years of the nineteenth century. Brother Edward, for example, owned a race horse, *Red Lancer*, that won several races up and down the country during its career, including the Glasgow Handicap at the Auckland Summer Meeting of 1899. For Grace, the security of her family's financial cushion probably meant she did not have to sell her work to survive, leaving her relatively free to pursue her artistic endeavours as and where she liked. The starving/struggling artist is a universal creature and so definitely not privileged enough to have a brewery-owning father.

Dunedin, for all its interest in the arts and patrons of such, was no match for the grandeur of Paris or London. And although being a professional artist for most was virtually synonymous with deprivation, especially in Paris and London, the tale of these two cities was such that, like the poles of superconducting magnets, they attracted budding artists from all over the world. Living on the opposite side of the Earth did not mean you could resist the attractions any more so than others living nearer these poles. Grace Joel was no exception. In fact, it was more the exception *not* to go abroad.

In 1898, in order to raise money for her forthcoming trip overseas, and evidence of her apparent desire to fend for herself as much as possible despite the backing of her well-heeled family, Grace held an 'art union' or raffle at her Liverpool Street studio, offering 16 of her paintings, all of which were won by fortunate recipients. O'Keeffe had done the same four years earlier in order to study in Paris at the Académie Julian. The following comment in the *Evening Star* captured the innocent and charming community atmosphere of the event:

> *Miss Grace J. Joel has decided to leave Dunedin for Europe at an early date, and a farewell art union is being promoted by her numerous friends and well-wishers. A private view of the pictures which form the prizes is given today in Miss Joel's rooms, Liverpool street. They include several important oil paintings that have been shown … and favorably commented on in Australia and New Zealand, and no doubt this opportunity of securing a memento of this rising artist will be seized upon by the numbers of Dunedin folk who respect Miss Joel personally and appreciate her endeavours to raise the standard of art in the community.*[64]

The reporter from the *Otago Daily Times* was not so gracious. Dipping his pen in the well of faint praise, he observed that *Youth*, 'a study of the nude, has been much commended, though it probably does not appeal to popular taste in New Zealand'. Spoken like a true Victorian. But as was previously observed, this view would have been a mainstream one. The nudes that Grace Joel regularly exhibited were therefore not, of course, to everyone's taste. However, the press was rarely particularly outraged, except if the skin tones were wrong and the feet too large.

Actually, nudes were problematic even in *gai Paris*, let alone colonial Dunedin. Witness the uproar over Manet's *Le déjeuner sur l'herbe* of 1863, of whose centre of controversy Émile Zola had this to say: 'This nude woman has scandalized the public, who see only her in the canvas. My God!'[65] Fifty years later, a study of a nude at the Paris Salon (no less) fell foul of the Police Commissioner of the Champs Élysées district at a 'private inspection' before the exhibition opened. The offending work 'he condemned and ordered to be removed'. This event did not escape notice in New Zealand.[66]

Even a century later, many of Grace Joel's works were still considered almost risqué and had the

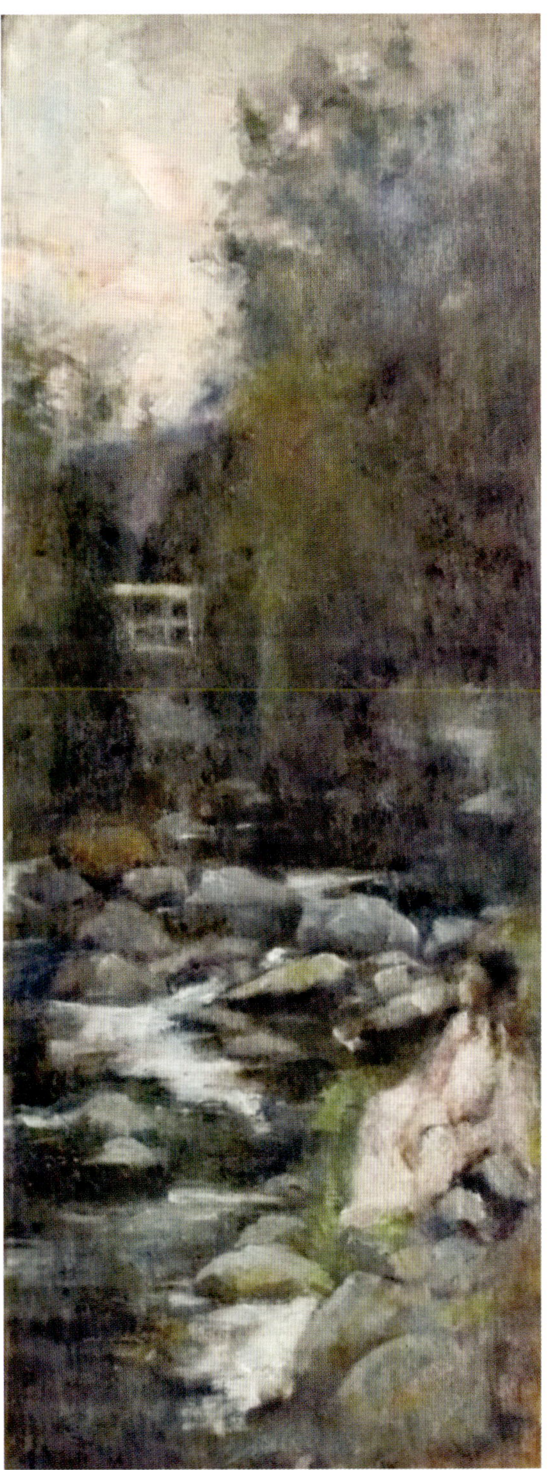

IMAGE 2.15

Girl by the Stream*, by Grace Joel, date unknown, oil on board, 50.5 x 19 cm. This work could be contemporaneous with *Waitati* (Image 2.10), as it seems to feature the same region. Ferner Galleries, New Zealand

WANTED, MODELS for the Life.—Apply Miss Joel's Studio, Liverpool street, between 4 and 5 p.m. 5s

Image 2.16

This *Otago Daily Times* advertisement appeared on 5 September 1899 after Grace Joel was already abroad.

power to get at least one reviewer feverish, as this item from the *Otago Daily Times* of 1984 testifies: 'Few New Zealand painters have given this subject much attention and Grace Joel is nearly singular in presenting it frequently as an object of sensual interest. Some of her works, little seen in her life time and still privately owned, are frankly erotic in their approach. They succeed sometimes at a sophisticated level, in expressing a languorous, knowing, sensuality that is disturbing for the worldliness it reveals.'[67] Take one look at her *Reclining Nude* (Image 6.9), and we can quickly see what the reviewer meant by 'sensual' and 'frankly erotic'. Sandra Chesterman singles out this particular work in her 2002 book *Figure Work: The nude and life modelling in New Zealand art*, which deftly traces the sexual maturity of a nation.[68]

It is perhaps not surprising, then, that as of the 1920s and 30s, few nudes were being exhibited on the New Zealand art scene by either men or women. However, one brave Christchurch artist, Evelyn Page (1899–1988), did take up the nudity baton from Grace Joel. Impressionism was well past its peak, but Page made this style all her own. Unfortunately, one of her nude works (*Summer Morn*, 1929), displayed at the Robert McDougall Art Gallery in Christchurch, was removed on request of solicitors acting for the model. She apparently was 'finding public exhibition of the work an embarrassment'.[69] Since the model was only portrayed from the rear, her embarrassment is somewhat difficult to comprehend. The year was 1943. The painting was taken down, put into storage and not returned to the gallery walls until 1978, after the model's death.

A most curious advertisement was published in the *Otago Daily Times* (Image 2.16) – curious because it appeared well after Grace Joel had left Dunedin to go abroad. While simple explanations can be advanced for this untimely occurrence, the most extraordinary aspect is that it was placed by a woman in the remote colonial outpost that was nineteenth-century Victorian Dunedin.

In order to find a more receptive outlet for some of the disturbing worldliness alluded to in the 1984 *Otago Daily Times* review, Grace Joel had to leave New Zealand. Now nearly 34 years of age, she perhaps was experiencing feelings of the kind Joanne Drayton ascribes to Frances Hodgkins: 'As a member of the OAS council, Frances was mixing with overseas artists and feeling her independence, and with her ties, holds and reasons for staying dropping away, a trip Home to Britain seemed the next step.'[70] Frances Hodgkins left for 'Home' two years later.

The minutes of the 21 March 1899 meeting of the OAS, at which Grace Joel was not present, record a note from her resigning her council seat, as she was leaving the country. The council accepted her resignation with regret.[71]

The prospect of moving to the other side of the globe must have caused Grace a good measure of trepidation as it would any colonial artist intent on trying their hand on the world stage. Even the Australian bohemian artist Charles Conder, who later befriended Oscar Wilde and Toulouse-Lautrec, confessed in a letter to Tom Roberts, written just before his departure overseas: 'I mean to work hard in Paris and do something, but I feel very doubtful about myself ...'[72]

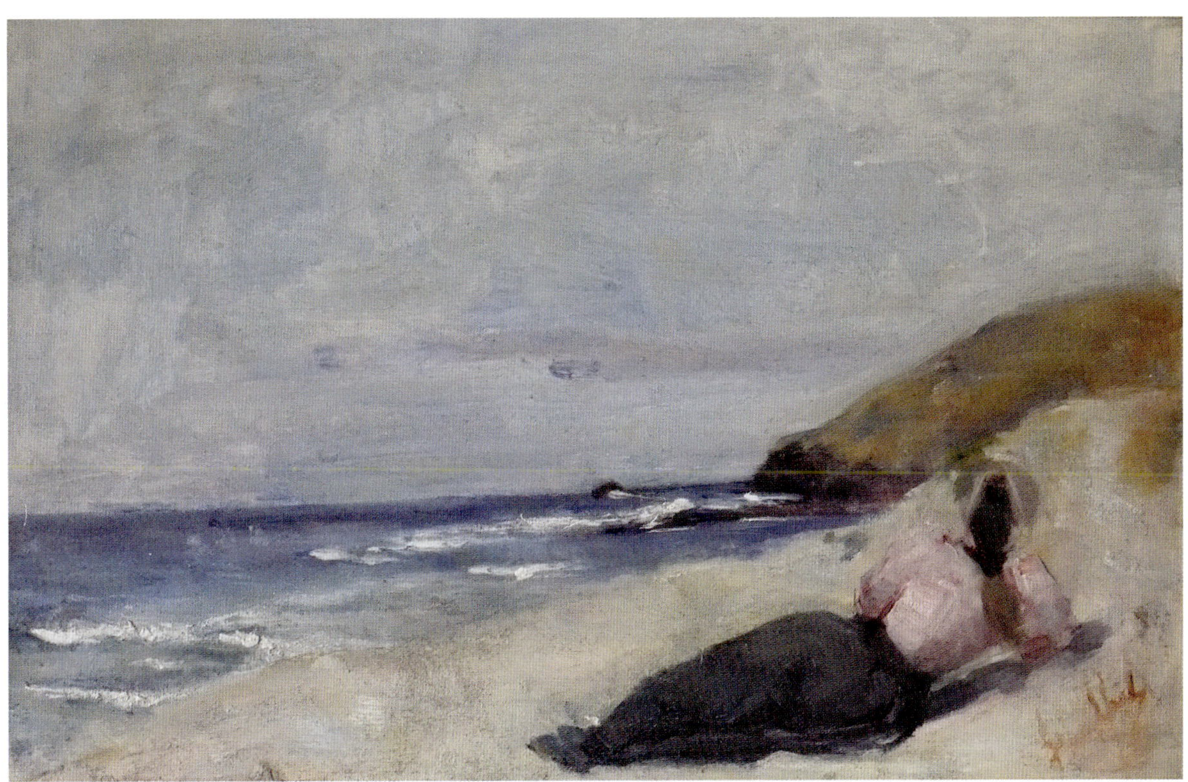

IMAGE 2.17

'*A Quiet Holiday* (No. 32) represents a young woman who employs her leisure time in lazily lolling about the Sandhills at the Ocean Beach, and who shows her contempt for the artist by turning her back on her' (*Otago Witness*, 17 November 1898, p. 21). Painted by Grace Joel, oil on canvas, 48.5 x 28.5 cm. Private collection

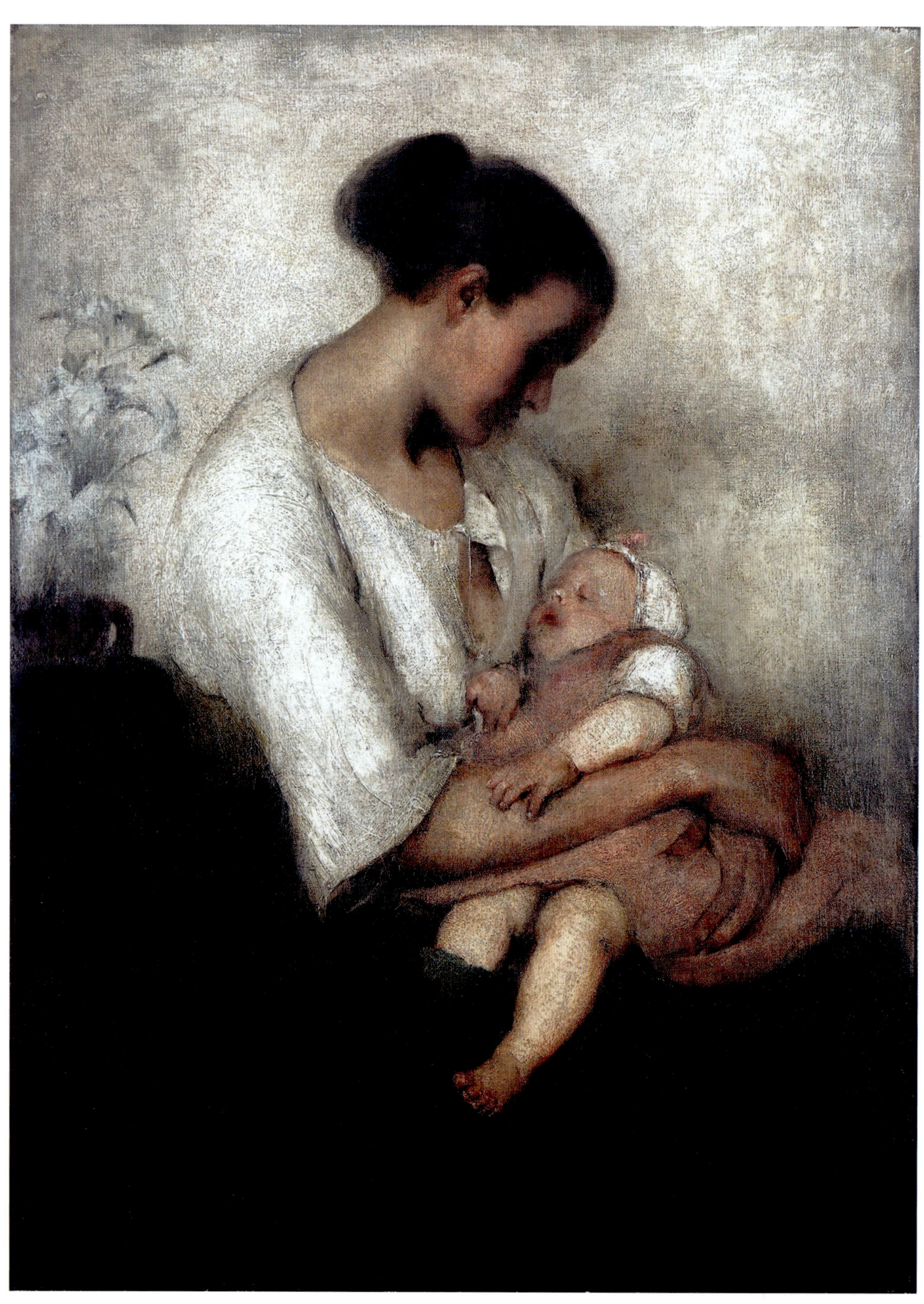

Son enfant (*Her Child*), 1901, oil on canvas, 105.4 x 76.2 cm, Grace Joel's first exhibited work at the Paris Salon. The folds in the dark-brown cloth do not appear in the colour photograph because of reproduction issues.

Private collection

Chapter 3

Europe Beckons

Mother and child: It is the most beautiful subject in the world – Grace Joel, 1909

On the last day of February 1899, Grace Joel sailed from Dunedin to Wellington and from there, on the second day of March, began the arduous six-week journey to England. '"Miss Joel – Dunedin" is one of the 99 passengers in the Saloon class aboard the Royal Mail Steamer, *Gothic*, stopping at Rio de Janeiro, Tenerife, and Plymouth.'[1] Grace did not travel well, long journeys often leaving her incapacitated for weeks after arrival. How did she prepare for such an event? 'I always have to pretend to myself I am not going.'[2] Some of the flavour of what this long journey was like not only for Grace Joel but for the thousands of New Zealanders who made the passage to (or from) England during this era can be found in excerpts from a passenger's diary.

The entries begin one year before Grace Joel's departure, 19 March 1898. The steamer was the RMS *Ruahine*, and the passenger Annie Beauchamp, who was travelling to England with her husband Harold. They happened to be the parents of Kathleen, the future Katherine Mansfield. (Nine-year-old Kathleen and her siblings had been left at home in the care of relatives.) Annie kept the diary up every day, but a few partial entries are sufficient to appreciate the rigours of the journey. She and Harold were travelling first class, as did Grace Joel, so we can imagine how those in steerage must have fared.

March 19th

After writing my last note we hoisted our anchor and steamed away … I had a most delightful bath, plenty of warm water … As I was dressing I was dreadfully ill several times but it did not seem to prostrate me very severely … Everybody was relatively miserable, no attempt made to keep up the Sabbath Day …

March 27th

Too rough for baths or even get up, until half past twelve, when I was terribly seasick again much to my disgust, but nearly everybody else was ill, the motion was fearful, and a frightful sea … I do hope it will soon improve …

April 5th

The days are gradually improving, today has been lovely and so much warmer … we saw dozens of whales the other morning, early morning they were playing around the ship … Colonel McDonald gave a lecture on the Maori War, not very interesting, he has not a talking voice …

April 6th

Plenty of sun and a fair wind at last with the sails set. [Steamships still had sails in those days as a safety measure in case the propeller broke as well as an aid to propulsion.]

April 8th

After coaling [the Ruahine *briefly stopped at the coastal port of Montevideo, Uruguay to pick up coal], we continue our voyage to Rio … As yellow fever is reported to be raging at Rio, it is possible that*

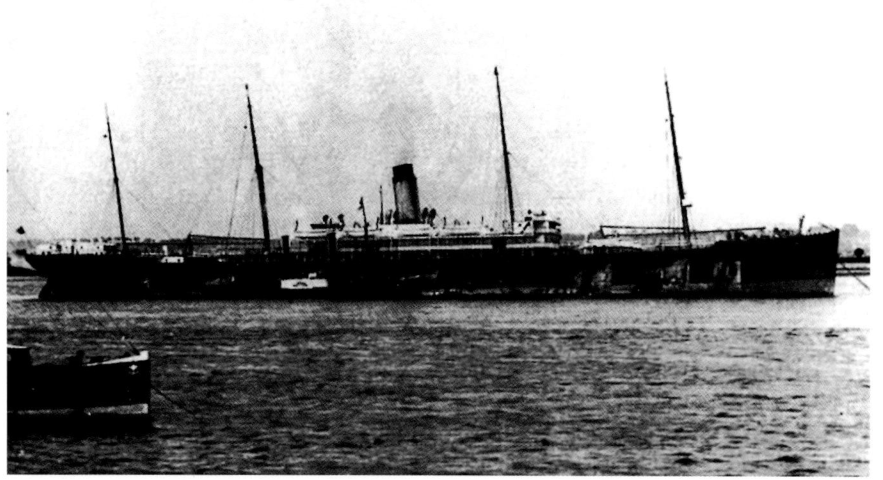

Image 3.1

The 7730-ton steamer RMS *Gothic* on which Grace Joel took passage to London in 1899. The four masts are for auxiliary sails.

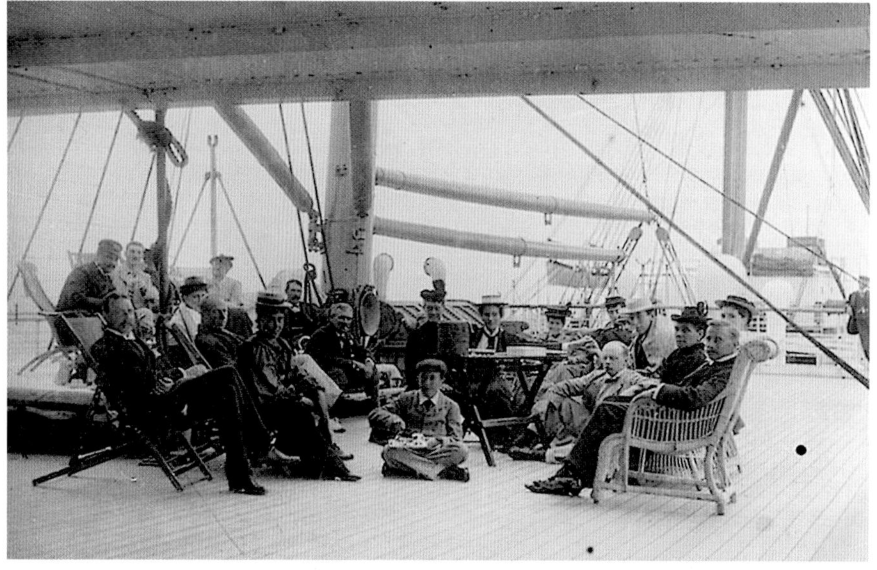

Image 3.2

Enjoying the good life on board the *Gothic* in 1896, at least for some passengers.

we may not be able to land at that port. Should there be much sickness at Rio, the authorities at Teneriffe [sic] [where the ship berthed next] would stop us from going on shore at that place also. This would mean that we should not set our feet on terra firma at any place between New Zealand and England …

April 13th

We heard conflicting statements as to the health of the city, some saying that yellow fever, alias Yellow Jack, was raging, whilst others said that there were very few daily deaths … However, we decided to risk matters … Once in the tram we had a glorious ride, and passed the most interesting part of the City … we passed shops, warehouses, cathedrals, churches, private residences, lovely parks and gardens in rapid succession … we engaged a wagonnette, drawn by four sturdy mules … and continued our journey. This drive was a poem …

April 15th

A fearful day, feeling worse, the heat so awfully trying … we are all flopping about quite prostrate … we just lie on the outside of our bunks and groan and can't sleep. Tonight is very rough and I feel quite sick …

April 19th

We have had a most trying day, we crossed the Line at 1:30 and it has been miserably hot and muggy, almost too hot to move or eat. We have passed five sailing vessels and 2 steamers, and they are such an interest – if we are near enough three cheers go up from either vessel …

April 26th

We woke up this morning to view Teneriffe [sic] Peak to perfection … immediately had to hoist our yellow flag and the health officer came alongside and declared us in quarantine as we had been to Rio, although we had not one case of sickness on board … we could not land, as the island is in a very disturbed and dangerous state owing to war has been declared between America and Spain. English people are not safe at Santa Cruz and are leaving the Island in droves …

May 2nd

Monday night was a gorgeous night, beautiful moonlight and calm, so it enabled us to see the beauties immediately we entered the Channel, which I would not have missed, for the pleasure of entering Plymouth … got up at seven next morning, to see all we could of River Thames this also was indescribably beautiful, seeing the coast towns and watering places gradually getting bigger and more important, until we entered the Royal Albert Docks [London] which crowned everything for magnitude and wonderment. Uncle Henry was down on the docks to meet us … There was a special train waiting for passengers and luggage, so we all met again in the train. We were landed at Liverpool St. Station, one of the most important stations. There we left Uncle, and took a handsome [sic, should be hansom] to …

Grace Joel's voyage would have been similar, of course, but without the presence of a comforting husband when Grace felt really indisposed, or a photo of five lovely children to boost her spirits.

Grace arrived in London mid-April 1899. Nothing got past the all-seeing and all-knowing correspondent of Dunedin's *Evening Star*, who mentioned (6 May) that Grace was staying at Quebec House, Old Quebec Street in London, and 'early next week she quits London for Paris'. Also mentioned was another New Zealander, Miss Annie Blacke, who was studying at the Westminster Art School but in the autumn 'proposes leaving for Paris'.

During her brief stay in England, Grace attended numerous art exhibitions, including one in Grosvenor House featuring works from the Duke of Westminster's collection. Here she viewed many of the old masters, such as Gainsborough's *Blue Boy*, now housed in the Huntington Library, San Marino, California. She visited the famed English artist G.F. Watts (1817–1904), then over 80 years of age. Shown one of her portraits, he asked her if she really did it herself. When she replied, 'It is my father,' Watts responded: 'It could not be better painted.' Watts also informed her that she would be a successful professional painter *if* she chose to be so. Along with the artist Solomon J. Solomon ARA, Watts expressed the view that Grace need not study painting under anyone.[3] Needless to say, cousin Emanuel Fox had met with Solomon some years earlier.[4]

Grace crossed to Paris a few weeks later and met up with Australian/New Zealand artist friend, Dora Meeson, 'with whom she has been taking counsel as to the best means of study'.[5] Meeson had been studying at the Académie Julian. She had earlier attended the National Gallery School in Melbourne, had a stint at the Christchurch School of Art, gone on to London's Slade School of Art and just experienced the honour of having one of her works – a portrait of her sister Ruth – hung at the Paris Salon. Perhaps influenced by the views of Watts, Solomon and Meeson, Grace revised her plans to continue studying painting and enrolled to study drawing at the Julian instead.

Art students had already been travelling to Europe from New Zealand for several years to 'complete their education'. Away from family and friends, often for years, sometimes for good, 'The price the artist paid for his escape is considered worthwhile.'[6] Invariably, their every triumph was heralded in the local press as if they had never left. To a very similar extent this was true also of the Australian media, who consistently claimed Grace Joel as one of their own: 'She is an Australian artist' sums up the collective attitude. This cultural hegemony by the Australians of New Zealanders, a sore point with Kiwis for more than a century, extends not only to the arts but also to horses, food and other such serious matters.

Another instance of cultural sparring occurred when Dora Meeson won first prize of £75 at an Australian-wide art competition judged in Sydney in 1895, the theme being 'Minerva, Goddess of Wisdom'. Dora had been in Melbourne studying at the National Gallery School for a few months by this time. The Christchurch *Star* reported the prestigious win under the heading 'A New Zealand Artist': 'We notice that Miss Meeson has been quietly laid claim to as a Melbourne artist ... for although the young lady has been studying for some little time in Melbourne ... her training was acquired here; and it was here that the bent of her talent won hearty recognition.'[7]

The Australian press faithfully recorded every work exhibited at a major venue by an Australian artist (and that included Grace Joel), but often included neither the title of the work nor even a brief description – just the venue and artist. The brevity may have been partially due to the fact that reports from the UK to the Antipodes and back again had to journey, in each instance, half way around the world along the overland and undersea cables that carried the dots and dashes of the electrical telegraph. As well, there were many Australian artists overseas to report on. From 1889 (when she won the prize for Best Charcoal Drawing), Grace Joel's name appeared approximately 240 times in Australian newspapers. However, it is fortunate that the media did follow Grace Joel as closely as they did because often this is all we have to tell of her activities.

Dora Meeson's good friend from Melbourne, George Coates, who won a three-year scholarship from the National Gallery School in Melbourne in 1896 and was now a Julian student, was also selected for the Salon exhibition of 1899. Dora and George, enjoying one another's company on strolls through Paris, where they 'studied old masters in the Louvre and new masters at the Luxembourg'[8] (as no doubt Grace Joel did also), became engaged to marry. On receiving a letter from Dora about the engagement, Frances Hodgkins revealed her own feelings about marriage in a letter to her mother, Rachel: '... poor foolish girl – her career done for'.[9] Yet only months later, when again writing to her mother, Frances advised that she had been 'reading Robt. Louis Stevenson's Letters just now – dear man – every day I fall more & more in love with him – & could I but have seen him I wld cheerfully have married him at sight.'[10]

Herein lies a singularly female dilemma of the era (and before and since for that matter). The necessity to remain single was very likely a haunting thought in the mind of many a serious woman artist. However, Dora had two aspects in her favour. For one, she and George vowed never to have children. Secondly, her husband was a more than capable artist in his own right and, unlike many other couplings of creative souls in marriage, then and now, never seemed threatened by his wife's talent or expected her to subsume it to his. Work by Dora and George can be found in all Australian state and national galleries as well as various regional galleries in Australia and England.

Dora introduced George to Grace some time after the latter arrived in Paris as this excerpt from Meeson's biography of her husband attests: 'During this last winter of his stay in Paris [1899] George's health gave way. He was finding it difficult to make ends meet on the scholarship. His studio was unhealthy ... and he had insufficient food. Miss Grace Joel, the New

Zealand artist to whom I had introduced him, when she went to see him, wrote me how shocked his mother would be to see the change in him.'[11]

George Coates fortunately was nursed back to health by friends, and he and Dora married in London in 1903. The wedding took place at St Peter's Church in Ealing, the subsequent wedding venue of E. Phillips Fox and Ethel Carrick in 1905 and to which Dora and George were invited. In due course the couple established themselves as professional artists at No. 9 Trafalgar Studios in Chelsea. A neighbour at No. 4 was artist Florence Haig, also an ardent suffragette, who joined raids, took part in window smashing and endured imprisonment for her beliefs. Both Dora and George were highly sympathetic to the ideals of the suffragettes. She became a member of the Women's Freedom League. He joined the Men's League for Women's Suffrage. However, because 'George would have been so upset' had Dora landed in prison,[12] she avoided any real militancy. New Zealand women had already been granted the right to vote in 1893, of course, and Australian women in 1902, so Dora held the moral high ground in this regard.

Dora and George's studio belonged to the Welsh painter Augustus John (1878–1961), who let it to them for the then relatively modest sum of £50 per year. Nevertheless, money was always tight, and the gold medal George won as part of his travelling scholarship from the National Gallery School was 'regularly pawned' and then redeemed as finances permitted. Chelsea at that time had many purpose-built studio-flats available for artists, and it was the artistic hub of London as a result. Soon Dora and George Coates were absorbed into the extensive network of expatriate Australian artists of the day.

The Royal Institute of Oil Painters, founded in London in 1882, named Dora Meeson as its first Australian female member. Both she and George were represented at the Paris Salon of 1907, 1908 and 1909. George went on to have many artistic successes in England, principally as a portrait painter and later as an official Australian war artist. In her 1906 review of Australian artists, Grace Joel praises George as 'having the highest qualities' as an artist and claims that one of his works hung at the Salon 'seemed to be one of the few there painted with soul'. However, she is quite frank when remarking on the painting he had to do to fulfil the conditions of his art scholarship: 'His subject composition, in accordance with the scholarship for the Melbourne Gallery, was not such a complete success.'[13]

In later years, the Coateses moved to Glebe Place, also in Chelsea, and within walking distance of Grace Joel's residence. Dora and Grace enjoyed a degree of friendship, but they certainly didn't live in each other's pocket. In Dora's biography of her (late) husband, Grace receives only one mention, and that is in the preceding citation. The bond of friendship between Dora and Grace was sufficient enough, however, for Grace to exhibit a sketched (NFS) portrait of George in 1909 at the London Salon, paint another of Dora's niece and then a portrait of Dora herself (Image 3.3).

Dora mentions in her biography of George, which she wrote in 1937, well after George's death, that while living in Chelsea she and he often strolled along the Embankment adjacent to Cheyne Walk in the evening, as did many of the people living in the area. So it was possible that they and Grace encountered one another from time to time as they 'watched the moon on the water, or the soft grey light of evening, when the lights came out one by one'.[14] Grace displayed these tranquil scenes in *Battersea Bridge from Cheyne Walk* and *Lights through the River Mists*, paintings that both featured in a solo exhibition in 1909 of her work at the Doré Gallery, which promoted itself as being situated in the 'Centre of [London's] Bond Street'. In her biography of George Coates, Dora laments: 'How different it was in those days to the roaring thoroughfare of thundering traffic and speed that Cheyne Walk has now become.'[15] And so it is still to this day.

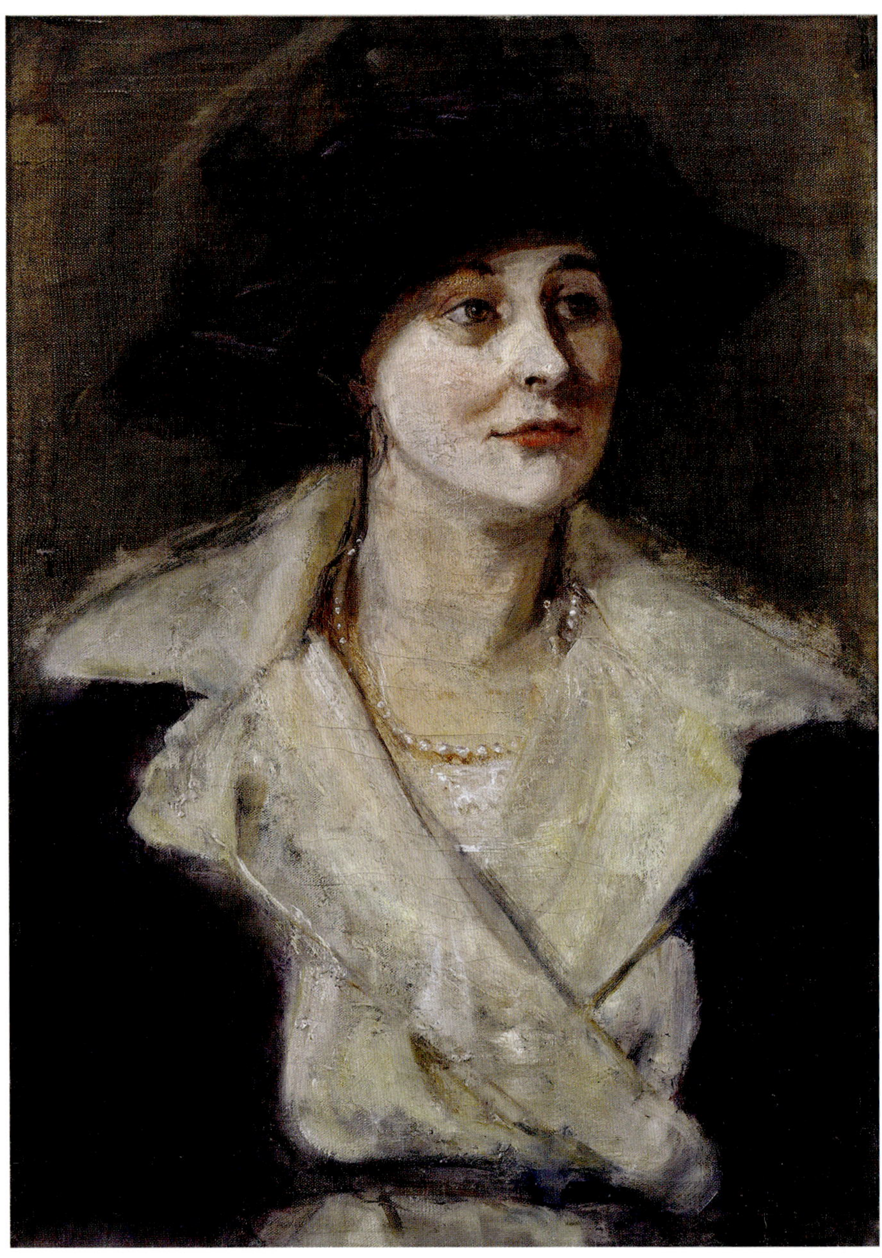

IMAGE 3.3

Mrs Coates of Chelsea, by Grace Joel, c. 1905, oil on canvas, 66 x 47 cm. This was not a woman to trifle with over women's suffrage and she accomplished a great deal for the women's movement in England. Private collection

Académie Julian

No part of the world is too remote, no social state too humble, no incapacity too glaring. Everyone is welcome at the 'Académie Julian' in Paris
– H.P. Sealy, 1901

The pre-eminent art academy in the world as the nineteenth century gave way to the twentieth was the École des Beaux-Arts in Paris. Entry was free (that is, it was subsidised by the French taxpayer), but it maintained a fearsome French language test and so attracted few foreigners. However, there was another contemporary yet outstanding French school of art – the Académie Julian, founded in 1868 by Rodolphe Julian, a former wrestler and painter of undistinguished works.

The Académie excelled because it employed some of the same master teachers as those at the École. They included Gustave Moreau, Jean-Paul Laurens, Jules Lefebvre and William-Adolphe Bouguereau, all of whom embraced the traditional academic style, with the latter arguably the most highly regarded painter of his era. Bouguereau (1825–1905) was the first president of the Société des Artistes Français, the group of painters and sculptors that ran the highly prestigious annual exhibition at the Grand Palais des Champs-Élysées known as the (Old) Salon. The Salon judges considered themselves the guardians and arbiters of the civilised world's artistic standards. These well-established and well-connected artists served another important function, that of introducing their students at the Julian to potential clients and giving them access to important exhibitions, including the Salon's.

Because the École des Beaux-Arts did not deem it worthwhile to admit women until 1897, the Académie Julian was especially popular with women and foreigners, as well as French nationals. One of the basic tenets of the Julian was for women to receive the same training as the men so that afterwards they would be competitive with them. In return, the 'women's immense respect for Bouguereau, Lefebvre, and other artists who taught at Julian's became legendary ... The fact that Bouguereau, for one, had known many of the century's leading academic painters and those who were considered old masters by the 1890s added greatly to the degree to which the women idolized him.'[16]

Over the years, various branches of the Académie Julian sprouted up throughout the Paris environs. It became a magnet for aspiring men and women artists from around the world. Among its various notable students were John Singer Sargent, Giovanni Giacometti, Sir Jacob Epstein, Henri Matisse, Pierre Bonnard, Édouard Vuillard, Marcel Duchamp and many others. Although the training for men and women was the same, it was done separately, and included drawing and painting from nude models, with women even painting from the male nude. This was Paris, remember!

Some of the flavour of life for students at the Académie Julian is captured in the following excerpt from *The New Zealand Illustrated Magazine*, October 1901, by H.P. Sealy:

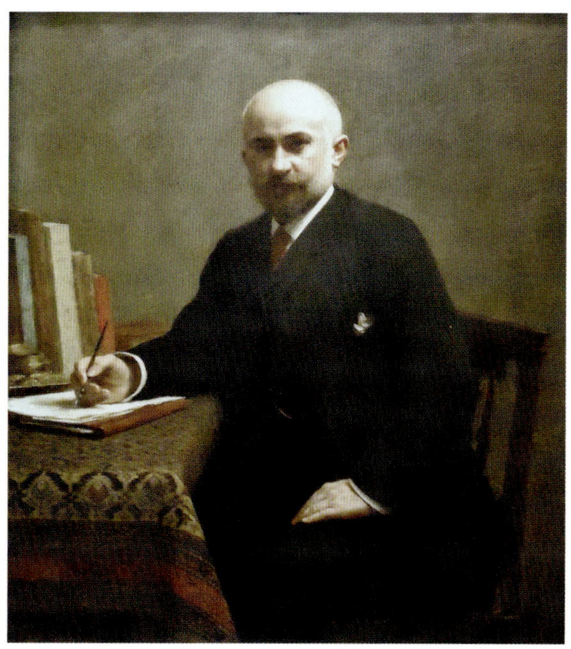

Image 3.4
***Monsieur Julian*, by Henri Fantin-Latour, 1887, oil on canvas, 160 x 150 cm.** Musée d'Orsay, Paris

There can be no possible mistake about which professor it is that attended that morning. A student would know with his eyes shut. M. Ferrier enters quickly, energetically, full of life and action. M. Bouguereau, a fatherly old gentleman, and looking as much like a hearty Scotchman as anything else, comes slowly up behind the nearest student, and gives his opinion in the kindest manner. He hails from the North, and has the more phlegmatic temperament of the Norman. M. Ferrier, on the other hand, comes from the South of France, is more demonstrative, and generally ends by seizing the charcoal if the drawing is hopelessly out, and putting it right in a few touches.

Upstairs the professors are Messieurs Benjamin Constant (the Queen's portrait painter) and Jean-Paul Laurens; thus the student in Paris can have the highest talent in France to come and look at him twice a week for a mere trifle. They work in the interests of Art, the pay is merely nominal.

... Side by side they peg away – bald heads and curly heads, the duffer and the genius, the beggar and the Count, the Australian and the Parisian. No part of the world is too remote, no social state too humble, no incapacity too glaring. Everyone is welcome at the 'Academy Julian' in Paris.

Sealy goes on to relate that, in the early 1890s, the Académie hosted two other students from New Zealand besides himself. One was Charles F. Goldie, who had 'pronounced success as a medallist at the Academie' and who subsequently became highly popular in New Zealand for his detailed portraits of Māori.

Of teaching master Jean-Paul Laurens (1838–1921), the painter of public works for the French Third Republic, Grace Joel was rather critical, saying from the perspective of six years later: 'I feel that the influence of Jean-Paul Laurens was to crush the individuality of those working under him.'[17] Fortunately, she was not his pupil, but her contemporaries Rupert Bunny, George Coates, Dora Meeson, A.H. O'Keeffe and Cristina Asquith Baker were; whether or not they were crushed to any extent by Laurens can be left for others to judge. As we have already seen, Coates and Meeson had very successful careers, their work represented widely throughout Australian galleries. Bunny had a career of great distinction both overseas and in Australia. So it is not clear whom Grace had in mind when she wrote these comments.

It is noteworthy that the Fauvist painter Henri Matisse (1869–1954) came from the traditional and conservative grounding offered by the likes of Moreau, Lefebvre and Bouguereau at the Julian. In addition, a revolutionary group that included Bonnard and Vuillard was hatched in the studios of the Académie Julian during 1888/89. Known as *Les Nabis* (*Nabi* is the Hebrew word for prophet, referring to the group's messianic zeal), its members were considered to be avant-garde Post-Impressionists by the art community.

Not everyone made a complete go of it. As student artist Clive Holland, who was a *nouveau* in the Quartier Latin in 1902, observed in an issue of *The Studio* from that year: 'There is plenty of human wreckage floating about in the Quarter; and the tragedy of unfulfilled promise, unaccomplished hopes, is closely known with student life.'[18]

It was into this heady atmosphere of La Belle Époque that Grace Joel stepped in 1899, having crossed the Channel to Paris, taken counsel with Dora Meeson and then enrolled at the Académie Julian in order to study drawing. Here she came under the tutelage of not only Marcel-André Baschet (1862–1941), formerly a vice-president of the Salon, but also the notable decorative artist François Schommer (1850–1935), whose works could be found hanging in Paris's public buildings, including the Hotel de Ville. The Julian *atelier* that Grace attended was located at 55, rue du Cherche-Midi, and it was certainly within walking distance of a known early 1901 address for her – 9, rue Campagne-Première in Montparnasse. Parisians commonly referred to this building, a densely inhabited nest of artist studios built around a central courtyard, as *le cité d'artistes*.[19]

The sole documentary evidence for Grace Joel's attendance at the Académie Julian has only recently been discovered (see Image 3.6). The '55' in the

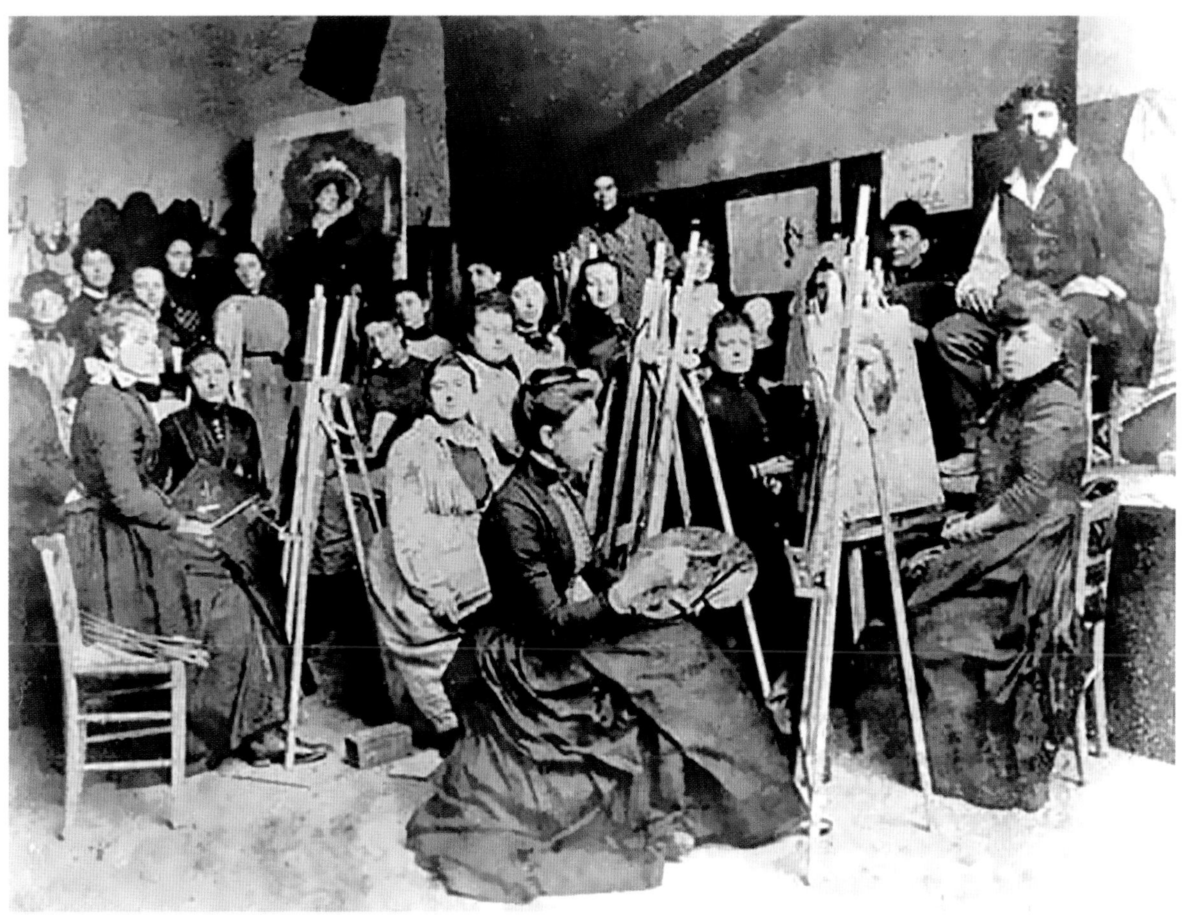

IMAGE 3.5

A women's atelier of the Académie Julian, rue de Berri, Paris, in 1889. The high-seated male appears to be the model. André Del Debbio Collection, Paris

column is the street number of the studio on the rue du Cherche-Midi. Miss 'Sievwright' exhibited with the Otago Art Society in the late 1880s and won a third prize for an oil study from life at the New Zealand South Seas Exhibition of 1889/90.[20] Perhaps it was this event that inspired her to spend five years studying at the Julian. Miss Daisy Fitchett, also a former member of the OAS, exhibited with Grace Joel in the late 1890s after Daisy's return from study at the Julian and elsewhere. Grace's time at the Julian overlapped with that of another Dunedin compatriot, A.H. O'Keeffe, in the men's section.

Was there ever a more exhilarating time to be a young artist in Paris? The Universal Exposition of 1900, at which James Whistler won the Grand Prix in painting, and which included a gallery full of impressionist paintings, was surely an added delight. And then there was the Parisian pastime of shopping: 'The endless shops lining the streets offered clothes, jewellery, pictures, and all manner of consumer spectacles.'[21] It was also the year and place in which the Great Aesthete, Oscar Wilde, died, ending an era characterised by fashionable decadence.

An artist, musician and feminist who preceded Grace Joel at the Julian was the Russian, Marie Bashkirtseff (1858–1884). Her stirring journals were much admired and provided inspiration for another expatriate New Zealander, author Katherine Mansfield (1888–1923). In her diary,

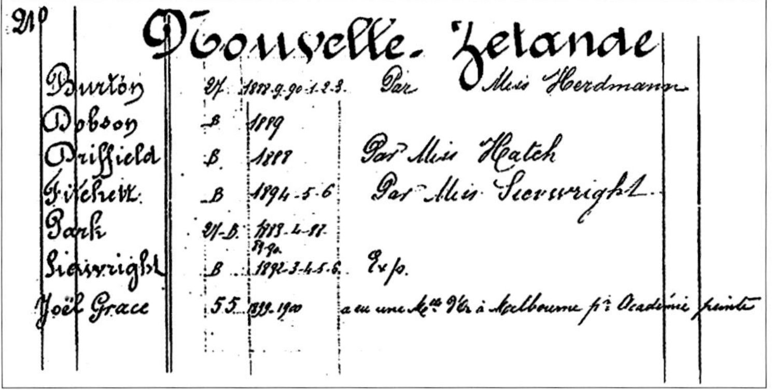

Nouvelle-Zelande

Burton 21. 1889-90-1-2-3. Par Miss Herdman
Dobson B 1889
Driffield B 1888 Par Miss Hatch
Fitchett B 1894-5-6 Par Miss Sievwright
Park 21-B 1893-4-95
Sievwright B 1892-3-4-5-6. Exp.
Joël Grace 55 1899-1900 a eu une Mlle d'or à Melbourne p. Académie peinte

IMAGE 3.6

The only known tangible evidence of Grace Joel's attendance at the Académie Julian. The text to the right states: ***a eu une Médaille d'or à Melbourne pour Académie peinte.*** Gabriel p. Weisberg/André Del Debbio Collection, Paris

Bashkirtseff brooded over whether or not she was a genius, and quintessentially manifested the anguish of many an art student: 'This is killing me! O Art! I shall never attain to a mastery of it.'[22]

One means Monsieur Julian employed to toughen up his students for the realities of the art world was to encourage competitions within each studio, the winners of which went on to larger competitions of the entire school. Those who won received cash prizes. New Zealander H.P. Sealy wrote that in his studio the best seats in the house for painting from a model were decided each week by an *esquisse* (in this case a painted sketch) done the week before and placed in order of merit by the professor. Those doing the best work got the best seats. Each week, new, different male and female models appeared before the students.

Of the time Grace spent at the Julian, we know very little. One report that did filter back mentions that the students in her *atelier* were mostly French and that, 'Before she was there long it was her good fortune to be one of those selected to represent her studio in the *concours* for drawing, and her study from life was placed first by the judges.'[23] Perhaps as a result of her Julian experience and her teachers' support, Grace developed a propensity for exhibiting at the Salon. This was no mean feat:

> *You fill in a form, send it in to the proper address, and then await a reply. Usually the aspirant receives inside of ten days a letter notifying that the picture is not accepted. If this letter does not arrive in ten days, the applicant begins to hope that he has a chance of a place on the walls. As a rule there are about 14,000 applicants, and only from 1500 to 2000 are successful. The selection is made by a jury of forty or fifty men who have attained to high honor in the art world …*[24]

Lest an impression be conveyed of the august body of Salon judges sitting deliberating with equanimity on the artworks before them, the truth is rather more disturbing. In *Mary Cassatt: A life*, author Nancy Mowll Mathews describes the situation prevalent in the mid-1870s when Cassatt, who had come from America, was finding acceptance by the Salon difficult: 'Those paintings that were not "protected" in some way – through an elaborate system of friendships and favors – were fair game for ridicule … In [Emile] Zola's view … paintings were very likely to be passed over unless a juror had a particular interest in a picture done by a student of his or a woman he was acquainted with in some other way.'[25]

Cassatt herself noted: 'In front of the women's paintings the gentlemen were particularly prone to sneer, never displaying the least gallantry.'[26] If a juror (all men of course) did vote in favour of a painting by a woman, Cassatt averred: 'He was interrupted by loud jeers. Was she pretty?' It would seem that even the giants were but mortals with feet of clay. What is ironic is that the works of these very same men were resplendent with women, women and more women. Of course, the scene being described was in the 1870s; by the turn of the century, women's participation in various spheres of broader society had become more accepted and less ridiculed.

Yet even male artists without a patron found acceptance by the Salon difficult. Lamenting the plight of her friend and fellow student in Melbourne, Arthur Streeton, Grace Joel wrote in her 1906 article on Australian artists living in London:

It is difficult always for a complete outsider to get the corner of the wedge in. He had studied with no professor, either in Paris or London, so that there was no one to be proud enough of their pupil to lend a helping hand, as all other Australians have had. Where thousands of pictures are looked at in one day by a jury, however expert, it is impossible that they can be judged on their merits; so that where the picture or name is not known, it is mere chance what is accepted or hung. This has been proved in all parts of the world in the case of the greatest artists, such as Puvis de Chavannes (France), Segantini (Italy), Burne-Jones, Whistler (England), and many others, some of whom have been rejected fifteen times, and in some instances it has been the same picture that has been accepted. It is now almost impossible to purchase these artists' pictures, as such a high value is set on them.[27]

These difficulties make remarkable the fact that Grace Joel's first ever submission, *Son enfant* (*Her Child*), to the Salon de la Société des Artistes Français was accepted and exhibited in 1901. She was in august company: the likes of Salon president W.-A. Bouguereau also had work on show. While the inclusion of *Son enfant* would have brought Grace considerable pleasure, it must have been tempered by the news of the death of her brother, Edward Alexander, shortly before he reached the age of 39.

On the other side of the world, an Australian critic effused over *Son enfant*: 'Here a woman of the people has hushed her child to sleep, her strong, toil-worn arms hold the babe with all a mother's tenderness, and her lowered head exhibits the sweet solicitude of a mother's love. A calm, quiet-compelling picture, for the child sleeps softly, and a loud word or an incautious step might break its slumbers.'[28] Yet acclaim beyond acceptance and exhibiting could also be garnered. Owing to the large number of paintings on display, some exhibition spaces were more desirable than others. Having one's work shown at eye level was more desirable than not, and being 'well hung' at the Salon meant something other than what it does today, as does 'on the line', meaning at eye level. Thus, with *Son enfant*, Grace 'was also fortunate in that her exhibit was hung in a good room and in a capital place on the wall – not too high.'[29] It was with this painting and its success at the 1901 Paris Salon that Grace Joel took the first step along the path to establishing her Anglo-European artistic career.

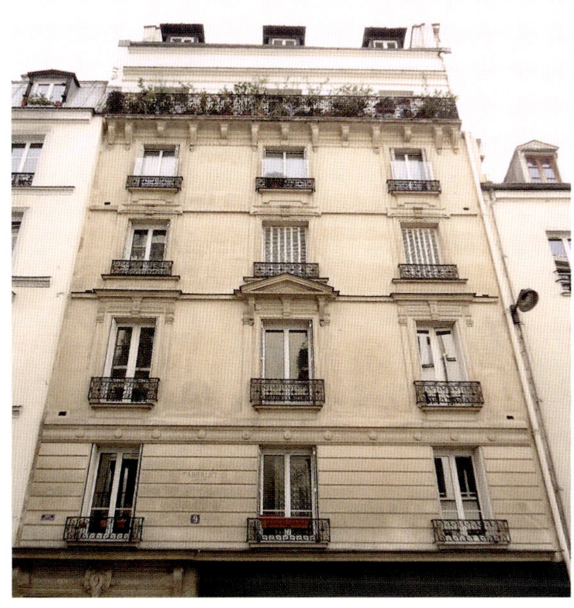

IMAGE 3.7
The address 9, rue Campagne-Première where Grace Joel lived while studying at the Académie Julian.

In the case of *Son enfant*, we have absolute certainty as to the identity of this painting, something that cannot be said of many of her other works. An article based on a rare interview with Grace Joel that appeared in a 1909 edition of *The Woman Worker* includes a photograph of the painting with the caption 'Her Child'. The interviewer, Georgia Pearce, stated that a few weeks after Grace arrived in Paris, 'she had a portrait commission offered her, and not long after a picture hung in the Salon … This is the very picture which is here reproduced.'[30] And if this were not enough, a black and white illustration of *Son enfant* could be found in the Salon's catalogue of 1901 (Image 3.8).

When exhibiting in France, Grace gave her allegiance to the Salon de la Société des Artistes Français, which over time accepted 15 of her works. Her loyalty to the Salon is interesting given that she could have approached more than one French salon

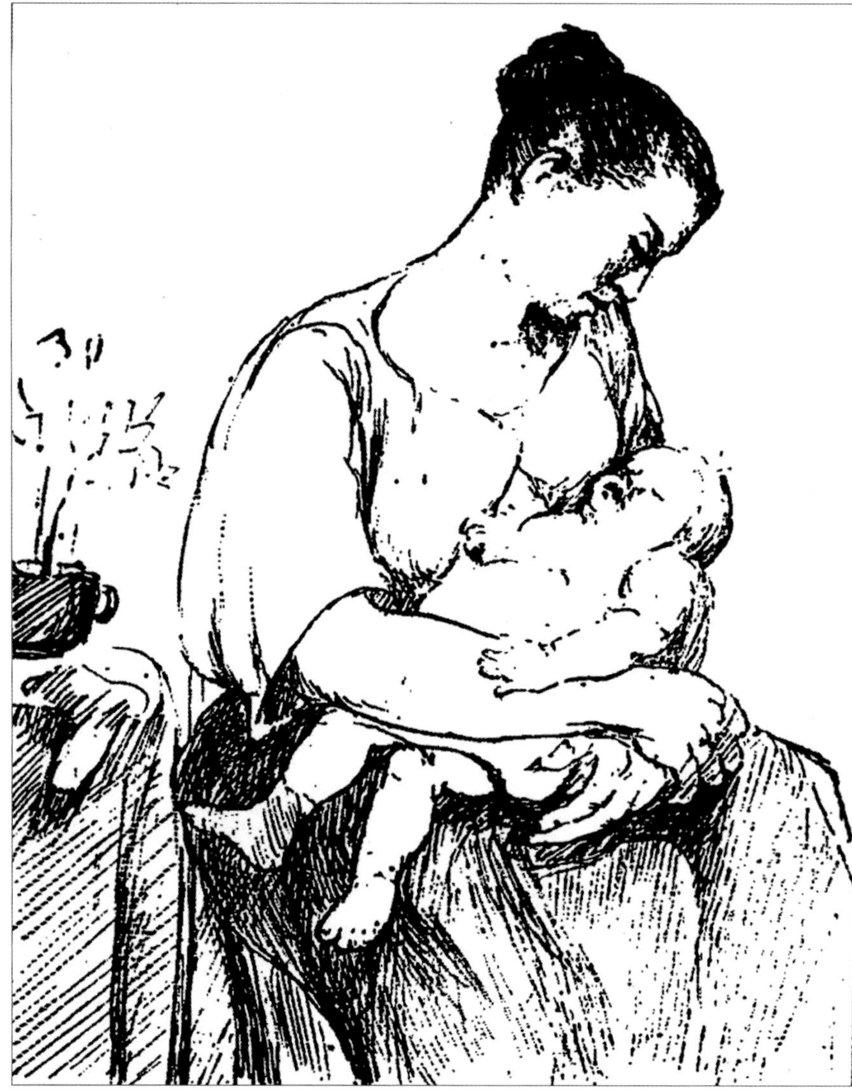

Image 3.8

Drawing for *Son enfant* (*Her Child*), 1901, (see page 60 for the painting). The drawing is reproduced from the illustrated edition of the 1901 exhibition catalogue.

Private collection

at this time. In 1890, Messieurs Ernest Meissonier, Puvis de Chavannes and Auguste Rodin among others formed a splinter group, namely the Société Nationale des Beaux-Arts, founded on values that were less traditional and conservative than those of the Salon. The society hosted its own rival salon. In 1903 another breakaway group was created, the Salon d'Automne. It gained the support of Renoir and Rodin. All three salons still exist today, and to the nouveau have been a 'veritable mine of pleasure and information'.

A possible explanation for Grace's fidelity to the (Old) Salon is that its traditional sensibilities were consonant with her own. Until her death in 1924, she never wavered in her commitment to the same set of thematic values, dominated by the sentiments of maternal love and a deep sense of empathy. The theme of mother and child was a recurring one in Joel's *oeuvre*. In the aforementioned interview in *The Woman Worker* in 1909, she proclaimed that, for her: 'It is the most beautiful subject in the world.' This sentiment was echoed by interviewer Georgia Pearce: 'The old Italian masters used to paint Madonnas. Where is the difference? They, too, found it the most beautiful subject in the world.' Indeed.

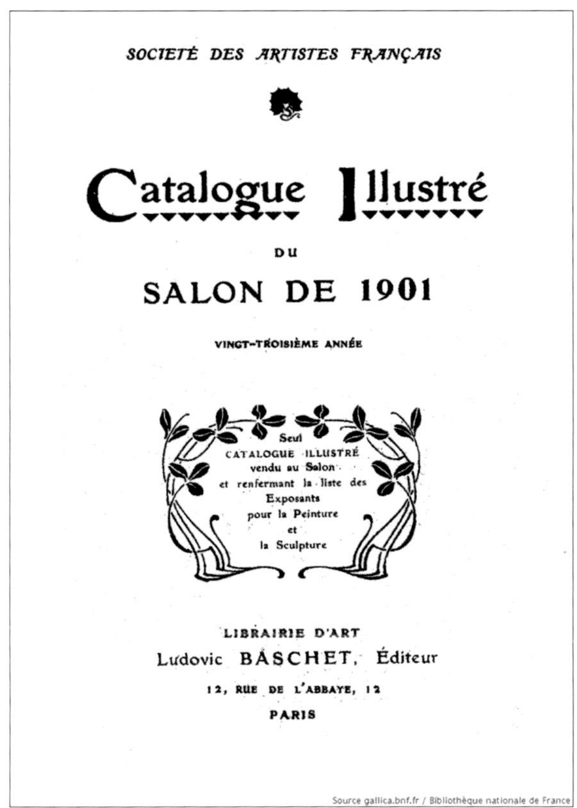

SOCIETÉ DES ARTISTES FRANÇAIS

Catalogue Illustré

DU

SALON DE 1901

VINGT-TROISIÈME ANNÉE

Seul CATALOGUE ILLUSTRÉ vendu au Salon et renfermant la liste des Exposants pour la Peinture et la Sculpture

LIBRAIRIE D'ART
Ludovic BASCHET, Éditeur
12, RUE DE L'ABBAYE, 12
PARIS

Image 3.9

A Paris Salon catalogue cover during the Belle Époque. One of the entries in the catalogue noted the first work Grace Joel exhibited at the Salon, in 1901 **(see page 60).**

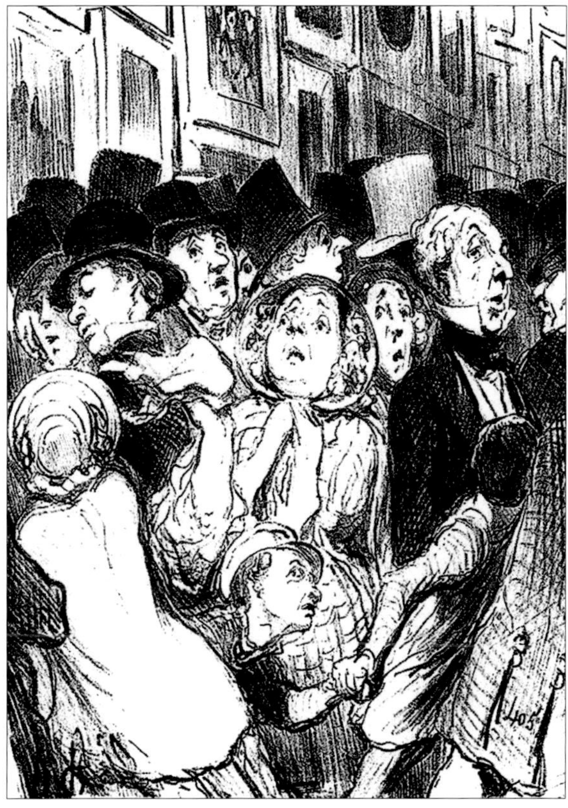

Image 3.10

***Free Day at the Salon*, satirised by Honoré Daumier, published in *Le Charivari*, 17 May 1852. This was one of several caricatures of the Paris Salon done by Daumier.**

Pearce described Grace Joel as 'distinctly petite. A little woman full of restless energy.' Grace told Pearce that for a break in subject matter she sometimes painted flowers. 'They are such a refreshment and keep you from getting mannered with your flesh painting.' Grace created several compositions of roses. One of these, titled simply *Roses*, attracted the following observations at the Otago Art Society's annual exhibition of 1895: '... the representation of an armful of bloom-laden twigs thrown down carelessly to await assortment for the bouquet. The absence of formality in regard to composition, the happy treatment of the flowers themselves, and the delicacy of the tints ... '[31] This commentary says it all with regard to Image 3.11.

Étaples

> *Art, even in the case of the humblest of its votaries, elevates the soul, and makes one superior in some degree to those who are not of the sacred fraternity*
> – Marie Bashkirtseff, Journal entry for 6 January 1882

Although Grace Joel neither lived nor travelled as extensively on the Continent as her compatriot Frances Hodgkins, she did travel to the coast of France in order to paint at Étaples. This charming fishing village and port north of Paris in Picardy hosted a flourishing artists' colony, especially but not exclusively for those from the English-speaking world. Fishermen's cottages had been turned into studios or rented out for low cost. The little town

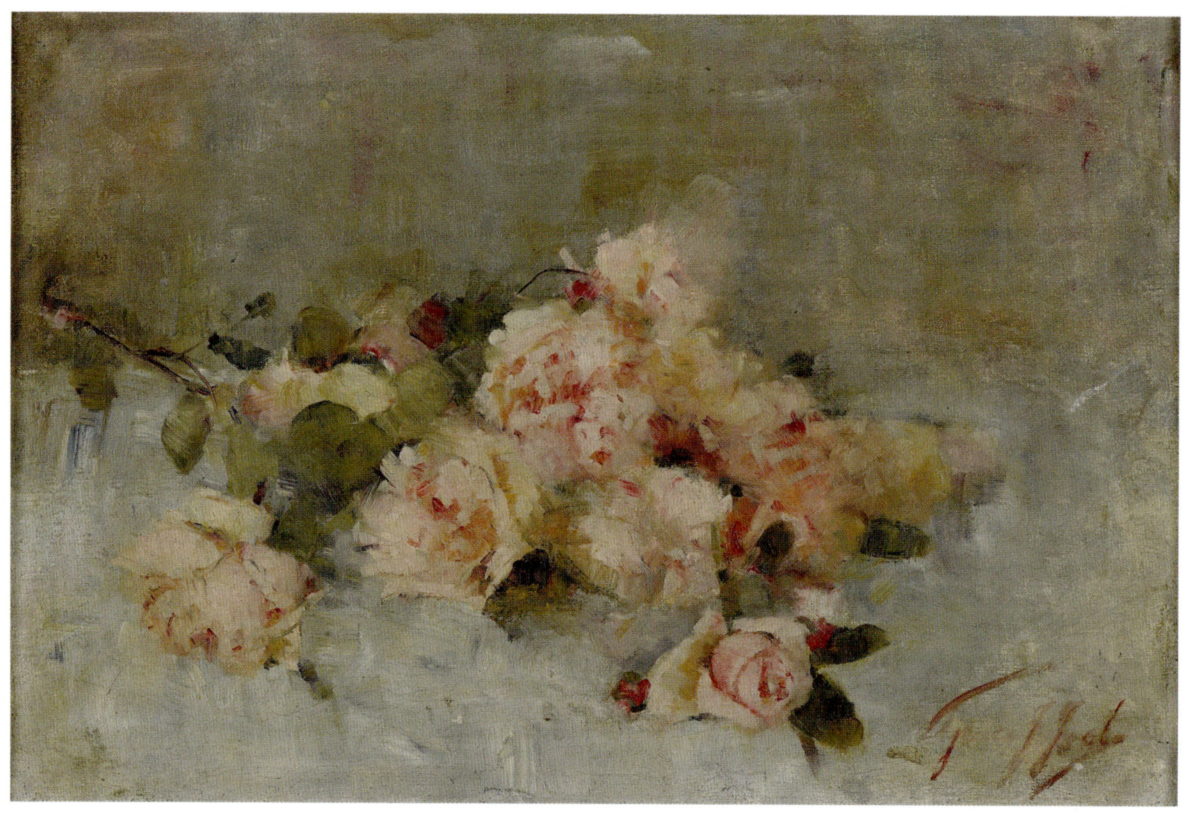

Image 3.11

***Flower Study of Roses*, by Grace Joel, c. 1895, oil on linen on canvas, 33.5 x 49 cm. The painting at one time sold at Sotheby's, London.** Dunbar Sloane Galleries, Wellington; painting now at the Museum of New Zealand Te Papa Tongarewa, Wellington

earned its living principally from fishing. The men, 'with strongly marked features, well bronzed and weather-beaten, are fine specimens of toilers of the sea.' Each day, weather permitting, they took out their fishing boats, distinctive with their large patched sails, and returned with the tide to land their catch. Ashore they were assisted by wives and daughters, both young and old, who carried off baskets of fish for auction in the market place. The costumes, the customs, the natural rhythms of daily life – it was no wonder that artists had flocked there for years to paint – and to escape the daily rigours of life in London and Paris.

At least 22 Australian artists spent time working at Étaples during this era; several stayed on for years. Iso(bel) Rae, for example, a former student of the National Gallery School in Melbourne (1877–87) and a contemporary of Frederick McCubbin, who taught Grace while she was in Melbourne, moved to Étaples with her mother and sister in 1890. The outbreak of war in 1914 ended the artistic idyll at Étaples, but the Rae women stayed on, the only foreigners to do so. As a port, Étaples became an important strategic supply base for the Allies during the Great War, and Iso Rae documented the activity of those years in the village through her art; all this, despite having what Grace Joel described as 'an extremely sensitive and retiring' disposition. It is highly likely that Grace met up with Iso Rae while in Étaples, since NGS students were no strangers to the village, and Rae by then was one of the locals. Given the attraction that Étaples had for artists in

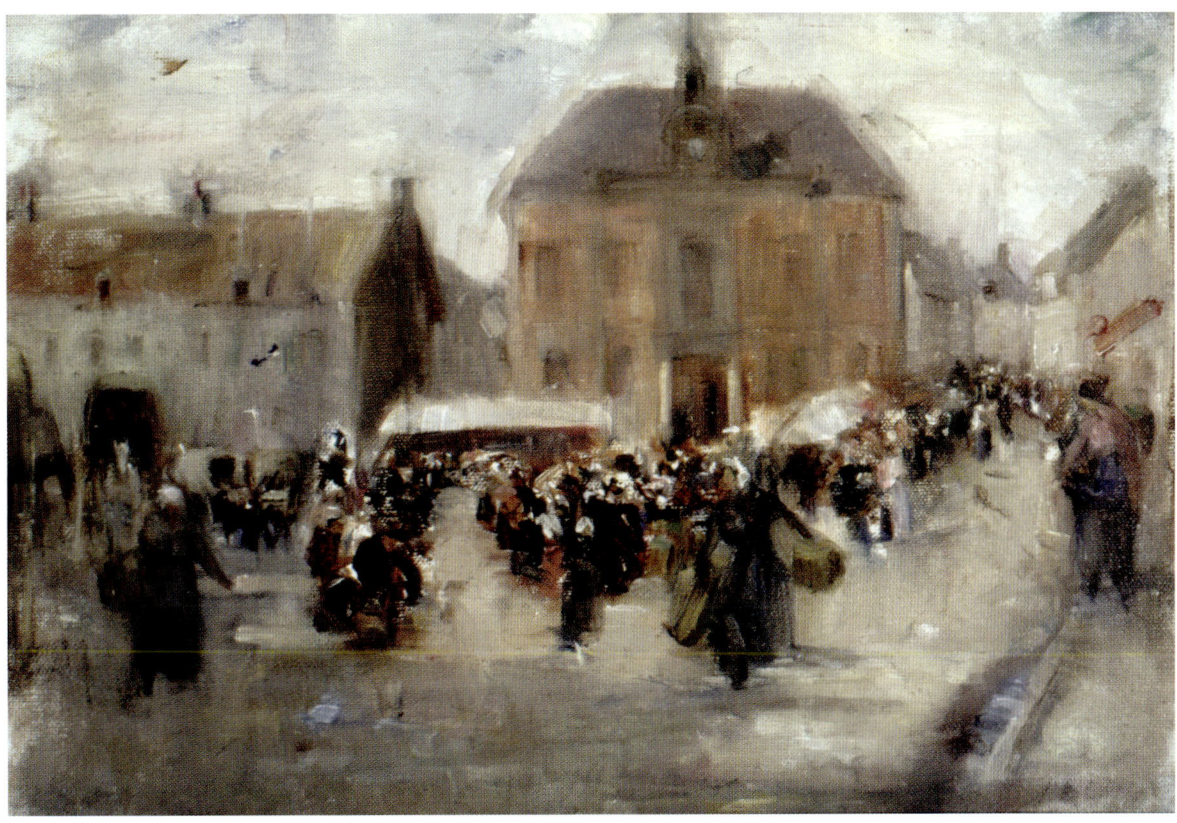

IMAGE 3.12

Marketing, Étaples, by Grace Joel, c. 1901, oil sketch of the public square and town hall, 27.8 x 36.2 cm. Private collection

the pre-war years, it is no surprise to find that cousin E. Phillips Fox had made the pilgrimage some years before Grace.

The *London Express*, commenting favourably on a solo exhibition of Grace's work at the Doré Gallery in 1909, noted that she had 'spent a summer [of 1901] at Étaples among the fisher folk and country people, and made many studies of young girls, resting among the sheaves after a long day's gleaning, and of peasant mothers with their babies'. The newspaper also made an astute observation of Grace Joel's artistic sensitivity: 'The pathos and poetry of peasant life in European countries … appealed strongly to her.' Here was a woman capable of deep emotional understanding, who communicated the 'poetry of peasant life' not with words but paint.[32]

Grace's time in Étaples saw her producing a number of works, including two of the town square's market place. One of these was a *plein air* unsigned oil sketch (Image 3.12). Some years later, D.H. Souter (1862–1935), art editor of *Art and Architecture*, described the other, more accomplished work (Image 4.2) as 'shewing the wide street of a provincial town in the soft mellow atmosphere of a summer day. Peasants sit at their stalls laden with the produce of field and byre, busy purchasers hurry here and there, and the picture is full of quiet movement painted in subdued tones, restrained in effort, excellent in effect, and one of the gems of the exhibition.'[33] Both paintings were called *Marketing, Étaples*. E. Phillips Fox had painted his own version of *Market Place, Étaples* in 1890.[34]

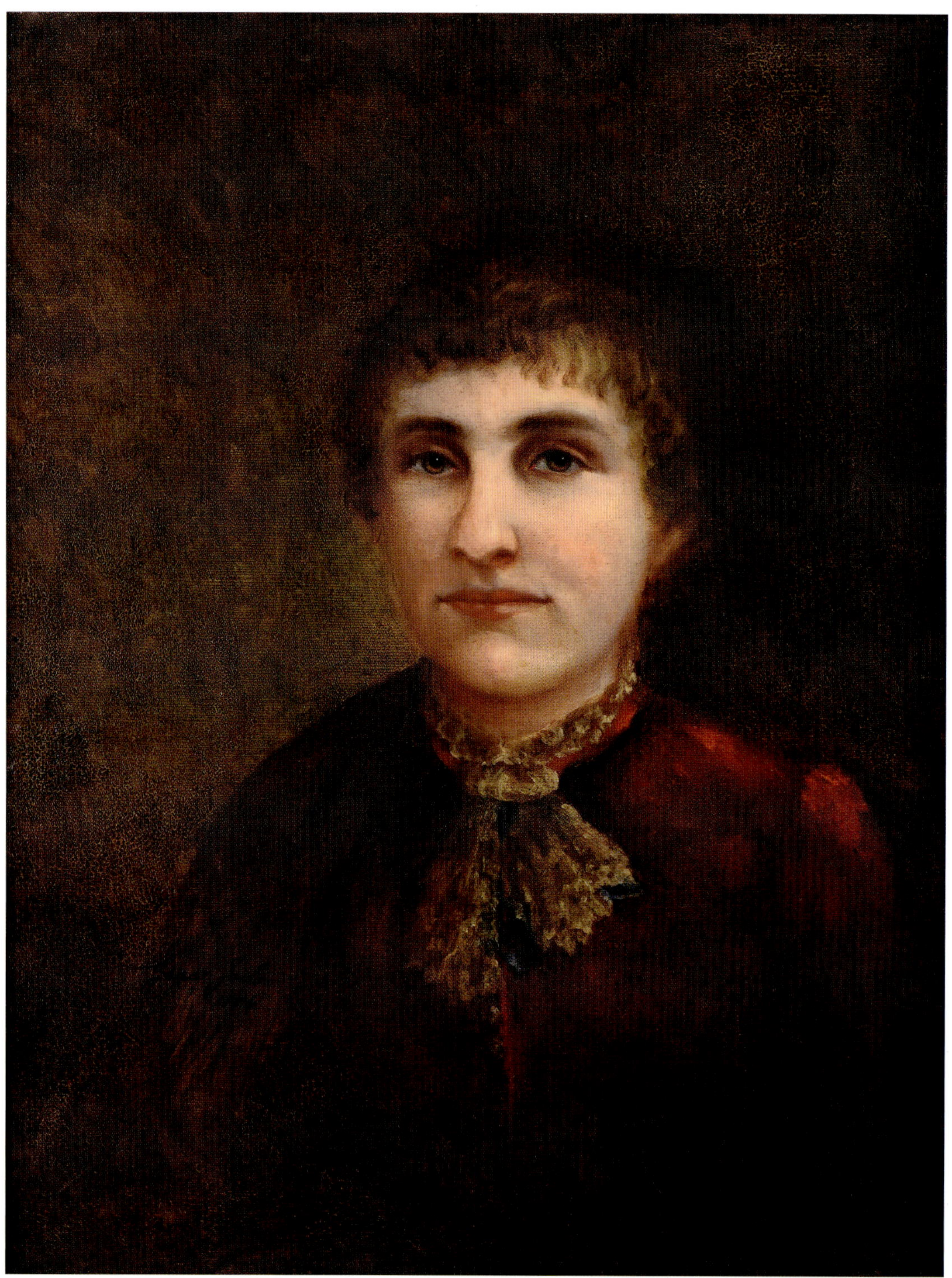

IMAGE 4.1

Girl in Red Dress, by Grace Joel, dated 1886, 60 x 45 cm. The portrait bears a strong resemblance to Grace's sister, Blanche, in Image 1.9, especially if the fringe is returned to the exposed forehead in the photograph. Because the work has remained in the family and is not the face of a Madonna that one would paint for exhibition or sale, the sitter was more than likely Blanche. Private collection

Chapter 4

Life in England

She paints in a low key with rich quiet tones reminiscent of the Old Masters – Edith Fry in 'The British Australasian', 1921

Grace returned to London in 1901, 'where it is her present intention to remain permanently in the artistic profession'.[1] With an annual income from her father, she was in the enviable position of not having the worry of sole reliance on her work as an artist for her livelihood. But then her works were for sale whenever exhibited, on occasion at a price amounting to a workingman's yearly wage. Grace had no doubt been in contact with her sister, Blanche, who arrived towards the end of the year with her children and with the intention of engaging in studies at the Royal Academy of Music in London. Grace took a studio at No.7 Stanley Studios, Park Walk, S.W. London, and soon began receiving various commissions, including two portraits. According to the *Otago Daily Times*, the distinguished English painter Solomon J. Solomon (who had advised Grace previously) continued to take a benevolent interest in her work at this time.[2]

Solomon was noted for painting grand theatrical depictions of scenes from the Bible, such as Samson and Delilah. One might ask, what good was such a transcendental artist when the Great War rolled around? If you were Solomon J. Solomon, you introduced the military to the techniques of camouflage, such as covering gun emplacements with netting, painting schemes for tanks and disguising observation posts as trees. You also published a book on the subject after the war. Solomon's techniques became standard features of modern warfare.

As planned, Blanche enrolled at the Royal Academy of Music in London, studying the piano under Signor Albanesi. She won a handful of medals and honours in pianoforte, harmony and singing during her three-year course. She was also elected an Associate of the Royal Academy of Music (ARAM) for her distinguished studies there. In a case of fruit not falling far from the tree, Blanche's daughter, Kathleen, who was perhaps even more musically gifted than her mother, also became an ARAM after winning a clutch of prizes, including a gold medal from the academy for best playing by a female student. She won three top Royal Academy of Music prizes in 1920 alone, and for many years thereafter continued gracing the London concert stage. Owing to the marvels of short-wave transmission, a BBC Empire broadcast featuring Kathleen's piano virtuosity could be heard on the radios of her distant homeland at 5:45 p.m., 11 August 1936.[3] Grace completed a Rembrandt-like portrait of Kathleen around 1921 (Image 6.21).

Grace, along with Dora Meeson, exhibited mid-year at the 1902 British Colonial Art Exhibition in Piccadilly. The media's London correspondent reported that 'special praise is accorded to "the portraits of Miss Grace Joel"'.[4] But Frances Hodgkins, who was 'missed over' for the occasion, had other views on the exhibition:

> *Tell Sis there is a Colonial show on at the Institute for water colors [in Piccadilly] just now run by Wadham & Sinclair … I went to see it this afternoon & blush to think how badly the Colony is represented – most of them are truly awful … Miss Stoddart & I were feeling a little annoyed at being missed over but I now feel so no longer – the papers are all very down on it and it will only do Colonial art more harm than good I fear … Miss Joel has a big canvas representing 'Maternity' – it is fine color but too clumsily painted. Dora Meeson's work is not good …*[5]

According to the same London correspondent, Miss Stoddart *was* represented at the exhibition, so perhaps Margaret Stoddart felt no such annoyance; after all, she already had a reputation as New Zealand's pre-eminent floral artist.

October found Grace exhibiting her scenic *Marketing, Étaples* (more than likely not the sketch version) and four other works at the John Baillie Gallery Bayswater. An equal number of paintings were exhibited by former Dunedin compatriots Frances Hodgkins and Annie Blacke. Friend Dora Meeson was not left out either, being represented by three of her works. In a letter to her mother on 23 October 1902, Frances Hodgkins wrote: 'It was odd to find oneself flanked, as in the old Dunedin days by Miss Joel & Annie Black[e] …'[6] Another exhibitor, Dorothy Kate Richmond, who had studied with James Nairn in Wellington, was Hodgkins' frequent travelling companion. Summing up the exhibition, the London correspondent for the

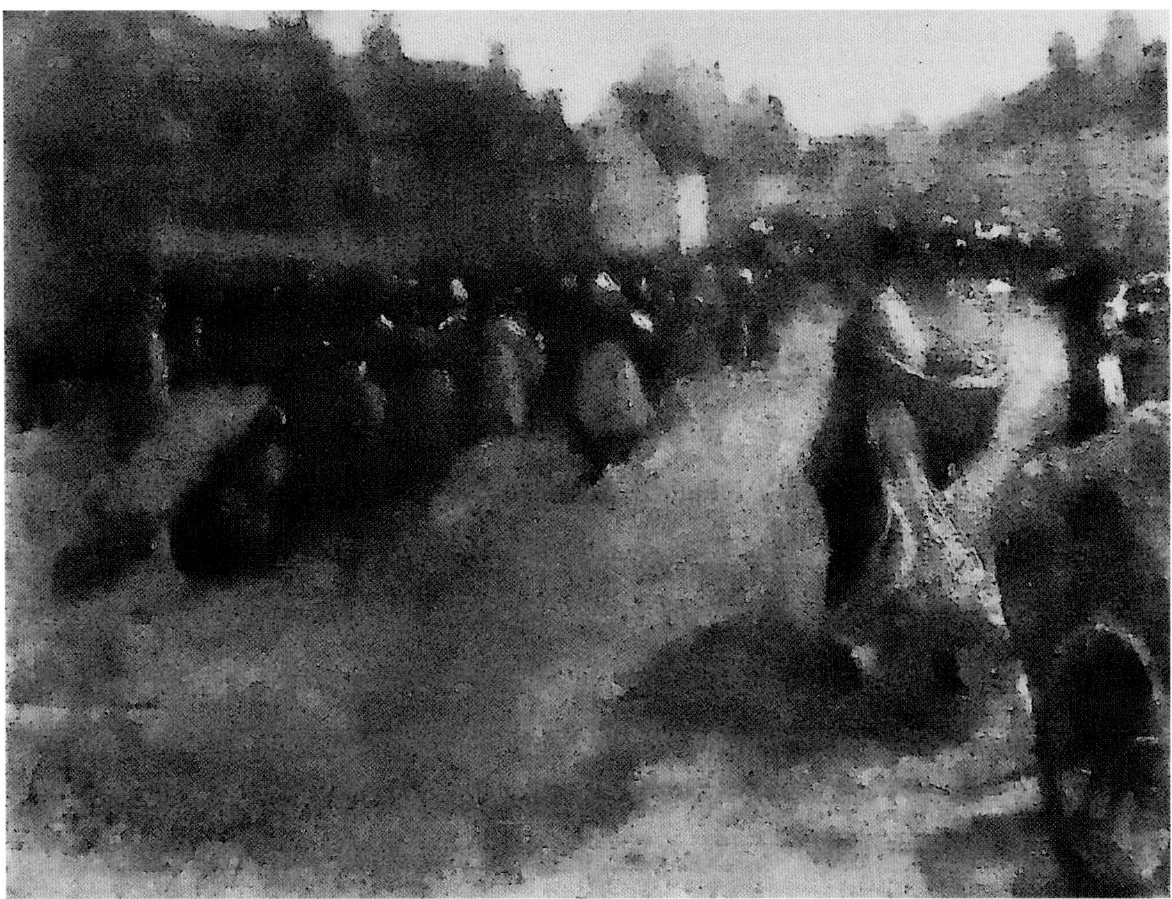

IMAGE 4.2

The best image we have of the main painting titled *Marketing, Étaples*, by Grace Joel, c. 1901, oil on canvas, whereabouts unknown. This black and white photograph accompanied D.H. Souter's article about Grace and her work, published in the periodical *Art and Architecture*.

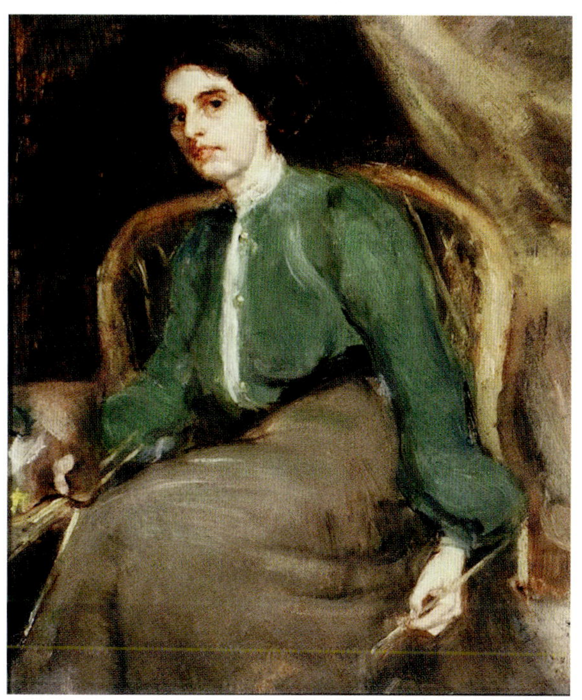

IMAGE 4.3

***Self-portrait, Seated in a Cane Chair*, c. 1901–02, oil on wood, 22 x 18.5 cm. According to Frank Dickinson (*Grace Joel: Paintings and drawings*, 1980), the artist's style of blouse provides the approximate date.**

Private collection

Auckland Star concluded: 'The cleverest piece of work in the exhibition is Miss Joel's *Marketing, Étaples* … Her *Moonlight and Sheep* is something of a tour de force.'[7] Grace had not forsaken her homeland at this time. She exhibited three works at the Otago Art Society in November 1902. One, titled *Saint Tasie*, portrayed the head of a French peasant girl and was possibly one of the studies she had made in Étaples the year before.

When, on 1 May 1903, the Grand Palais Paris Salon opened, Grace's address was listed there as 60 Alexandra Road, St John's Wood, N.W. This well-heeled part of London is now famous as the location of the recording studio Abbey Road, forever associated with the Beatles. The work by Grace on display at the Salon was *Le retour par le sentier crayon* (although *crayon* should have been *crayeux*). In the dusty and remote colonial outpost of Perth, Western Australia, the presence of *Homeward Bound by the Chalky Path* (to give the painting its English translation) in the Grand Salon was duly noted in the local press.[8]

Of this latest Salon conquest, the London correspondent for the *Evening Post* remarked that Grace Joel had 'scored a marked success with a large landscape picture, which has been well hung.' No longer could she be regarded strictly as a figure painter. But the gracious correspondent then expressed sympathy for the disappointment she must have experienced when one of her paintings was crowded out 'at the last moment' from display at the 1903 Royal Academy exhibition: 'In this stroke of ill-luck, however, Miss Joel has many eminent British associates. The available space is in fact much too small to accommodate all that is worthy of exhibition.'[9]

A few weeks before the Salon exhibition, Grace set 18 paintings on view at her St John's Wood residence for a gathering of friends. One of these works, a full-length portrait of a boy, met with sufficient approval to warrant a commission to paint the boy's sister.[10]

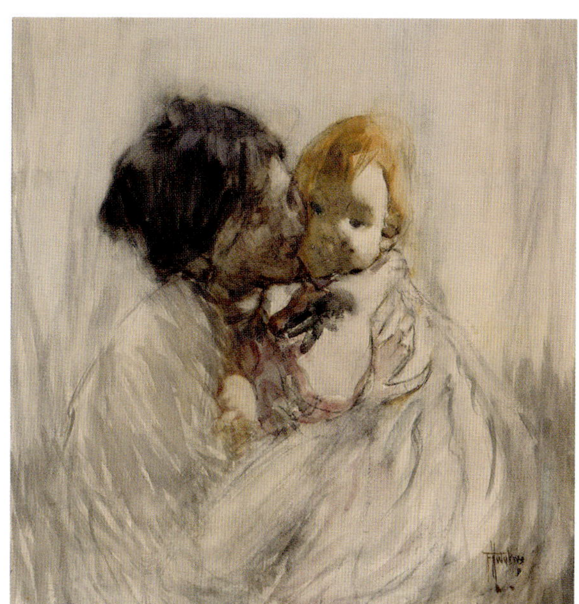

IMAGE 4.4

***Woman and Child*, by Frances Hodgkins, c. 1912, watercolour and charcoal, 47.5 x 45.9 cm, is one of several of her mother and child thematic works.**

Dunedin Public Art Gallery, Dunedin

Excursion to Holland

As autumn took hold in London in 1903, Grace embarked on a six-week sojourn to Holland where she visited various centres of art and was pleased to find paintings by the Dutch emigrant to New Zealand, Petrus van der Velden, highly regarded by other artists in his home country. She met with the contemporary Dutch master Jozef Israëls (1824–1911), who viewed some of what she had painted locally and spoke 'very highly of the work.'[11] Five years later, Grace recalled 'the bright eyes and marvellous vitality of her kind host, though he was over eighty; of his extraordinary dignity and distinction of bearing.'[12]

Returning to England in October, Grace launched a major exhibition of her works, 33 in all, at the John Baillie Gallery in London. The paintings included some from her recent travels in Holland. Of particular note are *Marketing, Étaples*; *Le grandpère*; *Eleanor* (NFS), 'daughter of Hilaire Belloc, Esq., lent by Hilaire Belloc, Esq.'; *Her Child* (Ex Salon 1901); *Homeward Bound by the Chalky Path* (Ex Salon, 1903); *Mrs Maurice Joel* (NFS, very likely the portrait of Grace's mother Catherine, painted in 1895, and taken with her when she left New Zealand); *A Dutch Woman, Prinzengracht – The Hague*; *Household Chores*; *On the Thames*; and *Westminster*. *Le grandpère*, for sale at £21, possibly corresponds with *Le grandpère d'Étaples*, shown at the Paris Salon in 1908.

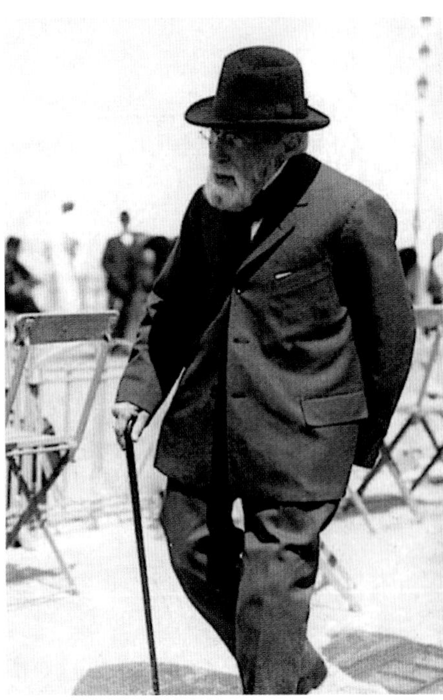

Image 4.5

The Dutch master Jozef Israëls in 1911, shortly before he died.

As we will become increasingly aware, identifying works by Grace Joel is more a matter of trying to minimise the degree of uncertainty regarding any particular work. There is the historical record from exhibition catalogues and media accounts on the one hand, and the actual painting in question on the other. On rare occasions, as for example, *Son enfant* (*Her Child*), the identification can be regarded as 'absolutely certain' and so at the extreme end of the spectrum (zero uncertainty), whereas with others we have to be content with equivocating terms such as 'reasonably certain', 'very likely', and so on down to 'possibly corresponds to' and 'we may as well be hunting the Snark'. In this regard, to this day, disagreement remains over the precise determination of Rembrandt's *oeuvre* (and that of many other artists), so the problem of identification is just part of the artistic territory. In fact, 'Jan Hulsker, the doyen of Van Gogh studies, claimed that the artist's accepted *oeuvre* was littered with fakes.'[13] At least we can be 'reasonably certain' that this issue is one we do not have to contend with in regard to Grace.

A small work at the Baillie that was again shown at the Doré (in 1909) was *In the Garden of the Luxembourg*. These gardens, within painting distance from where Grace Joel lived during her time in Paris, were very popular with the public and especially so with artists, who could sit on the benches for free, unlike in other parks, where the sitter had to pay. This attribute helps to explain the many painted scenes one comes across of the Jardins du Luxembourg (see Image 4.6).

Grace also exhibited a portrait of *Mrs Yeatman Woolf*, 'lent by Mrs Yeatman Woolf Esq.', who also contributed *A Miniature* for the exhibit. What makes

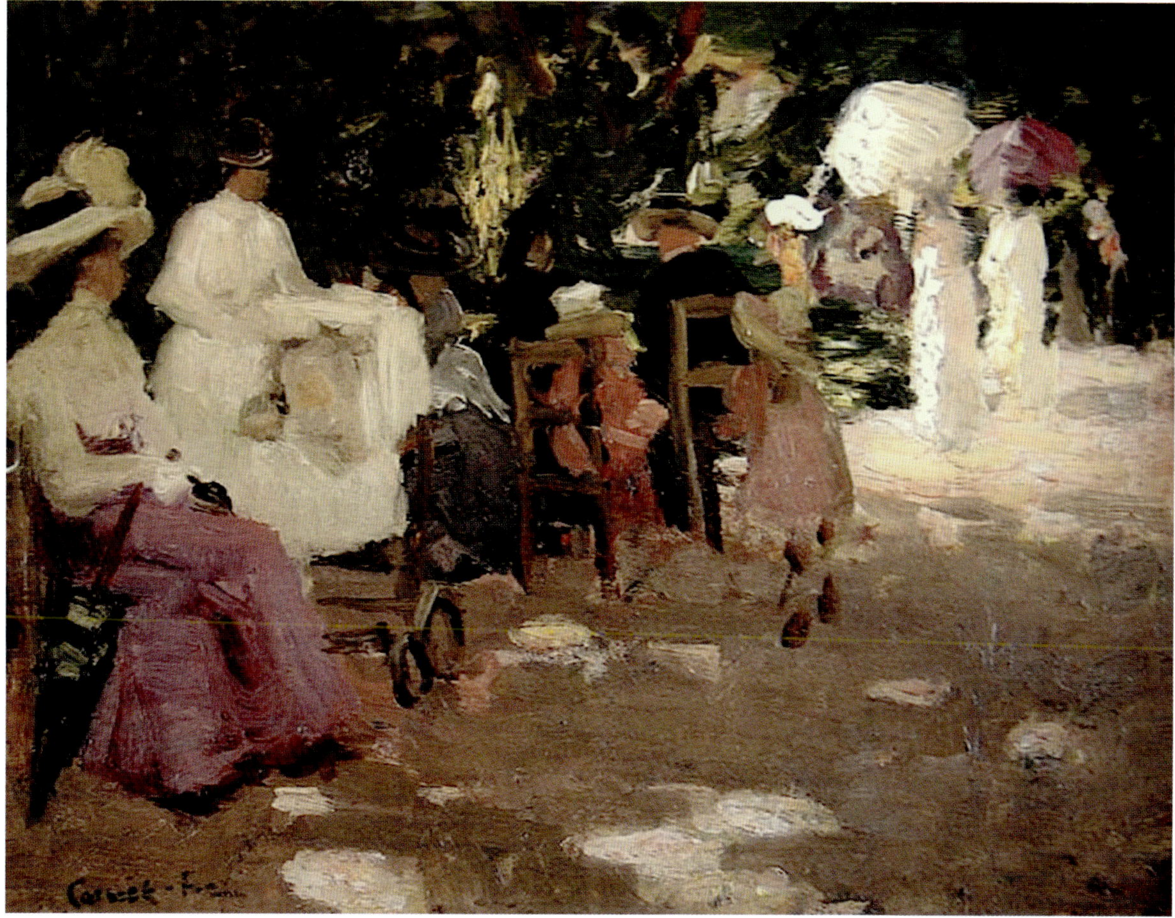

Image 4.6

The amygdala-stimulating *Les Jardins du Luxembourg*, by Ethel Carrick Fox, c. 1905, 34.5 x 42.5 cm. Ethel was married to Grace Joel's second cousin, Emanuel Phillips Fox. She was a talented and successful painter in her own right. Private collection

Mrs Woolf (*née* Nashelski of Auckland, New Zealand) a person of interest was that she was close enough to Grace Joel to be the recipient in Grace's will of her Limerick lace fichu – a Victorian woman's triangular neck-covering worn over a dress. Mrs Woolf was also involved with an organisation called the Sick Room Helps Society: 'The contributors, mostly female, constitute a representative group of middle-class Anglo-Jewry in Edwardian times.'[14] The society's main function was to provide maternal care for Jewish women in London's East End at a time when other sources of such care were scarce. By 1911, the Helps Society had evolved into the Jewish Maternity Hospital in Whitechapel. A check of the 1907/08 list of contributors does not show Grace Joel's name, but she may have been a contributor at other times. Certainly, her artistic contribution to the theme of maternity was substantial.

The year 1904 found Grace painting commissioned portraits, which provided her with additional income. 'On the completion of an important portrait recently painted by her she was agreeably surprised at the substantial amount of the cheque which was promptly tendered to her.'[15] In late May, Grace again met with the distinguished English Victorian painter and member of the Royal Academy, George Frederick Watts, at his residence. Just over a month later, he was dead at age 87.

> *Miss Grace Joel, the gifted New Zealand artist, had a most gratifying interview a few days ago with Mr G.F. Watts, the famous veteran painter. He took much interest in Miss Joel's work, and gave her great encouragement as to her future. One of her pictures he described as 'charming' and he sent for Mrs Watts to come and see it, and she was equally pleased. The great English painter spoke most kindly and encouragingly to the young New Zealand artist, and assured her that, in his opinion, she need have no fear of failure. On the contrary, he was convinced that she would have considerable success – how great it was impossible for him yet to judge. But that she WOULD succeed he entertained no doubt at all. Subsequently, Mrs Watts wrote to Miss Joel a charming letter expressing the pleasure Mr Watts had experienced in looking at her work. Miss Joel leaves London next week on a visit to Holland.*[16]

Several years later (1909), Grace showed Mrs Watts' letter to Georgia Pearce, the interviewer from *The Woman Worker*, who felt inclined to share it with readers: 'It is pleasant to think your visit gave you pleasure and encouraged you to go on further and higher on the way to the gate of the Temple called "Beautiful". I think the pleasure my husband found in looking at your work must help you, too.'

Holland Redux

In August 1904, Grace gave up her studio in St John's Wood and travelled to Holland for several months. She intended to meet up with former National Gallery School attendee, the red-haired beauty, Ada May Plante. Ada had been studying at the Julian (1902–04) and was sharing a studio with another Julian student who was also one of Grace's Melbourne acquaintances, Cristina Asquith Baker (1868–1960). Interestingly, E. Phillips Fox, Cristina's former art teacher and Grace's second cousin, had an adjoining studio. Just like old times in Melbourne. Both Ada (1875–1950) and Cristina went on to achieve significant artistic recognition in their lifetimes. On 18 August 1904, Grace sent Christina a postcard from Laren, Holland that read, in part: 'Have not heard from Miss Plante. I suppose she is not coming. Sold a small picture in London.'[17]

While in Holland, Grace painted a number of works, which she exhibited once back in England. One life-size canvas, *Hollandaise* (*Dutch Woman*), caught the attention of the Paris Salon and was well hung there in one of the main viewing rooms in 1905. The *Otago Daily Times* reported that as 'soon as the picture was in position Miss Joel received a letter from the agent of the Paris Salon asking her to accord to that body the first right of sale.'[18] Grace apparently had no desire to part with the painting, however, as it was one of an ensemble of Salon triumphs that she exhibited in Australia and New Zealand during her return to the Antipodes in late 1905. Back in England by spring 1907, she exhibited it at the London Salon in 1908 and at the Doré Gallery a year later. Both times it was for sale but remained unsold. In her 1920 will Grace donated this work to the Christchurch Art Gallery, which had expressed a desire to purchase one of her paintings.

This large work was subsequently renamed *A Time of Prayer*, and there is no question that the two paintings are the same because of the media entries which identify them as such.[19] The work portrays a woman whose piety has been governed by the book in her lap and who faces life with the stoical attitude that so imbues the work of Jozef Israëls. Indeed, the latter's own *Après la Messe*, which also features an older woman who is wearing both a head and neck scarf and is seated front on with her Bible, is surely the source of inspiration for Grace Joel's similar composition.[20] Both are equally stark. The *Evening Star* effused over *Prayer*: 'The facial expression is excellent, the painting of the one visible hand is a perfect triumph, and, in fact, examined in every particular this is a strong and clever piece of work, well designed and skillfully finished.'[21] The same woman and facial expression also appeared in the watercolour sketch *Dutch Woman, Arms Akimbo*, but this time the one visible hand is not such a triumph, being rather too large. However, the work is interesting for its rare use of the word 'akimbo' and again the sombre tone of Israëls.

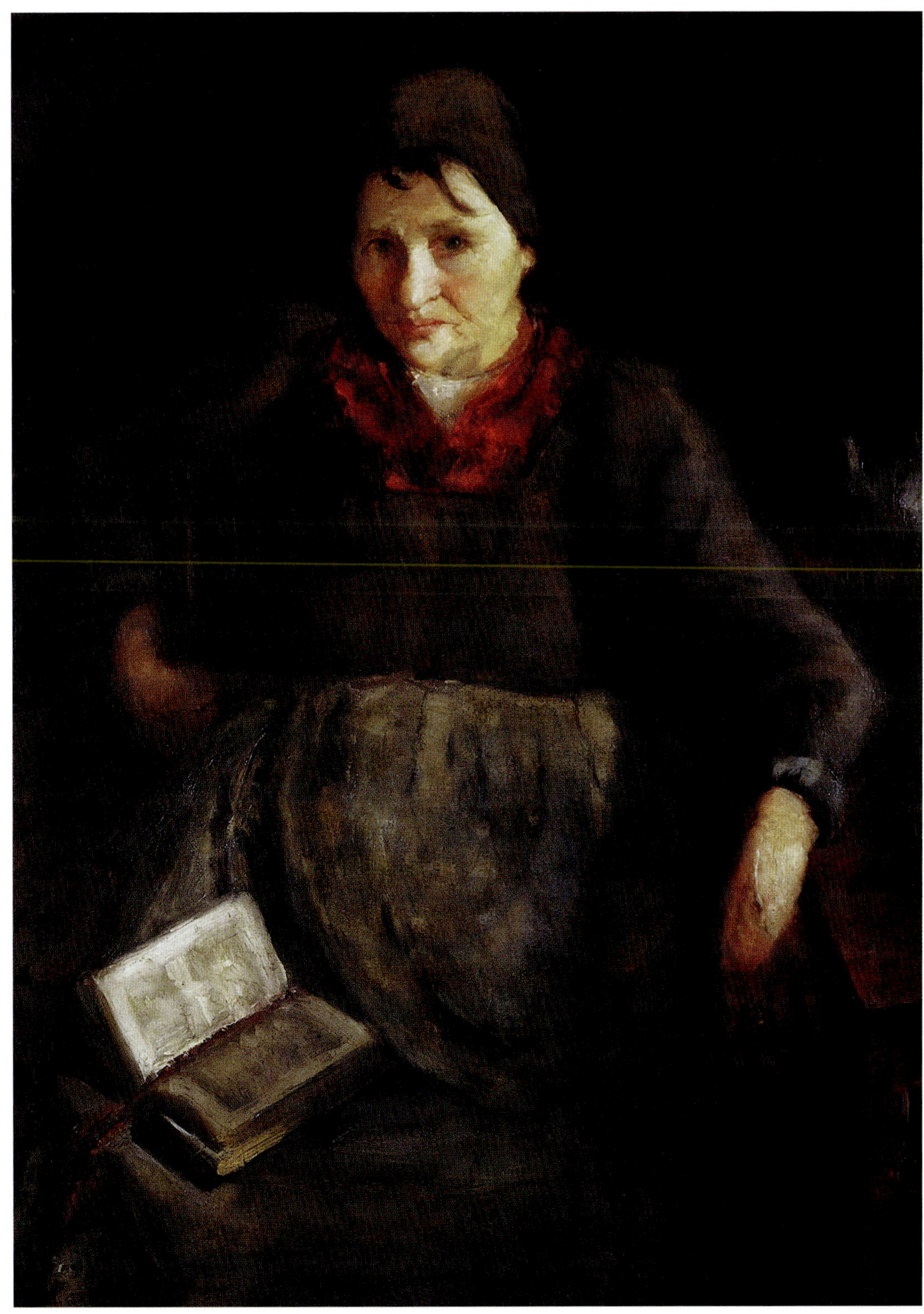

IMAGE 4.7

***A Time of Prayer*, by Grace Joel, 1903–04, oil on canvas 106 x 76.8 cm, exhibited at the 1905 Salon under the title, *Hollandaise* (*Dutch Woman*). The composition derives from a similar work by Dutch master Jozef Israëls.**

Collection of the Christchurch Art Gallery Te Puna o Waiwhetu; purchased 1996

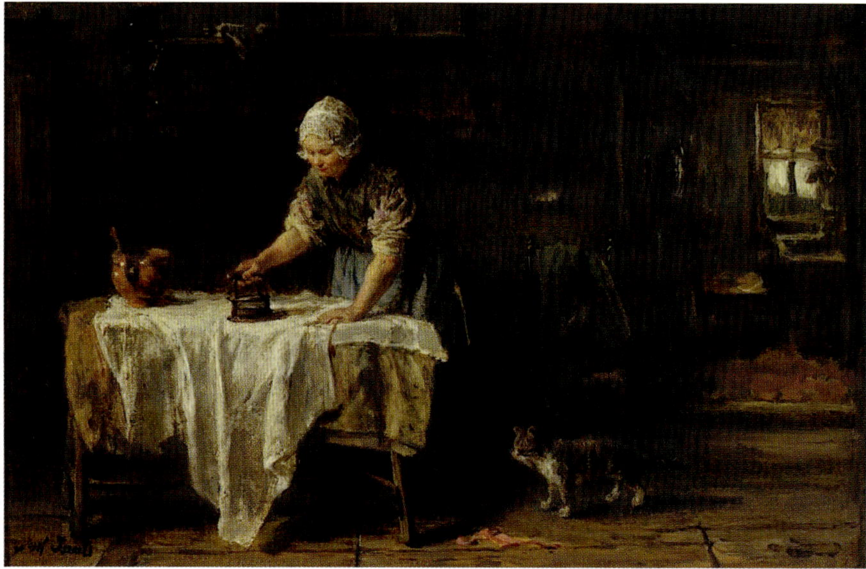

IMAGE 4.8
***Het strijkstertje/The Ironing Girl*, by Jozef Israëls, 1886, oil on canvas. Israëls imbued a simple domestic chore with a quiet dignity.**

By the time Grace met with Jozef Israëls for a second time, in 1904, she had acquired three of his etchings. In her will, she bequeathed one to her brother Louis, another to Melbourne's National Gallery of Victoria and the third to the Otago Art Society. Israëls was arguably the finest Dutch artist of the latter half of the nineteenth century, and so these gifts carry a certain cachet. The *Jewish Chronicle* observed that 'Miss Joel is susceptible to the influences of those painters in whose countries she has travelled ... The spirit of Josef Israëls is strongly dominant in her Dutch pictures.'[22]

Return to England

In the second half of the 19th century, the motherhood theme had become the secular counterpart of the traditional image of the Madonna and child – Ruth Zubans, 1995

Once more back in England, as of 1904, Grace spent a month in the cathedral city of Canterbury, although her residence was now at No. 12 Milton Chambers, 128 Cheyne Walk, Chelsea, London. Cheyne Walk is a very distinguished historical location. This road along the Thames River runs roughly between the Chelsea and Battersea bridges, and part of it merges with the Embankment. Since the fifteenth century, it has featured some of the grandest and most elegant houses in London. A former prominent resident was Henry VIII, who built a new manor house there facing the river in 1543.

Over the centuries Cheyne Walk became the location of many aristocratic family mansions and palaces sited along the river front. By the early eighteenth century, however, Georgian townhouses (today, the Walk's oldest residences) were replacing the palaces as the grandeur of the sixteenth and seventeenth centuries waned.

In more modern times, Cheyne Walk residents have included artists, among them J.M.W. Turner, James McNeill Whistler and John Singer Sargent. There have also been writers, including Oscar Wilde, Henry James, George Eliot, Mark Twain, Bertrand Russell, Katherine Mansfield, Hilaire Belloc, Sylvia Pankhurst ... In 1968, Mick Jagger and his girlfriend Marianne Faithfull, together with Jagger's good friend David Bowie from just around the corner, began to imbue Cheyne Walk with a somewhat different tone.

The Great Man of Letters and parliamentarian Hilaire Belloc and his wife Elodie lived a short

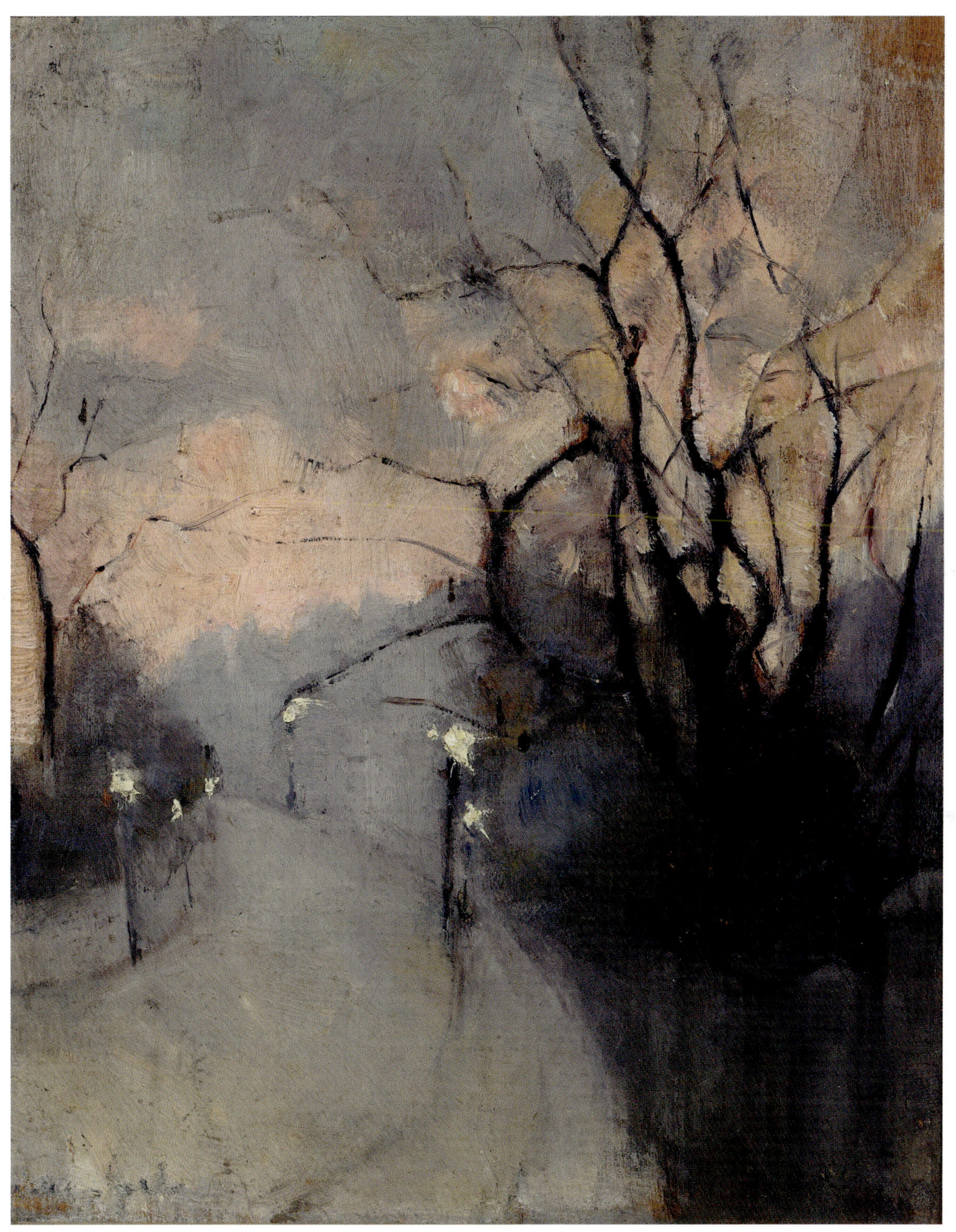

Image 4.9

***Autumn Twilight, Hampstead,* by Grace Joel, c. 1905, oil on wood panel, 26 x 20.9 cm.**

Given by Professor F.N. Fastier, Dunedin, 1980; Hocken Collections Uare Taoka o Hākena, University of Otago, Dunedin

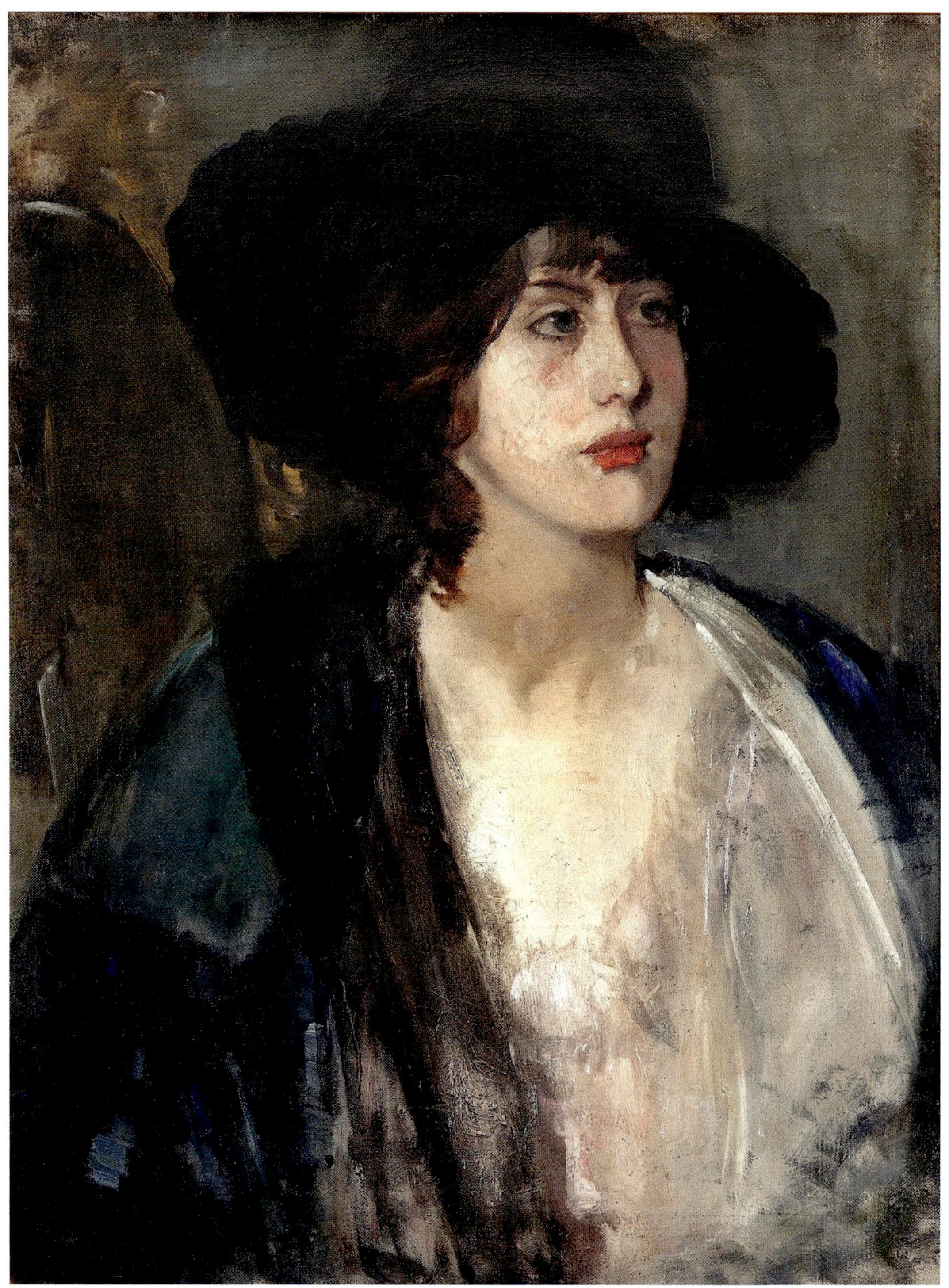

IMAGE 4.10

Woman Wearing a Hat, early twentieth century, by Grace Joel, oil on canvas, 58.4 x 43.2 cm. On the reverse side is written, 'painted in Paris'. In her Master's thesis, Kirsten Fergusson argues for the sitter to be Grace's old National Gallery School colleague, Christina Asquith Baker, who was a student in Paris from 1902 to 1905. A photo of Asquith Baker does show a resemblance. Private collection

distance down the road from Grace Joel, at 104 Cheyne Walk. Their daughter, Eleanor, was the subject of a portrait by Grace, who also painted the outdoor scene viewed from their drawing room. Of the latter, Elodie wrote to Grace on 25 May 1905 after the Bellocs had moved to the countryside: 'I wish that you could see our picture of Chelsea. It is quite charming and has the place of honour in our dining room ... I brought it here as a sort of memento of all my life in dear old 104, Cheyne Walk.'[23]

The Belloc biographer Robert Speaight prefaces this note from Elodie by saying that 'On May 25 (1905) she wrote to her friend Grace Joel, a New Zealand painter and pupil of Renoir.'[24] However tantalising this comment may be, no evidence has been found confirming Joel as one of Renoir's students. In his notes in the catalogue accompanying the 1980 New Zealand-based exhibition of Grace Joel's work, Frank Dickinson mentions that 'the empiricism of Renoir and the Impressionists imbued Grace Joel's attitude to painting'. This connection to the Impressionists may be all there is to the Renoir remark.

Of the painting itself, Eleanor Belloc later had this to say in her *Reminiscences of H.B.* (1956): 'My mother had the view from their drawing-room in Cheyne Walk painted by Grace Joel, a charming scene of the river with the brown sailed barges of that date and the misty grey of a wintry London.'[25] Two years later Elodie again wrote to Grace informing her that Eleanor's portrait now hung in their newly oak-panelled dining room.[26]

Grace's brief friendship with the Belloc family requires some comment. Hilaire Belloc was the son of a French barrister and English mother. Educated at Oxford, he became a writer, poet, politician and activist, yet it was his conversion to Catholicism that had the most profound effect on his life. But could he keep his religious views at a personal level? He could not. His quarrels with H.G. Wells over the latter's secular account of mankind's history became legendary. Belloc also held strong anti-Islamic views, which he published. When it came to the Jews, of whom Grace Joel was one, the situation was far more complex. Belloc wrote a book on her people that shows he held the stereotypical view of Jews exerting excessive power through the world of finance. Some people saw him as an unequivocal anti-Semite, an epithet he bore for the rest of his life. However, he was an outspoken critic of the institutional anti-Semitism that he saw on the rise in Germany. Let us leave it at that.

As art writer Anne Kirker has noted, Grace Joel habitually worked in the mornings and left the afternoons free for socialising with friends, visiting galleries and dropping in and out of other artists' studios.[27] Grace, very well acquainted with the Australian artists working in London and on the Continent, knew who had exhibited where and

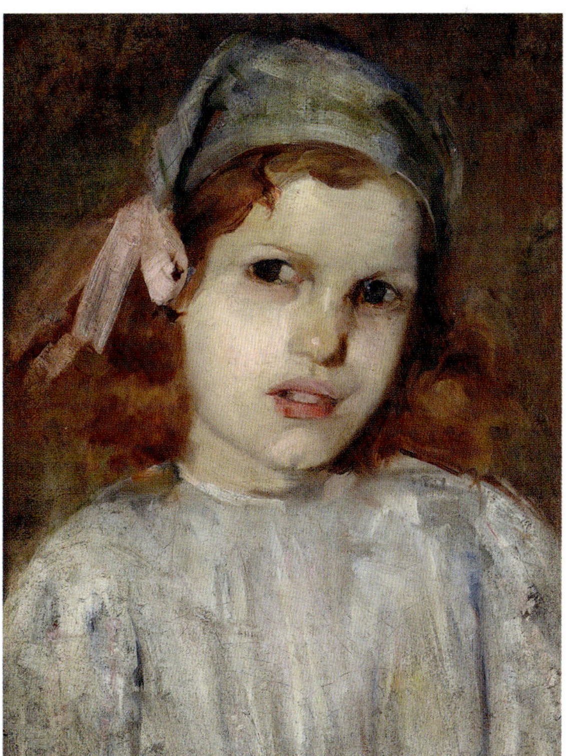

IMAGE 4.11

***Portrait of a young girl*, c. 1905, oil on canvas, 45 x 34 cm. This is one of the paintings shown at Grace Joel's Trafalgar Studios invitational viewing for friends before she left for Australasia in 1905.** Private collection

when and what they were doing next. All this was gleaned first hand, which denotes a diverse circle of artistic friendships. Not having the pressure to sell her works allowed her the freedom to fully engage in a rich artistic life without the travails that went with it. This is not to say that she did not take her painting seriously, as an interview with a former sitter of Joel's testifies (see p. 101). Grace Joel made a life from painting rather than a living.

In March 1905 Grace issued cards inviting her friends to come to No. 6 Trafalgar Studios in Chelsea to view some of her paintings and sketches, as she was about to return to Australasia for a spell. Trafalgar Studios was a noteworthy address. For one thing, Dora and George Coates lived down the passageway at No. 9, quite possibly by this date or a short time later. More enticingly, the studio was one 'which Mr Charles Conder placed at her disposal'.[28] Conder's working activities were somewhat erratic. According to Dora Meeson, Conder shut himself in, worked until very late at night and was said to be ill 'and in a pitiable state'.[29]

Dora claimed that Conder's condition was a result of a drug he was taking (he very well may have been), but the truth is that Conder's brain was gradually becoming deranged due to the terminal effects of syphilis. The artist, one of the founders of the Heidelberg School, subject of a painting by Henri de Toulouse-Lautrec and praised in death by Pissarro and Degas, spent the last three years of his life in and out of a sanatorium where he eventually died in 1909, at the age of 40. He seemingly contracted the disease from his former 'friendly and accommodating' landlady in Sydney when, as a cash-strapped artist, he paid her in a less than conventional manner.[30] In the end, Conder paid the ultimate price for his art. Ironically, a year later, in 1910, Dr Paul Ehrlich developed Salvarsan as an effective treatment for syphilis.

Once in the Northern Hemisphere and before he married and 'settled down' with wealthy widow Stella Maris Belford in 1901, Conder lived a decadent existence in the demimonde with like-minded friends Toulouse-Lautrec, Aubrey Beardsley and Oscar Wilde, all of whom also died young. However, in 1905, Conder was still well enough for him and Stella to throw a high-profile fancy dress party at their Cheyne Walk address. The beautifully illustrated invitation card specified 'Disguise Imperative' for both artists and patrons. Did our Grace, as a fellow artist living just down the road, receive an invitation? If she did, did she attend? If she attended, who did she dress as? Conder dressed as Eugène de Rastignac, a socially ambitious fictional character of Honoré de Balzac's, which was most appropriate.

Grace Joel was obviously acquainted with Conder, although one would hesitate to say *well* acquainted, as even Oscar Wilde called him 'unknowable'.[31] At this time Conder's home was, like the Bellocs', also along the road from Grace's, at No. 91 Cheyne Walk. The house itself dated from the eighteenth century. As the Conders were often away as guests at country estates, Conder may have made his studio available so that Grace's gathering of friends could view her 18 artworks on March 25 and 26 from 3 to 6 p.m.

The paintings included a 'very striking portrait of Vera, daughter of Mr Arthur Lazarus: the subject is a little girl dressed in white and holding in her arms her doll.'[32] As Vera was in a 'piquant scheme of blue and white' and the work was likely in oil, it would not have been Image 4.12, although the similarities are striking enough to suggest that the latter could be a watercolour sketch for the former. There were also some Dutch scenes, watercolour sketches, another portrait of a young girl with Titian hair and dressed in pale-blue muslin (Image 4.11), and an oil painting of the Thames and Battersea bridges in the early evening light, which was very likely a view from Grace's Cheyne Walk neighbourhood.

Meanwhile, Grace's sister Blanche Levi continued to make her own mark upon the musical world, fulfilling an invitation by the Scottish composer Sir Alexander MacKenzie to perform the Tchaikovsky Concerto No. 3 for piano and orchestra at the Royal Academy Orchestral Concert.[33] Grace, in

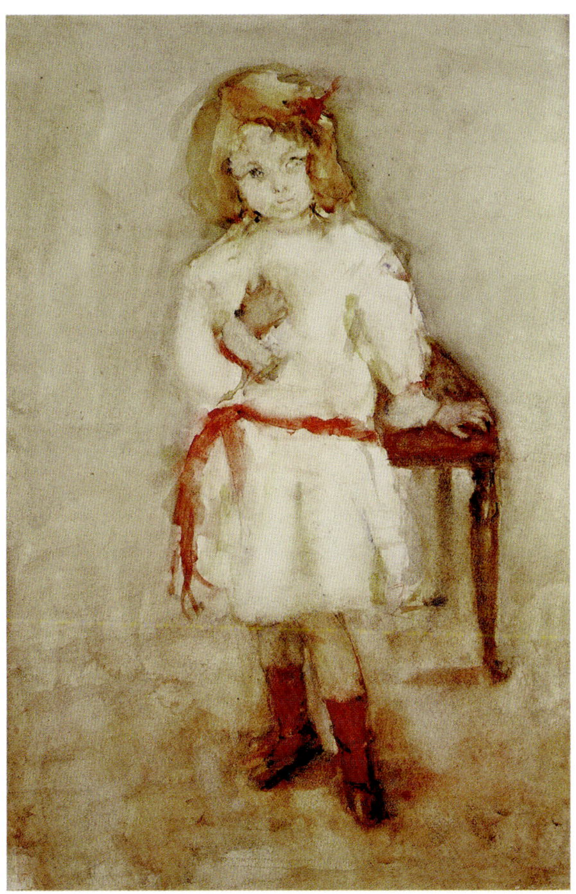

IMAGE 4.12

***Portrait of a Young Girl*, watercolour on paper by Grace Joel, possibly 1905, 37 x 24.5 cm. The girl is clutching her teddy bear. The work was perhaps a sketch for an oil portrait of Vera Lazarus.** Ferner Galleries, New Zealand

turn, was engaged on a portrait of The Hon. Sir John Cockburn KCMG, MD, a former premier of South Australia, now living in London. However, because Grace would shortly be returning to New Zealand, 'Sir John's latest portrait is likely to remain unfinished for a long time.'[34] True enough, but it was finished eventually and exhibited at the Doré Gallery in 1909.

Not to miss a beat, the *Otago Daily Times* announced that the Royal Academy had accepted one of Joel's pictures for its 1905 annual exhibition.[35] It may have been 'crowded out', however, as there is no mention of any of Grace's work in the exhibition catalogue for that year. Grace's first exhibited work with the academy, *Autumn*, had to wait until 1908. This non-acceptance seems similar to Grace's previous experience in 1903. The work she submitted in 1905 may be the one she mentioned when writing to Royal Academician George Clausen in 1922. She describes it as a painting of two children that 'has twice been kept to the last & crowded out' – a pity given that more than 300,000 people witnessed the 1905 Royal Academy exhibition at Burlington House.[36]

Just a few weeks later, the *Otago Daily Times* announced that 'The clever New Zealand artist had recently been elected a member of the Royal British Colonial Society of Artists.'[37] Grace's activities could not have been followed more closely had she remained in Dunedin. Indeed, mid-year Grace was reported to be staying in Woldingham, Surrey, 'taking some spring studies for a picture' and enjoying a pleasant stay in the country. Also noted was an account from *Connoisseur Magazine* (founded the year before in London) of the recent Jubilee Exhibition of the Society of Women Artists at Suffolk Street Galleries. While critical of the exhibition for 'wavering between tedious sentimentality ... and studied ugliness', the *Connoisseur* reviewer did say that 'if the exhibition will be remembered, it will be only due to the efforts of some half-dozen artists out of the vast number of exhibitors'. One of the five women artists mentioned who saved the day from tedious sentimentality and studied ugliness was Grace Joel.[38]

To the city of her birth she subsequently returned.

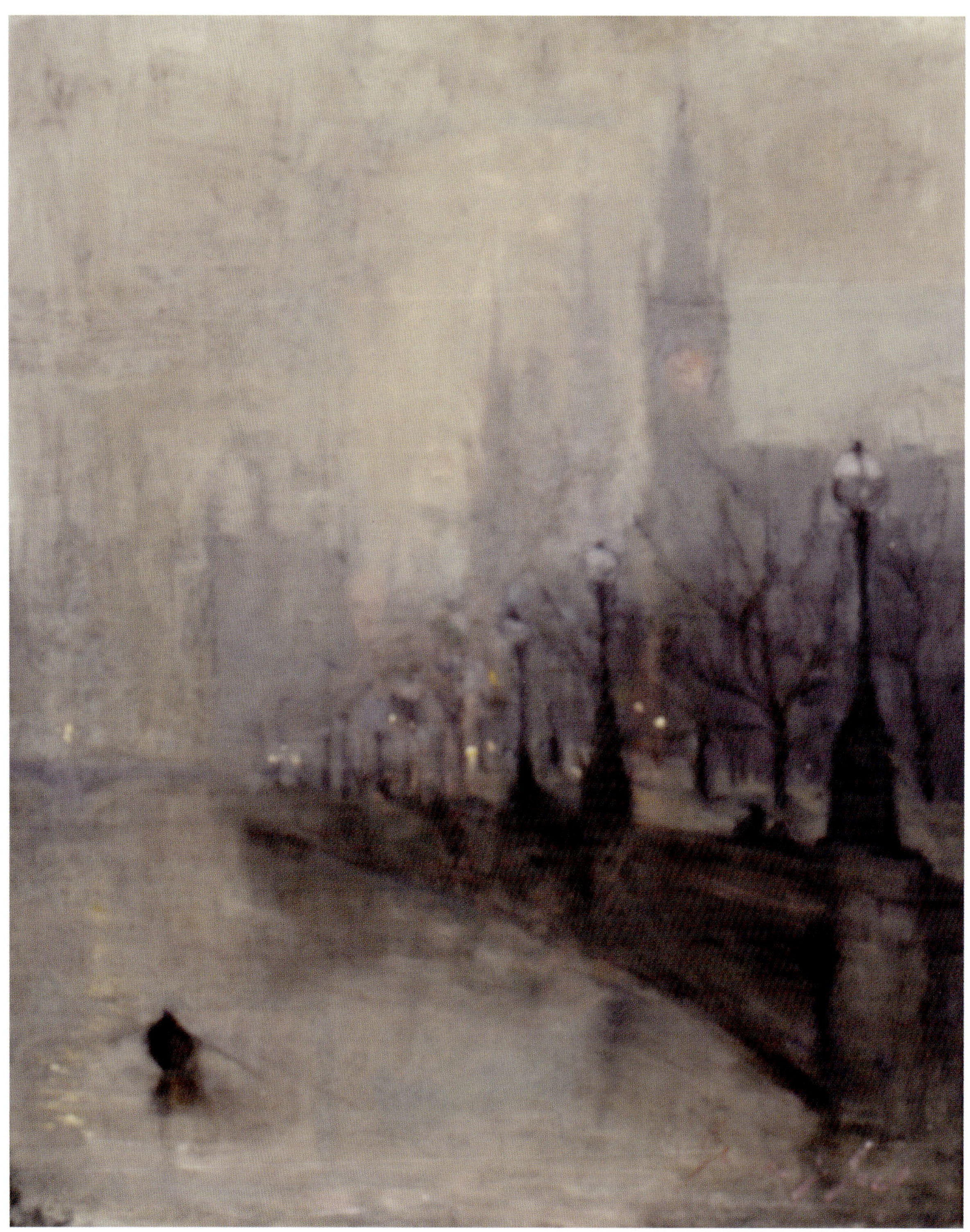

Image 5.1

The very Whistlerian *Westminster, Early Winter's Evening*, by Grace Joel, c. 1903–05, 45 x 34.7 cm. This could well be the same work as *Westminster*, exhibited at London's John Baillie Gallery in 1903, the year of Whistler's death in that city. Private collection

Chapter 5

Visit Down Under

The artist, Miss Grace Joel, a clever lady hailing from the antipodes, has been suddenly called to New Zealand on account of her father's health, and is likely to remain in Australasia for some time. She travelled out by the Persic, *and takes with her a selection of her paintings, including those which have been exhibited in the Paris Salon and the London galleries* – 'The Advertiser' (Adelaide), 22 November 1905

On 26 October 1905 Grace Joel left London aboard the twin-screw steamer *Persic*, so beginning the long journey back to New Zealand. Grace's father, 76 and in poor health at this stage, presented a compelling reason for her return to Dunedin. While she was still on the high seas in November, four of her works were on exhibition at the Otago Art Society: *Westminster, Early Winter's Evening* (Image 5.1), *The Truant* ('a delightful little picture of a little Dutch boy' who had run away from school), *A French Beggar Boy* (perhaps a result of her visit to Étaples) and *The Usual Meal, Holland* ('one of those low-toned, cool, and dim Dutch interiors perfectly harmonious, and the sitting figure especially well drawn'[1]).

Grace arrived in Sydney on 14 December and then travelled to Melbourne. She seemed in no hurry to reach Dunedin, as she remained in Australia for the next nine months. Sister Blanche had just boarded ship in London at this time with the intention of going directly to Dunedin,[2] so perhaps Grace felt there was no urgency to her own arrival there.

While in Sydney in the early part of the new year, Grace had a 'well-received' solo exhibition at the Society of Artists' headquarters in Vickery's Chambers. Among her works was a sketched portrait of Arthur Streeton (Image 5.5), *Her Child, Marketing Étaples, Lights through the River Mists,* which D.H. Souter when reviewing the exhibition described as showing 'the Thames from Cheyne Walk, with the lights of London scintillating in a scheme of Whistlerian greys',[3] and the rural idyll, *The Day is Done*. Of the latter, the *Australian Town and Country Journal* claimed that the painting attracted a great deal of attention, being the artist's principal picture. Souter concurred. It also caught the attention of the art critic of *The Sydney Morning Herald*, who welcomed Grace back as if she were a conquering heroine. He commented at length on her works, especially:

> *'The Day Is Done' (No. 19), is a large canvas showing a cornfield, work finished, and the standing sheaves leaning together in mutual interdependence, like praying hands. Two little girl gleaners, one child seated against a sheaf, the other standing, are in the foreground, and are drawn with such tender yet purposeful softness of outline as to suggest the effect of fading light. Indeed, the painting owes its value and charm to this expression of the sentiment of a reposeful hour, and the rosy glow that suffuses the western sky tells the same story.*[4]

Grace herself must have also thought highly of *The Day is Done*, for it commanded the single highest price she placed on any of her paintings for sale – 200 guineas at the Doré exhibition of 1909. It was likely to have originated at Étaples, given the previously mentioned *London Express* account of Grace's summer spent at this quaint French fishing

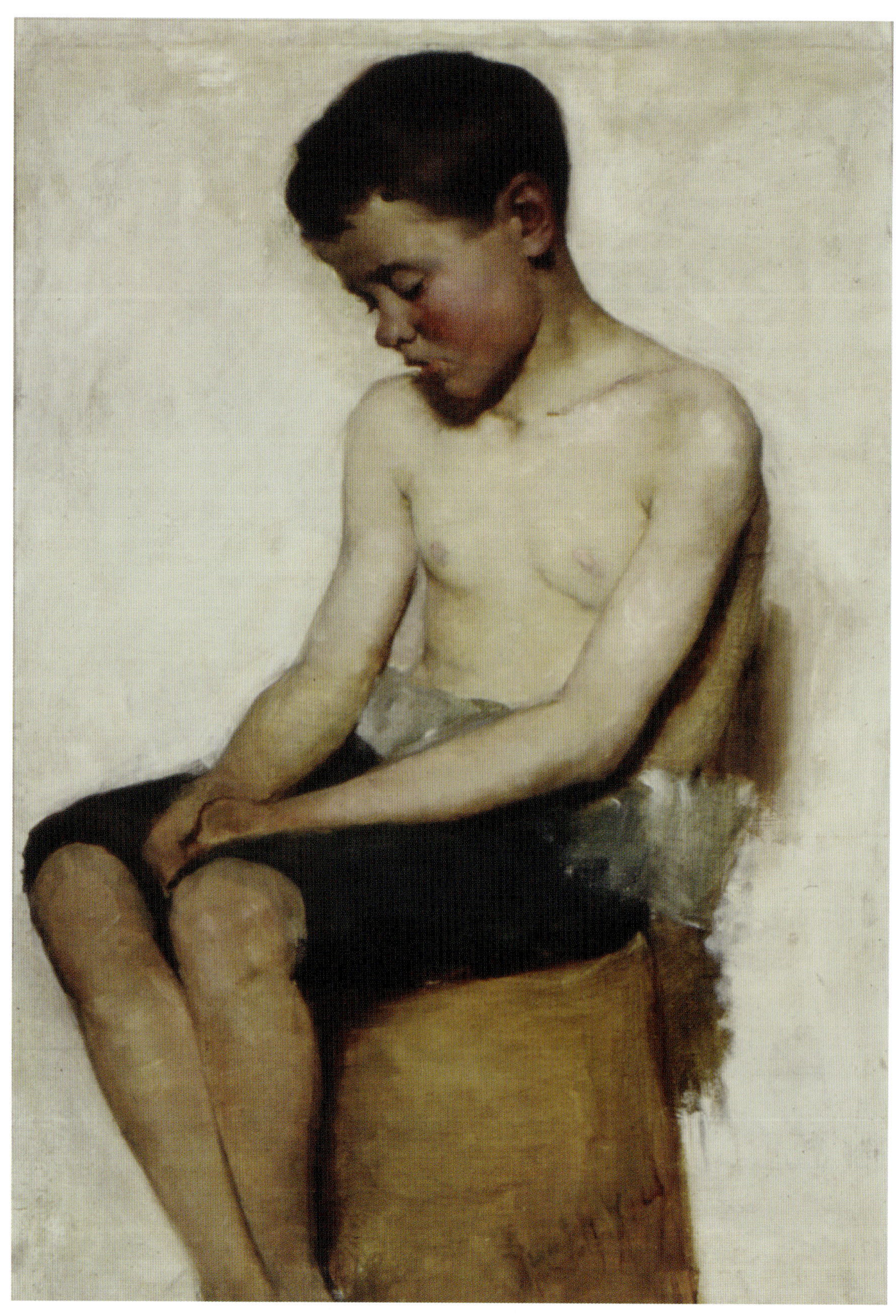

village and her 'many studies of young girls, resting among the sheaves after a long day's gleaning'.[5] Unfortunately, the painting's whereabouts today is unknown.

The Article of 1906

> *Joel was one of Australia's most successful and gifted female impressionist painters, admired for her treatment of the nude and mother and child themes*
> – OCULA, www.ocula.com

During her Australian visit, Grace published a review titled 'Australasian artists in London: A reminiscence' in the journal, *Art and Architecture*.[6] The journal's co-editor, D.H. Souter, knowing Joel was back Down Under, had doubtless requested an update from her on the current status of his overseas compatriots, a subject on which she was particularly well versed. But the article is also revealing of Grace Joel, the person.

It portrays an artist of some authority within the community of London-based Australian artists. In the article, Grace mentions her attendance at these artists' inaugural annual dinner, which began 'With the burning of gum leaves ... How suggestive this must have been, bringing back their dreams and ambitions in that sunny land!' The article also makes clear that Grace was on very personal terms with many of them, one such being John Campbell Longstaff (1861–1941). She fondly recalls visiting him at his workplace, where she stood 'ringing at the outer door, with the lion's head' for admittance to 'his magnificent studio in St. John's Wood'.

Image 5.2

***Study of a Boy Nude to the Waist*, by Grace Joel, oil on canvas, c. 1894, 75 x 50 cm. This study was likely done when Grace attended the National Gallery School in Melbourne. According to Frank Dickinson (Dunedin Public Art Gallery catalogue *Addenda & Errata*), Hugh Ramsay completed a study of apparently the same model while at the NGS (1895–99).**

Private collection

Grace's assessment of Longstaff's work is forthright, but not without sincere praise. After all, he had painted portraits of King Edward VII and Queen Alexandra just two years earlier, and she certainly knew which of his works had been hung on the line at the Royal Academy. Furthermore, he had been the first winner of the Melbourne National Gallery School overseas scholarship in 1887. In time, Longstaff went on to be appointed an official war artist by the Australian government. He also won, five times over (starting in 1925), Australia's highest award for portraiture, the Archibald Prize, and secured a knighthood. In short, he became one of Australia's most highly regarded artists.

Grace Joel's cousin and art teacher from Melbourne, E. Phillips Fox, did not attend the inaugural expatriate event, as he was 'now settled in Paris ... having already gained distinction in England'. Grace advises in her article that Fox had been offered a commission to paint the portrait of the Sultan of Morocco and that he might have to pay a visit there to finish the work.[7] She is also keenly aware of what he had exhibited in London and where. His pictures, she writes, 'have that sincerity, earnestness, and simplicity without which no artist can be great'.

Fox was a true Impressionist in the French sense in that he was enchanted with the *en plein air* transient qualities of sunlight and vivid colour effects. Grace never truly embraced this style of painting, preferring instead to create muted tonal compositions of her own subjects. This middle course between the extremes of the Impressionists and the older conservative regime so cherished by the Paris Salon served her well.

Emanuel Phillips Fox exhibited many works in Paris and London and was a regular exhibitor at the Royal Academy. In 1910 he became the first Australian full member of the secessionist body, the Société Nationale des Beaux-Arts. Sadly, Fox died from lung cancer in 1915, at the age of 50.

In her article, Grace reports on another visit, this time to the St John's Wood studio of Heidelberg

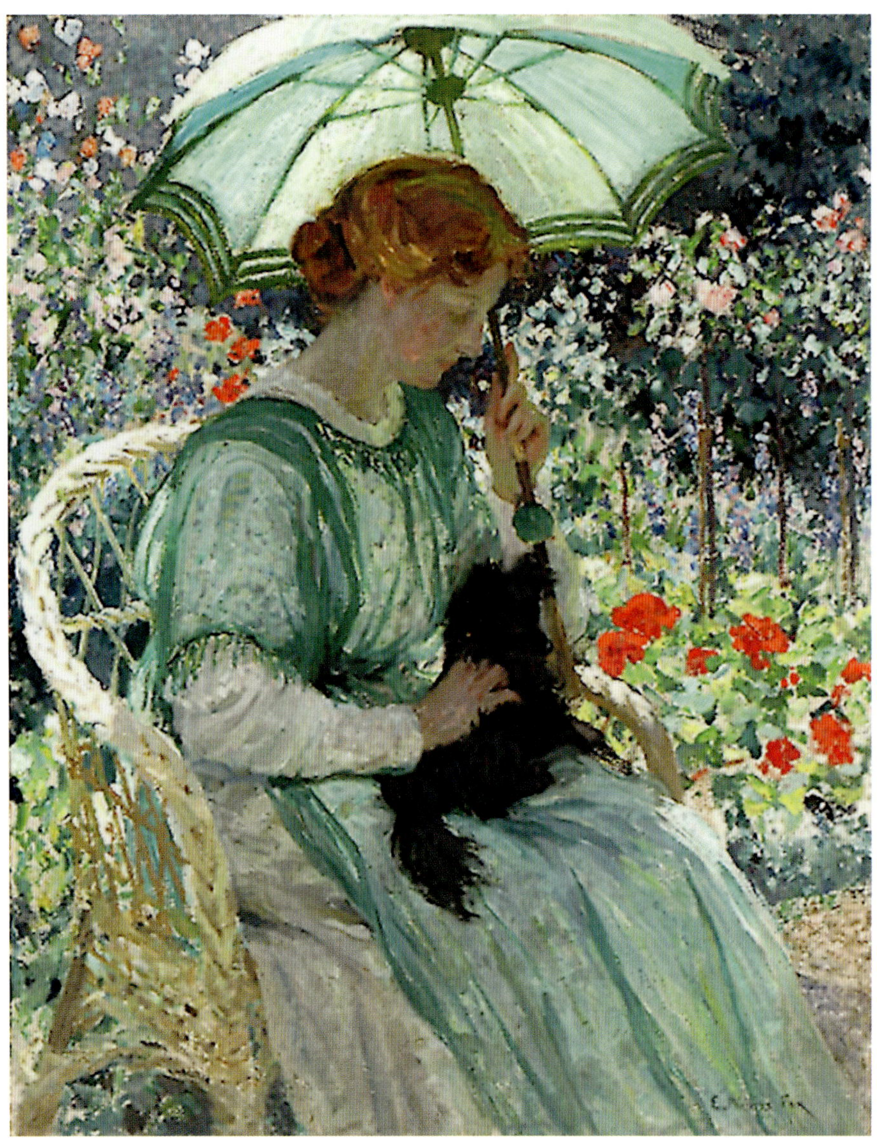

Image 5.3

The subtly variegated *The Green Parasol*, by E. Phillips Fox, 1912, oil on canvas, 117 x 89.5 cm. Australian artist Violet Teague said of this work in 1916: 'I have never seen a picture that solves the problems of full sunlight, pure and lively color, and reflected light in more masterly fashion' (quoted in Len Fox's book about E.P. Fox, 1985, p. 80).

National Gallery of Australia, Canberra

Image 5.4 (Opposite)

Rainy Weather at Étaples, oil on canvas, 56 x 73 cm, by Rupert Bunny, 1902.

painter and Melbourne Art School partner of Fox, Tudor St George Tucker. He 'appears so frail,' she remarks, before kindly commenting that 'his best works have a charm and tenderness about them.' In a similar vein of compassion, Grace says she is glad to convey that Tom Roberts had 'recovered from the attack of eye trouble when I last saw him with Mrs Roberts in London.'

James Quinn, over whom Grace had won first prize in painting from the nude during her time in Melbourne a little more than a decade earlier, was another frequent exhibitor in London and Paris. His work sometimes appeared at the same venues as Joel's. Commenting on her visit to his studio in Putney, Grace maintains that 'a mother with a little boy on her lap, teaching him to read, had much more refinement, tenderness, and feeling than some of his work.' Grace seemed to make a habit of getting about town in order to visit the studios of serious Australian artists, her interest in their work and their progress as artists obviously genuine.

One of the superstars of the expatriate community of Australian painters and a regular visitor to Étaples was Rupert Bunny (1864–1947). He 'paints the highest art most, the ideal with charm, feeling, and mystery ... He had gained honours in France that no other Australian had. His work was always admired and appreciated by art critics, but it is not of the kind that sells.' Bunny had studied alongside E. Phillips Fox at the National Gallery School, and later in Paris under J.-P. Laurens. The Luxembourg Gallery purchased his *After the Bath* in 1904, and he became one of the most celebrated artists to come out of Australia.

As we have already observed, Grace was not one given to idle flattery, tending to speak with candour yet affection. Another example adds credence to this apparent characteristic of hers. Having claimed in her article that former Melbourne art student colleague Arthur Streeton had not 'yet reached the eminence his Australian admirers expected of him', Grace then, as if to qualify her comment and

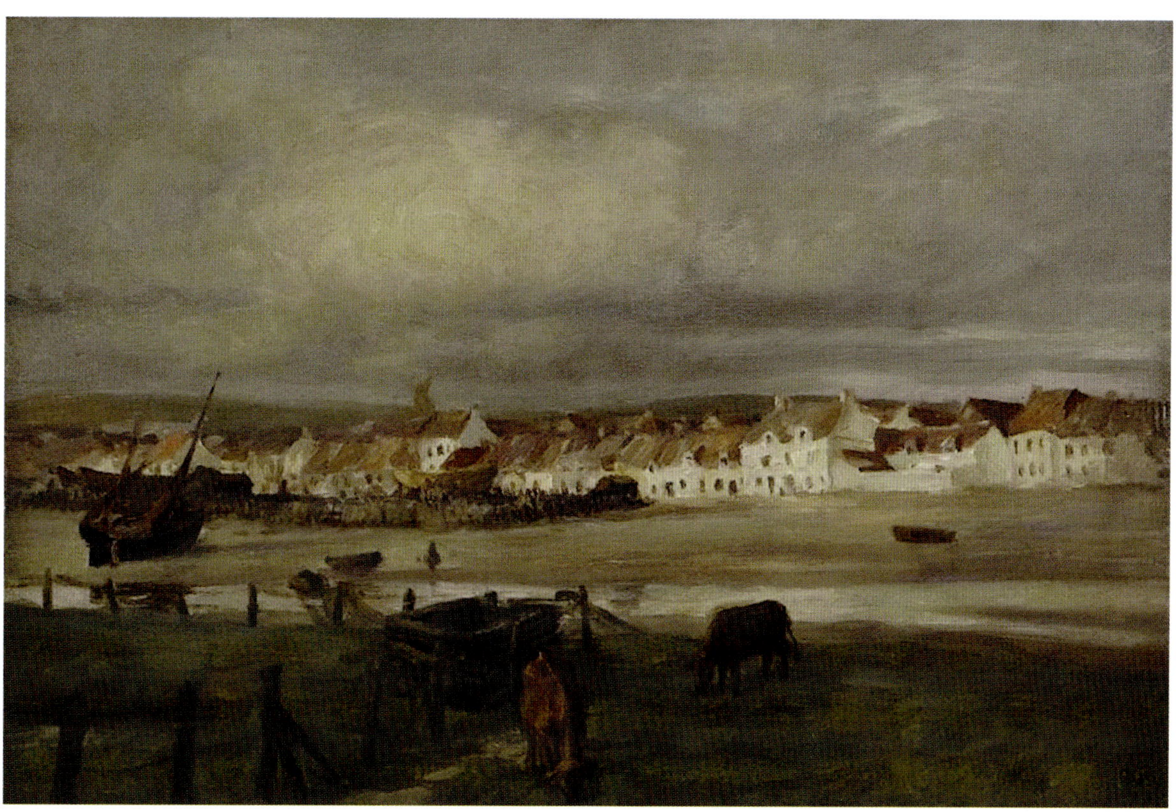

express feminine concern, observes that 'his intensely sensitive nature has suffered from London life.' Well informed about the details of Streeton's life and his works, she reports his most recent address in Cheyne Walk as being 'three doors from where the genius Turner lived'.[8] She knows where his paintings have been exhibited, which of them have hung at the New Gallery and when he changed studio.

Grace knows, too, that Streeton had spent 'a good deal of time at Windsor' and that he had finally exhibited a work at the Royal Academy 'of delicate grey harmony, unfortunately not advantageously hung ... [It has] charm of colour, beauty, tenderness, and suggestiveness.' Kind words most welcome considering the frequency with which Streeton's works were rejected. In contrast, author Susanna de Vries bluntly, and perhaps too harshly, claims that Streeton 'spent twenty-two monumentally unsuccessful years overseas'.[9] Perhaps the tender, sensitive side of Streeton appealed to Grace's own caring nature. Be that as it may, Streeton married the Canadian prodigy violinist, Nora Clench, in 1908, and later received a knighthood for his services to the arts in 1937, chiefly for his painting while working in Australia.

We are starting, at this point of Grace's article, to build up a picture of a very sincere, sociable, compassionate woman, well versed on the expatriate Australian art community. She is well acquainted with those painting in London. As a habitué of the London gallery scene, she has an intimate knowledge of their work. And she speaks as one who possesses a very discerning artistic eye of works imbued with the qualities of earnestness, sincerity, spirit, suggestiveness – terms that are not part of the lexicon of the average gallery viewer.

Another artist attracting Grace's praise in the article is George Lambert (1873–1930), whose full name was George Washington Thomas Lambert. Yes, his father was American, but he was born in St Petersburg. Lambert exhibited with the Paris Salon and Royal Academy, became an official Australian war artist and went on to have a stellar career, winning the Australian Archibald Prize for portraiture in 1927. The catalogue for a retrospective of his work held in 2007 includes a particularly apt quote from Grace Joel's 1906 article about one of his paintings. Obvious here is the respect accorded to her words.

Further acknowledgement of Grace's artistic judgement comes from the fact that Charles Conder's biographer Ann Galbally quotes Grace's words about Conder almost in their entirety. Grace refers to his paintings as 'charming, graceful in design, delicate in colouring and feeling'. And so they were. However, she also notes his deteriorating state of health, the cough he has had for months and the fact that he is scarcely recognisable with 'his long, straight hair'.

Finally, Grace focuses her attention on her dear friend of long acquaintance, Girolamo Nerli.

> *There is one other artist I might draw attention to, who spent at least twenty years on this side of the world, and is now back in his native land, Italy. I mean Nerli, now il Marchese Girolamo Pieri Nerli. This Italian artist did much to raise art in this part of the world, and I am surprised that so little recognition has been shown him. His portraits have always been characterized by their originality in harmony and arrangement; he never repeats himself with a new sitter. They were always full of colour suggestiveness – were what the French call* très sensible *– vibrated with life and blood, and were graceful in design. His portrait of Robert Louis Stevenson was one of his best-known, and won distinction for him in London, being favourably compared in* The Athenaeum *with Sargent's picture of the same. He is happy now in his native home, which doubtless he will never leave for Australia. In the beautiful palaces in which he resides ... He paid London a short visit, and while there he and his wife were the guests of Lady North. The report of his death [Lord North's] caused great annoyance to him in Italy, he told me in one of his letters.*

Grace was clearly in contact with Nerli while he was living in Italy, and he confided in her again over the death of Lady North's husband. The dead, dead past is gone, but their friendship had endured.

By the middle of 1906 Grace was still in Melbourne, where she showed two works in July

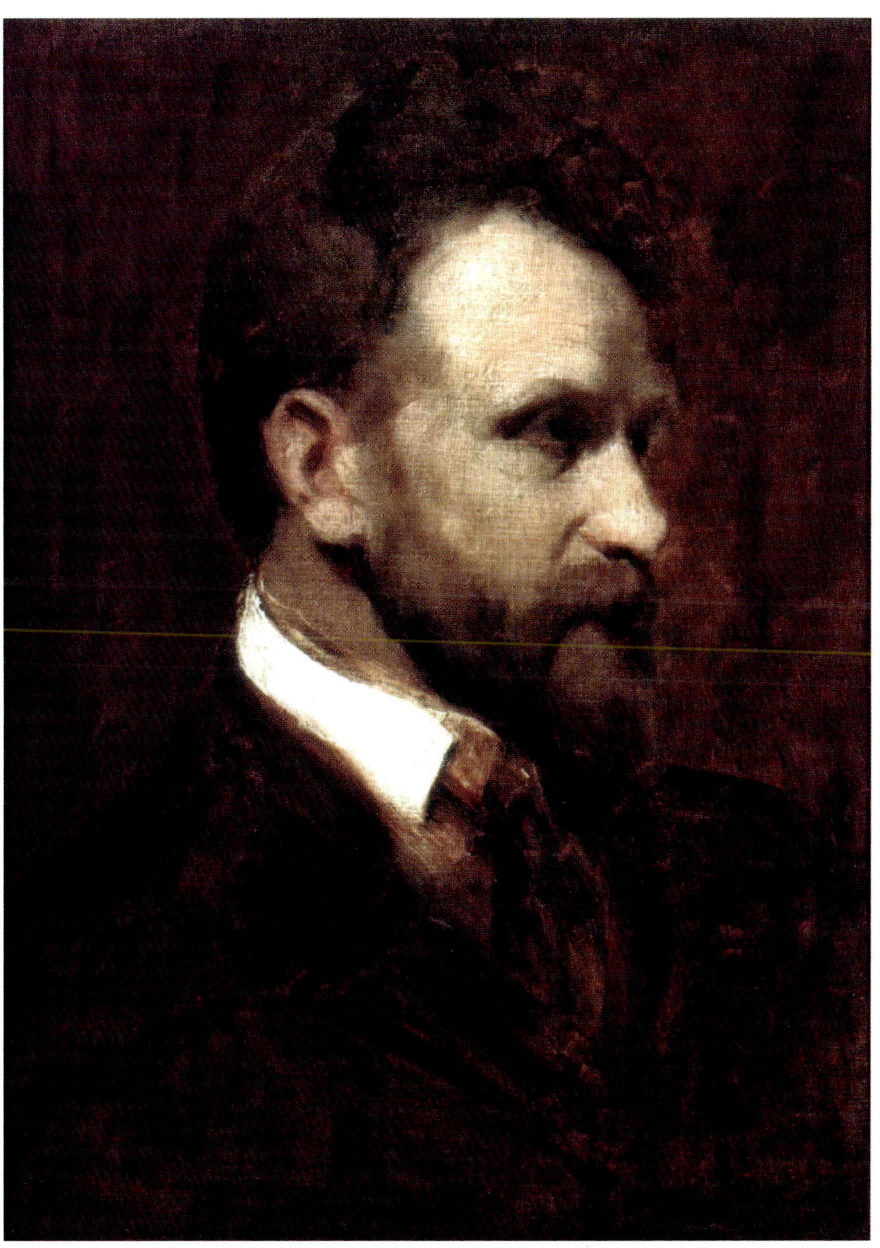

Image 5.5

Portrait of Arthur Streeton (1867–1943), by Grace Joel, oil on canvas on hardboard, 55.5 x 40.6 cm, almost certainly painted in England prior to 1906. Streeton's 'intensely sensitive nature' is rendered with great care. Streeton, then, was perhaps an incongruous choice for selection as an Australian official war artist. Bequeathed to the Art Gallery of New South Wales. Art Gallery of New South Wales, Sydney

at the annual exhibition of the Victorian Artists' Society. Of more significance, however, was a large solo exhibition, mounted in the same month at the Athenaeum Hall and visited by Lady Talbot, wife of the governor of Victoria. Joel's Paris Salon winners were on display, perhaps to demonstrate that she was now taken as a serious artist overseas: *Her Child* (Ex Salon 1901), *Homeward Bound by the Chalky Path* (Ex Salon 1903), *A Time of Prayer* (Ex Salon 1905), *Battersea-bridge on a Foggy Morning*, the praiseworthy *The Day is Done*, and a *Portrait of Maurice Joel* (most likely Image 6.5). There were a few new titles as well, which may have been old standbys by another name. So, for example, *Their Daily Meal* is quite possibly the work formerly titled *The Usual Meal, Holland*. The Athenaeum was a big success for Grace, as the show was extended and four of her paintings sold.[10]

Finally, on 5 September 1906, Grace returned to Dunedin aboard the SS *Monowai* with her sister Blanche, who had joined her in Melbourne. The *Otago Daily Times* advised its readers, once Grace was back in the city, that 'She has not made her plans yet for the future.' She visited with family who were now living at 17 Onslow Street in St Clair, one of Dunedin's seaside suburbs. The family home in Regent Road had become the St Helen's Maternity Home, the opening of which one year before was formally inaugurated by the Prime Minister himself, Richard J. Seddon. 'Healthy mothers – and he used that term in its broadest sense: healthy morally, intellectually, and physically – would breed good healthy youngsters, the pride of the country, a credit to the race from which we sprung. – (Applause).'[11] Was it just coincidence that Grace Joel painted the portrait of Seddon (see page 11) the following year?

The *Evening Star* was pleased to find that the local girl made good remained untainted by overseas success:

> *As a Salon exhibitor she is entitled to speak with authority. But her honors have not made her either vain or dictatorial. Personally she is just the same as ever when chatting to old acquaintances. Her present visit to Dunedin is purely in the nature of a holiday, for she has no idea of settling here to teach, but we understand that if suitable rooms are procurable she will give an exhibition before leaving.*[12]

She did indeed. The room procured was in the Choral Hall, where Grace staged a triumphal homecoming by exhibiting 44 of her works transported half way across the globe. These included some of her finest paintings, such as *The Day is Done*, as well as Salon winners: *A Time of Prayer*, *Her Child* and *Homeward Bound by the Chalky Path*. *The Day is Done* certainly resonated in an agricultural land such as New Zealand. The *Otago Daily Times* called it 'a finely successful rural landscape and figure study depicting peasant girls resting in the fields, while the soft glow of sunset steals over the scene'.[13]

The exhibition was the subject of lengthy features in the *Otago Daily Times* and *Evening Star* eulogising Grace's return; she who, from her modest Dunedin origins, had prevailed abroad over the 'great world of Art'.[14] On the first afternoon's viewing by invited friends, seven paintings sold, including *A French Beggar Boy*.[15] In the ensuing fortnight, more paintings sold; the exhibition attracted large crowds and was deemed 'one of the best that has been shown in this city from the brush of any one artist'.[16] Upon conclusion, an 'art union' (lottery) was held in order to dispose of further works.

Despite this great flurry of purchases, Grace still had seven paintings up her sleeve for exhibition at the Otago Art Society annual exhibition early the following month. One of her most ambitious works, *Among the Flowers*, was rather steeply priced for Dunedinites at £75, but was surely worth it, given its status as 'a picture that at once attracts attention. The attitude of the figure, the graceful pose, the natural fall of the clinging pink drapery, and the harmony of the surrounding detail, all combine to constitute one of the most delightful bits of colour and composition in the gallery.'

Once again, we have evidence in this review of Grace's love of the colour pink combining with

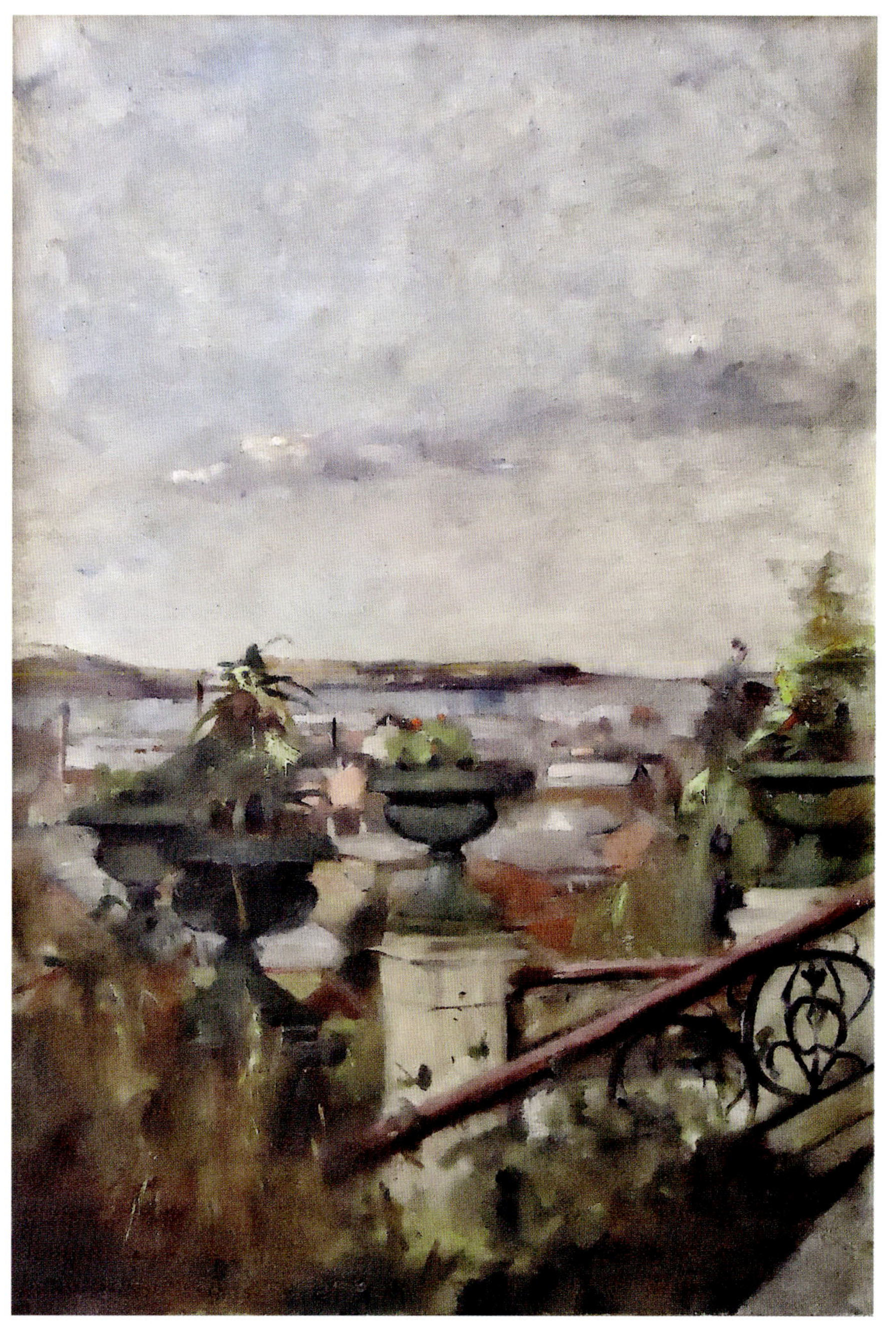

Image 5.6

Not the Côte d'Azur but rather a view of Otago Harbour from the Joel family residence, Eden Bank, Regent Road, Dunedin, by Grace Joel, date unknown, oil on canvas, 68 x 47 cm. Possibly *A Summer Morning*, 1896. Grace went abroad in 1899, and the house became a maternity hospital in 1905, so c. 1896 would be a reasonable date. This view overlooks the urns and balustrade that can be seen in the photograph of the house (Image 1.3). Private collection

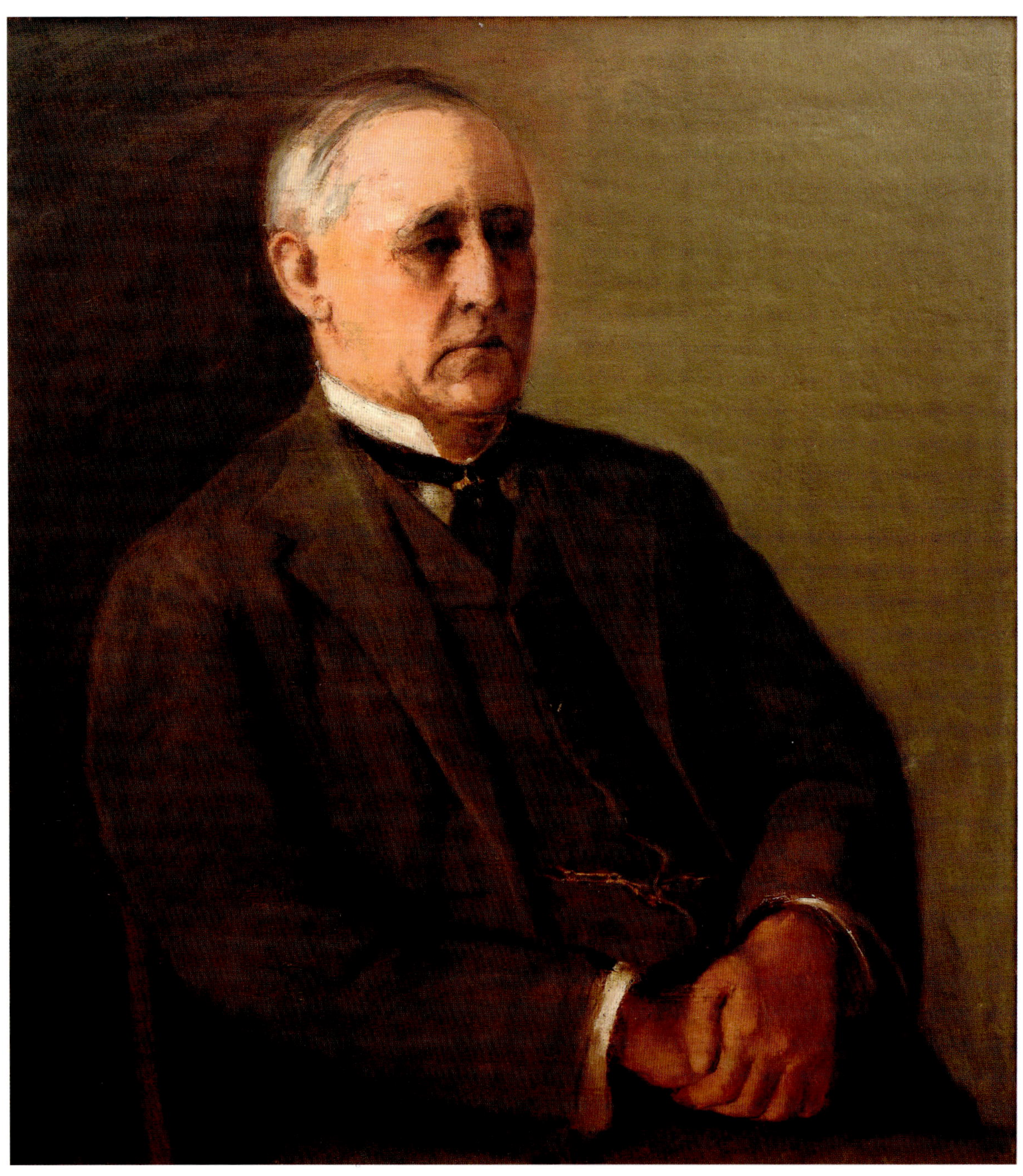

IMAGE 5.7

John Tonkin Roberts CMG, Mayor of Dunedin, 1889/90, painted by Grace Joel in 1906/07, oil on canvas, 81 x 71 cm. The *Otago Witness* (27 March 1907, p. 32) commented: '[It] requires no great effort of the imagination to fancy the man himself getting up from the chair and doing the honours of the place.' Private collection

one of her favourite themes – that of a young girl 'midst flowers. *The Apple Gatherers* (Image 5.8), more modestly priced at £10 and 'another work of outstanding merit',[17] was subsequently sold. Joel's portrait of Dr Hocken was published in the *Otago Witness*,[18] but may not have been to his liking, as it is nowhere to be found in the Hocken collections of today.

During this visit to the Antipodes, Grace had a studio in town, which a reporter from the *Otago Witness* visited. There he was privy to 'three admirable portraits of prominent New Zealanders' painted by Joel. One was the previously mentioned portrait of the late Right Hon. Richard Seddon; another was of Dunedin lawyer and political activist, Mr John MacGregor. However, the very best was 'unquestionably' of Mr John Roberts, CMG (former mayor of Dunedin during the New Zealand and South Seas Exhibition of 1889/90), whose 'dignity, ease and naturalness of the pose are most striking ... Upon entering the studio with the portrait facing one, it requires no great effort of the imagination to fancy the man himself getting up from the chair and doing the honours of the place. The portrait does Miss Joel so much credit that it is not surprising to find that she proposes exhibiting it abroad.'[19]

During this period in Dunedin, Blanche's daughter Kathleen studied piano under her mother. Later, she would be the subject of one of Grace's paintings (Image 6.21).

Interview of 1998

This was also the period in which Grace executed a figure painting of local Dunedin eight-year-old Irene Searle and her sister, Elsie. What makes this young girl's presence a singular one in the Grace Joel story is that Irene was interviewed by the Dunedin Public Art Gallery curator Peter Entwisle in 1998, when Irene was 100 years old. More precisely, 100 years and four months. Not only that, but in Irene's own words: 'I've got a very good memory for the past.' And so she did. What follows is a selection of lightly edited excerpts from this interview that took place in Dunedin on 22 December 1998. It gives us some insight into Grace Joel's persona and her working habits. It is also a testament to Mrs Irene Ross and her recollections of 92 years into the past when she was little Irene Searle being painted by the internationally recognised artist, Grace Joel.

Peter Entwisle: *When were you born Irene, what year?*

Irene Ross: *Eighteen ninety-eight.*

PE: *Eighteen ninety-eight. So that's a hundred years ago this year?*

IR: *Yes. I had a wee celebration.*

PE: *I bet.*

IR: *As you can see. The Queen.*

PE: *There's a message from the Queen. Congratulations. [Queen Elizabeth II sends a birthday card containing a personal message to all those living in the British Commonwealth who attain the age of 100.]*

PE: *Mrs Ross, when you were young, I believe you were painted by Grace Joel, the artist?*

IR: *Yes, I was.*

PE: *And what year was that Mrs Ross?*

IR: *I think it might have been round about 1906. I think I would be about eight at the time. I was never very impressed by this; as a matter of fact, I wasn't very pleased because she had asked my mother if she could paint me, and my mother wasn't too pleased. I think she had ideas that I might want to become an artist's model if I started then ... evidently she said it would take a week or two. My sister was in the background [of the painting], and she blamed me that we missed all our summer holidays.*

PE: *And how did Miss Joel come to pick you for her picture?*

IR: *Well, she had an aunt ... and she served in a drapery shop, and Miss Joel came out to New Zealand about that time and she happened to be in the shop. Miss Joel apparently looked at me and thought I would be suitable to do a portrait.*

PE: *Sorry, Miss Joel saw you in the shop?*

IR: *Yes … Mother said it would be all right … We had to go up every morning for a couple of hours. And we worked very hard. She wasn't really the sort of person you would take to very much. I suppose she had a fair load with all her fame. Even then she was quite famous. But we never had a laugh and didn't talk. We got a spell for about ten minutes about midday. We plodded on up and down, up and down every day until the end.*

PE: *And did she pose you? Did she arrange how you sat or how you stood for her picture?*

IR: *Oh yes. She said that I had to wear a white dress and a gold sash. I had really unusual hair; it was a dark auburn. I think that must have been what attracted her. And my sister, you could only see a hat and book. She was reading me a story. She had a large white hat on … A friend of my father's, Professor Moore, who lived in England, was coming out to New Zealand to judge music exams. He stopped off at Paris and saw the portrait. I had ceased to take any interest in it by that time.*

Irene mentions at this point that Grace Joel called the painting *La Leçon*, but the painting was selected for the Paris Salon of 1910 under the name, *La Légende*. This is unequivocally the same work, for it was described as 'an oil painting of two children, life-size, seated, and is called *La Légende*. One of the children is looking out with dreamy wondering eyes, while the other is reading to her. The two little girls are New Zealanders, daughters of Mr and Mrs Searle of Dunedin.'[20]

PE: *Were you interested in it while Miss Joel was painting it?*

IR: *Well, she never let us see it until she was finished. And we were heartily sick of it by that time. We had to try to look the same all the time. And we were very serious while this person was working … not the sort of thing we were used to at all. When she invited my parents up to have a look, I can't remember what their reaction was … I wanted to be out playing … A few years after, this piece was in the paper that this picture was hanging in the … some salon. I don't know where it was.*

PE: *It was in Paris.*

There is some discussion about how Irene came to the attention of the Dunedin Public Art Gallery for the interview. Entwisle then asks Irene Ross about the artist's personality.

IR: *Personality … she wasn't a striking person. She was just an ordinary middle-aged woman as far as I was concerned.* [Bear in mind Irene was eight years old and Grace Joel was 41 at the time.]

PE: *When the picture was finished and you looked at the picture, did you like it?*

IR: *Oh, can't remember. My mother didn't like it.*

PE: *Your mother didn't like it?*

IR: *Yes. She didn't think it was very like me.*

PE: *Did your sister like it?*

IR: *I don't remember. She didn't appear in it really.*

PE: *Just the book and the hat.*

IR: *[In] the background. I think she had just intended to do a quick one of me, and then we arrived up there together. My sister had to come with me because I was too small to go out on my own, and she [Grace] decided to do a real painting.*

PE: *And you're supposed to look spellbound in the story that your sister was reading?*

IR: *Yes, that was the idea.*

PE: *Was the painting in oils?*

IR: *Yes.*

Entwisle and Ross endeavour to determine the location of Grace Joel's studio where the painting was done. They eventually agree that it was the studio at 3 Stafford St, Dunedin, that Grace was using at the time, and which she advertised as such, to give art lessons.

PE: *And in the studio there was a chair for you to sit on?*

IR: *Yes, my sister and I were both seated … and I had to wear this same dress, with the wide golden sash … And my sister just happened to be in white too … She had no idea that she was to be in the picture when she took me along there.*

PE: *And your sister was wearing a hat of the sort that Miss Joel wanted?*

IR: *Yes, I was wearing a bonnet, a white bonnet, which was well off my face, because I had the idea it was my hair, the colour of my hair, that she was taken with. And in those days I had large brown eyes to match.* [Laughter]

PE: *And Miss Joel had her canvas on an easel?*

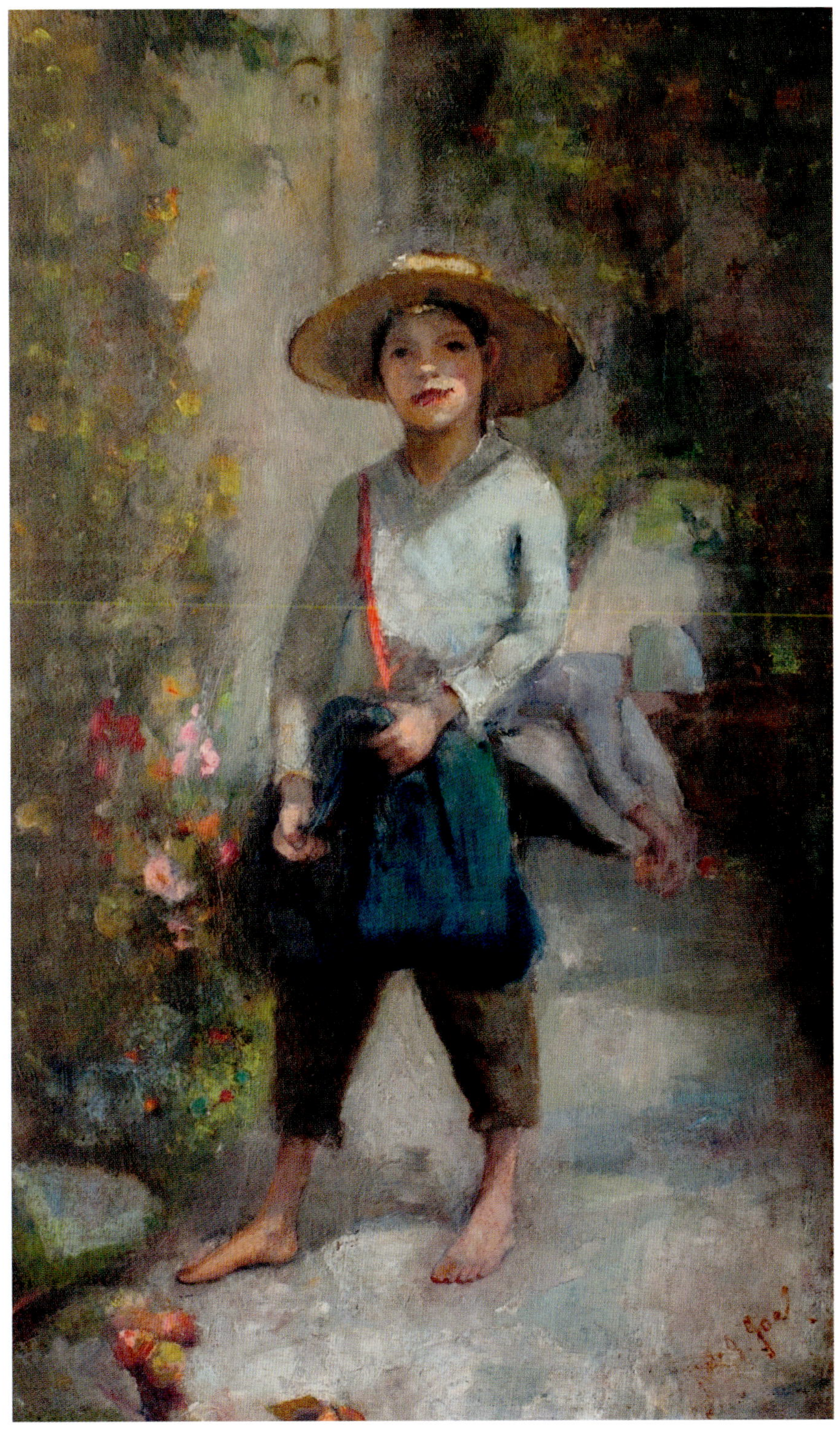

Image 5.8

The Apple Gatherers, by Grace Joel, c. 1906, oil on canvas, 65.5 x 39 cm. Numerous paintings bearing the same title were done in the nineteenth and twentieth centuries, including one by French Impressionist Camille Pissarro, in 1891. Private collection

IR: *Yes ... on an easel; the last week I was there she also painted a panel–just narrow, like that ... but it wasn't a bit like me. It was tall and thin, and I was short and fat.*

PE: *Maybe she was making you fit the proportions of the panel?*

IR: *Well, I think she must have been.*

Discussion ensues about artistic licence and bringing out the character of a sitter.

PE: *Even though you were a bit bored sitting for Miss Joel, do you think you managed a good smile?*

IR: *One day, she must have thought it was a bit boring and she bought us a bag of cherries. And I can remember quite well, she said, 'Now start to eat the stalk end.' I don't know whether it was to make the cherries last longer or what. But we put these stalks in our mouths on our ten-minute break.*

She wasn't a very good personality. I mean she didn't put herself about to entertain us or stop us from being bored. She got on with her painting and that was a very serious job of course.

PE: *Did she talk to you a bit?*

IR: *No, she didn't talk to us much at all.*

PE: *Miss Joel offered nothing in the way of a present or reward?*

IR: *Just those darn cherries. No ... I thought, you know, she could of perhaps bought us a few sweets to eat or something like that. No.*

PE: *And she didn't give your parents anything?*

A: *Not a thing.*

Ross and Entwisle continue to discuss how Grace Joel arranged Irene and her sister to make the picture tell a story.

IR: *I think the first day we went up she didn't start painting at all. I think she was arranging us to make the picture that she wanted.*

PE: *The first day she tried different poses. Did she try different arrangements?*

IR: *Well, I think she did at the beginning ... once she had started painting ... we had to take up the same positions and wear the same clothes.*

PE: *Did she begin by making a drawing?*

IR: *I couldn't see. I never knew what went on, on the canvas side ... But I know that I had to go straight home and my dress had to be ironed, ready for the next day. It always had to be the same dress.*

PE: *And did Miss Joel wear a smock over her clothes to protect her from the paint?*

IR: *I couldn't tell you that ... I only took interest in myself and my sister ... I dare say she was not a personality that you would remember much about. I mean she was just ordinary in everything really. I mean she was all right, but you know there was nothing that a child would notice about her. She didn't have a nice smile or anything like that, that you would remember.*

PE: *Did she seem severe?*

IR: *No, more serious than severe.*

PE: *And quiet, not very talkative?*

IR: *No, not talkative at all. But I imagine she talked to us in this ten-minute interval. Because she would have a spell too.*

Ross says her sister didn't mind being roped into the picture as she was of a 'rather retiring nature'.

PE: *And you went along every day of the week?*

IR: *Monday, Tuesday, Wednesday, Thursday, Friday and Saturday. We didn't go on Sunday.*

PE: *You went for two hours each day.*

IR: *In the morning, yes. As far as I remember we used to go quite early about ten o'clock and sit till twelve o'clock.*

This schedule coincides with the view expressed previously by Anne Kirker that Grace Joel preferred working in the mornings, leaving the afternoons free for other pursuits. The painting seems to have been done over the summer holidays after New Year 1907, with the arrangements having been made late in 1906. Ross then describes how she and a friend started the women's division of Federated Farmers in the South Island.

IR: *In my very small way I'm getting quite famous.*

PE: *But I'm sure your reputation would be perfectly intact; you can admit now that you were an artist's model once when you were young.*

IR: *I don't think I'll wander astray now.*

Irene Ross's words show us a woman artist who was truly dedicated to her craft and single-minded in her approach. Perhaps a bit on the stern side with children and rather oblivious to their personal needs. Nor did she relate to them particularly well. These characteristics could be construed as at odds with her many mother and child paintings and abiding empathy for young children, as expressed in *Enfants sans mère/Mitherless Bairns*, *Two Little Waifs*, *Portrait of a Young Girl* and various other works. But to be human is to be contradictory. 'Do I contradict myself? / Very well, then I contradict myself, / (I am large, I contain multitudes)', wrote American poet Walt Whitman.[21] Rather, Grace Joel demonstrated her abiding affection for children through her art rather than her manner. Although motherhood had passed her by, *her* children were her paintings.

What is also clear from the interview is the prevailing attitude towards a female becoming an artist's model. Modelling was associated with nudity, and nudity with sex; no caring Victorian mother would want her daughter to indulge in such a tainted activity. Even in today's liberated twenty-first century, being a female 'life model' is probably still considered a salacious activity in some quarters. A painting of a vase and a painting of a nude woman do not evoke the same visceral response even though they both display pleasing curves.

Grace's thoughts, meanwhile, were turning back towards the Northern Hemisphere. She had lived in Paris and London, exhibited in each at the highest levels, toured their famous galleries, been in the midst of a thriving circle of gifted Australasian painters and met the likes of Hilaire Belloc, G.F. Watts and Jozef Israëls. Was it any wonder then that on 12 December 1906 the *Otago Witness* announced Grace Joel's intention 'to leave for London early next year to take up her quarters permanently in the world's metropolis'.

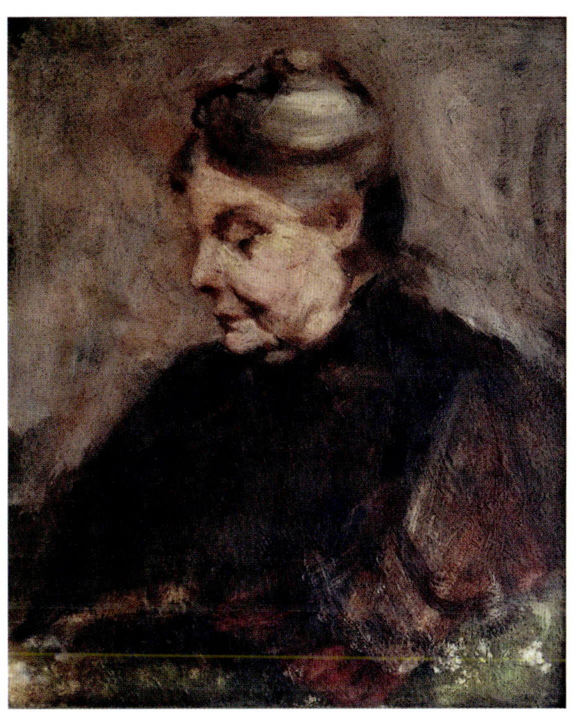

Image 5.9

Catherine Joel, portrait of the artist's mother, oil on canvas. A reasonable guess for the date would be c. 1906 when Grace was back in Dunedin and her mother was age 75. The style is in stark contrast to the formal 1895 portrait of her mother (Image 2.4), and is much more sympathetic to elderly subjects.

Private collection

This desire to flourish long term in a larger and less restricted arena was also present among a handful of Australian artists of the time such as E.P. Fox, Rupert Bunny and George Lambert. The Australians, 'despite their clear loyalty to their country, found the Australian cultural *milieu* stultifying and constraining'.[22] So, like Grace Joel, they too sought their futures abroad, as did Kiwi contemporaries Frances Hodgkins and Raymond McIntyre.

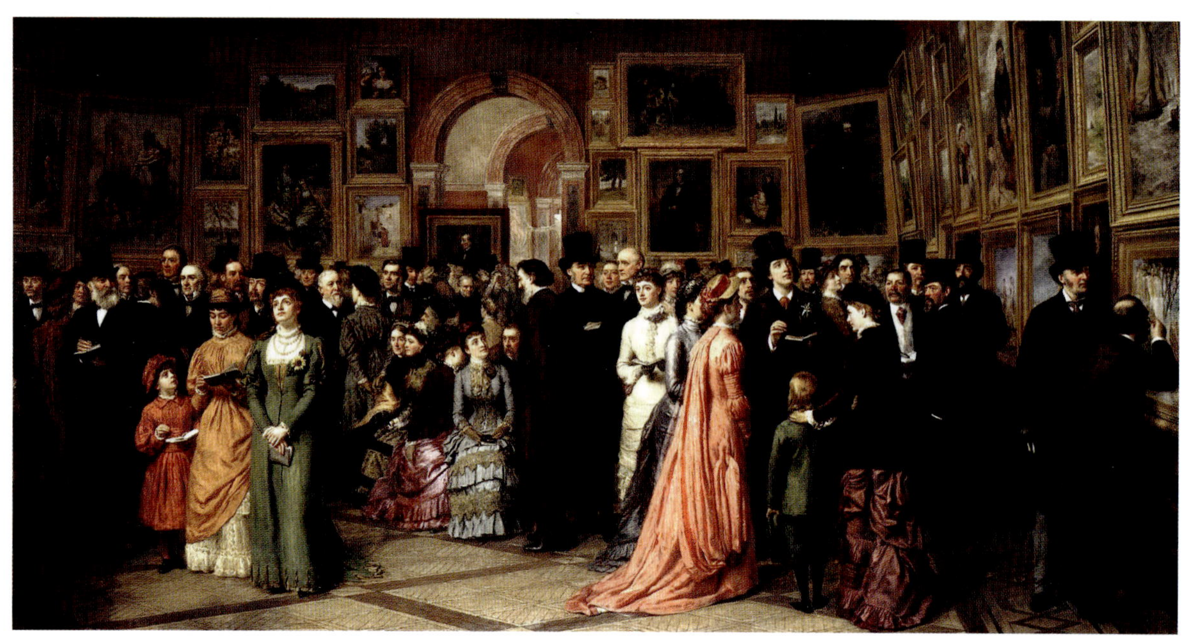

IMAGE 6.1

A Private View at the Royal Academy, by William Powell Frith, RA, 1881, oil on canvas, 60 x 114 cm. Frith intended the painting to mock the extravagant dress style of the Aesthetes as well as the tall Oscar Wilde (right of centre), probably discoursing on the finer points of the Aesthetic Movement. Private collection

Chapter 6

Back to the Future

In spite of Miss Joel's own lack of interest in her personal reputation and success, it is somewhat surprising that her outstanding talent is not more widely recognised in this country – Catalogue notes, Auckland Society of Arts Exhibition 1968

The period when Grace Joel was a working artist coincided with an era in the history of art characterised by a seething cauldron of manifestos, movements, and 'isms' – Pre-Raphaelism, Aestheticism, Impressionism, Post-Impressionism, Fauvism, Modernism, Cubism, Dadaism and Futurism, with Surrealism just squeaking in before Grace's death. Despite the artistic ferment swirling about her, Grace was only lightly touched by three of the developments – Pre-Raphaelism, Impressionism and Aestheticism. Her style also varied considerably along her own personal spectrum of subject matter. The painting of her mother (Image 2.4) is Grace at her formal, realistic portraiture best. At the other end of the spectrum, we have her charming impressionistic *A Rose 'midst Poppies* (Image 2.7) and her portrait of Nerli (Image 1.21) In between, we can find echoes of Rembrandt, Whistler's aestheticism, Renoir … But whatever influence can be discerned in Grace Joel's work, the end result is undeniably hers.

Grace left Dunedin for London on 27 March 1907. Although she was departing New Zealand for good, she kept back a few works for the art exhibitions held in Canterbury and Wellington each year.[1] Eight months later, her father Maurice died at the age of 78 on 13 November at his residence in St Clair. The total value of his estate was £11,678,[2] which represented the sale of a considerable quantity of beer over the years. His will awarded each of the three Joel daughters a fixed sum of £50 per annum for life or until they married.

By at least May of the following year, Grace's address was 7B Stanley Studios, Park Walk, Chelsea, London. Access to the studios, situated behind Stanley Mansions, a five-floor brick building dating from 1892, was through an archway under the northern end of the mansions, a short distance from Fulham Road.

The Royal Academy selected Grace Joel's *Autumn* for its 140th annual spring exhibition (May 1908). The Dunedin *Evening Star* fulsomely described it as 'a study in the nude depicting a woman lying on the grass bewailing the departure of summer's verdure'.[3] Keeping Grace's nude woman company on the walls of Burlington House were works by E. Phillips Fox, George Coates, John Longstaff, George Lambert, James Quinn and Arthur Streeton. A flower study by Dunedin artist (and former Grace Joel student) Jean Rollo Fisher had also 'found acceptance by the authorities of the Royal Academy'.[4] Evidence suggests that Grace assisted Jean in this matter, and would do so again when she helped Jean secure exhibition space for her work at the Paris Salon on two later occasions. In both instances, Jean sent the paintings directly to Grace from New Zealand.[5] Being exhibited at the Royal Academy and the Salon was no mean feat for an outsider, of course, so it seems fair to say that Joel was now favourably regarded by members of both establishments.

Around this time, a new avenue opened up to artists intent on exhibiting their work. The Allied Artists Association, formed in London by *Sunday Times* art critic Frank Rutter, was open to all painters and sculptors. Significantly, there was no jury – the scourge of all artists; anyone who paid the annual subscription of one guinea could exhibit up to three of his or her works. Rutter established the association in reaction to the conservatism of the New English Art Club, which itself was formed in 1885 as a reaction to the conservatism of the Royal Academy. The association's first London Salon in July filled the Royal Albert Hall with more than 3000 items. Grace signed herself up and exhibited *A Time of Prayer* for a sale price of £150 as well as *Motherhood*, priced at £80, a price differential indicating the latter work as a substantially more modest one than the former.

The year 1908 was turning into an altogether successful one for Grace Joel. In addition to gaining Royal Academy acceptance, she was 'the only Antipodean artist to have a canvas on view at the New Gallery (Regent Street, London) exhibition of the Society of Portrait Painters'.[6] The 'interestingly original' *Mdlle. la Comtesse de M* (NFS), to give the 'canvas' its title, featured a large portrait of a young girl. Described as 'a harmony in pink', it could be found hung on the line in the New Gallery's west room. Given that the society had some 50 members and each could exhibit up to three paintings, it was indeed an honour for Grace to be one of the chosen outsiders. In the view of *The Studio*, 'No preceding work of hers challenges it, but the fact of such a standard being once attained invites us to anticipate successes in the future for this artist.'[7] That the painting was not for sale and retained by the sitter's family suggests that the young girl could have been a personal friend, perhaps Cristina Asquith Baker, of whom Grace may have been very fond.

The New Gallery, founded in 1888, nevertheless ran afoul of Joel, who lamented in her 1906 article that it 'is now exactly opposed to the original intention of the founders, Burne-Jones and G.F. Watts'. Like many other salons, it too had become capricious in its choice of exhibitors, a situation that bedevilled many a working artist. Expressing this frustration with the arbitrariness of the art world, Grace chastised the New Gallery: 'It is useless to send without an invitation, as I have known more than one case where the picture sent without was rejected, and afterwards invited by the visiting committee, who were unconscious of the fact that the painting had previously been submitted.'[8] Nevertheless, it had served in the past as a haven for artistic followers of the Aesthetic and Pre-Raphaelite movements.

The title of the portrait that Grace exhibited at the New Gallery exhibition of 1908 is also 'interestingly original'. As far as can be ascertained, there was no such *Mdlle. la Comtesse de M* ... living at the time. However, there is a somewhat unusual association with the monograph *Mémoires de Madame la comtesse de M**** (Image 6.3), written in 1697 by Henriette Julie de Castelnau, Comtesse de Murat. Her *Mémoires*, partly autobiographical, 'contest the narrow confines and contradictory expectations her society placed on women',[9] making Castelnau surely one of the first feminists to appear in print. But what is also noteworthy is that it is only legend she married Nicolas de Murat, who in fact married the daughter of one of his cousins. As a consequence, Henriette was no longer *Madame* but *Mademoiselle*. *Et voilà*, it is possible, at least in principle, to derive the epithet *Mdlle. la Comtesse de M*, albeit with some linguistic sleight of hand.

Image 6.2

A possible candidate for *Mdlle. la Comtesse de M*, by Grace Joel, only inasmuch as it fits the known criteria of being a large canvas of a young girl in 'harmonies of pink'. A diaphanous garment covers the dress. The use of the reflection in the mirror is an 'interestingly original' touch. However, there are several possible alternative titles for this exceptional work. Oil on canvas, 125.7 x 76.2 cm. Private collection

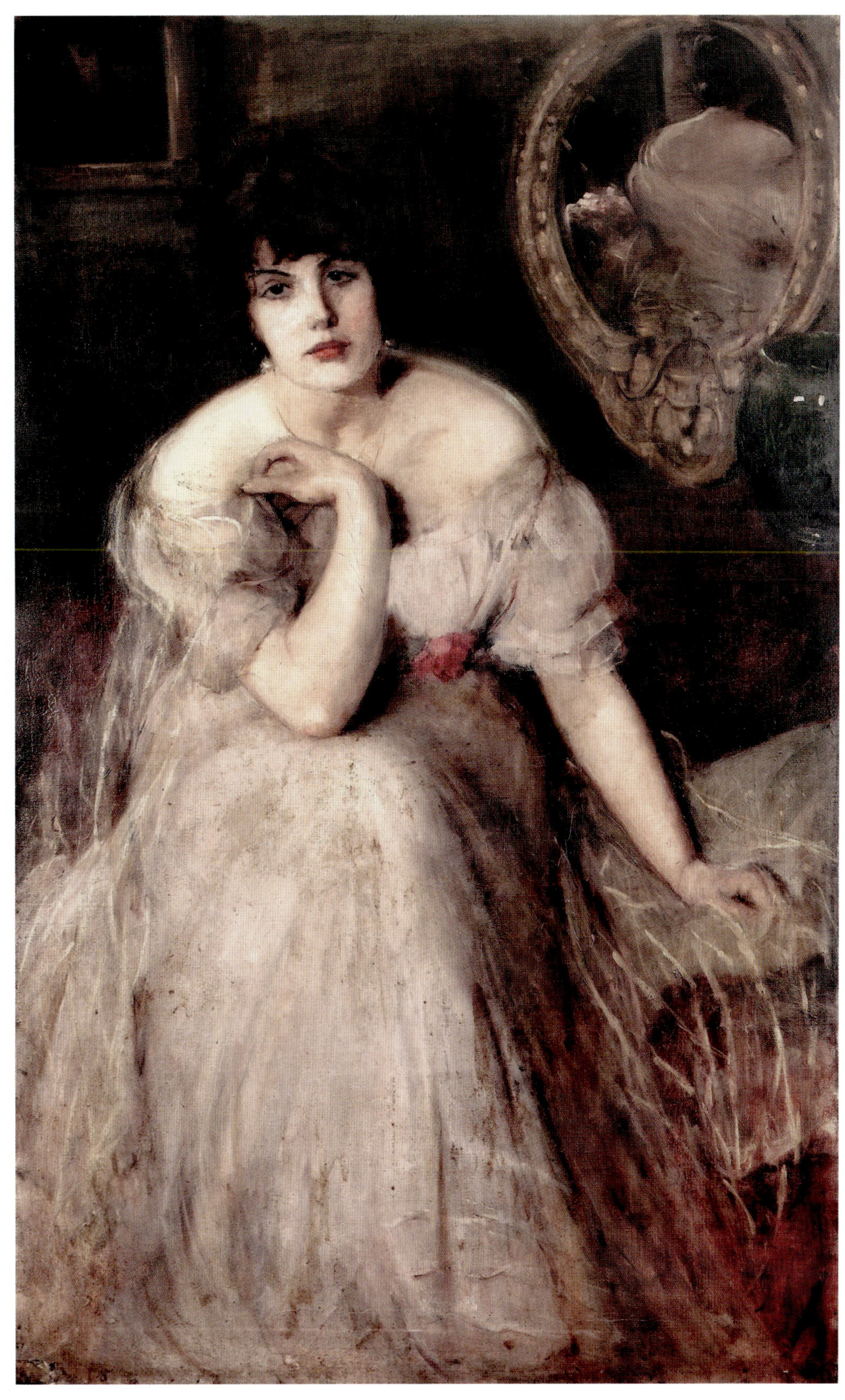

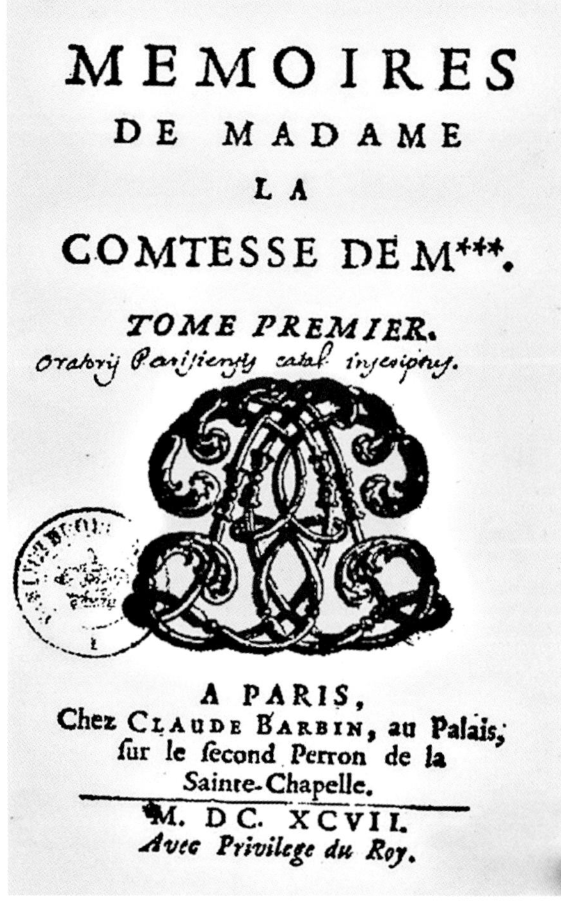
MEMOIRES
DE MADAME
LA
COMTESSE DE M***.

TOME PREMIER.

Oratorij Parisiensis catal. inscriptus.

A PARIS,
Chez CLAUDE BARBIN, au Palais;
ſur le ſecond Perron de la
Sainte-Chapelle.

M. DC. XCVII.
Avec Privilege du Roy.

IMAGE 6.3

The title page of the book by Henriette Julie de Castelnau published in 1697, from which Grace Joel may have taken the title of her 1908 portrait *Mdlle. la Comtesse de M.*

While this is all starting to look like the proof of a mathematical theorem, and a fanciful one at that, we have just learned something interesting about Henriette Julie de Castelnau and her *Mémoires*, so let's conjecture a little more. Perhaps Grace Joel, strolling along the avenues of Paris or London, chanced upon a second-hand bookshop where she spied a copy of the 200-year-old *Mémoires*. The plight of this woman described in de Castelnau's 'autobiography' may have resonated with Grace, who decided to honour her in the only way she knew how, with a portrait. A final, more prosaic yet plausible variation of this scenario is to have the sitter a *mademoiselle* who simply replaces the *madame* taken from the title of the book.

Having over-indulged in academic speculation about the title of this painting, we should refrain from so doing with respect to the work itself, except to say that the painting in Image 6.2 may not be *la Comtesse de M* at all. However, because the pink gown appears in other works, such as the *Girl in Pink Dress*, Image 6.4,[10] it is possible that this sitter is the same sitter as in Image 6.2 but painted years earlier, given that her somewhat limp left arm is much thinner, and the face appears younger and thinner too. What we can say with a greater degree of certainty is that Grace liked pink, as it appears in several of her works – recall the hapless nude *Youth* spread out on the pink coverlet for crucifixion by the critics?

Back from the realm of speculation, we find Grace exhibiting yet more of her works in May at the Paris Salon: this time, *Enfants sans mère* and *Le grandpère d'Étaples*. The latter would have been painted either during Joel's trip to the fishing village of Étaples when she visited there in 1901 or sometime later.[11] A painting titled *Le grandpère* shown at the Baillie Gallery in 1903 may be the same work. A year later, in March 1909, the following description of it appeared in her interview in the *Woman Worker*: 'Her last Salon picture [1908] was the "Grandfather of Étaples", a portrait of an old man with a fine, firm old face, tanned and withered, rather in the Rembrandt style. The Portrait was painted in a little shed of the French fishing town, and so named because "all the little children there seemed to claim him as their grandfather."'

This passage makes clear that Grace Joel did paint a portrait of an elderly French peasant during one of her trips to Étaples. Its whereabouts are now unknown, although after its Salon debut, the Doré Gallery exhibited *Le grandpère d'Étaples* in 1909 for an asking price of 50 guineas. It was exhibited again with the International Society of Portrait Painters in 1911, and yet again at the London Salon of 1921, where the asking price had risen to £100. The work

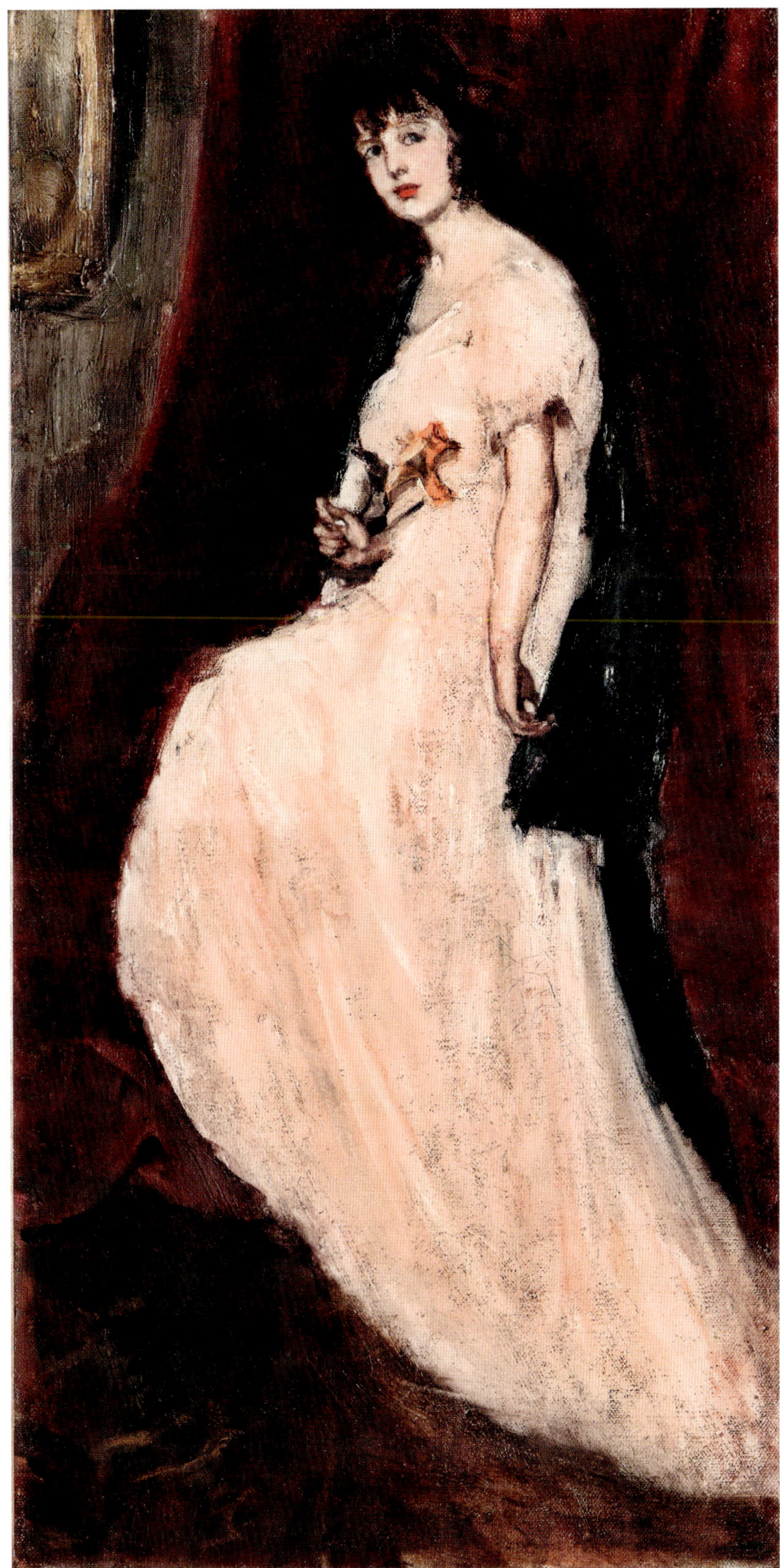

IMAGE 6.4

Girl in Pink Dress, by Grace Joel, oil on canvas, early 1900s, 58.8 x 29.3 cm. This mademoiselle is not a candidate for *la Comtesse de M*, as the canvas is not large enough (nor good enough) to qualify. The girl is perched on a tall black chair. It, the red velvet backdrop and the rolled-up theatre notes in hand give the illusion of being at the theatre. But the game is given away by the mirror in the background, which has reappeared from the preceding *Mademoiselle*, both of which were likely staged in Joel's studio.

Museum of New Zealand Te Papa Tongarewa, Wellington

had also been earlier described as a portrait of an old peasant 'in low brown tones'.[12] Unfortunately, over the years, Grace's portrait of her father (Image 6.5) has become misaligned in the literature and at art exhibitions with the portrait of *Le grandpère d'Étaples.*

What makes the case that Image 6.5 is Grace's father and not *Le grandpère d'Étaples* more compelling is that the label on the back of the painting gives the name of the picture framer –James Bourlet & Sons Ltd. Because 'Ltd' was not appended to the establishment's name until 1911, the picture frame would not have come into existence until after that date.[13] But *Le grandpère* was exhibited on two occasions before then, in 1908 and 1909. Did Grace change the frame of *Le grandpère* for its next appearances with the International Society of Portrait Painters and finally at the London Salon? It's very unlikely.

As a further nail in *Le grandpère's* coffin, let us recall when Grace Joel met the elderly G.F. Watts during her brief stay in England in 1899, and the portrait (unframed?) she showed him. 'It is my father,' she had said, to which Watts replied: 'It could not be better painted.' Image 6.5 was almost certainly the portrait Watts saw at the time, which implies that Grace painted it in the mid- to late 1890s. In her Master's thesis, Kirsten Fergusson argues that the painting stylistically is contemporaneous with Grace's portrait of her mother, painted around 1895. No other portraits in oil of her father are known, although there is a watercolour, done while Grace was visiting her family in 1906. There are also some fine sketches in charcoal.

The final nail in the coffin is the fact that *Mrs Maurice Joel* (very plausibly the painting mentioned above), exhibited at the John Baillie Gallery in 1903, was not for sale, nor ever offered for sale, whereas *Le grandpère d'Étaples* had a price attached on at least two more occasions. All of this is further evidence that this portrait of Maurice Joel was the one Watts saw at the turn of the century and had nothing whatever to do with *Le grandpère d'Étaples. Le grandpère* was painted at a later date in a little shed in a French fishing village, and is thus a separate work altogether. The prosecution rests its case.

Several reviews in French media, such as the following one in *La Revue Moderne Universelle,* commented favourably on *Le grandpère* and *Enfants sans mère*: 'Mdlle. Grace J. Joel a deux toiles "Le grandpère d'Étaples", et "Enfants sans mère" dans lesquelles elle a mis toute son âme d'artiste et de femme; la deuxième surtout de ces toiles emotionne [sic] par l'impression qui s'en dégage.'[14]

Frances Hodgkins and Grace Joel, both now working in London and having studied together for years in Dunedin, still seemed distant associates. In a 1908 letter to her mother, written from her lodgings at 3 Cheyne Walk, Chelsea, not far from Grace Joel's Stanley Studios, Hodgkins told of a brief encounter with Grace the previous day.

> *Yesterday I found myself on the top of [a] bus beside who do you think Miss Annie Black[e] – mutual recognition & smiles ... We had a long talk & I promised to go & see her if I have time & meet her husband. A funny thing happened. I asked after Grace Joel & she was telling me all about her & giving me her address when I looked down & there in the street was the little lady herself – Joel all over, but much better dressed & more prosperous looking. More recognitions – she looked up & caught my eye & we waved to each other. In this great big London it really was rather odd!*[15]

Unlike Grace, Frances struggled for survival as a woman career artist; hardly surprising, then, that she noticed and then commented on Grace's state of dress and aura of prosperity.

The ever observant London correspondent for the *Otago Daily Times* informed readers (18 September 1908) that Joel was painting a portrait of a Colonel Woods in the Suffolk town of Lowestoft. On completing it, she was to do a commissioned portrait of another colonel, named Pitman. The owner of this work (presumably Pitman) lent the portrait for Joel's exhibition at the Doré the following year. The *ODT* correspondent also noted that the Walker Art Gallery in Liverpool had Grace's *Her Child* on

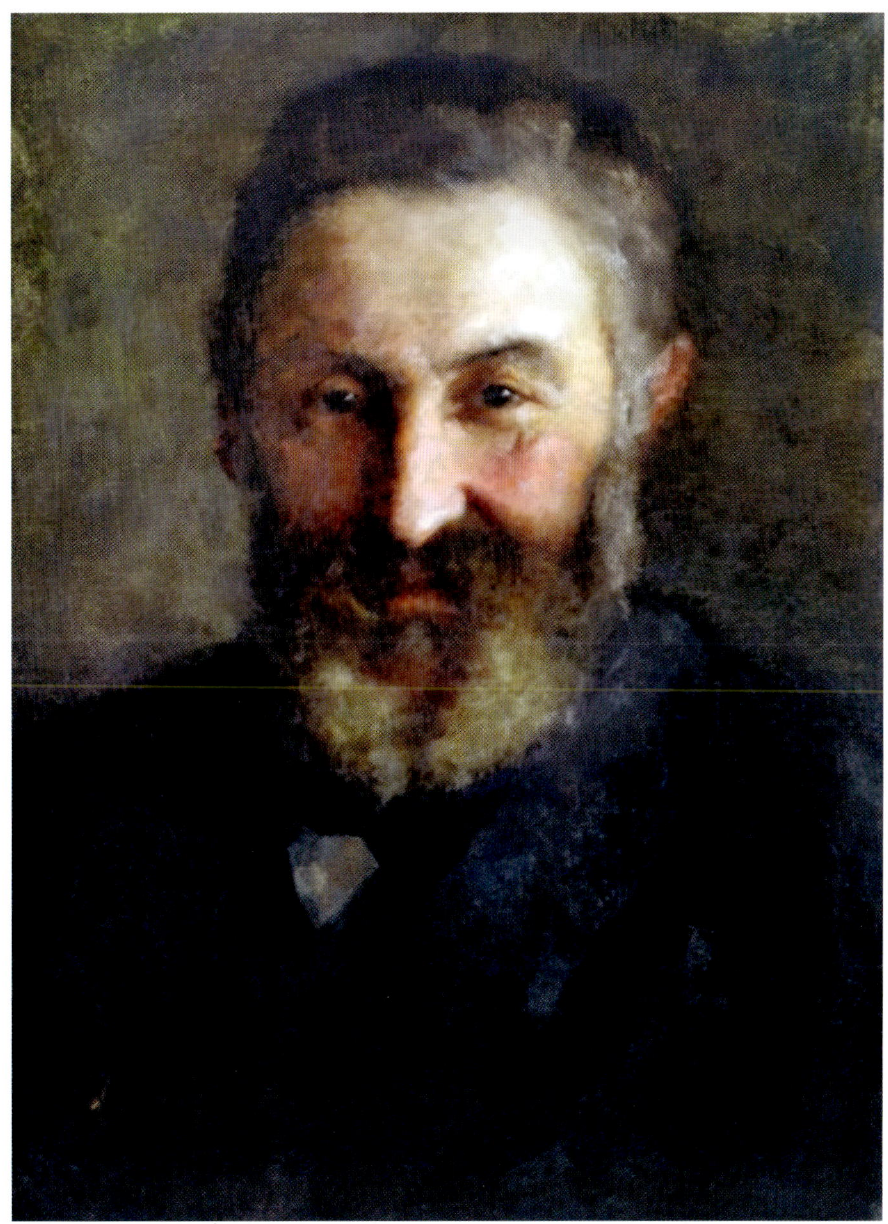

Image 6.5

This is not *Le grandpère d'Étaples* that was exhibited at the 1908 Paris Salon, but Grace Joel's father, Maurice, painted in the mid- to late 1890s. The original *Le grandpère* has been confused with this portrait of Maurice Joel for half a century. Oil on canvas, 53 x 41 cm. Private collection

display.[16] However, he took particular umbrage to *The Guide to the Salon*, when praising *Le grandpère d'Étaples* ('treated with a joyous and sympathetic air'), giving the artist as an Australian. But surely the writer of the guide can be excused the error, given that the work of three *bona fide* Australian associates, James Quinn, George Coates and George Lambert, could be found alongside Grace's painting at the Walker. Artistically, Grace Joel had come a long way from her studio in Liverpool Street, Dunedin, to a national gallery in Liverpool, England.

As London moved deeper into spring, Joel was visited in October by David Edward Hutton, half-brother of Dunedin artist, Nellie Hutton, who had been attending an international congress of art masters. Hutton reported that he found Grace 'busy with a fine portrait of a lady and child'.[17] We'll return to this encounter later.

In early January 1909 the International Society of Sculptors, Painters and Gravers held its annual exhibition at the New Gallery, London. Several New Zealand newspapers gave an account of the single work that Grace Joel showed at this event – *Mother and Child*.[18] The following month she embarked on a large solo exhibition at the Doré Gallery. An entry in the exhibition catalogue reads 'WIDOWED (Ex International 1909)'. It was priced at 100 guineas. If we take the justifiable liberty to identify the two works, we find there is actually only one – a 'widowed mother and child'. The sale price suggests a painting moderate to large in size.

Just as Grace's exhibition at the New Gallery on Regent Street was coming to an end, Augustus John arrived with his celebrated *Woman Smiling*, destined for display at this same venue for another exhibition ('Fair Women'), also organised by the International Society. Perhaps Joel and John crossed paths as they moved in and out of the gallery, a not inconceivable possibility given that John had not long previously rented a studio to Grace's friends Dora Meeson and George Coates.

Contrary to the typical Grace Joel portrayal of mother and child that exudes tenderness and love, Image 6.6 is the only extant one imbued with despair. This difference makes it a candidate for the aforementioned *Widowed/Mother and Child*. However, this argument has one caveat: just a few months later, the Paris Salon exhibited *Veuvage* (*Widowhood*), a 'lifesize mother and child'.[19] Therefore, if *Widowed/Mother and Child* is the same work as *Veuvage*, it follows that Image 6.6 is *not* that work because of the latter's modest size. Then again, if *Veuvage* is a separate work, Image 6.6 could very well be *Widowed/Mother and Child*. Determining which option has the most veracity is somewhat constrained by the exhibition record for that period.

Image 6.6 certainly carries some of the sombre overtones of Jozef Israëls and of a Dutch interior setting, and we know that Grace produced 'some very successful pictures of Dutch home interiors' during her 1904 visit to the Netherlands.[20] Perhaps Image 6.6 is one of them, as the household appliance sitting on the table appears to be a Dutch coffee pot of the late nineteenth century.[21] One etymology (but not the only one) of the English word 'coffee' is the Dutch *koffie*; the Dutch East India Company was, after all, heavily involved in coffee production from the early eighteenth century. If the interior depicted in Image 6.6 is indeed a Dutch interior, we can date it to circa 1904. But why is there a lone coffee cup on the table? Is it meant to signify that the woman portrayed has been left on her own? If so, could this work actually be *Widowed/Mother and Child* after all? Yes … perhaps. And as for the 'fine portrait of a lady and child' seen earlier by David Hutton in Grace's studio? A modest guess is that it was *Veuvage*.

It was not unusual for Grace Joel to change the names of her works to suit particular circumstances. For example, *Enfants sans mère* exhibited at the Paris Salon in 1908 became *Mitherless Bairns* at the 1909 Doré exhibition. Some of her works went through these name transformations from time to time, making identifications all the more difficult. The one description we do have of *Enfants sans mère* is

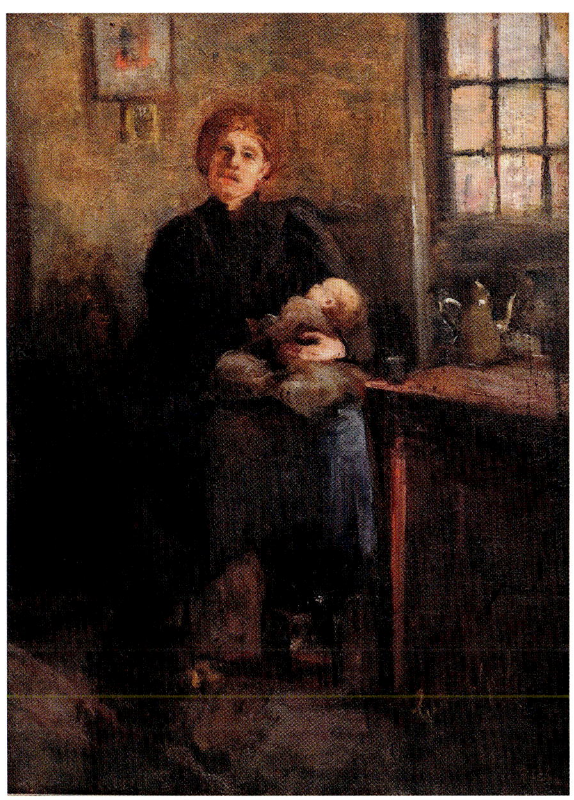

Image 6.6

***Mother and Child*, by Grace Joel, oil on canvas, 54.6 x 40.3 cm.** Auckland Art Gallery Toi o Tāmaki, Auckland

from *The Argus* of 1908: 'It is a simple but charming "Mother and Child" [sic]. A captious critic would no doubt suggest that "sister" would be a more accurate description of the very youthful "mother", but he could still take pleasure in the softly-lighted interior and the wee mite in the pink dress which Miss Joel has placed in the centre of her canvas.'[22] Evidently something has been lost in translation here. Despite the muddled description, this could be the work in Image 6.25, which does feature a wee mite in a pink dress positioned more or less in the centre of the canvas and imbued with the tones of a softly lit interior.

In February, following on the heels of the International Society's exhibition, came the celebratory 'Exhibition of Pictures/English, Dutch, French/and Figure Subjects/by Grace J. Joel/ Exhibitor at Royal Academy and/Paris Salon/ The Doré Galleries/35 New Bond Street, London, W., 1909.' This gallery showing was a tour de force for Grace Joel and a clear demonstration of her achievements as an artist.

Grace assembled 56 works, including *Autumn's Grief at the Dying Year* (Ex Royal Academy 1908 under the title *Autumn*), *Le grandpère d'Étaples* (Ex Paris Salon 1908), *Mitherless Bairns* (Ex Paris Salon 1908 under the title *Enfants sans mère*), *Homeward Bound by the Chalk Path* (Ex Salon 1903), *Her Child* (Ex Salon 1901), *A Time of Prayer* (Ex Salon 1905), *Mdlle. la Comtesse de M.* (Ex Society of Portrait Painters 1908), *Widowed* (Ex International Society of Sculptors, Painters and Gravers 1909), *The Day is Done* (Ex Australia/New Zealand), *Une madonne moderne* and 10 watercolours.

According to *The Studio*, the exhibition was 'dominated by Grace's portrait of *Mdlle. la Comtesse de M.*',[23] which was not for sale. *The Hon. Sir John Cockburn KCMG, MD* also had no price on his head, as he was doubtless going to a good home. Four of Joel's portraits in the exhibition were lent by their current owners: *Mrs Yeatman Woolf*, *Colonel Pitman, RA* [Royal Artillery], *Kate (Daughter of Mr Albert Woolf)* and *Mrs C. Batchelor*. It seems that Grace Joel had made a name for herself as a portrait painter of note in London. Adding gravitas to the whole affair, the High Commissioner for New Zealand paid the exhibition a visit.

Grace's work *Une madonne moderne* made its first appearance at the exhibition, and this showing, along with the painting's subsequent acceptance at the Paris Salon of 1914 and the Royal Academy in 1920, bought it a distinguished pedigree. *Une madonne moderne* can now be identified with certainty from the gallery stamps on its reverse side as Image 6.7.[24] Note the halo effect forming the background, and also the pink flower, an adornment that Grace often used in her work. The softly muted tones give the painting an ethereal quality, which was surely the intention.

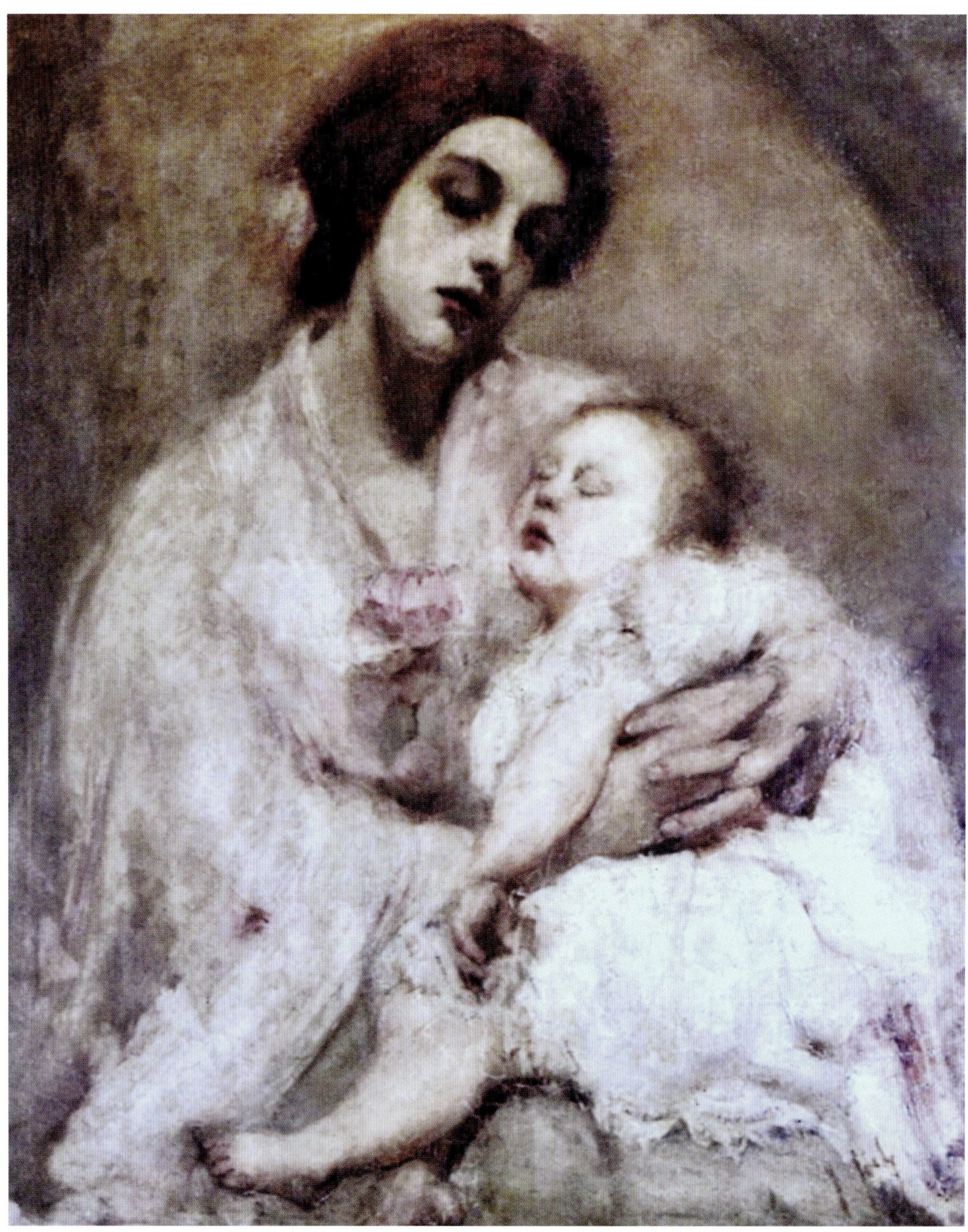

Image 6.7

Une madonne moderne, by Grace Joel, c. 1909, oil on canvas, 91.5 x 77 cm. First shown at the Doré Salon exhibition of 1909, where it was priced at 70 guineas, and subsequently at the Paris Salon (1914) and Royal Academy (1920). A stamp imprint on the reverse side from the Société des Artistes Français, 1914, positively identifies this work. The depiction of mother and child takes on the aura of a religious icon. Private collection

The watercolours included *Trafalgar Square, Roses* and *Two Little Waifs*, the latter one of Grace's recurrent motifs. Two other works titled *French Shrimp Gatherers* and *Mending the Nets* were almost certainly scenes from the shores of Étaples, which Grace had visited in 1901 and possibly sometime after that.[25]

The Doré exhibition did not go unnoticed by the *Jewish Chronicle*, which had been following Grace's artistic career: '... in her landscapes there is a decided tendency toward the school of French impressionists ... She has also grappled with the nude ... and we feel she has done it with a certain decided success, both in her poetical and impressionistic renderings of the theme. A conspicuous feature of her exhibition is her feminine and tender treatment of the beautiful subject of motherhood.'[26]

Perhaps of some psychological interest is the fact that both Grace Joel and Mary Cassatt created many sensitive works on the theme of mother and child, yet neither of them married and neither of them had children. The two women's interest in this subject matter possibly indicates unfulfilled desire, or grew from knowledge that their chosen path would always render them observers of the beatific scenes they depicted. According to Cassatt biographer Nancy Mathews, 'Cassatt surely saw the irony in making maternity her signature theme.' Grace Joel probably did as well. The unmarried Frances Hodgkins was no stranger to mother and child themes, either.

During the late 1940s, art historians began debating if Cassatt's 'sacrifice' was worth her while; maybe, they argued, her mother and child paintings 'were really an acknowledgment that women *should* have children, and that she had made a serious mistake in her life.'[27] Had these male critics known of Grace Joel's work, they'd probably have said the same about it ... and her. As if this were not male-centric enough, another biographer wrote of the Cassatt era (a generation preceding Grace Joel's but no doubt applicable to hers) that 'It was still maintained in some quarters, that the greatest contribution to the world of art that could be made by any woman was to be the mother of a genius.'[28] Would Julius Vogel's vision of total equality between the sexes ever be realised?

Lest one think that artists such as Joel, Cassatt and Hodgkins depicted mothers and children as a means of expressing their unfulfilled desire for motherhood and that this phenomenon was the preserve of women artists of the time, Grace's cousin Emanuel Fox painted numerous works on this theme. His marriage to Ethel Carrick was a childless one, although both were from large families. Fox's principal biographer, Ruth Zubans, claims that 'Fox's repeated depiction of motherhood leaves no doubt about the personal significance of this theme, perhaps a wish for an existence he knew would never be fulfilled.'[29] It is interesting that the artistic ideal for Fox was still motherhood and not fatherhood, a

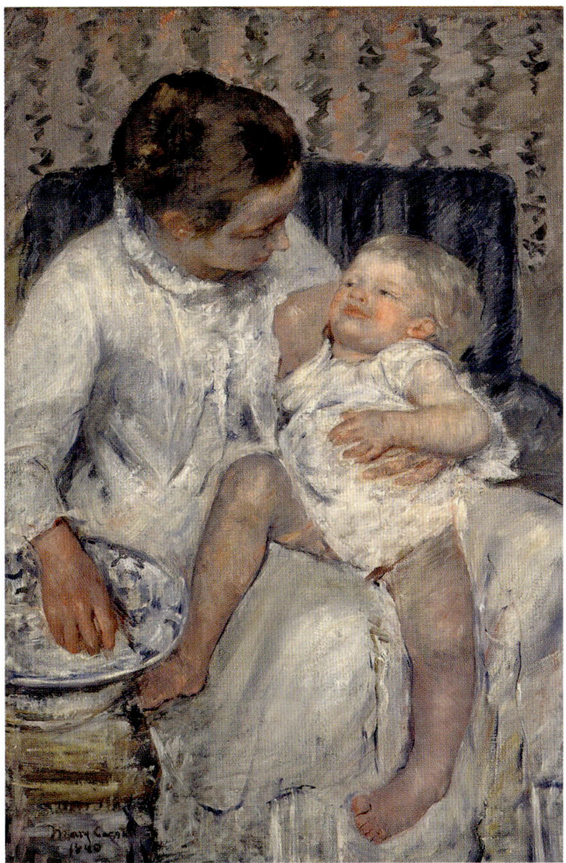

Image 6.8

Mary Cassatt's *The Child's Bath*, 1880, oil on canvas, 100 x 65 cm.

theme receiving scant attention from artists down through the years.[30]

The essence of Fox's treatment of motherhood differs significantly from Grace Joel's. The latter's renderings of the subject are suffused with love, *l'amour divin*, representing the deep emotional, even spiritual, bond between mother and child. Fox's portrayals present more of a social ideal, depicting the mother as 'the core of the family – generous, sharing, embodying the value of civility'.[31] Certainly, many other male artists were drawn to the theme of motherhood, including the nineteenth century's Bouguereau, Renoir and Monet, among others.

It seems reasonable to state that even the mother and child works of Frances Hodgkins and Mary Cassatt do not express the same intensity as Grace Joel's. If we take Peter Entwisle's interview with Irene Ross as evidence, we can assume that Grace was not disposed to the simple domestic pleasures of childcare. For her, it was the burning fervour of the mother/child love relationship that mattered most. The fact that Grace never experienced maternal love for herself adds poignancy to her later works titled *L'amour maternel*, *L'enfant adorée* and *L'amour divin*.

Towards the end of April 1909, Grace readied herself to visit the Paris Salon where her works *Veuvage* (*Widowhood*) and *Présage* (*Omen*) would be on show at its May exhibition. As mentioned, the former painting could be the *Widowed* (*Mother and Child*) exhibited earlier in the year at the International Society and the Doré Gallery. Of *Présage*, all we know is that it was a watercolour.[32] According to commentary in the *The Argus* on the exhibition, 'There are certain things that women paint better than men because of the special way they interpret them.'[33]

The Paris Salon exhibition of May 1909 also hosted work by often-rejected (by galleries) good friend Arthur Streeton. George Coates and Frances Hodgkins were there too. The observant Miss Hodgkins, with two watercolours on exhibit, reported spying in the crowd at the Salon 'a weird and familiar little figure', who turned out to be Grace, although 'she passed in the crowd before I could stop her.'[34] Frances's comments about Grace in her letters suggest some antipathy, but why she might have been so inclined is uncertain. Hodgkins also wrote in the same letter that she loved the freedom of living among strangers, and having no one know about one's private affairs (Grace Joel may have felt likewise). Perhaps the genesis of Frances's acerbic observations of Grace lies here.

After her Paris visit in May, Grace headed to northern France once more to paint in the idyllic village of Étaples.[35] Arriving back in London in time for Christmas, she had the pleasure of finding her full-length portrait titled *Miss Kitty Bridges* hung on the line at the Society of Portrait Painters' showing at the New Gallery. The only other Antipodean artist represented was George Coates. Frances Hodgkins also shared wall space with Grace during December, but this time in the Rendezvous room at the London office of the *British Australasian*. The exhibition was the first such for the newspaper, which intended it to become a permanent event.[36]

Even while in France, Grace managed to exhibit three works at the July London Salon, held in the Royal Albert Hall. One of these was a 'clever' *Sketch Portrait of George Coates* (NFS). Frances Hodgkins had 'three pleasing water-colours'. Several years later, in 1914, George Coates repaid the gesture by painting a portrait of Grace Joel; where it is now is unknown.[37]

It was at the Paris Salon of 1910 that Grace exhibited *La Légende*, depicting little Irene Searle and her sister Elsie. Works by nearby Chelsea dwellers Dora Meeson Coates and husband George also featured. Grace's address in Chelsea was now 12 Milton Chambers, 128 Cheyne Walk, where she would reside until her death in 1924. Grace by this time had a housekeeper, whose daughter posed for her from time to time.[38]

In August of that year, another New Zealander moved into a flat further along Cheyne Walk. The newcomer was writer Katherine Mansfield, and the flat belonged to her painter friend, Henry Bishop.

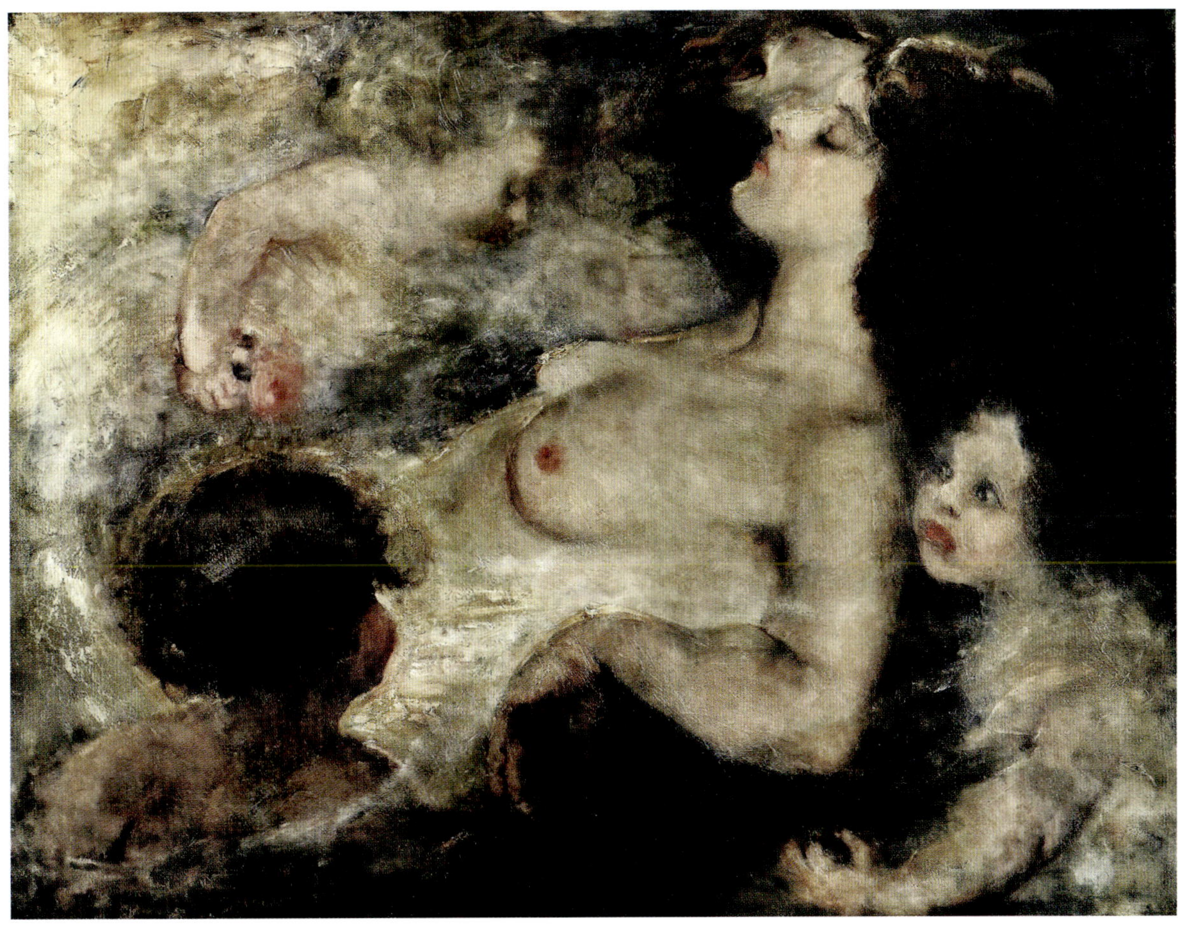

IMAGE 6.9

Reclining Nude, by Grace Joel, undated, oil on canvas, 71 x 92 cm. The woman is thought to be the daughter of Grace Joel's housekeeper at Cheyne Walk, which would make the painting post 1910. The subject is reclining in a pool of water, and the cherub at the top is gazing at its own reflection. This more allegorical and erotic rendering of motherhood is a wide departure from Joel's previous works. The artist may be a single woman, but she is no prude. Interestingly, George Coates exhibited a nude with cherubs in 1909 (*Joie de vivre*). Dunedin Public Art Gallery, Dunedin

Mansfield stayed here for five months while Bishop was abroad.[39] There is no evidence that Grace ever met Katherine, however, or Bishop for that matter, despite the proximity of her home to Bishop's. According to Mansfield's close companion Ida Baker, Bishop's flat was at the 'Kings Road end of Cheyne Walk'. So, too, was Grace's. The address no longer exists.

Several months earlier, Grace Joel was one of those present at a reception in honour of the Governor-Designate of New Zealand, Lord Islington, at the Westminster Palace Hotel in London. The New Zealand artist Raymond McIntyre (1879–1933), also based in London at this time, wrote home frequently. In a letter to his father dated 5 May 1910, he reported: 'Last night at ten o'clock I was at Westminster Palace Hotel, being presented to the new Governor of New Zealand ... I found Miss Joel wandering forlornly about like Lottie might do.[40] She was thrown out at the R.A. too, but escaped without injury ... I saw E.W. Christmas ... I introduced him to Miss Joel. He, like all of us, has heard of her, but never met her.'[41]

Ernest William Christmas (1863–1918) was an Australian-born painter whose striking landscapes attracted a commission from the New Zealand Tourism Department. He had exhibited and travelled widely, and the previous year had been elected to the Royal Society of British Artists, which allowed him to append the initials RBA to his name. Such letters were sought after because they helped artists get their work accepted at the highest levels.

How should we interpret McIntyre's claim that Grace was 'thrown out at the R.A. too, but escaped without injury'? One possibility is that the academy rejected her work but her dignity remained intact. Another is that the academy accepted her work but then crowded it out for want of space, a situation Grace had already experienced twice. In either event, McIntyre's comment is somewhat harsh because Grace had exhibited at the Royal Academy as well as the Paris Salon, so perhaps what he said reflected envy or antipathy. Was McIntyre even aware that Grace Joel was his new neighbour, just a few doors down from his No. 120 Cheyne Walk studio? Yet again, in the absence of information, we cannot really say.

But let us hope that Grace Joel and Raymond McIntyre did become acquainted, as they both enjoyed the same view of the Thames. What Grace witnessed from the Thames Embankment was a brooding vista, whose 'foggy days are dreams of colour, with sun struggling to appear, making the ever-changing river like a beautiful opal; sometimes the light appears the palest pink of a delicate rose, another time of the most evanescent yellow.'[42] Grace had already rendered this scene in oils, of course, in her *Battersea-bridge on a Foggy Morning*, formerly shown in Melbourne.

McIntyre was an interesting personality. He was an ardent admirer of Whistler and undaunted by the big names in the art world. When writing a review of an exhibition of Paul Gauguin's work in 1924, he asked if the Frenchman's Tahitian work was 'pictorially interesting quite apart from the man who produced it. Yes! Undoubtedly some of it is.'[43] The self-assurance of this immigrant from the Antipodes was also evident in his review of the works displayed by The New Society of Artists, a *Salon des refusés* for those rejected by the Royal Academy: 'Because of the type of work it encourages this society has not justified its existence.'[44]

A few years previously, the well-known suffragette Sylvia Pankhurst had been living in the same apartment building as McIntyre – when she was not touring the country giving lectures, demonstrating or spending time in prison, that is. Pankhurst trained as an artist, and a portrait of her close friend, the British politician and women's suffragist supporter Keir Hardie, hangs in the National Portrait Gallery in London. There is no tangible evidence that Sylvia Pankhurst knew Grace Joel, although family lore claims they did meet and that Pankhurst enlisted Joel into the cause of women's suffrage.[45]

This notion has entered the annals of New Zealand art history through Gil Docking's book, *Two Hundred Years of New Zealand Painting*, where he wrote that Grace took 'an interest in the suffragette movement' but provided no evidence that she did.[46] *The Suffrage Annual and Women's Who's Who* of 1913 contains the name of Dora Meeson Coates with a brief biography, but there is no mention of Grace Joel.[47] If Grace was involved with the woman's suffrage movement, it's likely she played a minor role and was probably a suffragist rather than the more activist suffragette.[48]

Throughout the years preceding the Great War, women (and some men) in Britain continued to campaign for female suffrage, but the *zeitgeist* of early twentieth-century England seemed unable to countenance the prospect of women voting. The London *Times* editorial of 22 June 1908 proclaimed that enfranchising women 'would weaken the moral fibre of the nation if the supreme decisions of the State were determined partly by women who could not feel the same responsibilities for seeing them carried through as men'. There it was – the moral fibre of the nation would be in peril. As a consequence, the struggle for women's suffrage in England was a titanic one, and Dora Meeson, with full support from her husband George Coates, was at its forefront. Even if, as a friend of Dora's, Grace did not participate in the suffrage movement, she could not have been oblivious to the political maelstrom going on around her.

Family lore also has it that Grace Joel toured Europe with the famous dancer, Isadora Duncan, but there is no such mention in various texts on Duncan. So the question of whether or not Grace ever knew Sylvia Pankhurst or Isadora Duncan remains open. That said, on a July afternoon in 1910 Anna, Lady Stout held an 'At Home' in a Kensington residence for about 100 guests. Lady Stout and her husband, the former New Zealand Prime Minister and Chief Justice Sir Robert Stout, had long championed women's rights in New Zealand. Numerous New Zealanders were in attendance, including Grace Joel.

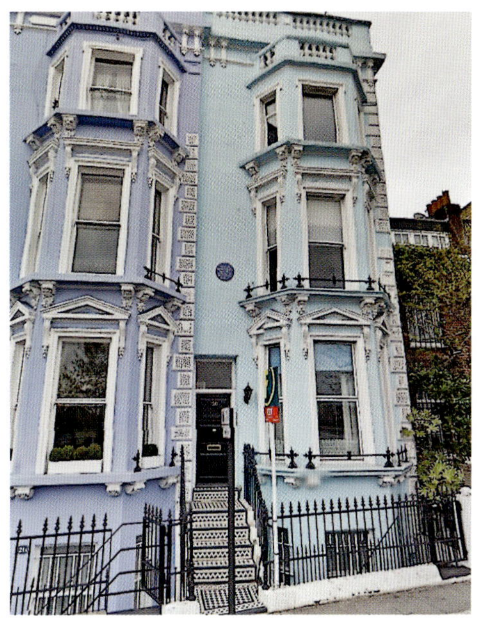

IMAGE 6.10

No. 120 Cheyne Walk, the house that Sylvia Pankhurst used as a base (noted by the blue plaque) and later the residence of New Zealand artist Raymond McIntyre. The house to the right (No. 119), directly behind the tree, was formerly occupied by J.M.W. Turner, and was where he died in 1851. Grace Joel's residence, No. 128, which no longer exists, would have been just a few dwellings to the left. Across the roadway in front of these apartments is the Thames at the Battersea Bridge end.

Speeches given by Constance, Lady Lytton and her sister Betty, Lady Balfour were a highlight of the afternoon. Although born into the highest echelon of British aristocracy and its attendant privileges, Constance Lytton became a militant member of the suffragette movement. She spoke that afternoon of her experiences being force-fed in prison. Dunedin's *Evening Post* reported that 'many of the guests promised to take part in the big procession through London tomorrow evening.'[49] After hearing such harrowing tales, Grace Joel could well have been one of them.

In 1910 the Dunedin-founded clothing retailer Hallenstein Brothers appointed Isidore de Beer, one

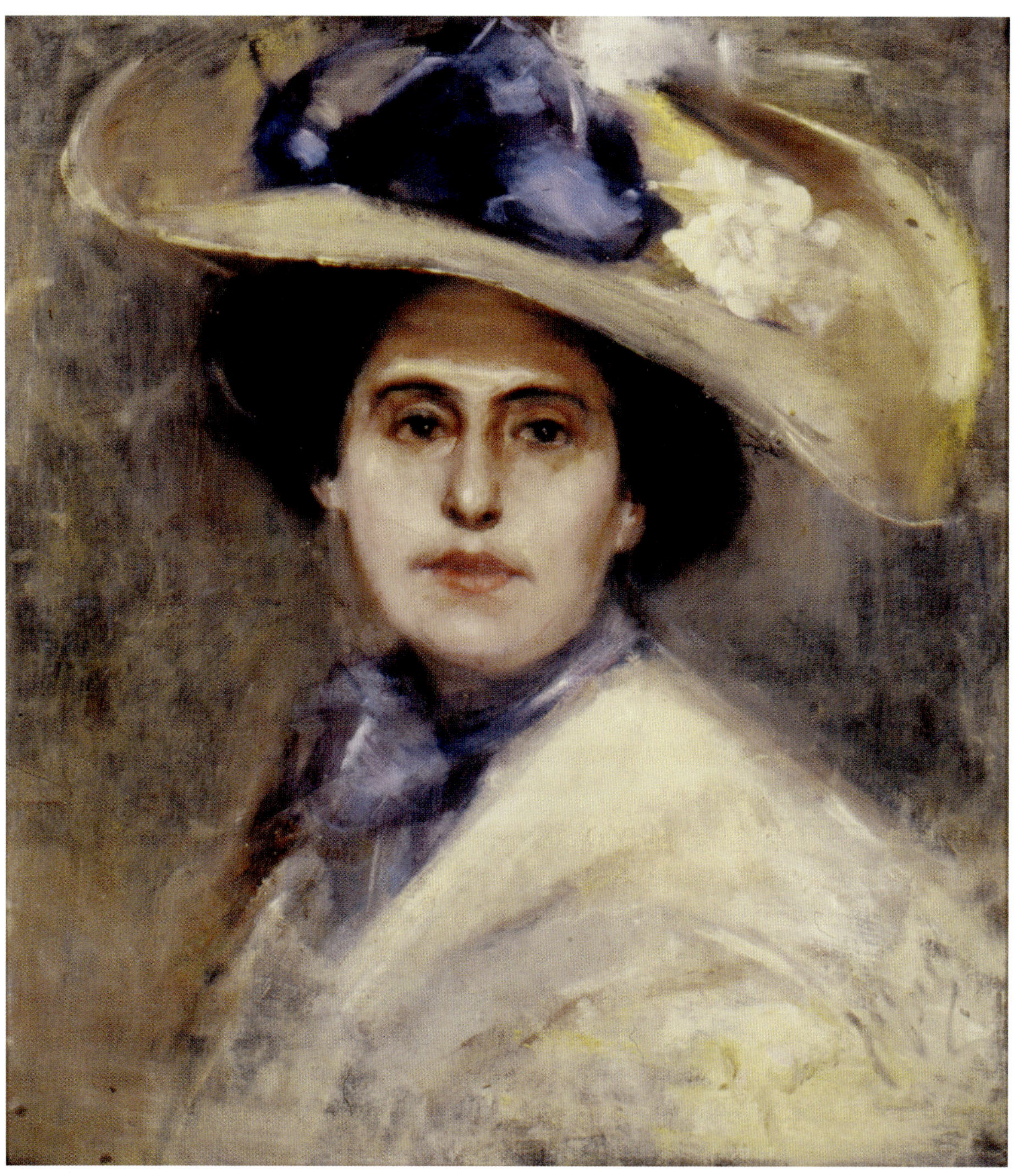

Image 6.11

A very stylish, *Self-portrait Wearing a Hat*, c. 1905–10, oil on canvas, 53.7 x 44.6 cm. The date is suggested by the large decorative Edwardian hat that was fashionable during this period. Frances Hodgkins wore one too. The hint of a moustache faithfully recorded indicates a certain lack of vanity on the part of the artist, who could easily have chosen to leave it out. Private collection

of its directors, to run the company's London office. For Isidore and his family, the posting meant leaving Dunedin to settle permanently in England.

Once in England, daughter Dora lived a life of shopping (although according to her diary she hated Harrods for some ungiven reason), walking, taking in art galleries, attending concerts, visiting relatives and receiving guests: 'Jos Friedlander and Miss G. Joel called – at separate times. Miss Joel entertained us with her experiences of sales.'[50] The routine was broken by the occasional trip to the Continent.

Another work that Grace exhibited during 1910, this time in July at the Royal Institute of Oil Painters in Piccadilly, was 'a pleasing little canvas' of the head of a child on the verge of tears called *I Want My Mummy*. The forlorn child was accompanied by a small painting of chickens by the aforementioned Mr E.W. Christmas, who had heard of Grace Joel but never met her.[51]

Within artistic circles, the year 1910 came to be associated with a degree of infamy. In November, painter and art critic Roger Fry[52] mounted an exhibition titled 'Manet and the Post-Impressionists' at London's Grafton Galleries. In addition to Manet, the exhibition featured work mainly by Cézanne, Gauguin, van Gogh and Matisse. These artists had gone beyond exploring Nature (the capital N is deliberate) through the Impressionist principles of light and colour and arrived at a more emotional Post-Impressionist expression of it.

The shock of the new was astounding. With but a few exceptions, the works produced comments of the kind expressed by critic Wilfrid Blunt, who classified the exhibition as 'Nothing but the gross puerility which scrawls indecencies on the walls of a privy.'[53] Other critics were even less kind, hurling words such as 'infection', 'madness', 'putrescence' at the works on display, while the British public were 'thrown into paroxysms of rage and laughter'.[54] Literally. 'One gentleman … laughed so loud at Cézanne's portrait of his wife that he had to be taken out and walked up and down for five minutes in the fresh air.'[55]

Not all London denizens were so afflicted. For writer Katherine Mansfield the exhibition was a revelation. She visited 'again and again', realising 'as she stands in front of a Van Gogh … that these paintings can teach her about narrative structure'.[56] Nor did the new art perturb Frances Hodgkins. In subsequent years, she became one of its many and various proponents (see Image 6.14). Grace Joel, however, while certainly aware of the exhibition (what artist in London could not be), was seemingly uninfluenced by it if we take her own work as evidence. Roger Fry, undaunted by negativity, emerged the following summer to again hammer away at the British public with his 'Second Post-Impressionist Exhibition'.

In April 1911, just three months after the Post-Impressionists had vacated the Grafton Galleries, the International Society of Sculptors, Painters and Gravers set up its annual exhibition in the same venue. The only colonial artist to have an oil painting accepted by the society and hung on the line was Grace Joel, and the painting was none other than *Le grandpère d'Étaples*: 'The subject is the head of an old and withered peasant looking out from a harmony of brown. When this same canvas was hung in the Salon [of 1908] it was picked out for very complimentary comment by the French critics.'[57] Australian artist George Lambert also exhibited, but as a member of the International Society he could rightfully do so. To add significance to Grace's achievement, the Dunedin *Evening Post* declared, 'The exhibition of this society is the goal kept in view by nearly all artists from the colonies.'[58]

Soon afterwards Grace exhibited *La fleur écarlate* at the Paris Salon. The description of this large sympathetic rendering of 'a little girl standing amid some scarlet hollyhocks'[59] sounds reminiscent of her 1896 *A Rose 'midst Poppies*. One of Joel's former Dunedin pupils, Jean Rollo-Fisher, had sent Grace a floral painting, and it too appeared at the Salon. Rollo-Fisher's address in the exhibition catalogue was the same as Grace Joel's.[60] It appears that Grace was also becoming more at home with other

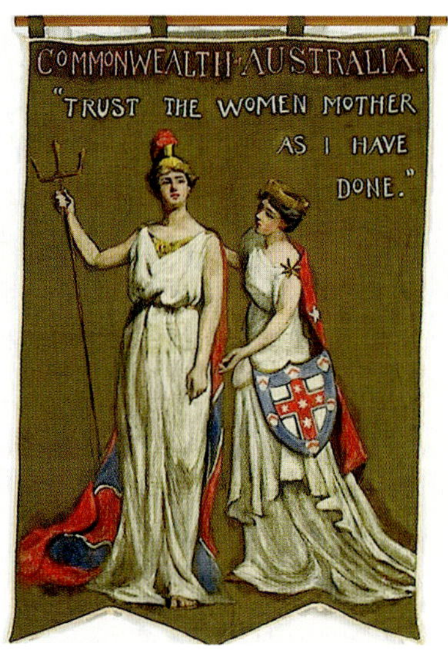

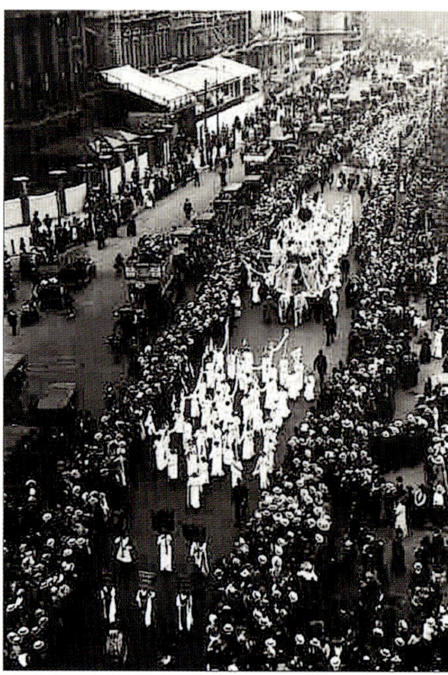

Image 6.12

The banner painted by Dora Meeson Coates for the Women's Suffrage march in London, 17 June 1911. The banner image was put on a commemorative one dollar coin by the Australian government in 2003 in celebration of a century of women's suffrage in Australia.

Banner in the Parliament House (Canberra, Australia) art collection

Dunedin expatriates, given this June 1911 entry in Dora de Beer's diary: 'Weather changed. Miss Joel to lunch.'[61]

That same month, 17 June 1911 to be precise, London was the venue for 'the greatest procession of women in support of the suffrage movement that the world ever has seen'. Dora Meeson, who was also a member of the Artists' Suffrage League, which created a number of banners, posters, booklets, leaflets and postcards in support of the women's suffrage movement, painted a large banner: *Commonwealth of Australia – Trust the Women Mother as I Have Done*. Its heavy bulk was carried by Dora, with the assistance of three others, at the head of the Australian and New Zealand contingents, husband George Coates walking at Dora's side. New Zealand was represented by Lady Anna Stout, whom we've encountered previously.

Almost a year on, in May 1912, the *Feilding Star*, the newspaper of a small town situated in the south of New Zealand's North Island, reported that the Paris Salon had accepted Grace Joel's *L'amour maternel*: 'It is a picture in oils of mother with nude child in her arms, and the subjects are of life size. The title was suggested by the absorbed expression of the mother holding her child and gazing at it.'[62] This is an accurate description of Image 6.13. The modernist emphasis on style over emotional content was certainly not for Grace.

Feilding (often voted New Zealand's most beautiful town, and the spelling *is* as given) was a long way from Dunedin in distance and culture, yet here it was following the triumphs (there had been other reports as well) of Grace Joel, a Dunedinite in London exhibiting in Paris. 'Miss Joel's work,' the *Star* continued, 'is held in high esteem by critics and artists in England and France.' Yes, the French critics, in particular, most definitely did praise *L'amour maternel*. Dunedin's *Evening Post*, unstinting in keeping a close eye on what the French had to say about Grace's latest Salon conquest, reported that the *Journal des débats* (among other sources) 'makes mention of the fine feeling, the colour, and the sweet expression of the mother looking at her child'.[63]

Image 6.13 (Opposite)

It is virtually certain that this is *L'amour maternel*, by Grace Joel, exhibited at the 1912 Paris Salon, oil on canvas, 113.6 x 78.4 cm (life-size).

Museum of New Zealand Te Papa Tongarewa, Wellington

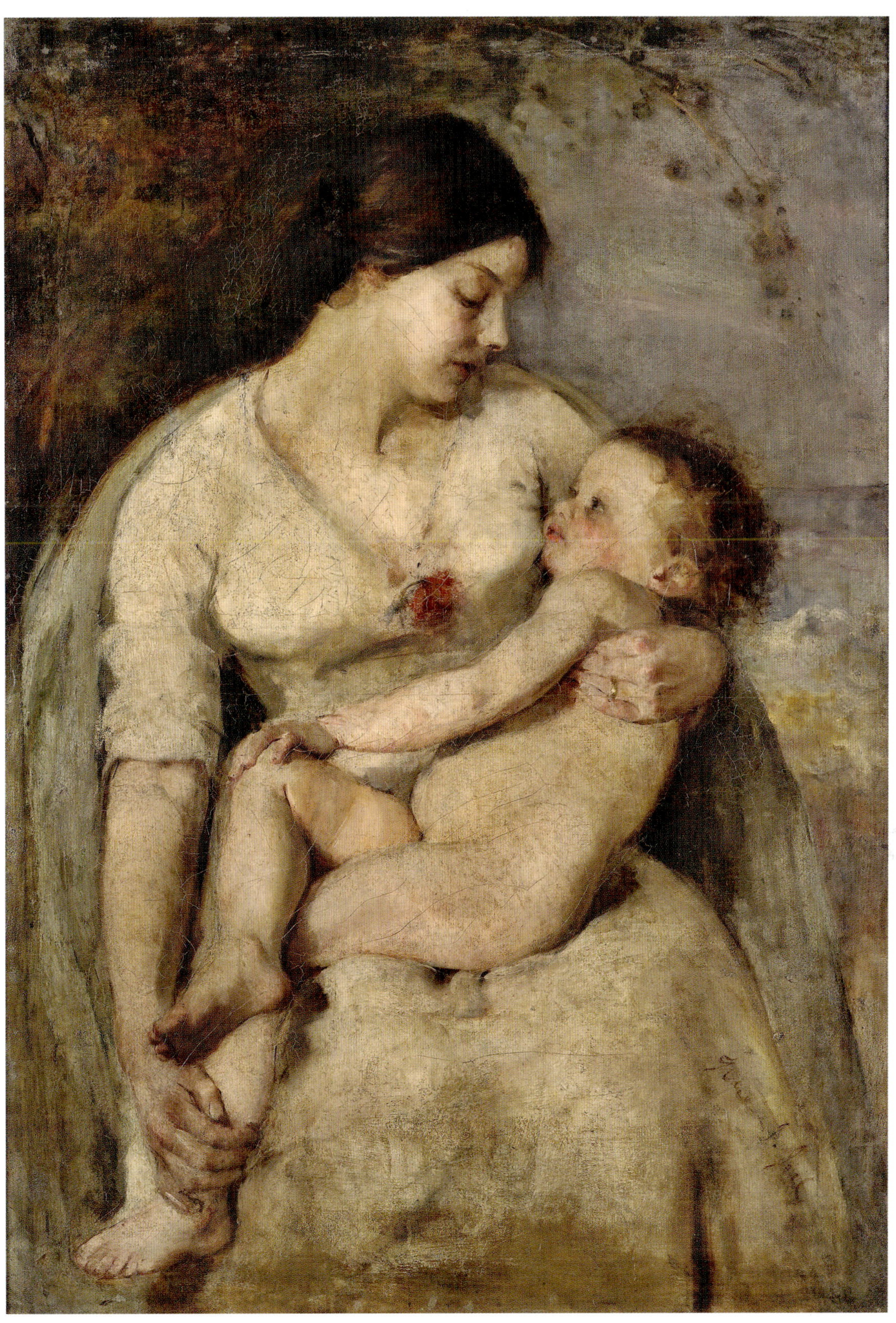

At the end of the year, Grace again attended a very large reception for the Governor-Designate of New Zealand, Lord Liverpool, at the same venue as before – Westminster Palace Hotel. The ladies' attire was faithfully recorded: 'Lady Hall-Jones was in black satin and lace ... Lady Mills in black satin with gold trimmings and diamonds ... Miss Grace Joel was in white satin with amber scarf, Mrs Chapple in black silk ...'[64]

Towards the middle of the following year (1913), the Paris Salon accepted another of Grace's mother and child paintings, this one being *L'enfant adorée.* A more or less complete description of this work exists courtesy yet again of the *Evening Post*: '[The painting depicts] a mother gazing with divine love at her little girl, their hands being clasped round each other's necks. The canvas is life-size, and is a golden harmony. The child has a wistful expression and is letting fall some pink blossoms which she has been holding in her hands.'[65] Another painting on view was a 'canvas of white flowers' by Jean Rollo-Fisher, pleasingly hung on the line. The latter's address was again that of Grace Joel, who clearly was continuing to act as an intermediary on behalf of her former pupil. *L'enfant adorée* under its English title of *The Adored Child* was also shown during 1913 at The Royal Institute of Oil Painters' exhibition. The telling description of the mother gazing lovingly at the little girl, their hands clasped round each other's necks, should assist in deciphering which of Grace Joel's many mother and child paintings are which.

By mid-year, Grace was again in the company of her sister, Blanche. Accompanied by daughter Kathleen, Blanche had just arrived back in London after spending seven years in New Zealand. She remained in England for the next 20 years, returning to New Zealand in 1933. On arriving in England, Kathleen discovered that she had been awarded one of three Australasian scholarships, 'which entitle[d] her to free tuition for two years or more at the Royal Academy of Music.'[66] Mother and daughter, Blanche and Kathleen, possibly made musical history in 1927 by performing a recital together for two pianos at Wigmore Hall, London.[67]

War Years

The curse was upon us. The war, destructive and overwhelming, had begun ... It was Leonardo da Vinci who called war 'frenzied madness', but we did not realize this then ... Dora Meeson Coates, 1937

Although war was about to break out, May still heralded the opening of the Paris Salon, which was displaying Grace Joel's *Une madonne moderne* (Image 6.7), previously exhibited at the Doré. In this work, the lowered eyelids give the painting an aura of sublime contentment in contrast to, say, *L'amour maternel* (Image 6.13), where the intensity of maternal love is writ large.

Also in May, Grace Joel attended an At Home hosted by Mrs Thomas (Ida) Mackenzie and her daughters at their residence in Hampstead. Husband Thomas Mackenzie had only a few years earlier been a government minister and briefly prime minister in New Zealand. Now resident in London, he held the post of High Commissioner for New Zealand. The afternoon gathering was for 'their New Zealand friends and visitors from the Dominion.'[68] Grace was clearly on the High Commissioner's A-list, as in December she attended a reception given by him for the captain and officers of HMS *New Zealand*. The occasion was also graced by a sprinkling of English lords and ladies. For the sartorially minded, the *Evening Post* noted that Grace Joel was in 'cream brocade' as were three others in attendance. Four years later, Grace was one of the distinguished guests who attended the wedding of Ida Mary Mackenzie, daughter of the High Commissioner and his wife, by then elevated to Sir Thomas and Lady Mackenzie.[69]

From 5 June to 11 July 1914, Grace and her long-time acquaintance, James Quinn, had paintings hanging at the Royal Society of Portrait Painters' 24th Exhibition, Grafton Galleries, London. The work Grace exhibited was *Mrs Bridges and Kitty.* Mrs Bridges was seemingly a very satisfied return customer; in 1909, the Royal Society had exhibited Grace's full-length portrait, *Miss Kitty Bridges.*

On the other side of the world, a curious art auction was taking place in Sydney, Australia. The more than 200 works of art awaiting the auctioneer's hammer included oil paintings, watercolours, engravings and such like, all from a 'well-known collector and connoisseur', and with many 'picked up by the collector in Europe'. Even the reporter of the *Sydney Morning Herald* was somewhat sceptical of the works reputed to be 'a Rembrandt, a Sargent, or a Turner'.[70] Such suspicion was warranted, as Turner's *The Shipwreck* had been gifted to the nation in 1856, yet here it was, up for auction; so, too, the *Head of Flora*, reputedly by Titian. At least this conned/conning connoisseur had good taste. Among the paintings grouped under Australian works was the still life, *Peonies*, by John Longstaff, and a painting by Grace Joel, *In the Cornfield*. The latter was possibly *The Day is Done*, which does depict a cornfield, where two young girls rest at day's end. Whatever the case may be, it is heartening that a work of Grace Joel's could be found trading amid the finest of artistic company on this winter's day at a Southern Hemisphere auction.

Spinning the globe back to Europe, we encounter the events of 28 June 1914, when the Gräf & Stift convertible carrying Archduke Franz Ferdinand of Austria and his wife, Sophie, Duchess of Hohenberg, executed a wrong turn in Sarajevo, with the resulting assassination of both. Within a month the floodgates of the 'war to end all wars' were unleashed. The Belle Époque had come to a frightening end; four years of trench warfare were to follow in the killing fields of Europe.

Dora became a policewoman at a munitions factory. '[T]here was a shifting all round of occupations,' she recalled. 'It had its good side, for the rich knew what it was like to be hungry and the poor to be well fed.'[71] Grace Joel's Australian circle disbanded for the time being, and the Paris Salon closed, remaining that way throughout the war years.

Chelsea, Grace Joel's home, changed as well. Soldiers could be seen bivouacked on the grounds of the local gardens, and hospital and army trucks rattled 'noisily' along the usually quiet Embankment. Chelsea residents Meeson and Coates lay awake on the hot summer nights, 'listening to the heavy, ominous rumble of laden troop-trains, all night long, slowly steaming out of Victoria Station'.[72] Streaming into London from the other direction came masses of refugees from Europe.

In September 1915 a unique auction of patriotic fervour took place at Christie's auction house in London. It was attended by 'dukes, duchesses, celebrated actors and actresses', and even leading artists. Grace, who had reached 50 years of age several months earlier, may have been one of those in attendance or even have given to the cause. Its purpose was to raise money for the Red Cross. Many items were donated by royalty, an interesting one being a wheel-lock sporting rifle dating from 1646 sent by King George. One of the fortunate bidders walked off with the gift proffered by Queen Mary: a 'magnificent tortoiseshell fan set with Her Majesty's monogram in diamonds, surmounted by a gold crown, the mount being composed of feathers from an eagle's wing'. All this majesty for only 190 guineas, less than the 200-guinea price tag on Grace Joel's *The Day is Done* at the 1909 Doré exhibition.[73]

Many of the works at that year's Royal Academy depicted scenes from the war. Yet, artistically, Grace continued to inhabit her own personal world despite the turmoil. Her substantial Royal Academy contribution was *Divine Love*, again on the mother and child theme and 'quite up to her standard'.[74] Grace exhibited the same work with the Society of Women Artists in 1917 and in 1920 with the Royal Scottish Academy, where it enjoyed 'great success'.[75] At each showing, it was presented under the same epithet – *Divine Love*.

Art consultant Anne Kirker says of Grace Joel's many mother and child works that 'an expressive, almost erotic undercurrent infuses the subject'. She describes the work in Image 6.15 as having a 'warmth and sensuousness'.[76] Dunedin art critic Peter Entwisle comments too on the suggested fullness of the mother's breasts and her 'knowing look'.[77] As will

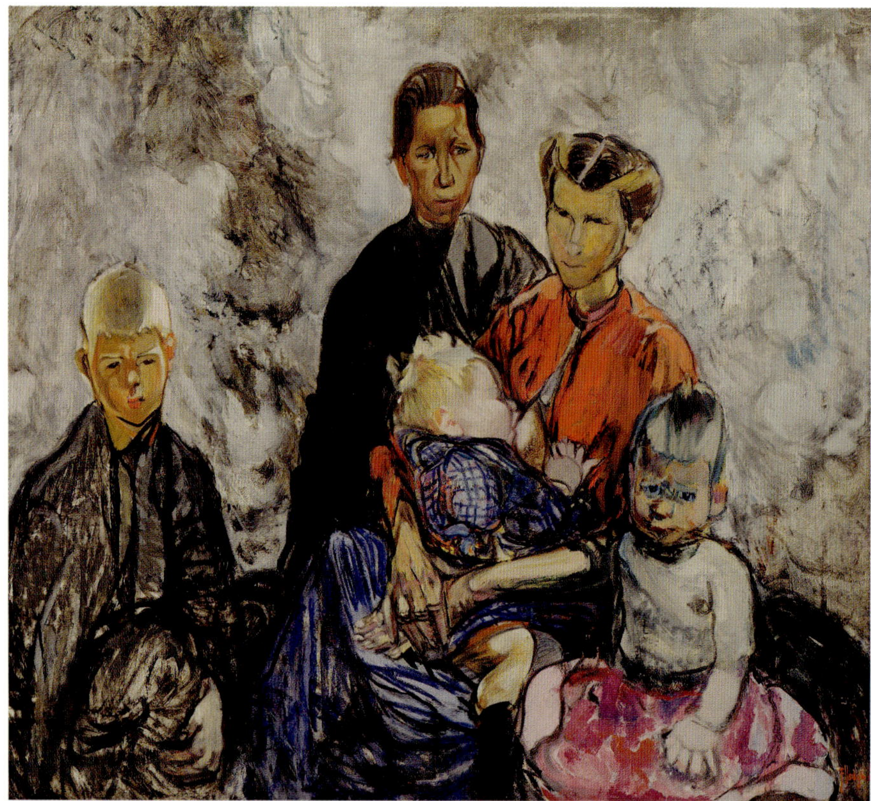

IMAGE 6.14

***Belgian Refugees*, c. 1916, by Frances Hodgkins, oil on canvas, 87.5 x 95 cm. Grace Joel did her own version of *Refugees* in 1919.**

Collection of the Christchurch Art Gallery Te Puna o Waiwhetu; purchased with assistance of the National Art Collections Fund, London, 1980

become apparent, it is very likely that Image 6.15 is the painting *Divine Love*. Years later, a reviewer appraising Joel's work in *La revue moderne* lists *Divine Love* (along with *Une madonne moderne* and *Son enfant/Her Child*) among her 'most important and most characteristic canvases'.[78] Readers can make up their own minds. However, with regard to Image 6.15, I completely agree.

Of a work as magnificent and compelling as Image 6.15, we would expect a commensurate exhibition pedigree. However, an examination of Grace Joel's *oeuvre* indicates that only three of her works secured exhibition space at three or more first-class venues – *Son enfant* (*Her Child*), *Une madonne moderne* and *Divine Love*. Because the former two have already been accounted for, we are left with *Divine Love*, with the preceding comments from *La revue moderne* adding to the weight of evidence.

Curiously, a mother and child work did enter the scene just before the Royal Academy exhibition. According to a report in *The Argus* reviewing works that Australian artists had given to the National Portrait Society, 'Miss Grace Joel sent a portrait of a mother and child which has apparently cost her a lot of trouble and much repainting, and which has produced certain rather messy passages of colour, but there is some good drawing, and the design is natural and effective.'[79] Could this be the same painting shown again at the Royal Academy as *Divine Love*? Just maybe, as the pose in Image 6.15 would not be easy to execute. If so, the 'messy passages of colour' are no longer in evidence.

Image 6.15 represents one of Grace Joel's most accomplished paintings and is perhaps a work that Grace herself cherished, as she apparently never offered it for sale.[80] The mother, uncharacteristically, is looking away from the child, yet her body position remains full of love and tenderness. It is this close emotional bond that makes the awkward position of the child appear natural. The face of the woman is that of Grace Joel herself and so could be a self-

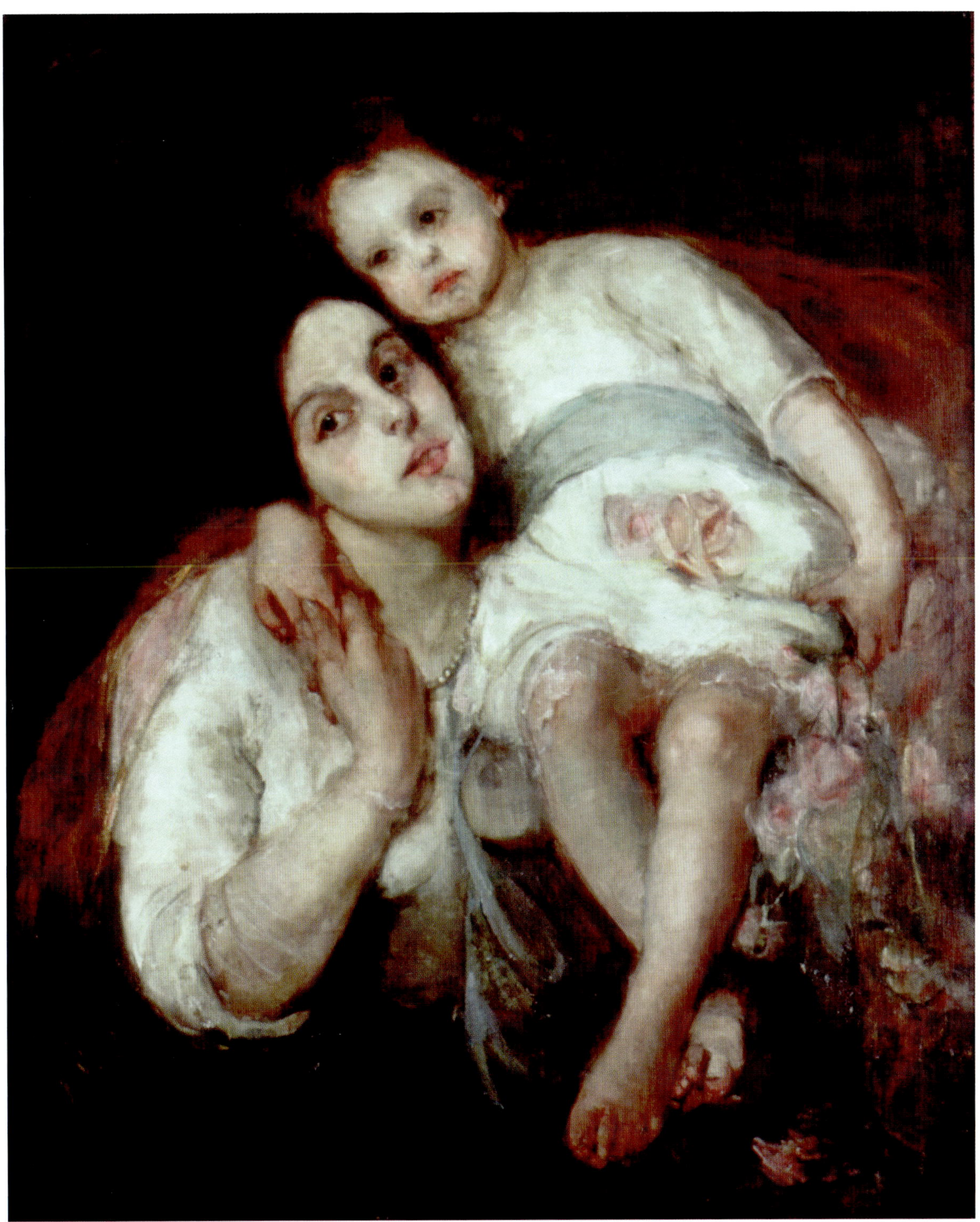

IMAGE 6.15

The voluptuous *Divine Love*, by Grace Joel, c. 1915, oil on canvas, 90.4 x 70.8 cm. Exhibited at the Royal Academy (1915), Society of Women Artists (1917) and the Scottish Academy (1920). In art historian Peter Entwisle's view, 'A reference to Titian would be apt.' Private collection

portrait featuring the child she never had. Had she in Image 6.15 finally blurred the distinction between rendering and reality? Is she saying to us that *this is my child?*

We might be inclined to associate Image 6.15 with *L'enfant adorée*, the mother and child painting exhibited at the 1913 Paris Salon. However, if we recall the requirements to be fulfilled by this work, then it fails on two counts. Firstly, the mother is gazing not at the child but to the side of the viewer. Secondly, it would be absurdly awkward for the mother to place her arm around the neck of the elevated child. However, Image 6.15 does contain some of the elements of *L'enfant adorée*. For example, 'The child has a wistful expression and is letting fall some pink blossoms which she has been holding in her hands.'[81] Also, the painting is nearly life-size, which is near enough for a newspaper description. And there *is* one arm around one neck. Image 6.15 thus could be a variation of the previously exhibited *L'enfant adorée*. What is certain is that the complete description of *L'enfant adorée* fits no extant painting by Grace Joel and its whereabouts remain unknown.

Stendhal's syndrome: *A psychosomatic disorder that causes rapid heartbeat, dizziness, fainting, confusion and even hallucinations when an individual is exposed to art, usually when the art is particularly beautiful …*

Despite the war, the annual round of art exhibitions continued in London. The pages of the 12 April 1916 issue of *The Argus* carried an article titled 'Australian Art in London'. The article featured the National Portrait Society's exhibition of May through June at the Grosvenor Gallery, London. It listed Grace Joel among the Australian artists, and Frances Hodgkins among the New Zealanders. Friend James Quinn was also represented, as was George Lambert. Grace showed a portrait of the stage actress Mabel Dunham,[82] and a year later at the same venue the portrait *Ethel*. Ethel Carrick married her second cousin Emanuel Phillips Fox in 1905, so this could have been a portrait of her.

Grace's mother Catherine died in May of 1916 in her 85th year. The obituary in the *Evening Post* commented that she was 'well known for her philanthropy'. In her will, she stipulated that Grace receive 'all my jewellery and all pictures of mine painted by herself'. In addition, after the payment of monetary bequests, debts and funeral expenses, the residue of the estate was to be shared evenly between the surviving siblings, Grace, Blanche, Lily and Louis Joel.

For women artists such as Frances Hodgkins, however, the war years were particularly difficult, and she struggled more than ever. Buying art was not the main concern of most citizens. Perhaps to keep up artistic spirits, Grace held a showing of 20 of her works at her studio in Chelsea. 'Of the eight portraits shown, the one that attracted most attention was of Miss May Hayman, daughter of Mr. Max Hayman. It was admired alike as a picture and a likeness, and the comment was made that it might have been a "Gainsborough". Another portrait which came in for much interest was that of Mr. Raymond McIntyre, the well-known New Zealand artist, who has been resident for some years in England …'[83] Grace and her Cheyne Walk neighbour Raymond McIntyre had obviously met in the ensuing years under more congenial circumstances than their fraught evening encounter at the Westminster Palace Hotel in London, when he had found her 'wandering forlornly'.

This was the year that Grace received the honour of being elected an associate of the Society of Women Artists. In return, the following year, she exhibited with them her sumptuous mother and child portrayal, *Divine Love*, which was unpriced. In time, it found its way to New Zealand and into the collection of Maurice Joel, Grace's nephew in Dunedin.

At the Royal Society of Portrait Painters' exhibition held from early June to early July 1916, Grace showed *Reflections*, which may be the same painting as the one now called *The Dressing Room*. The model, who appears to be looking at her reflection in a mirror, is wearing a pink gown; both it and mirror had appeared previously (Images 6.2 and 6.4). The work was further exhibited on two later occasions. If Image 6.16 is *Reflections*, it makes poignant, within the context of the hellish war of attrition raging in Europe, Lawrence Weschler's characterisation of the works of Vermeer as 'a zone filled with peace, a small room, an intimate vision.'[84] On 1 July when the exhibition closed, British forces sustained 58,000 casualties at the Battle of the Somme. And this was only the first day of that appalling event, which dragged on into mid-November.

In 1918, Grace was once again exhibiting at the London Salon, Grafton Galleries, this time, entering the painting *La jeunesse: Panneau decoratif* (Image 6.17). It appears that the *panneau* had been cut down from a larger-sized work. The figures are clearly posed, with the sex of the children left ambiguous, perhaps deliberately so. The child on the left has a stick propping up his or her arm in its elevated position. The device was one that artists often used during the long periods of time in which a subject had to remain still while a painting was being executed. The painting portrays three stages of youth, and its composition is daring.

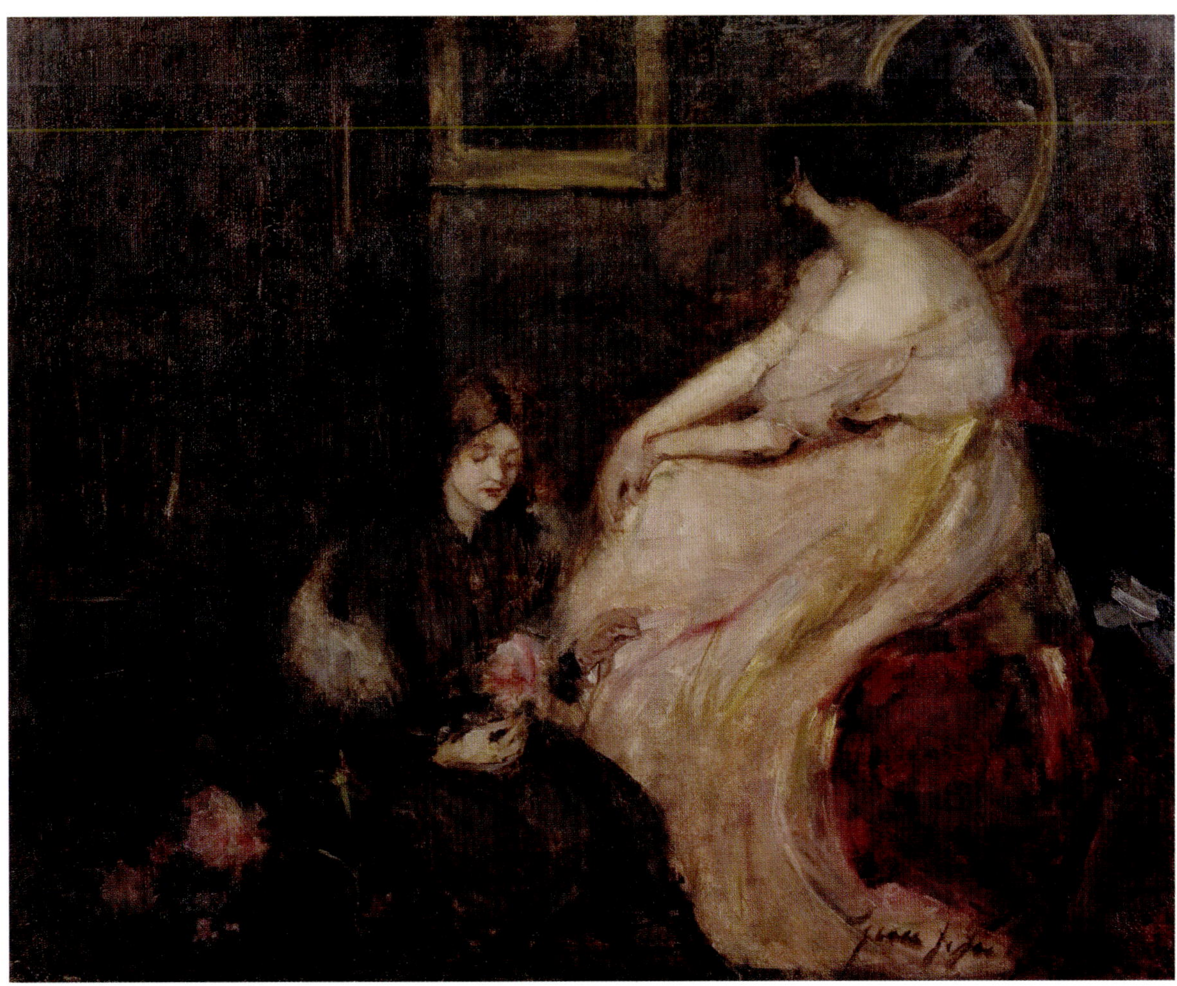

Image 6.16

Quite possibly *Reflections/The Dressing Room*, by Grace Joel, c. 1916, oil on canvas, 51 x 61 cm. The pink gown, mirror and possibly the sitter appeared in Images 6.2 and 6.4. Private collection

That same year Grace exhibited *Forebodings* with the Society of Women Artists, a title she used for a watercolour shown at the Doré in 1909. It is difficult to read anything into this title, as there is no information about the work.

Postwar Final Years

> *The world is a ghastly place for women without incomes ...* Frances Hodgkins in a letter to her mother, 13 January 1918

Shortly after the abominable war came to a halt with the signing of the Armistice of 11 November 1918, the Royal British Colonial Society of Artists, in conjunction with the newly formed Society of Australian Artists, mounted the exhibition 'War and Peace' at Burlington House under the auspices of the Royal Academy. It included the art of war painted for and lent by the Commonwealth of Australia. Grace, who had become a member of the Society of Australian Artists, exhibited *Widowed,* which is very likely the work we have encountered before. This was a most appropriate choice of painting for such an exhibition. Grace also again displayed the genteel *Reflections*, perhaps to balance out the horrors of war depicted by many of her male compatriots. Australian war artists completed more than 400 paintings between 1917 and 1919 ... lest we forget.[85]

Grace painted the luscious *Nude with Fruit* circa 1920. Australian artist and author Edith M. Fry, commenting on the painting in a 1921 article titled 'Australasian Artists in Europe', explained that the use of bright colour was due to Joel 'experimenting lately in a different vein. A study of a nude against an azure background, with some oranges in the foreground, and the portrait of a fresh-faced girl, have a brilliancy of colouring which even an advanced modernist might envy.'[86] Grace Joel at last seemed to have embarked on a more modern approach to her work. The muted palette of the past is gone, at least in this work. Matisse would have approved.

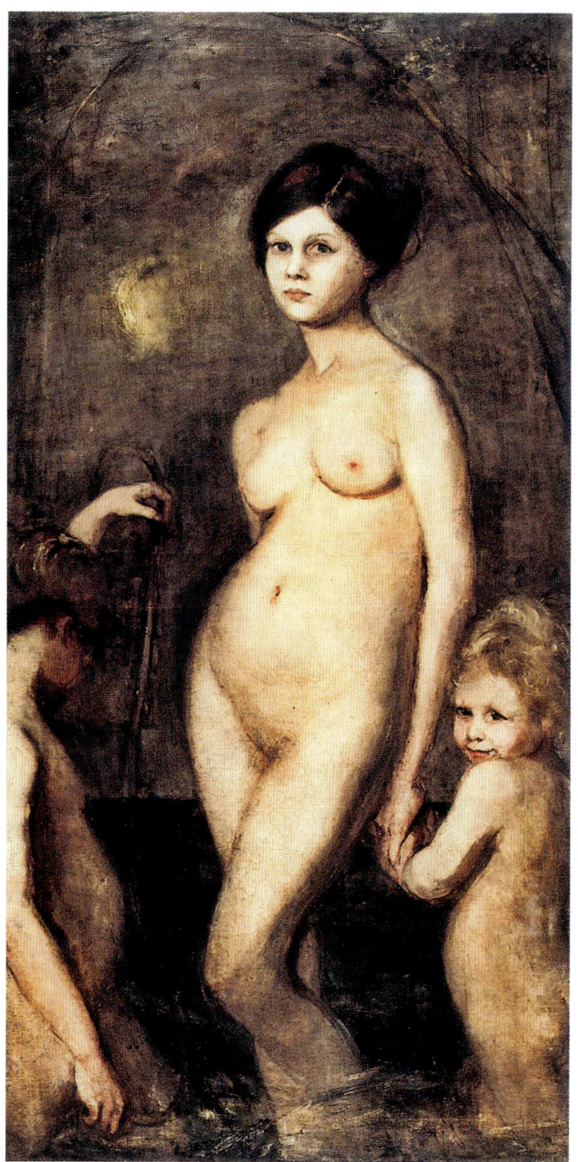

Image 6.17

***La jeunesse*, by Grace Joel, oil on canvas, 150 x 74 cm. The exhibition label on the stretcher bears the title.**

Private collection

Image 6.18 (opposite)

***Nude with Fruit*, by Grace Joel, c. 1920, oil on canvas, 102 x 75 cm. The sitter is possibly the same woman as in *Reclining Nude* (Image 6.9).** International Art Centre, Auckland

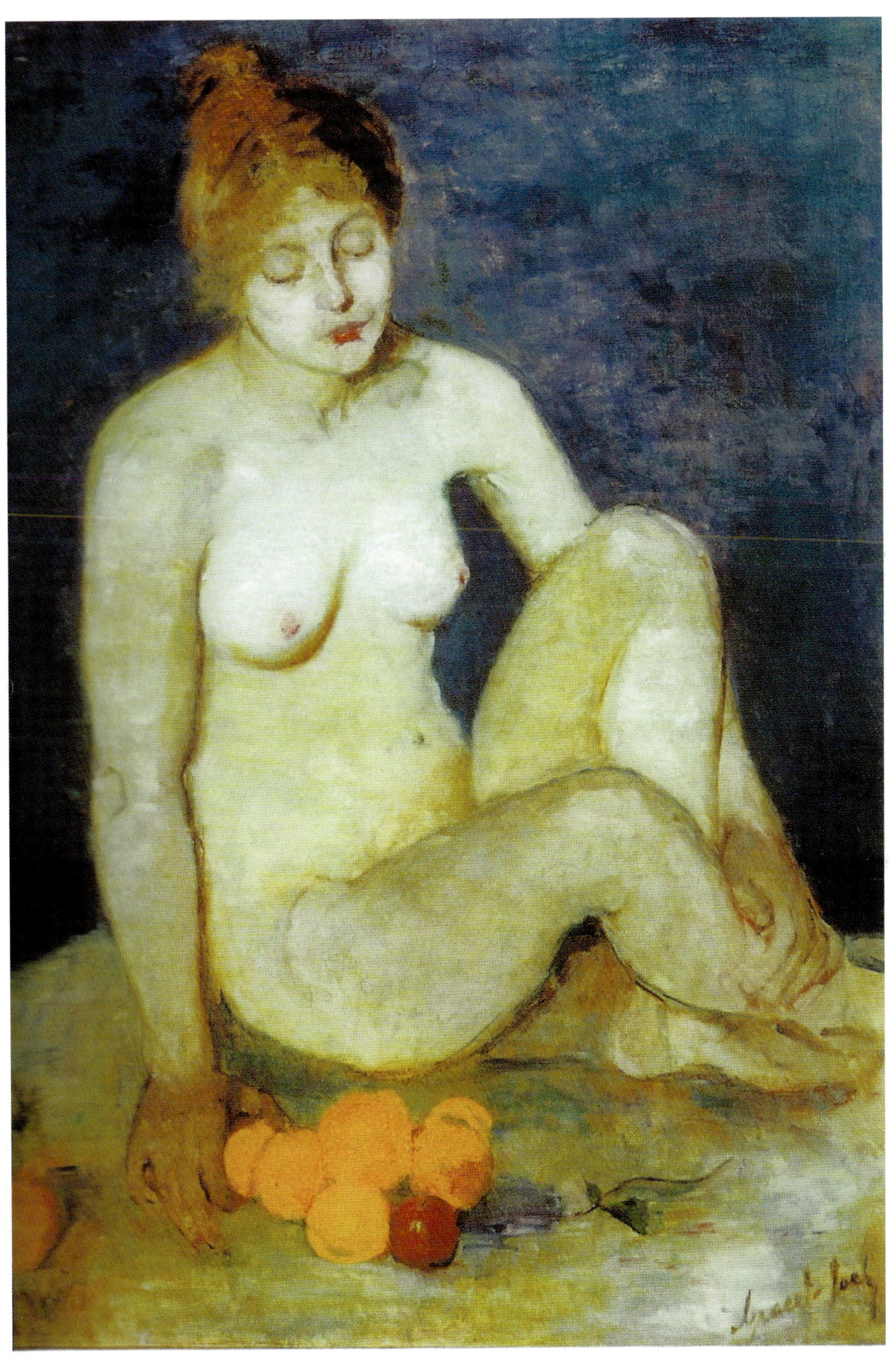

This nude was one of many that Grace Joel painted. According to Peter Entwisle, 'Her depictions of women and womanhood had a sensuality that made some critics uneasy.' Yes, this was daring territory for a woman to explore, especially in Grace Joel's time and to some extent even up to the present day.

In April 1920, members of the Society of Australian artists were out in force again with a representative showing of 91 works at Burlington House. Represented were many of Grace's London circle – George Coates and Dora Meeson Coates, John Longstaff, George Lambert and James Quinn, among others, and, of course, Grace Joel.[87] There were few war pictures, probably because people no longer wished to be reminded of its horrors. The fact that associates Arthur Streeton and Tom Roberts were in Australia at the time doubtless explains the absence of their work in the exhibition.

As painted by Frances Hodgkins some years earlier, Grace Joel's own portrayal of *Refugees* could be viewed in 1919 at the London Salon's annual showing in the Grafton Galleries, indicating that she was not oblivious to the sufferings caused by the war. However, she had not strayed permanently from her favoured themes, as the refugees were accompanied by a work titled *Sacred Love*.

In the following year, the Royal Academy accepted one of Grace's major works, *Une madonne moderne*. More works followed at the London Salon, Grafton Galleries (*Ariadne, Her Babe*), and with the Society of Women Artists (*The Pink Hat*). Although the signs were not apparent in her work at this stage, Grace seemed to be experiencing the

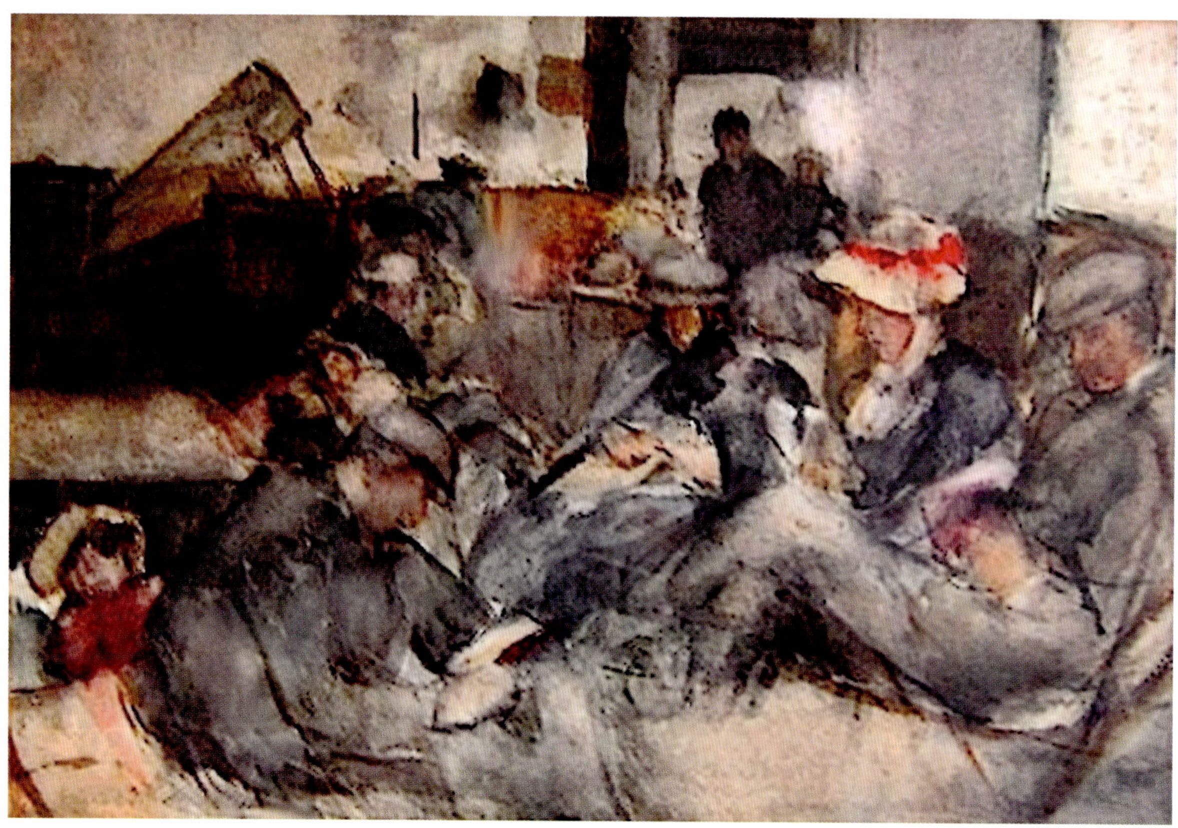

Image 6.19

A small watercolour sketch, possibly for the oil painting *Refugees*, which Grace put on sale at the 1919 London Salon for £150. The price indicates that this was a major work. Private collection

first symptoms of her impending mortality. Was her 1918 *Forebodings* an early clue? Whatever the situation was, Grace, 55 years old in 1920, drew up a will with the law firm of Aspinall and Sim of Dunedin. Ironically, the firm later became Aspinall, Joel and Hall, the Joel being the son of Grace's brother, Louis, who bore the same name as her father – Maurice Joel. Grace's sister, Blanche, who was still living in London, was the executor of the will in England; brother Louis was the executor of any New Zealand matters. Regarding her artworks:

> *I GIVE to my brother Louis the oil painting of my father which Hollyer photographed the water colour of my mother an etching by Josef Israels and the picture by J.W. North A.R.A. R.W.S. called 'A Windmill by the Sea' … I GIVE to the Sydney Gallery New South Wales (which expressed a wish to purchase one of my pictures) the portraits of Arthur Streeton and Signor G.P. Nerli (both Artists) painted by me and also the painting of Mr. Leech by the Artist Nerli I GIVE to the Melbourne National Gallery an etching signed and executed by the late Josef Israels I GIVE to the Christchurch Art Gallery (which also expressed a desire to purchase one of my works) 'A Time of Prayer' painted by me I GIVE to the Wellington Art Gallery the picture sketch water colour drawing by North A.R.A. (two subjects in one frame being a pencil sketch and a Windmill in South Wales) I GIVE to the Dominion of New Zealand representative in London the portrait of the late Right Honourable Richard Seddon to be hung in New Zealand House in London I GIVE to the Trustees of the National Gallery Melbourne Victoria FIVE HUNDRED POUNDS to found a Scholarship for the painting of the nude to be called 'The Grace Joel Scholarship' and the income thereof shall be awarded every two years alternately with the Travelling Scholarship AND I DESIRE that the principal qualities of this study of the nude shall be artistic feeling and beauty of colour and line and not technical exactness and in order to augment the said gift of Five hundred pounds …*[88]

The Grace Joel Scholarship was first awarded in 1930 with a prize of £50 and thereafter every three years until 1951. One of its notable recipients (1942) was Alan Moore, an official Australian war artist during World War II. The Grace Joel Scholarship Act of 1951, passed 'by the King's Most Excellent Majesty by and with the advice and consent of the Legislative Council and the Legislative Assembly of Victoria', allowed for minor variations in administering the will so that by 1986 the scholarship recipient received $AU500. The scholarship was awarded more than 20 times before ultimately being incorporated into The National Gallery of Victoria Art Prizes Fund, which amalgamated all the various National Gallery scholarship funds established by individuals over the years, including one bequeathed by the wife of E. Phillips Fox in honour of her husband.[89]

In addition to the bequeathed etchings by Jozef Israëls, there were also three gifted works by the 'idyllist' landscape painter John William North, an associate of the Royal Academy and member of the Royal Watercolour Society. He maintained a studio in London (as well as in Somerset and Algeria) and produced finely detailed poetical landscapes, mainly in watercolour. The English painter, G.F. Watts, who also figured in Grace Joel's life, is thought to have influenced North to take up oils, to which he applied his singular watercolour techniques.[90]

In 1916, Grace had worked in conjunction with the Dunedin Public Art Gallery to procure a watercolour landscape by North for its collection. Subscriptions for the painting's purchase were 'only being obtained from ladies', and the person charged with the obtaining in New Zealand was Mrs Arthur Fisher, better known to us as Jean Rollo-Fisher, Grace's onetime student in Dunedin.[91] One of the reasons given for purchasing such a work was that Dunedin had no watercolours by an associate of the Royal Academy, whereas Melbourne had two of North's and Sydney had one of his large oils. Colonial rivalry was obviously at play here, but in the end it came to nought, as the Dunedin Public Art Gallery never acquired the hoped-for watercolour.

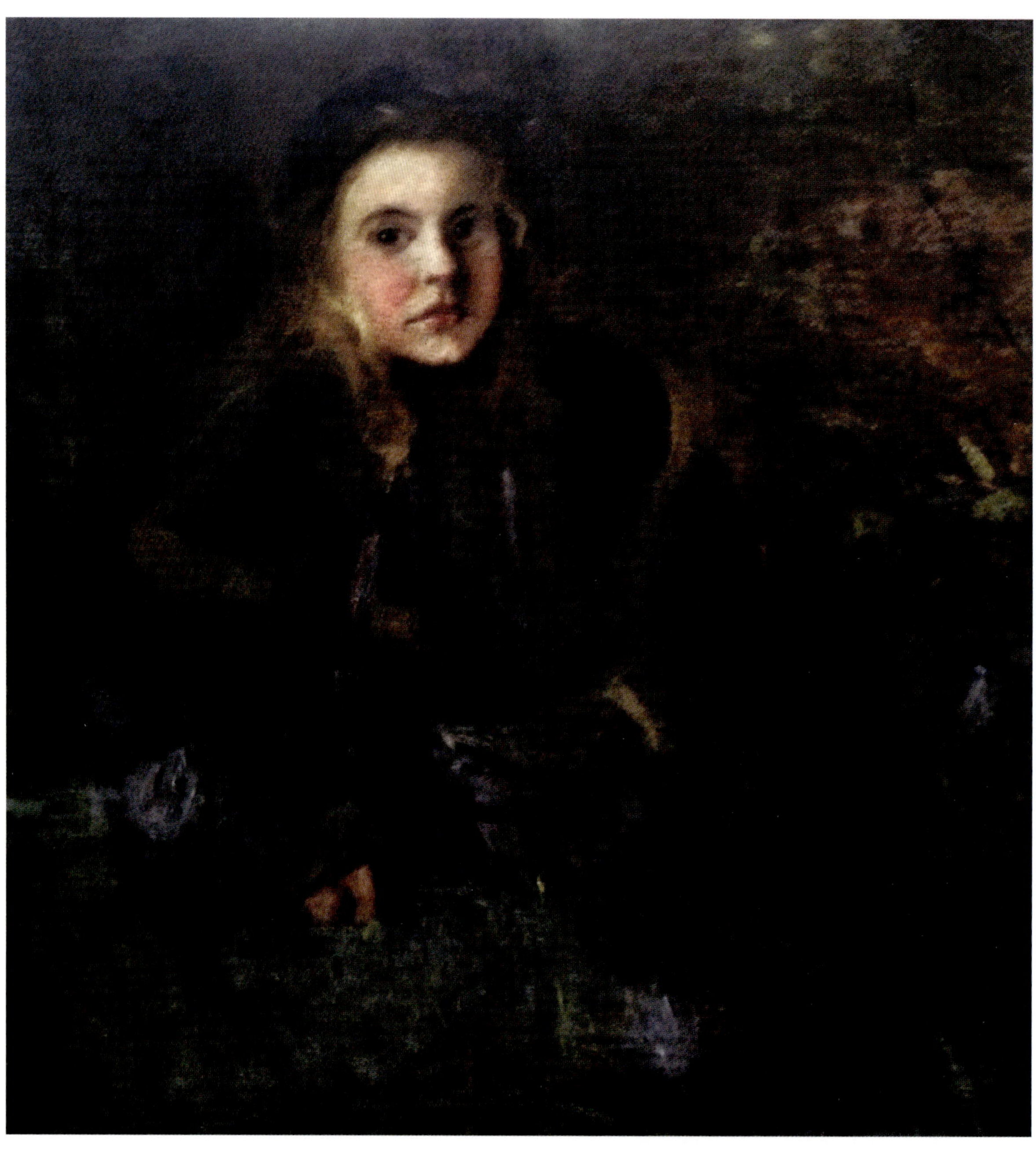

Image 6.20

Portrait of a Young Girl, by Grace Joel. This was one of her favourite themes. There is a hint of a tartan pattern in the girl's attire, which could place the painting from the early 1920s. Oil on canvas, 73 x 65 cm. Private collection

The year 1921 was the first time since the Great War that Grace had exhibited at the Paris Salon, this time with *Portrait d'un musicien*. The painting was probably the portrait (Image 6.21) of her niece, Kathleen, Blanche's daughter, as the title in English was written in Grace's hand on a visiting card attached to the back of the painting.[92] The work possesses some of the spiritual qualities of a Rembrandt. At the same time, Grace was completing a portrait of the talented violinist Gladys Chester, mentioned in the 1921 article by Edith M. Fry.

Portrait d'un musicien and its artist were singled out for special praise by noted critic, Clément Morro, in a 1921 commentary featured in *La revue moderne des arts et de la vie*:

> *There was naturally a fairly large number of portraits in this year's exhibitions ... Very few works in this genre could equal in psychological penetration the remarkable submission of Miss Grace Joel, whose Portrait of a Musician held my attention for a long time, during my visit to the latest Salon des Artistes Français.*
>
> *The melancholic grace of the face, the simplicity of the pose, the sobriety of the handling of paint, the fullness, the beautiful colour and the model's vitality, are the qualities which raise this work well above the average calibre of the portraits at the Salon.*
>
> *Indeed, Miss Grace Joel has already shown herself in her earlier works to be an artist with a very delicate taste, endowed with a remarkable sharp power of observation. A painter with a supple and varied talent, she has worked equally successfully in all the categories: portraits, landscapes, nudes, genre subjects. Her working method and her handling changing, moreover, according to the object represented.*
>
> *Among her most important and most characteristic canvases, we can note: Lights Through the River Mists, Une madonne moderne, Her Child, Autumn's Grief at the Dying Year, L'amour divin, Le grandpère d'Étaples which reminds one of Rembrandt, etc, etc ...*
>
> *As a watercolourist she has also produced exquisitely sensitive works.*[93]

The London Salon of 1921 was held at the Mansard Gallery in Tottenham Court Road. The talented Miss Joel exhibited three canvases: *In the Luxembourg*, *Le grandpère d'Étaples* and *La robe nouvelle*. Works by Picasso, Matisse and Modigliani had adorned these walls just two years earlier. Fry's article also mentions that Grace Joel was working on yet another portrait – Mrs Herbert Benjamin, of Portland Court.

In August 1921, Sir James Allen, appointed the previous year to the position of High Commissioner for New Zealand in London, invited a gathering of everyone in the arts (in the widest sense) from New Zealand to join him at his office for a spot of tea. More than 60 people turned up, including Grace Joel, Raymond McIntyre and Miss Jenny Wimperis from Dunedin days.[94] Ten months earlier, a distinguished gathering of lords, ladies, knights and captains had attended a welcoming reception for the new high commissioner that included Grace Joel but neither McIntyre nor Wimperis.[95] Because the reception was hosted by the outgoing high commissioner and his wife, Sir Thomas Mackenzie and Lady Mackenzie, with whom Grace was already well acquainted, her presence is not surprising.

In 1922 we find Grace again exhibiting her work titled *The Adored Child* (*L'enfant adorée*), this time with the Royal Scottish Academy, and also holidaying in Edinburgh with Sir James Lawton Wingate, president of the Royal Scottish Academy, and Anne, Lady Wingate. The visit (there had been several others[96]) engendered a portrait of Sir James by Joel. Grace was definitely moving within lofty circles of British society at this late stage of her life.

In March, Grace wrote to notable English artist George Clausen RA.[97] She introduced herself as a 'pupil of the late E. Phillips Fox' and also of the late Frederick McCubbin. She advised that Frederick McCubbin's students in Melbourne 'were all taught to look at your work with great reverence, and to him more than anyone else is due the sale of your works to the galleries there, as well as the

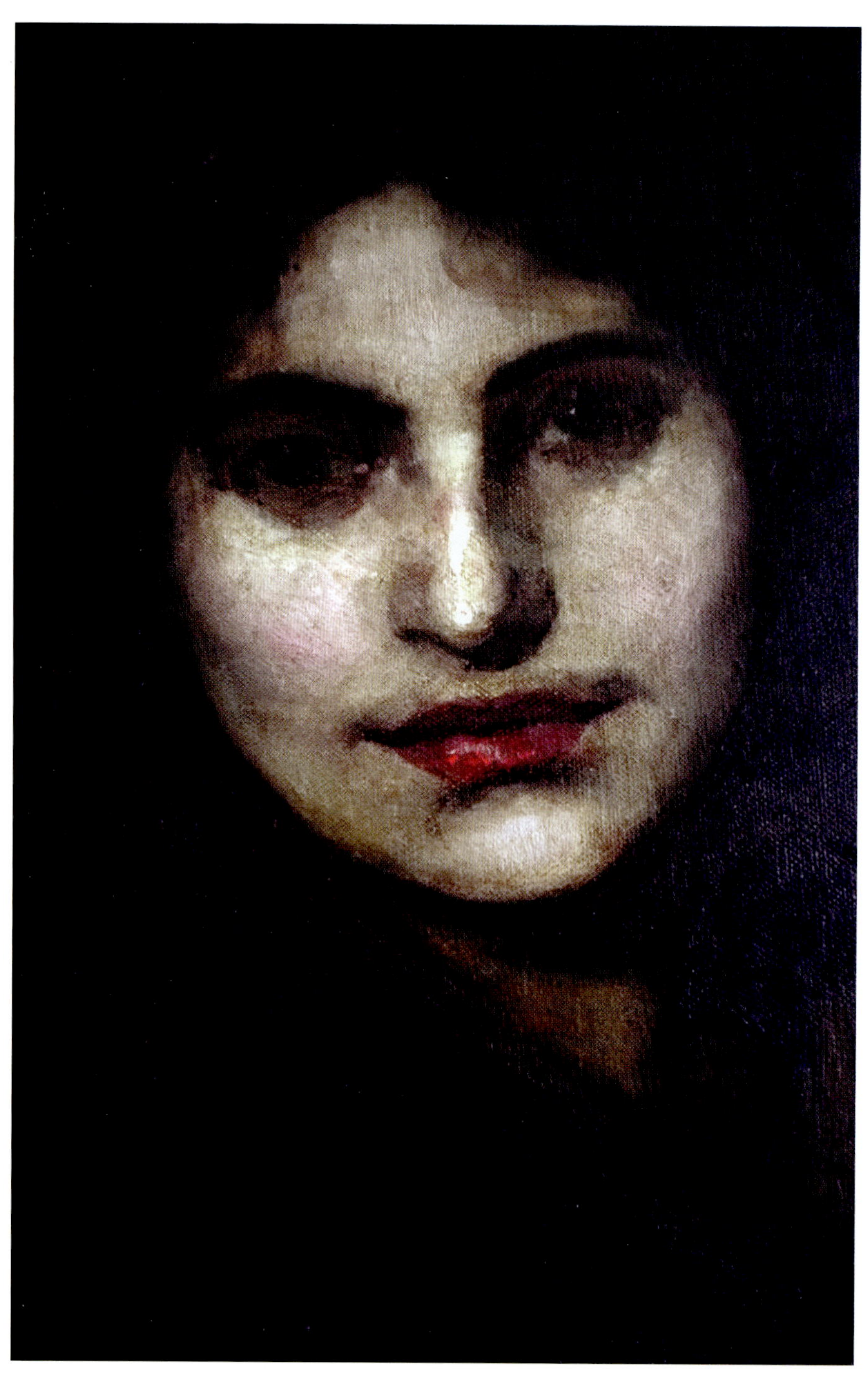

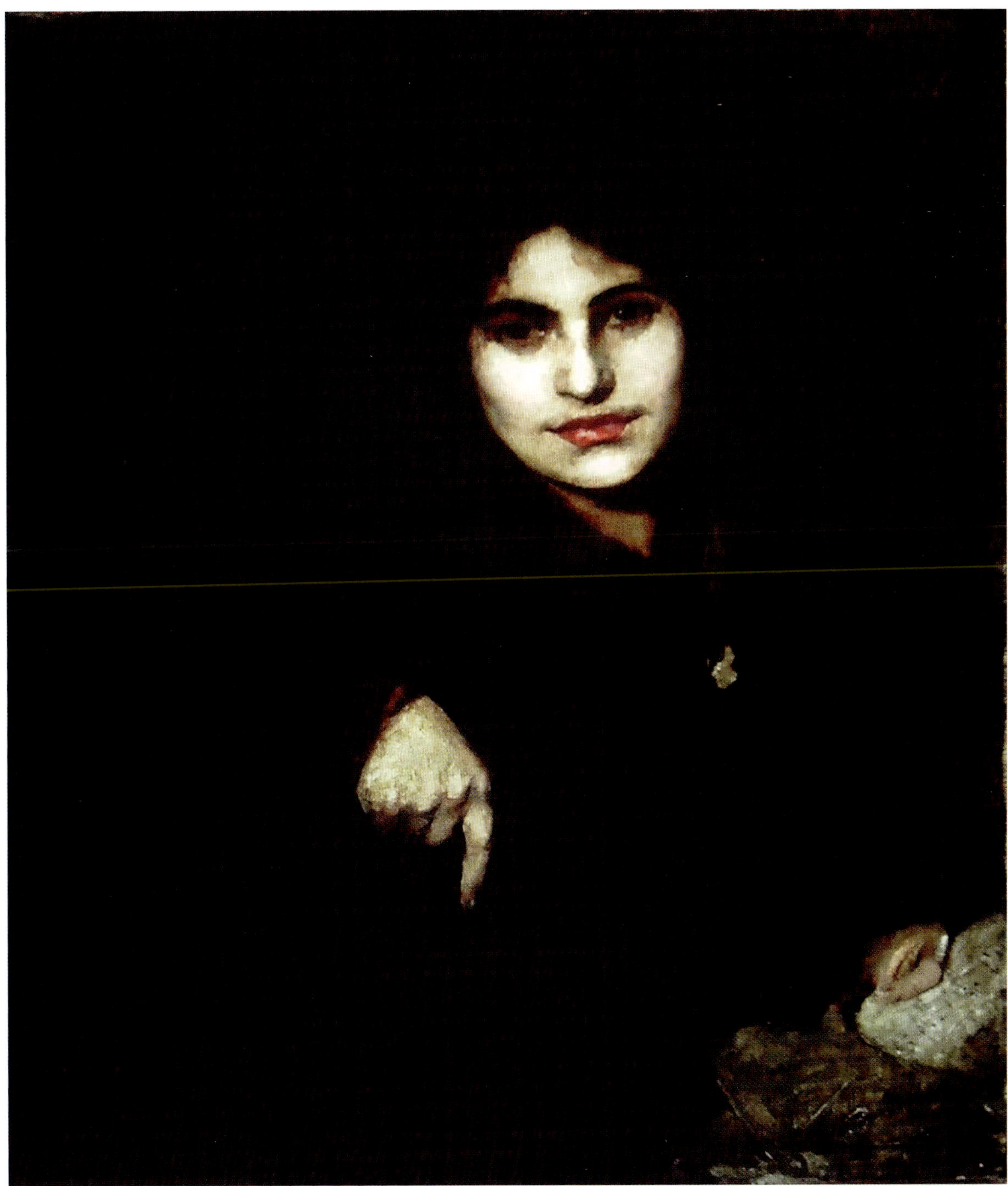

IMAGE 6.21

This *Portrait of a Musician* is of the artist's niece, Kathleen (daughter of Grace's sister Blanche), oil on canvas, 74 x 62 cm, detail at left. About the same time as Grace Joel did this painting, she painted a portrait of the violinist, Gladys Chester, but it is rather more likely this was the painting she exhibited at the 1921 Paris Salon. The Salon description in *La revue moderne* certainly fits this particular work; its title is written on the reverse side.

Private collection

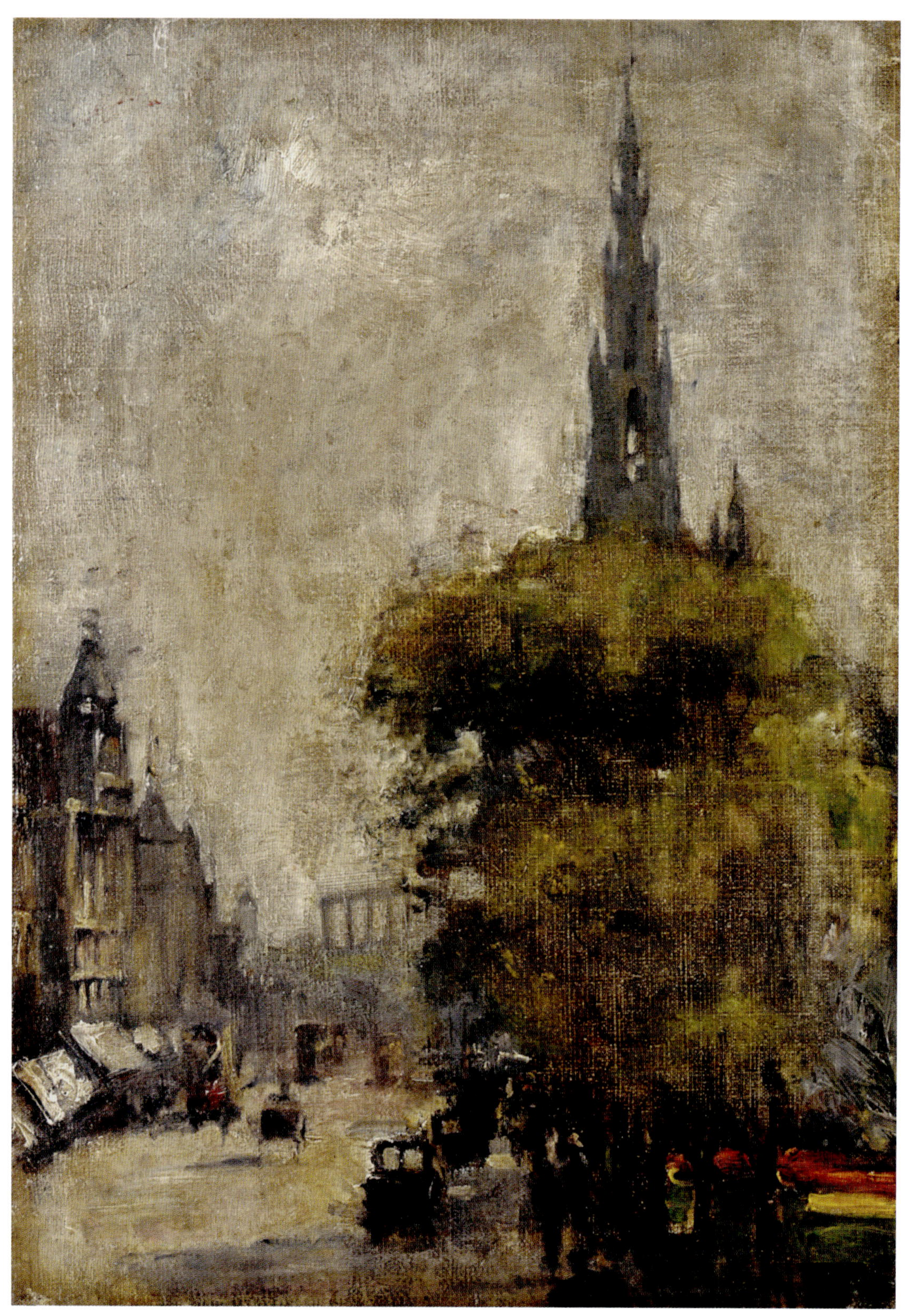

Image 6.22

***Princes Street, Edinburgh*, by Grace Joel, c. 1922, oil on canvas, 45.5 x 30 cm.** Private collection

admiration, most Australian artists have for your genius.'

If her words sound a tad sycophantic, they were intentional, as Grace wanted Clausen to put in a good word for her at the Royal Academy regarding one of her submissions – a painting of two children. She mentioned that she was going to send the painting to the Paris Salon that year, 'where I have exhibited so often'. However, she wished to send it to the academy, as 'it has twice been kept to the last & crowded out.' Grace admitted she heard that Clausen was on the selection jury and then mentioned that the late G.F. Watts, who 'thought highly of my work which he saw six weeks before his death', had promised her his support. Grace certainly understood the value of influence at the highest levels in the art world, and was trying to cultivate such, first with Watts and then Clausen, although Mary Cassatt would likely have disapproved of her efforts. Despite the Clausen letter, no Grace Joel works were exhibited at the Royal Academy that year or in the remaining two years of her life.

Another letter to Clausen followed in December on an entirely different matter, namely why Grace wished to purchase a watercolour done by Clausen. She had wanted to tell him why during the Royal Academy's prize-giving the preceding Saturday, but had not had the opportunity to do so. The explanation in her letter is long in the telling and at times vague. Her bank manager, on behalf of the sub-manager, had asked her, she told Clausen, to obtain two or three watercolours of English landscapes to take back to New Zealand. After quoting some condescending remarks by the bank manager as to whether the sub-manager would have 'sufficient appreciation to like them', Grace said that she had arranged with various notable artists to submit some of their works for consideration. Could she call on Clausen to inspect some of his works for the same purpose? She mentioned their mutual exhibiting at the Royal Scottish Academy that year and also reported having spent considerable time in the company of Sir James and Lady Wingate, painting a portrait of the former.

What are we to make of this rambling and unusual letter?[98] Why did Joel feel it necessary to narrate the details of the conversation between herself and her bank manager, especially as they were not that lucid? And the mention of her association with the Wingates? It smacks of name dropping. Perhaps a clue lies in the last line of the letter: 'I would have written before but have not been well.'

At the 1923 Paris Salon, Grace received a *mention honorable* for her work *Sympathie*. According to the *Evening Post*, she missed receiving the silver medal by two or three votes. The Australasian press widely reported this near miss, and letters of congratulations from French artists also brought her some consolation, referring 'to her picture as being original and distinguished, and as having the colouring of old masters'.[99] A candidate for this work would be Image 6.25, but this is pure speculation in the absence of any real evidence except for the sympathetic nature of the work and a possible handkerchief being held by the older child. Grace lingered in Paris, perhaps knowing that this would be her last trip there, as she was suffering from the illness that would take her life the following year.[100] Friends Dora Meeson Coates and George Coates were again exhibiting with her at the same venue.

So, too, New Zealander Sydney Thompson (1877–1973), who had three paintings on the line that year and had been accorded a *mention honorable* by the Salon the previous year. Thompson took lessons with van der Velden in Christchurch before studying in England and then Paris at the Académie Julian under Gabriel Ferrier and William-Adolphe Bouguereau. Thompson went on to have a very long and distinguished career, living in both France, principally Concarneau, where his three children were born, and in New Zealand, where he became a leading fixture of the country's art establishment. His work was very popular with the New Zealand public, and he received an OBE in 1937. Joel and Thompson would surely have been aware of each other's work, but whether their paths ever crossed is unknown.

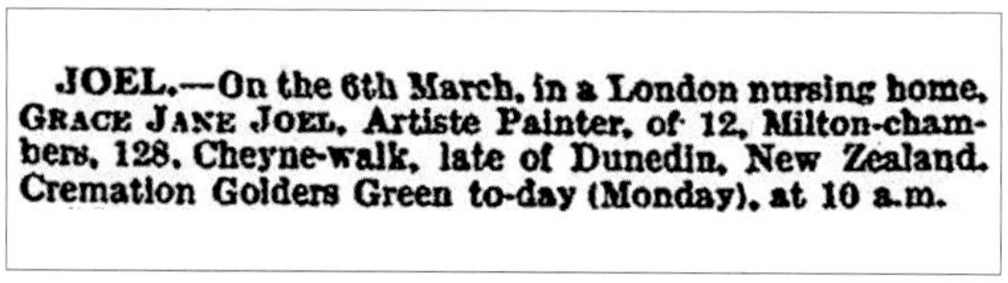

JOEL.—On the 6th March, in a London nursing home, Grace Jane Joel, Artiste Painter, of 12, Milton-chambers, 128, Cheyne-walk, late of Dunedin, New Zealand. Cremation Golders Green to-day (Monday), at 10 a.m.

Image 6.23

The Times (London) notice of 10 March 1924 of Grace Joel's death.

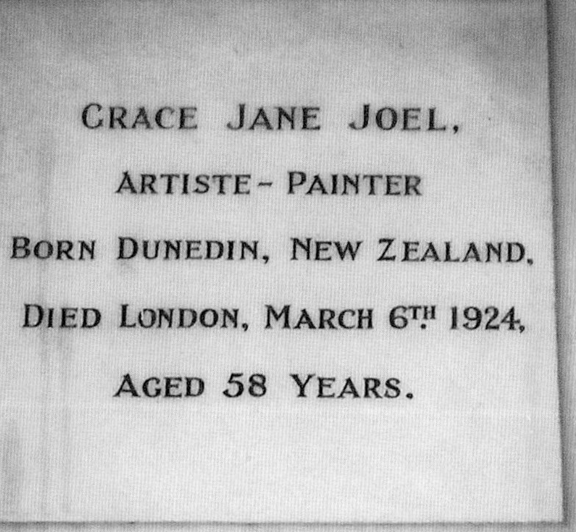

Image 6.24

The ashes of Grace Jane Joel, the 'little dark woman full of restless energy', finally came to rest in Columbarium A., Row A., No. 6, Liberal Jewish Synagogue, Willesden, London. According to Irene Levin, cemetery co-ordinator of the synagogue, the ashes are 'in a very exalted place – inside the prayer hall', in an annexe reached through a door in the hall.

On 6 March 1924 Grace Jane Joel succumbed to cancer at a London nursing home, 33 Redcliffe Gardens, which was just around the corner from her long-time residence in Cheyne Walk. 'There was genuine regret expressed down in Dunedin when cabled word came out that Grace Joel, one of our Southern Edinburgh's most gifted daughters, had been cut off just as she was mounting the ladder of success as an artist.'[101]

Upon application by her sister, Blanche, Grace was cremated at Golders Green Crematorium.[102] However, unlike the remains of Sigmund Freud and Anna Pavlova, which remained at Golders Green, Grace Joel's finally came to rest a few miles distant at the Liberal Jewish Cemetery in Willesden. Traditionally, Judaism did not approve of cremations, but among the more liberal elements of the faith it had become an accepted practice as a practical solution to the lack of available space. Grace does not appear to have been a member of the synagogue that is associated with the cemetery. Interred next door in the Willesden (Orthodox) Jewish Cemetery in the more traditional manner with grave site and head stone is Sir Julius Vogel in the company of a swathe of Rothschild family members. So whatever the relative relationship between the Joel and Vogel families is, two of their respective members rest in close proximity for all eternity.

Before her death, Grace sent one final work to the Paris Salon. The catalogue entry read: 'Joel (Mlle Grace-Jane), née en Nouvelle-Zélande, élève de MM. Baschet et Schommer. – Á Londres, 12, Milton Chambers, 128, Cheyne Walk, SW10. 1050 – *La première séance*.' The title is telling.

One criticism of Grace Joel's *oeuvre* is that she never really changed her style to suit the changing times as did her more well-known compatriot, Frances Hodgkins. The latter embraced Post-Impressionism when it came along, and moved her work through several transformations. Grace was aware of this need to progress, for she wrote:

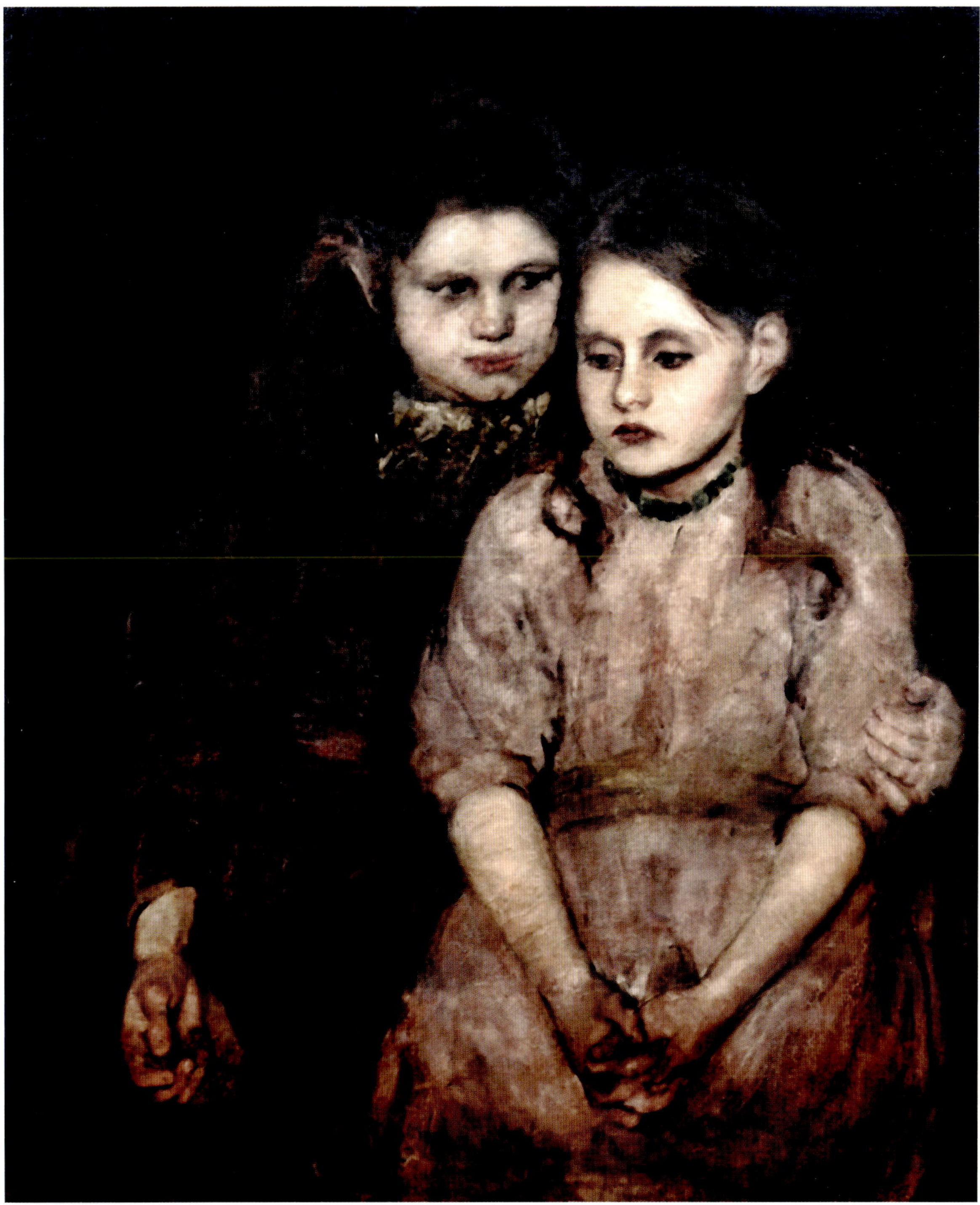

IMAGE 6.25

This work is most likely either *Enfants sans mère* or *Sympathie*, each having been exhibited at the Paris Salon in 1908 and 1923, respectively. The older child is holding what appears to be a handkerchief in her right hand. Oil on canvas, 91 x 72 cm. Private collection

'The wish to go further does not always show, but without that struggle one goes back; one does not stand still.'[103] But then, there was another painter whose works lost their popularity in his own lifetime because he refused to change his technique. His name was Rembrandt van Rijn.

Chacun à son goût.

It has often been said that Grace Joel and her works have never received the attention and credit they deserve. In 1979, long-serving Dunedin city councillor, Maurice Joel, penned a two-page biographical note on his aunt Grace: 'She affected to be indifferent to any reputation in her native land … One would not however be unjustified in saying at least that her general artistic achievement was of a very high order and that New Zealanders should be much more fully aware of her work.'

Perhaps this longstanding injustice has now been somewhat redressed, such that at long last Grace Joel can step out of the broad shadow cast by her contemporary, Frances Hodgkins. Even so, a great many known unknowns about this artist and her work remain, including the whereabouts of some of her finest paintings. And of the many unknown unknowns? About those, we can only muse.

Appendices

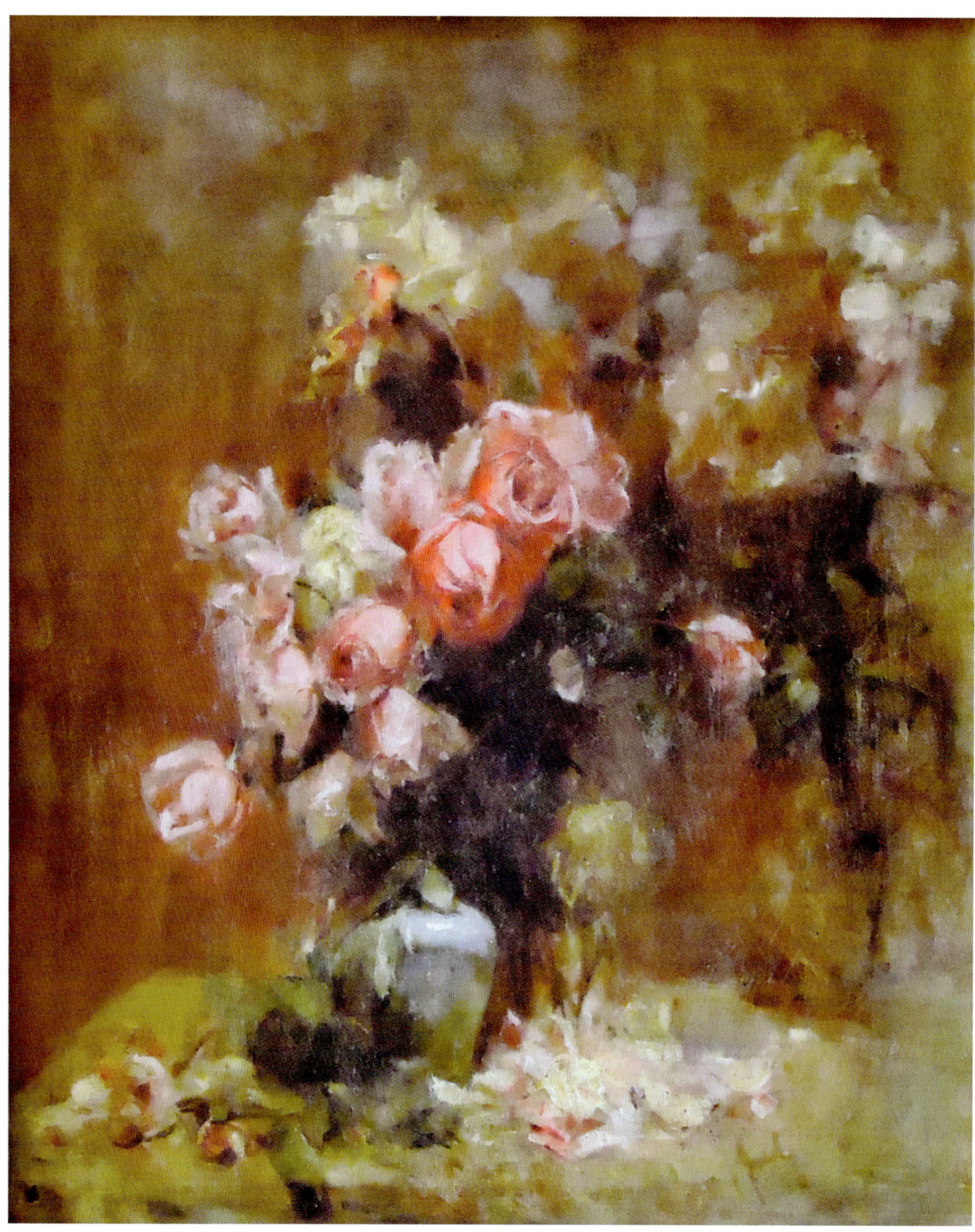

Untitled, undated painting by Grace Joel. Private collection

Appendix A

Exhibitions

Looking at paintings, then, is not a matter of finding something to impress the guests, or match the curtains, or increase in value at 18% per annum; it's a search for things worth hanging on the walls of your imagination – Justin Paton, 2008

1886

Annual exhibition, Otago Art Society, Dunedin

55 *Portrait* [unpriced]

79 *Portrait* [unpriced]

1887

Annual exhibition, Otago Art Society, Dunedin

123 *Spring*

134 *Marguerite*

141 *The Lovers' Walk* [£6-6]

142 *Peonies* [£5-5]

150 *Portrait*

197 *Prize Fruit*

236 *Trumpet Lilies*

245 *En Route for the High School* [£8-8]

1888

Annual exhibition, Canterbury Society of Arts, Christchurch

13 *Grannie's Pet* [£8-8]

1890

Annual exhibition, Otago Art Society, Dunedin

32 *Portrait*

39 *Study of Child's Head* [£2-2]

58 *Under the Spell* [£12] [reproduced in the catalogue]

67 *God Knows Best* [£30]

68 *A Literary Aspirant (An Impression)* [£3]

111 *Oh Memories! Oh Past that is!* [£15]

154 *Old Man's Head* [charcoal drawing, first prize, Melbourne Public Library, 1889]

1891

Eighth annual exhibition of paintings by the students of the National Gallery, under the direction of F. McCubbin, Melbourne

40 *Roses* [£5-5]

41 *Head* [£3-3]

42 *Study* [£2-2]

1894

Annual exhibition, Otago Art Society, Dunedin

61 *A Girl's Head* [£7-7]

75 *Portrait*

81 *Portrait*

290 *An Outcast* [watercolour] [£2-2]

1895

Annual exhibition, Canterbury Society of Arts, Christchurch

1 *Poppies* [£10]

7 *Head* [£10]

14 *Head* [£10-10]

18 *Grief* [£40]

50 *A Captive* [£30]

78 *Youth* [£35]

Annual exhibition, New Zealand Academy of Fine Arts, Wellington
96 *Roses* [unpriced]
180 *Grief* [£40]
183 *Gipsy* [£2-2]

Annual exhibition, Otago Art Society, Dunedin
13 *A Study* [£5-5]
23 *Little Nell* [£10]
30 *A Study* [£10-10]
43 *Roses* [£6]
55 *Aweary* [£10]
62 *An Impression of Golden Autumn* [£2]
78 *Sunlight and Shade* [£1-10]
87 *A Study on a Sunny Day* [£1-10]
103 *Harmony in Blue and Yellow* [£8]
125 *Poppies* [£5]
175 *Gipsy* [£2-2]
280 *Clay Model, Girl's Head*

1896

Annual exhibition, Auckland Society of Artists
27 *Youth* [£20]
33 *A Gipsy* [£3-3]
41 *Muriel* [£7-7]
50 *Grief* [£20]

Annual exhibition, Canterbury Society of Arts, Christchurch
16 *Little Nell*
70 *A Study*
80 *Shy*
207 *Study* [£15]
229 *Roses* [£7]
233 *A New Model* [£5-5]

Annual exhibition, New Zealand Academy of Fine Arts, Wellington
165 *A Captive* [£20]
169 *A Portrait* [unpriced]
177 *A Study* [£5-5]

Spring exhibition, Society of Artists, Sydney
25 *Muriel* [£7]
56 *Youth* [£20]
87 *Bess* [NFS]

Annual exhibition, Otago Art Society, Dunedin
13 *'The Dead, Dead Past is Gone; The Present –'* [£10]
21 *Portrait*
32 *A Rose 'midst Poppies* [£10]
48 *A Study* [£5]
60 *Between Faith And Knowledge* [£20]
75 *A Summer Evening* [£3]
99 *Evening* [£2]
109 *Home for the Holidays* [£15]
123 *'A vague unrest,/A nameless longing seiz'd her breast:/A wish, she hardly dared to own,/For something better than she had known'* [£10]
150 *A New Model* [£3]
155 *A Grey Afternoon* [£2]

Exhibition, South Canterbury Art Society, Timaru
26 *'The Dead Dead Past is Gone; The Present …'* [£10-10]
83 *A Rose 'midst Poppies* [£10]
95 *Girl in Blue* [unpriced]
96 *Head* [£5-5]
185 *A Summer Morning* [unpriced]
187 *Portrait* [unpriced]
201 *A Grey Afternoon* [unpriced]

1897

Annual exhibition, Canterbury Society of Arts, Christchurch
55 *'The Dead Dread [sic] Past is Gone, The Present –'* [£15-15]
61 *An Evening Idyll* [£3-3]
85 *Study* [£10-10]

Annual exhibition, Auckland Society of Artists
[Received too late for cataloguing]
A Rose 'midst Poppies
Our Father Which Art in Heaven
An Old Colonist

Annual exhibition, New Zealand Academy of Fine Arts, Wellington
174 *A Head* [£5-5]
180 *An Evening Idyll* [£3-3]
183 *Youth* [£20]
184 *The Close of a Grey Day* [£3-3]

Spring exhibition, Society of Artists, Sydney

23 *A dead, dead past is gone. A present is* [sic] [£15-15]

24 *An Old Colonist* [£5-5]

33 *Monthly Roses* [£7-7]

Annual exhibition, Otago Art Society, Dunedin

11 *Youth* [£20]

27 *Only We Two* [£10]

44 *Little Lily* [£3-3]

46 *Tired* [£3-3]

49 *Mitherless Bairns* [£2]

67 *A Summer Evening at St. Clair* [£3]

70 *An Evening Idyll* [£3]

75 *'Our Father which art in Heaven'* [£10]

95 *'Give Sorrow Words: The grief that does not speak/Whispers the o'er fraught heart and bids it break'* [£100]

109 *Beauty's Eyes* [£7]

114 *Yellow Sunbonnet* [£5]

238 *Primroses* [£7]

1898

Annual exhibition, Victorian Artists' Society, Melbourne

17 *A Girl in Brown* [unpriced]

48 *Between Faith and Knowledge* [£20]

57 *Study of a Head* [£10-10]

Otago Jubilee Industrial Exhibition, Dunedin

A Jolly Holiday

A Morning Idyll

Yellow Sunbonnet

Portrait of Mr E.B. Cargill [Mayor of Dunedin]

Study of an Interior

Annual exhibition, Otago Art Society, Dunedin

26 *My Sister and I* [£2-2]

30 *With the Past* [£7-7]

32 *A Quiet Holiday* [£3-3]

35 *The Close of a Sultry Summer's Day, St. Clair* [£7-7]

84 *She Pined in Thought* [£7-7]

126 *Rough Weather* [£2-2]

135 *Sweet Seventeen* [£10]

1900

Canterbury Jubilee Industrial Exhibition, Christchurch

275 *Little Nell* [Lent by G.H. Elliott]

1901

Société des Artistes Français, Paris

1095 *Son enfant* [This work was reproduced as a line-drawing on page 158 of an illustrated edition of the catalogue, a matter of some distinction]

1902

British Colonial Art Exhibition, London

A painting representing 'Maternity' plus unknown others

Exhibition, John Baillie Gallery, London

Marketing, Étaples

Four unknown others

Annual exhibition, Otago Art Society, Dunedin

4 *When the Sun goeth down* [£5-5]

7 *An Eavesdropper* [£6-6]

63 *Saint Tasie* [£12-12]

1903

Société des Artistes Français, Paris

981 *Le retour par le sentier crayon* [sic; should be *crayeux*]

Autumn exhibition, John Baillie Gallery, London

1 *Harmony in Blue & Yellow* [£5-5]

2 *The Little Dancer* [£3-3]

3 *Marketing, Étaples* [£7-7]

4 *Le grandpère* [£21]

5 *In the Garden of the Luxembourg* [£5-5]

6 *Monthly Roses* [£7-7]

7 *The Day is Done* [£157-10]

8 *Spinning* [£3-3]

9 *Moonlight and Sheep* [£6-6]

10 *Eleanor, Daughter of Hilaire Belloc, Esq.* [Lent by Hilaire Belloc, Esq.]

11 *Mrs Yeatman Woolf* [Lent by Yeatman Woolf, Esq.]

12 *Her Child* [Ex Salon 1901 as *Son enfant*] [£84]
13 *Evening* [£3-3]
14 *Household Cares* [£4-4]
15 *Homeward Bound by the Chalky Path* [Ex Salon 1903 as *Le retour par le sentier crayon* (sic)] [£42]
16 *When the Sun is Down* [£2-2]
17 *The Dispute* [£3-3]
18 *Dawn* [£5-5]
19 *A Dutch Woman* [£50]
20 *Spring* [£5-5]
21 *Harvesting Time* [£4-4]
22 *Mrs Maurice Joel* [NFS]
23 *Weary* [£2-2]
24 *Evening at the Old Farm* [£31-10]
25 *Baby*
26 *The Culprit* [£3-3]
27 *On the Thames* [£21]
28 *Solitude* [£2-2]
29 *Prinzengracht, The Hague* [£3-3]
30 *Westminster* [£3-3]
31 *Anchored* [£2-2]
32 *A Miniature* [Lent by Mrs Yeatman Woolf]
33 *A Drawing*

1905

Society of Women Artists Jubilee Exhibition, London
436 *Her Child* [Ex Salon as *Son enfant*] [£100]

Société des Artistes Français, Paris
1012 *Hollandaise*

Carfax Gallery, London
One of the pictures now on exhibition at the Carfax Gallery, London, has for its subject a Dutch woman. The artist is Miss Grace Joel, and the picture was painted last year when the talented Dunedin lady spent some little time in Holland. I hear it is very well spoken of by visitors to the Carfax Gallery. (*Otago Daily Times*, 13 October 1905, p. 2; datelined London 9 September)

Annual exhibition, Otago Art Society, Dunedin
89 *Westminster, Early Winter's Evening* [£4-10]
121 *The Usual Meal, Holland* [£10-10]
143 *The Truant* [£4-4]
163 *A French Beggar Boy* [£5-5]

1906

Vickery's Chambers, Sydney
A Time of Prayer (Ex Salon 1905 as *Hollandaise*]
Her Child [Ex Salon 1901]
Sketch-portrait of Sir John Cockburn
The Day is Done
Lights through the River Mists
Arthur Streeton – a sketch-portrait
Marketing, Étaples
A Dream of Spring
Saint Tasie
Evening at the Old Farm
Homeward Bound by the Chalky Path [(Ex Salon 1903]
In the Luxembourg
Battersea-bridge on a Foggy Morning
Dawn
Possibly others ...

Upper Athenaeum Hall Exhibition, Melbourne
Her Child [Ex Salon 1901]
Homeward Bound by the Chalky Path [Ex Salon 1903]
A Time of Prayer [Ex Salon 1905]
Trafalgar Square [sold]
Marlborough Road, St John's Wood [sold]
Who's Calling [sold]
The Dying Year [sold]
Battersea-bridge on a Foggy Morning
Evening at the Old Farm
Portrait of Sir John Cockburn
Portrait of Maurice Joel
The Beaten Path of Years
The Day is Done
Their Daily Meal
Saint Tasie
One of London's Many
Possibly others ...

Annual Exhibition, Victorian Artists' Society, Melbourne
27 *Falling of the Leaf* [£15-15]
71 *A French Beggar Boy* [£10-10]

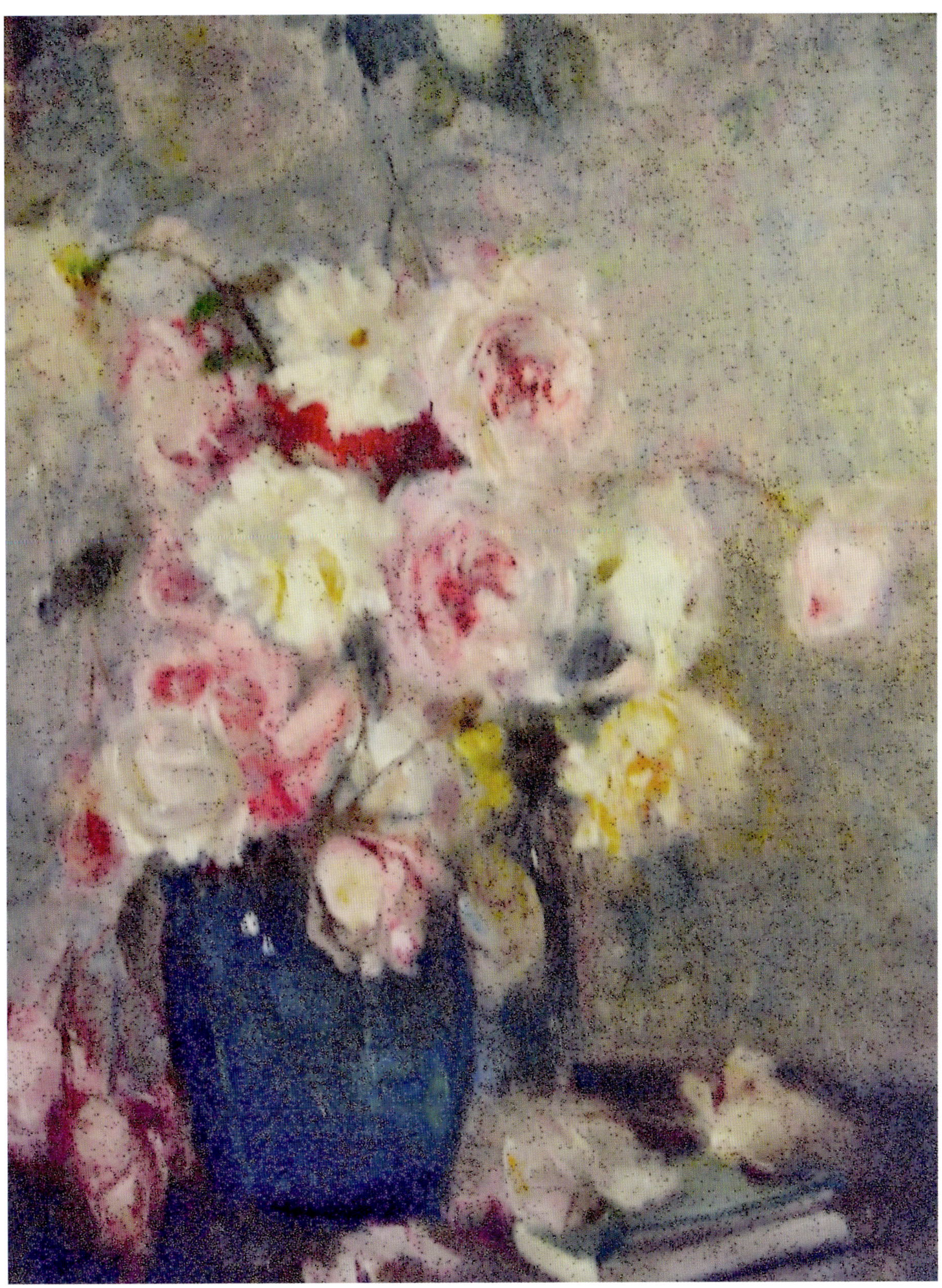

Untitled, undated painting by Grace Joel. Private collection

Choral Hall, Dunedin – exhibition of 44 pictures
Her Child [Ex Salon 1901]
Homeward Bound by the Chalky Path [Ex Salon 1903]
A Time of Prayer [Ex Salon 1905]
The Day is Done
Sketch Portrait of Arthur Streeton
Portrait of Sir John Cockburn
Evening at the Old Farm
The French Beggar Boy [sold, along with several others]
Eileen
Saint Tasie
Lights through the River Mists
Dawn
Moonlight and Sheep
Night by Moonlight
The Sun Goeth Down
Others …

Annual exhibition, Otago Art Society, Dunedin
40 *Portrait, Dr Hocken* [unpriced]
60 *A Dutch Maiden* [£3]
67 *The Culprit* [£4]
93 *Among the Flowers* [£75]
100 *Sunrise on the Thames* [£3]
112 *The Apple Gatherers* [£10]
119 *The Primrose Dell* [£8]

1907

Annual exhibition, Canterbury Society of Arts, Christchurch
24 *A Little Belle of Naples* [unpriced]
63 *The Eavesdropper* [£4-4]
137 *The Culprit* [£4-4]

Annual exhibition, New Zealand Academy of Fine Arts, Wellington
195 *A Little Belle, Naples* [unpriced]
271 *My Lady Disdain*
274 *The Eavesdropper* [£4-4]
282 Unknown [?]

1908

Exhibition of the British Art Gallery & Royal British-Colonial Society of Artists, London, held in Melbourne
145 *Roses* [£21]

Royal Academy, London
490 *Autumn*

Société des Artistes Français, Paris
922 *Le grandpère d'Étaples*
923 *Enfants sans mère*

London Salon, Royal Albert Hall
910 *The Day is Done* [£200]
911 *A Time of Prayer* [£150]
912 *Motherhood* [£80]
913 *Portrait* [sketch] [£5]
914 *Summer* [sketch for] [£5]

Royal Society of Portrait Painters Exhibition, London
20 *Mdlle. la Comtesse de M.*

Thirty-Eighth Autumn Exhibition of Modern Art, Walker Art Gallery, Liverpool
81 *Her Child* [Ex Salon 1901] [£150]

1909

International Society of Sculptors, Painters and Gravers, London
Mother and Child

The Doré Galleries, London
[Prices in guineas]
1 *When the Sun Goeth Down* [8]
2 *Mitherless Bairns* [Ex Salon 1908 as *Enfants sans mère*] [15]
3 *Portrait of Mdlle. la Comtesse de M.* [Ex Society of Portrait Painters 1908] [NFS]
4 *Roses* [15]
5 *Hyde Park (Summer)* [6]
6 *Widowed* [Ex International 1909 as *Mother and Child*] [100]
7 *The Day is Done* [200]
8 *The Hon. Sir John Cockburn KCMG, MD* [NFS]

9 *Evening at Durham* [6]
10 *Spring's Touch Bringeth Joy* [70]
11 *A Jolly Holiday* [6]
12 *Une madonne moderne* [70]
13 *When all the World is Young* [5]
14 *Autumn's Grief at the Dying Year* [ex-Royal Academy 1908 as *Autumn*] [80]
15 *Le grandpère d'Étaples* [Ex Salon 1908] [50]
16 *The Child and the Poppies* [10]
17 *The Road to Caterham* [6]
18 *Mrs Yeatman Woolf* [Lent]
19 *The Rest in the Shade* [6]
20 *Homeward Bound by the Chalky Path* [Ex Salon 1903] [70]
21 *Roses* [12]
22 *Summer* [sketch for] [5]
23 *The Hague, Princessen Gracht* [5]
24 *Her Child* [Ex Salon 1901] [125]
25 *Battersea Bridge from Cheyne Walk* [7]
26 *An Impression of Trafalgar Square in Fog* [6]
27 *Colonel Pitman, RA* [Lent]
28 *A Time of Prayer* [Ex Salon 1905] [125]
29 *Constance on Hearing the Death of her Son Arthur ('I am not mad, etc')* [10]
30 *In the Garden of the Luxembourg* [15]
31 *View of Westminster* [5]
32 *Orpheus and Eurydice* [6]
33 *Evening at the Old Farm* [70]
34 *Lowestoft* [5]
35 *Étaples (Market Place)* [6]
36 *Kate (Daughter of Mr. Albert Woolf)* [Lent]
37 *Preparing the Daily Meal* [7]
38 *Miss Dorothy Eliot*
39 *French Shrimp Gatherers* [7]
40 *Baby's Kiss* [12]
41 *The Day is Done* [sketch for] [6]
42 *Lights Through the River Mists* [20]
43 *Mending the Nets* [7]
44 *St. Clair Baths, New Zealand* [10]
45 *When the World is Old* [10]
45a *Miss C. Batchelor* [Lent]

WATERCOLOURS
46 *Trafalgar Square* [10]
47 *Two Little Waifs* [6]
48 *The Picture Book* [6]
49 *And God Loves Little Children* [6]
50 *Purple and Gold* [7]
51 *Forebodings* [20]
52 *Roses* [5]
53 *At the Seaside* [6]
54 *Notre Dame at Sunset* [4]
55 *Evening Near Westminster*

The Goupil Gallery, London
23/26 *Trafalgar Square in Autumn* [£12-12]

Société des Artistes Français, Paris
961 *Veuvage*
[?] *Présage* [watercolour]

The London Salon, Royal Albert Hall
206 *Evening at the Old Farm* [£80]
207 *Sketch Portrait of George Coates* [NFS]
208 *Roses* [£20]

Royal Society of Portrait Painters, London
214 *Miss Kitty Bridges*

1910
Société des Artistes Français, Paris
1037 *La Légende*

The Royal Institute of Oil Painters Exhibition, London
91 *'I want my Mummy'* [£15]

1911
International Society of Sculptors, Painters and Gravers, London
Le grandpère d'Étaples

Société des Artistes Français, Paris
1004 *La fleur écarlate*

1912
Société des Artistes Français, Paris
956 *L'amour maternel*

1913

Société des Artistes Français, Paris
969 *L'enfant adorée*

The Royal Institute of Oil Painters Exhibition, London
28 *The Adored Child* [Ex Salon 1913 as *L'enfant adorée*] [£95]

1914

Société des Artists Français, Paris
1088 *Une madonne moderne*

Royal Society of Portrait Painters Exhibition, London
165 *Mrs Bridges and Kitty*

1915

Royal Academy, London
657 *Divine Love*

National Portrait Society Exhibition, London
150 *Mrs Bridges and Kitty*

1916

National Portrait Society, Grosvenor Gallery, London
118 *Mabel D.* [Mabel Dunham]

Royal Society of Portrait Painters Exhibition, London
125 *Reflections*

Collection of works by Australian artists loaned to the trustees by Sir W. Baldwin Spencer, KCMG, FRS, Melbourne University, National Gallery
130 *The Truant*

Society of Women Artists Exhibition, London
182 *Roses*
585 *The Picture Book*

1917

Society of Women Artists Exhibition, London
237 *Divine Love*

National Portrait Society, Grosvenor Gallery, London
125 *Ethel*

1918

London Salon, Grafton Galleries
89 *La jeunesse: Panneau decoratif* [£150]

Society of Women Artists Exhibition, London
30 *Forebodings* [£21]

Royal British Colonial Society of Artists & Exhibition: 'War and Peace'
32 *Widowed*
83 *Reflections*

1919

National Portrait Society, Grosvenor Gallery, London
79 *Portrait of a Musician*

London Salon, Grafton Galleries
67 *Refugees* [£150]
68 *Sacred Love* [£150]

Society of Women Artists Exhibition, London
100 *Reflections* [£150]

1920

Society of Australian Artists, Burlington Galleries
Unknown work(s)

Royal Academy, London
109 *Une madonne moderne*

Royal Scottish Academy, Edinburgh
261 *Divine Love*

London Salon, Grafton Galleries
80 *Ariadne* [£150]
81 *Her Babe* [£100]

Society of Women Artists Exhibition, London
560 *The Pink Hat* [£100]

1921

Société des Artistes Français, Paris
1040 *Portrait d'un musicien* [sic]

London Salon, The Mansard Gallery
107 *In the Luxembourg* [£30]
108 *Le grandpère d'Étaples* [£100]
109 *La robe nouvelle* [£20]

1922

Royal Scottish Academy Exhibition, Edinburgh
328 *The Adored Child* [Ex Salon 1913 as *L'enfant adorée*] [£200]

1923

Société des Artistes Français, Paris
926 *Sympathie* [*Mention honorable*]

1924

Société des Artistes Français, Paris
1050 *La première séance*

Number of Works Exhibited

Britain

J. Johnson and A. Greutzner, *The Dictionary of British Artists 1880–1940*, indicate that Grace Joel exhibited the following number of works in Britain between 1903 and 1922:
Baillie Gallery, 33
Goupil Gallery, 1
Walker Art Gallery, Liverpool, 1
London Salon, 14
Royal Society of Portrait Painters, 4
Royal Academy, 3
Royal Institute of Oil Painters, 2
Royal Scottish Academy, 2
Society of Women Artists, 4 (by my count from the preceding list of exhibited works, the SWA number here should be 7).
The 56 paintings that Grace exhibited in 1909 at the Doré Galleries, London, have been mistakenly omitted. A few others from 1902 are mentioned above.

France

Société des Artistes Français, Paris, 15

Number Exhibited in Total (including posthumous exhibitions)

Well in excess of 400 paintings by Grace Joel were shown at formal public exhibitions, but many were displayed more than once. The 49 works catalogued for the 1980/81 exhibition, 'Grace Joel: Paintings & Drawings', that toured the major art centres of New Zealand has been counted only once in the preceding total. A very crude estimate of approximately 250 paintings can be made for the total number of individually distinct works, both oil and watercolour. Included in this figure are various works that seemingly have never been exhibited, such as *Mrs Coates of Chelsea* and *Portrait of a Woman Wearing a Hat*, among others. More than a dozen fine drawings also form an important part of the Grace Joel *oeuvre*.

Posthumous Exhibitions

1948

'Centennial Exhibition Art in Otago 1840–1948', Otago Museum, 9 March to 5 April
Grace Joel's work included *Mother and Child* (Image 1.23).

1954

'Artists by Artists', National Art Gallery of New South Wales, 4 November to 5 December
Grace Joel's portrait of G.P. Nerli shown at the exhibition was reproduced in the exhibition catalogue.

1962

'Six New Zealand Expatriates: Grace Joel, Rhona Haszard, Frances Hodgkins, Francis McCracken, Raymond McIntyre, Owen Merton', Auckland City Art Gallery, 1 April

The catalogue, prepared by Colin McCahon, included a biographical note on Grace Joel. Nine of Grace Joel's works were exhibited. They included *Self-portrait, Seated in a Cane Chair* and the portrait of the artist's mother, Catherine Joel. *Westminster, Early Winter's Evening* was exhibited under the title, *Embankment London*.

1967

'Exhibition of Works by Grace Joel, Frances Hodgkins and A.H. O'Keeffe', Dunedin Public Art Gallery, February
Sixteen of the works were by Grace Joel. The

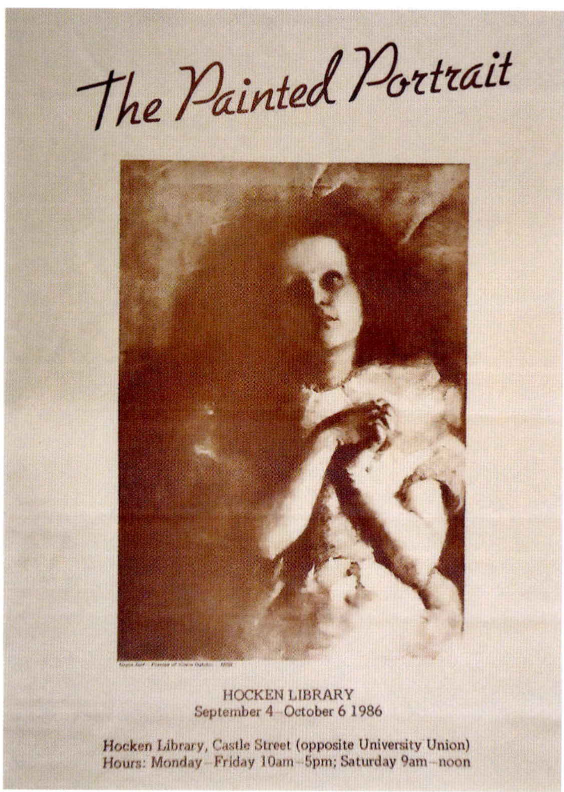

Portrait of Vivien Oakden **was used to advertise the Hocken Library Exhibition of 1986.**

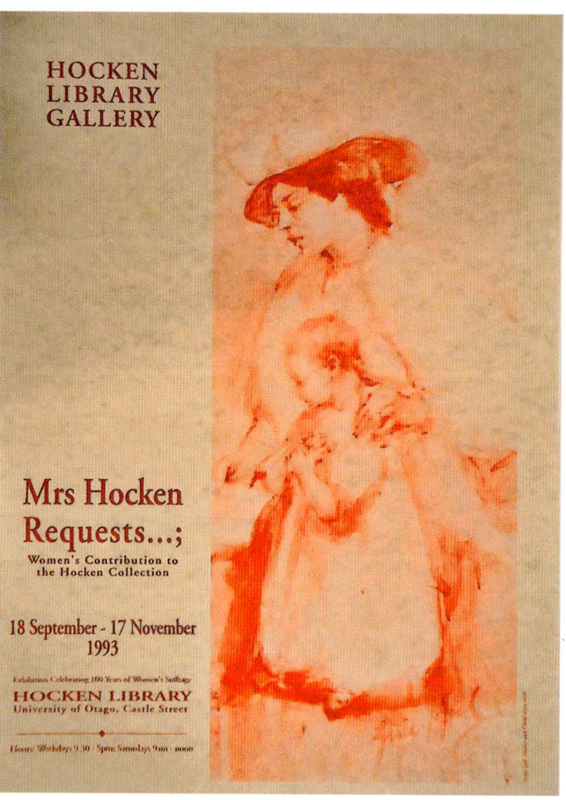

Mother and Child, **by Grace Joel, appeared on the Hocken Library exhibition catalogue cover of 1993.**

painting, *Westminster, Early Winter's Evening* was titled *Westminster Bridge* in the exhibition. Subsequent to the exhibition, viewed by some 4000 people, the gallery wrote to Mrs Louis Joel requesting first option on purchasing three of Grace's works –*Self-portrait Wearing a Hat* (Image 6.11), *Westminster Bridge* (Image 5.1) and *The Bon Vivant* (Image 2.2). The letter to Mrs L.J. Joel from the gallery's director, Chariton Edgar, 6 March 1967, described *The Bon Vivant* as 'gentleman with beard in top hat' and so is very likely to be the work depicted in Image 2.2.

1968

'New Zealand Women Painters 1845–1968', Auckland Society of Arts Festival Exhibition, 18 March to 14 April
The exhibition included seven of Grace Joel's oil paintings, among them the portrait of *Richard John Seddon, Portrait of a Gentleman* (i.e. *The Bon Vivant*), *The Nurse*, and *Girl with Scarf*. A number of Grace's charcoal and pencil sketches also featured in the exhibition. The Joel family supplied the exhibition notes.

1980

'Grace Joel: Paintings & Drawings', Dunedin Public Art Gallery, 26 January to 17 February
The catalogue listed 49 works and included an essay on the artist by Frank Dickinson. The exhibition subsequently toured all the major art centres of New Zealand, ending in Auckland on 4 September 1981.

1984

'William Mathew Hodgkins and His Circle: An Exhibition to Mark the Centennial of the Dunedin Public Art Gallery', Dunedin Public Art Gallery, 14 October to 15 November
The book by Peter Entwisle that accompanied the exhibition included a biography of Grace Joel.

1986

'The Painted Portrait', works drawn from The Hocken Library Collection, Hocken Library, Dunedin, 4 September to 6 October
Grace Joel's *Portrait of Vivien Oakden* was used on the poster advertising the exhibition.

1987

'Under the Spell: Frances Hodgkins, Nellie Hutton & Grace Joel: Three women artists influenced in the 1890s by G.P. Nerli', Hocken Library, Dunedin, 16 July to 31 August
The exhibition featured works held in The Hocken Library Collection, Dunedin.

1991

'Bohemians in the Bush: The artists' camps of Mosman', Art Gallery of New South Wales, Sydney, 6 June to 25 August
The Grace Joel painting on show was her portrait of G.P. Nerli.

1993

'Mrs Hocken Requests ...; Women's Contributions to the Hocken Collection', Hocken Library, Dunedin, 18 September to 17 November
The exhibition catalogued 100 years of women's suffrage. One of Grace Joel's mother and child works appeared on the cover of the catalogue.

'The Italian Connection: Italian artists in 19th-century Australia', S.H. Ervin Gallery, Sydney, 24 September to 14 November
The exhibition featured Grace Joel's portrait of G.P. Nerli.

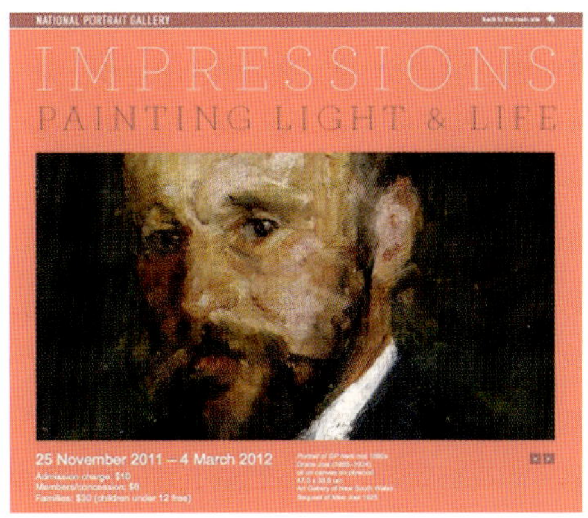

One of the images used to publicise the National Portrait Gallery Exhibition, Canberra, Australia, 25 November 2011 to 4 March 2012.

1995

'Review: Works by women from the permanent collection of the Art Gallery of New South Wales', Art Gallery of New South Wales, Sydney, 8 March to 4 June
The exhibition included Grace's portrait of Arthur Streeton.

2004

'From Life: Works by early generations of students at the National Gallery Art School', Victorian College of the Arts, Melbourne, 29 October to 13 November
Grace Joel, along with George Coates, James Quinn and Hugh Ramsay, was among the 20 selected former students featured in the catalogue. Her painting, *Nude*, winner of the 1893 Ramsay Prize, was exhibited.

2011–2012

'Impressions: Painting light & life', National Portrait Gallery, Canberra, 25 November to 4 March
The exhibition featured works by Rupert Bunny, Charles Conder, E. Phillips Fox, Grace Joel, George Lambert, Frederick McCubbin, Girolamo Nerli, Tom Roberts, among others.

Appendix B

Letters

Eden Bank
Regent Road
Dunedin

May 12th 1896

Dear Mr. Richardson

Will you let me know when the next Victorian Artists Exhibition takes place. I am thinking of becoming a member again. Thank you very much for the trouble you took with my pictures.

In gt haste

Yours sincerely

Grace J. Joel.

Victorian Artists' Society papers, La Trobe Library, State Library of Victoria, Melbourne, MS 7593 584/3a

***

12 Milton Chambers
128 Cheyne Walk, N.W.

March 14th 1922

To: Mr George Clausen R.A.

Dear Sir,

I hope you will forgive the liberty I take in writing, but I have always heard you were such a kind man, that it gives me courage! In the enclosed letter, you will see I was a pupil of the late E. Phillips Fox (after I had gained the first prize for the nude, Mr Quinn being placed second at the National Gallery Melbourne Australia). It was in Melbourne we as pupils of the late Mr Fred. McCubbin, were taught to look at your work with great reverence, and to him more than any one else is due the sale of your works to the galleries there, as well as the admiration, most Australian artists have for your genius.

We all wanted to paint figures out of doors like you, that was at the time when you painted 'The girl at the gate'. I am sending you under separate cover also a photograph of a painting of two children taken before it was finished. I was going to send it to the Salon this year where I have exhibited so often, but kept it to send to the Academy as it has twice been kept to the last & crowded out. I have heard you are on the jury but you may not like it but I shall feel flattered if you do. The late G.F. Watts thought highly of my work which he saw six weeks before his death which was unfortunate for me as he had offered me his influence which a letter from Mrs Watts at the time confirms. I know several R.A.s visit the studios before Academy but it is very difficult for them I am sure & it take[s] up so much of their valuable time. But should you be in any [sic] near I should feel it a great honour if you would come offer me your opinion & also I should feel everlastingly in your debt.

Hoping you will not think I am taking an unpardonable liberty. I am dear Sir

Yours truly

Grace J. Joel

I shall be much obliged if you will return incl.
E. Phillips Fox letter.

Letters written to George Clausen 1890–1940, CL/1/64, Royal Academy of Arts Archive, GB/0397

***

12 Milton Chambers
128 Cheyne Walk, N.W.

December 17th 1922

Dear Mr Clausen

I was not able to explain to you properly (about the purchase of one of your watercolours for ten guineas) at the distribution of prizes at the R.A. Saturday. I was at my bank a few weeks ago when my bank manager showed me some watercolours & asked me my opinion on them, & I told him they were no good & valueless. He then told me that the submanager was going back out to New Zealand, & wished to take two or three watercolours of English landscapes by someone good & what price I thought it possible to get them. I answered "I might at 10 guineas, but was not sure." He then said would I see about it. I said I would inquire & choose, only the submanager might not "look [like?]them." He then said, "he (the submanager), could see them because [but?] of course he might not have the sufficient appreciation to like them just because they were by notable artists." I considered this very natural, & so I promised to ask two or three artists of note to submit something at that price. I have already received some from one of the younger members of the Royal Academy & R.W.S. [Royal Watercolour Society]. As he lives in the country I could not go to his studio, but they are charming. Another of the R.W.S. has submitted some at this studio & I have chosen, but I have not taken them until I have made arrangements with the submanager about seeing them (who will have just returned from Paris) as I do not care for the responsibility of them. So, will you let me know when I could call & see what I thought would be likely to please. Naturally, if they appealed specially to me, I would be more enthusiastic in pushing the purchase.

I hope you are better, as I hear you were not well. I liked much the charming peasant's head you had in the Royal Scottish Academy this year where I was also exhibiting. I saw a good deal of Sir James & Lady Wingate & painted his portrait the day before I left. I would have written before but have not been well.

Yours truly,

Grace J. Joel

Letters written to George Clausen 1890–1940, CL/1/65, Royal Academy of Arts Archive, GB/0397

Notes

Prelude

1 Translated from the French. The original letter is held by a Joel family member.
2 *Evening Post*, 16 December 1924, p. 3 (datelined 5 November); *Otago Witness*, 30 December 1924, p. 68.
3 www.archives.govt.nz/womens-suffrage-petition
4 Personal communication.

Chapter 1

1 Mark Twain, *Following the Equator: A journey around the world* (Hartford, CN: American Publishing Company, 1897), p. 287.
2 The tragic account of Joseph Woolf's suicide by strychnine is documented in the *Otago Daily Times*, 16 August 1864, p. 4.
3 Advertisement by 'Madame Lubecki', placed in the *Otago Daily Times*, 4 July 1863, p. 8. Substantial brick additions and verandas were added in 1874.
4 New Zealand's Prime Minister at the time of this writing, John Key, is Jewish by birth, a matter irrelevant during his election campaigns, if even known by some of the electorate.
5 Julius Vogel, *Anno Domini 2000 or Woman's Destiny* (London: Hutchinson & Co., 1889), p. 36.
6 'Dunedin Hebrew Congregation', *Otago Witness*, 3 April 1901, p. 68.
7 Poet Charles Brasch founded *Landfall* in 1947 and served as its editor for the next 20 years. Noted author Janet Frame said in her autobiographical *An Angel at my Table* (Auckland: Hutchinson, 1984): 'I sensed that if you didn't appear in *Landfall* then you could scarcely call yourself a writer', p. 44.
8 'Otago Girls' High School prize list', *Otago Daily Times*, 29 December 1882, p. 2. This prize is referred to in Georgia Pearce's interview of Grace Joel, published in *The Woman Worker*, 10 March 1909, p. 229. However, it is stated there as the prize for drawing.
9 Letter from Edward Joel to his brother Maurice Joel, dated 2 June 1878.
10 'Shipping news', *Otago Witness*, 19 May 1883, p. 14.
11 Public records office, Victoria, Australia: passenger list of ships leaving Victoria; 'Shipping intelligence', *The Argus*, 23 May 1883, p. 4.
12 *The Argus*, 27 December 1883, p. 4. The *Parramatta* sailed from London via Colombo and could have picked up the Joel family at Port Said after their travel from Brindisi.
13 Statement made to Elizabeth Jerram, the daughter of Grace's nephew, Maurice Joel.
14 *Marlborough Express*, 30 November 1886, p. 2. The opening address of the Jewish Bazaar was delivered by Sir Julius Vogel 'in the course of which he replied to Bishop Neville's recent utterances on bazaars'.
15 *Otago Daily Times*, 4 April 1893, p. 3.
16 Peter Entwisle, *William Mathew Hodgkins & His Circle* (Dunedin: Dunedin Public Art Gallery, 1984), p. 118.
17 Georgia Pearce interview, *The Woman Worker*, 1909, p. 229.
18 A.H. O'Keeffe, 'Art in retrospect, early Dunedin days: Paint and personality', *Art in New Zealand*, vol. 12, no. 3, 1940, p. 160.
19 Joanne Drayton, *Frances Hodgkins: A private viewing* (Auckland: Random House, 2005), inside front cover.
20 'By M.R.', *Otago Daily Times*, 27 November 1889, p. 3.

21 Quoted in Victoria Hammond and Juliet Peers, *Completing the Picture: Women artists and the Heidelberg era* (Hawthorn East, VIC: Artmoves, 1992), p. 61.

22 Public Records Office, Victoria, Australia: passenger list of ships leaving Victoria, 1889.

23 Michael Dunn gives reasons for uncertainty regarding these details in his book *Nerli: An Italian painter in the South Pacific* (Auckland: Auckland University Press, 2005), p. 6.

24 Entwisle, *William Mathew Hodgkins*, p. 22.

25 O'Keeffe, 'Art in retrospect', p. 160.

26 *Otago Daily Times*, 11 February 1890, p. 6.

27 In the 1890 list of students, Dora Meeson is given as a free place student. Her scholarship was divided with Edith E. Munnings, and there is a note that 'Miss Meeson leaves at the end of ½ year.' In 1891, Dora was listed as an evening class student in the second and third terms. Information provided by Erin Kimber of the Macmillan Brown Library, University of Canterbury, Christchurch, New Zealand.

28 The Christchurch *Star*, 13 May 1890, p. 3, reports that Dora Meeson of Christchurch picked up two first prizes, one in the Class II section and one in Class III.

29 Christchurch *Press*, 26 April 1895, p. 6. Meeson was elected to the committee at this meeting; 'the meeting closed with a vote of thanks to the lady who presided.'

30 Or, to give the institution its full name, the National Gallery of Victoria Art School.

31 *Otago Witness*, 12 August 1882, p. 16.

32 *Otago Daily Times*, 14 September 1882, p. 3; *Otago Daily Times*, 30 January 1885, p. 4, advertisement for Bathgate & Meeson.

33 Nairn reputedly painted a portrait of Grace Joel circa 1896 but it is nowhere to be found, including in Victoria Hearnshaw's *James McLauchlan Nairn: A catalogue of works* (Dunedin: Hocken Library, 1997). In a letter dated 5 September 1896, Frances Hodgkins mentions the portrait to her sister Isabel and asks her if she had seen it. Letter (No. 33) in Linda Gill (ed.), *Letters of Frances Hodgkins* (Auckland: Auckland University Press, 1993), p. 45.

34 Quoted in 'An impressionist exhibition', *The Argus*, 17 August 1889, p. 10.

35 Patrick Cavanagh, 'The artist as neuroscientist', *Nature*, vol. 434, 17 March 2005, pp. 301–07.

36 *Otago Witness*, 17 November 1898, p. 21.

37 *Timaru Herald*, 12 December 1896, p. 3.

38 Quoted in Gordon H. Brown and Hamish Keith, *An Introduction to New Zealand Painting 1839–1980* (Auckland: David Bateman and William Collins, 2nd ed., 1982).

39 *Otago Daily Times*, 8 November 1892, p. 3.

40 Entwisle, *William Mathew Hodgkins*, p. 44.

41 Quoted in Eric H. McCormick, *The Expatriate: A study of Frances Hodgkins* (Wellington: New Zealand University Press, 1954), p. 33. This letter is to her sister Isabel. It is dated 9 June 1893 and is Letter 10 in Gill, *Letters*, p. 27.

42 Gill, *Letters*, Letter 33, 5 September 1896, p. 45.

43 Dunn, *Nerli*, p. 10. Neither Nerli's English nor his spelling was perfect.

44 G.A.K. Baughen, 'Baeyertz, Charles Nalder', Te Ara–the Encyclopedia of New Zealand: www.TeAra.govt.nz/en/biographies/2b1/baeyertz-charles-nalder

45 Gill, *Letters*, Letter 12, 29 April 1894, p. 29.

46 Christchurch *Press*, 27 February 1909, p. 7.

47 Dunn, *Nerli*, p. 42.

48 Exhibition catalogue.

49 In a personal communication at the time of writing, art historian Peter Entwisle said he now believes the nudes at the Dunedin School of Art were partially draped at this time, and that models were only fully nude during a later period at the time of Nerli.

50 Related to nephew Len Fox by Mr Solomon Phillips of Sydney, in Len Fox, *E. Phillips Fox: Some recollections and reminiscences* (Potts Point, NSW: Author, 1969), p. 6.

51 William Moore, *The Story of Australian Art* (Sydney: Angus & Robertson Ltd, vol. 1, 1934), p. 226.

52 Fox, *E. Phillips Fox*, p. 17.

53 The letter is in Appendix B of this book.

54 Daniel Thomas quoted from the Sydney *Sunday Telegraph* of 23 June 1963 in Fox, *E. Phillips Fox*, p. 21.

55 Thomas quoted in Fox, p. 21.

56 Kirsten Fergusson, 'Grace Joel 1865–1924: A reassessment', *Art New Zealand*, vol. 70, Autumn 1994, p. 87. Fergusson sighted the book when in Melbourne in 1992.

57 Hammond and Peers, *Completing the Picture*, p. 82.

58 Georgia Pearce interview, *The Woman Worker*, p. 229.

59 Grace Joel, 'Australasian artists in London: A reminiscence,' *Art and Architecture*, vol. 3, no. 3, May 1906, p. 102.

Chapter 2

1 *Otago Daily Times*, 18 August 1894, p. 1.
2 *Otago Daily Times*, 11 August 1894, p. 2; *Otago Witness*, 16 August 1894, p. 15.
3 This work fits the description by a reporter for *The Triad* (15 August 1894, p. 8): '... whilst opposite the door is a study of a child with a sweet face, sitting in a chair. This is one of the best in the room but is spoilt by the careless way the canvas has been stretched.'
4 *Evening Star*, 20 August, p. 3; *Otago Daily Times*, 22 August 1894, p. 1, and other dates.
5 'Minute Book', Dunedin Public Art Gallery archives.
6 *Otago Daily Times*, 28 January 1899, p. 1.
7 *Otago Daily Times*, 26 January 1895, p. 6, and other dates.
8 *Otago Daily Times*, 26 January, p. 6.
9 Linda Gill (ed.), *Letters of Frances Hodgkins* (Auckland: Auckland University Press, 1993), Letter 24, 23 July 1895, p. 38.
10 *The Triad*, 25 July 1895, p. 7.
11 Gill, *Letters*, footnote, p. 36.
12 Ibid., Letter 21, 5 May 1895, p. 36.
13 Ibid., Letter 128, 27 June 1906, p. 189.
14 Joanne Drayton, 'The haunting: Frances Hodgkins & Jenny Wimperis', *Art New Zealand*, no. 110, 2004, pp. 78–81.
15 *The Triad*, vol. 3, no. 6, 25 August 1895, p. 13.
16 *Auckland Star*, 29 April 1896, p. 2.
17 *Evening Star*, 14 November 1895, p. 4.
18 Grace remained on the Art Society Council until she left the country in 1899.
19 'Minute Book', Dunedin Public Art Gallery archives.
20 *NZ Freelance*, 29 December 1900, p. 3.
21 *NZ Herald*, 24 April 1896, p. 5.
22 *The Triad*, vol. 4, no. 2, 1 May 1896, p. 10.
23 *Otago Daily Times*, 21 March 1896, p. 6.
24 *Evening Star*, 29 May 1896, p. 4.
25 Personal communication.
26 *Little Nell* may have been procured by Mr Elliott at a later date but what is known is that he 'lent' it to the Canterbury Jubilee Industrial Exhibition held in 1900, by which time Grace Joel was overseas.
27 Christchurch *Star*, 8 September 1896, p. 2.
28 *Evening Star*, 2 November 1896, p. 2.
29 *Otago Daily Times*, 10 November 1896, p. 2.
30 *Otago Witness*, 12 November 1896, p. 24.
31 *Evening Star*, 12 November 1896, p. 2.
32 *New Zealand Herald*, 15 April 1897, p. 6.
33 *Evening Star*, 12 November 1896, p. 2.
34 *Sydney Morning Herald*, 2 October 1897, p. 7.
35 Michael Dunn, *Nerli: An Italian painter in the South Pacific* (Auckland: Auckland University Press, 2005), reference no. 102, p. 54.
36 In his book *The Expatriate: A study of Frances Hodgkins* (Wellington: New Zealand University Press, 1954), Eric McCormick asserts that Nerli had 'outlived his welcome – and his credit – in Dunedin' (p. 34).
37 Owen Marshall, *The Larnachs* (Auckland: Random House, 2011), pp. 176–77. *The Larnachs* is described in the *New Zealand Listener* (25 June 2011) as 'a sensitive, compassionate and discreet reworking of fact'.
38 *Evening Star*, 14 November 1896, p. 6.
39 The former title of the work was *Home for the Holidays* when exhibited with the OAS in 1896, as evidenced by the reviewer's comments in the *Evening Star*, 14 November 1896, p. 6: 'Everybody admires Miss Joel's "Home for the Holidays". The little girl in blue, carrying over her shoulder a strap of books, forms an interesting and at the same time a truly pictorial subject that needs no interpreter. A great deal of skill is also manifested in the workmanship, which, though off-hand and broad, leaves no trace of coarseness or vulgarity upon the picture, and altogether it is a spirited and highly-pleasing example of Miss Joel's aptitude in regard to this particular class of work, possessing the merit of originality without its too frequent accompaniment of mere fancifulness'. The price of £15 was also commensurate with the size of the painting.
40 Dunn, *Nerli*, p. 148.
41 *Timaru Herald*, 12 December 1896, p. 3.
42 In recent years, the John Leech Gallery has been absorbed into the Gow Langsford Gallery, although the picture-framing activities still trade under the John Leech name in a separate part of Auckland.
43 The name has also been spelled 'Leach', but such variation is not uncommon.
44 Harold Leech, the son of the original founder, John Leech, would have been 39 or 40 years of age in 1897. The portrait depicts a man with a full white beard, thinning white hair and bags under his eyes. If it is Harold Leech, then the picture-framing business certainly exacted its toll. The father, John Leech, died in 1879, so the portrait is unlikely to be him either, although it could have been done from a photograph.

45 Frank Dickinson's *Addenda & Errata* to his *Grace Joel, Paintings and Drawings* (Dunedin: Dunedin Public Art Gallery, 1980) includes the following note: '...an inventory of "Olveston" has been discovered in a deed box in the basement of the Perpetual Trustees office, Dunedin. It contains an entry in Mr Theomin's hand, "The Yellow Sun Bonnet Grace Joel 12gns". The inventory was compiled in about 1905'.

46 *Observer*, 2 May 1896, p. 11. The *Observer* critic of the Auckland Society of Arts Exhibition lambasted nearly all the works on show that year.

47 *New Zealand Herald*, 24 April 1896, p. 5.

48 *Evening Post*, 14 September 1897, p. 2.

49 'Miss Grace Joel has apparently been drinking inspiration from the pre-Raphaelites for her picture labelled "Between Faith and Knowledge". There is a suggestion of Holman Huntism "in petto" about this undraped youth, who stands with eyes raised to Heaven ...' *The Argus*, 7 January 1898, p. 5.

50 *The Sydney Mail*, 9 October 1897, p. 765.

51 D.H. Souter, 'Grace Joel, painter: Some notes on her work', *Art and Architecture*, vol. 3, no. 2, March–April, 1906, p. 54.

52 D.H. Souter quoted in William Moore, *The Story of Australian Art* (vol. 1, Sydney, Angus & Robertson, 1934), p. 168.

53 Moore, *The Story of Australian Art*, p. 245.

54 *Otago Daily Times*, 1 November 1897, p. 2.

55 *Otago Daily Times*, 13 November 1897, p. 2.

56 The descriptions of 'There is no grief ...' given in the *Otago Daily Times*, 1 November 1897, p. 2, and 'Give sorrow words ...', as stated in the *Evening Star*, 25 November 1897, p. 5, indicate that the two titles represent the same work.

57 *Evening Star*, 12 November 1897, p. 1.

58 *Otago Daily Times*, 13 November 1897, p. 2.

59 *Otago Daily Times*, 5 February 1898, p. 4. The advertisement says she was 'resuming' classes at her Liverpool Street studio.

60 *Otago Witness*, 10 March 1898, p. 24.

61 *Otago Daily Times*, 24 February 1898, p. 3.

62 *Official Record of the Otago Jubilee Industrial Exhibition Held in Dunedin New Zealand from March 22nd to June 4th, 1898* (Dunedin, Mills, Dick & Co., 1898), p. 39.

63 *Otago Daily Times*, 16 December 1899, p. 2.

64 *Evening Star*, 14 November 1898, p. 2. One of the works was *Girl with Scarf* (Image 2.6) and was a third prize offering at the art union according to Frank Dickinson's *Addenda & Errata*.

65 Émile Zola, 'A New Manner in Painting: Édouard Manet', *Revue du XX siècle*, January 1867, p. 91.

66 *Evening Post*, 17 November 1913, p. 7.

67 *Otago Daily Times*, 22 October 1984, p. 4.

68 Sandra Chesterman, *Figure Work: The nude and life modelling in New Zealand art* (Dunedin: University of Otago Press, 2002), p. 40.

69 Pricilla Pitts, 'Evelyn Page: Reflecting the human presence', *Art New Zealand*, vol. 26, Autumn, 1983, pp. 22–27.

70 Quoted in Joanne Drayton, *Frances Hodgkins: A private viewing* (Auckland: Random House, 2005), p. 52.

71 'Minute Book', Dunedin Public Art Gallery archives.

72 'Austral', 2 May 1890, Roberts papers, as quoted in Ann Galbally, *Charles Conder: The last Bohemian* (Melbourne, VIC: Melbourne University Press, 2002), p. 63.

Chapter 3

1 www.freepages.genealogy.rootsweb.ancestry.com/~nzbound/gothic.htm

2 Georgia Pearce interview of Grace Joel, *The Woman Worker*, 1909, p. 229.

3 *Evening Star*, 24 June 1899, p. 7 (datelined 12 May), and 13 September 1906, p. 3.

4 Ruth Zubans, *E. Phillips Fox: His life and art* (Carlton, VIC: Melbourne University Press, 1995), p. 18.

5 *Evening Star*, 7 July 1899, p. 4 (datelined London 3 June).

6 Colin McCahon, *Six New Zealand Expatriates* (Auckland: Auckland City Art Gallery and Pelorus Press, 1962).

7 Christchurch *Star*, 19 September 1895, p. 2.

8 Dora Meeson Coates, *George Coates: His art and his life* (London: J.M. Dent & Sons, 1937), p. 12.

9 Linda Gill (ed.), *Letters of Frances Hodgkins* (Auckland: Auckland University Press, 1993), Letter 82, 25 December 1901, p. 111.

10 Ibid., Letter 89, 29 May 1902, pp. 128–29.

11 Meeson Coates, *George Coates*, p. 17.

12 Ibid., p. 43.

13 Grace Joel, 'Australasian artists in London: A reminiscence', *Art and Architecture*, vol. 3, no. 3, May 1906, p. 102.

14 Meeson Coates, *George Coates*.

15 Ibid., p. 193.

16 Gabriel P. Weisberg and Jane R. Becker (eds.), *Overcoming all Obstacles: The women of the Académie*

Julian (New York and New Brunswick, NJ: Dahesh Museum and Rutgers University Press, 1999) p. 38.

17 Joel, 'Australasian artists in London: A reminiscence,' p. 102.

18 Clive Holland, 'Student life in the Quartier Latin', *The Studio*, vol. 27, no. 115, October 1902, p. 38.

19 John Milner, *The Studios of Paris: The capital of art in the late nineteenth century* (New Haven, CT and London: Yale University Press, 1989), p. 220. It was built from materials salvaged from exhibition buildings demolished after the 1889 Exposition Universelle.

20 Una Platts, *Nineteenth Century New Zealand Artists: A guide & handbook* (Christchurch: Avon Fine Prints, 1980); *Otago Daily Times*, 2 April 1890, p. 3.

21 Nancy Mowll Mathews, *Mary Cassatt: A life* (New York: Villard Books, 1994), p. 97.

22 Marie Bashkirtseff, *The Journal of a Young Artist 1860–1884* (New York: Cassell Publishing Company, 1889), entry for 21 June 1882.

23 *Evening Star*, 13 September 1906, p. 3; also *Sydney Morning Herald*, 6 April 1906, p. 3. The *Wanganui Chronicle*, 2 February 1906, p. 5, reported that Grace Joel was 'first in the concours of her second year'.

24 *Evening Star*, 13 September 1901, p. 3.

25 Mowll Mathews, *Mary Cassatt*, p. 104.

26 Ibid., p. 104.

27 Grace Joel, 'Australasian artists in London', p. 100.

28 As quoted in the *Otago Daily Times*, 11 October 1906, p. 9.

29 *Evening Star*, 13 September 1906, p. 3.

30 Georgia Pearce interview, p. 229.

31 *Evening Star*, 14 November 1895, p. 4.

32 *London Express* report reproduced in its entirety in the *Evening Post*, 13 April 1909, p. 9.

33 D.H. Souter, 'Grace Joel, painter: Some notes on her work', *Art & Architecture*, vol. 3, no. 2, March–April 1906, pp. 58–59. A black and white photograph of this work accompanies the article on p. 58 that is reproduced in Roger Collins, 'Grace J. Joel and France', *Bulletin of New Zealand Art History*, vol. 21, 2000, p. 17.

34 Ruth Zubans, *E. Phillips Fox*, cat. no. 20.

Chapter 4

1 *Evening Post*, 10 January 1902, p. 5.

2 *Otago Daily Times*, 13 January 1902, p. 8 (datelined London 29 November).

3 *Evening Post*, 11 August 1936, p. 4.

4 *Evening Post*, 28 July 1902, p. 2 (datelined London 21 June).

5 Linda Gill (ed.), *Letters of Frances Hodgkins* (Auckland: Auckland University Press, 1993), Letter 90, 27 June 1902, p. 130.

6 Ibid., Letter 97, 23 October 1902, p. 141.

7 *Auckland Star*, 24 November 1902, p. 5.

8 *The Western Australian*, 29 April 1903, p. 5: 'Miss Grace Joel, an Australian artist, has had a picture accepted by the Paris Salon.'

9 *Evening Post*, 17 June 1903, p. 6.

10 *Auckland Star*, 17 April 1903, p. 2.

11 *Evening Post*, 29 October 1903, p. 2.

12 Georgia Pearce interview of Grace Joel, *The Woman Worker*, 10 March 1909, p. 229.

13 *The Art Newspaper*, No. 72, July–August 1997: www.vggallery.com/misc/fakes/fakes2.htm

14 Contributors listed in the annual report of 1907/08 and available on the website titled 'Contributors to the sick room help society': www.jeffreymaynard.com/sick07ad.htm/

15 *Otago Daily Times*, 24 March 1904, p. 8.

16 *Otago Daily Times*, 29 July 1904, p. 3 (datelined London 2 June).

17 Private collection, Melbourne.

18 *Otago Daily Times*, 9 June 1905, p. 2 (datelined London 6 May).

19 *Sydney Morning Herald*, 6 April 1906, p. 3: '"A Time of Prayer" (No. 1) was originally shown at the last Paris Salon (1905), under the title of "The Dutchwoman"'; *Doré Gallery Catalogue 1909*: 'A Time of Prayer' (Ex Salon 1905).

20 Kirsten Fergusson makes this point on page 66 of her Master's thesis: 'Grace Joel: Portraits and figure studies', University of Canterbury, Christchurch, New Zealand, 1993.

21 *Evening Star*, 9 October 1906, p. 4.

22 Quoted in the *Evening Post*, 28 May 1909, p. 9.

23 Robert Speaight, *The Life of Hilaire Belloc* (London: Farrar, Straus & Cudahy, 1957), p. 196.

24 Ibid., p. 195.

25 Eleanor Jebb, 'Reminiscences of H.B.', in Reginald and Eleanor Jebb, *Testimony to Hilaire Belloc* (London: Methuen and Co., 1956), p. 107, quote page 112.

26 Speaight, *Hilaire Belloc*, p. 247.

27 Anne Kirker, *New Zealand Women Artists* (Auckland, Reed Methuen, 1986), p. 35. This is borne out in the interview of Irene Searle, 1998.

28 *New Zealand Mail*, 24 May 1905, p. 1.

29 Dora Meeson Coates, *George Coates: His art and his life* (London: J.M. Dent & Sons, 1937), p. 37. Dora Meeson is seemingly referring to her own

witnessed account of Conder's odd behaviour, but her narration is possibly hearsay, recalled from many years past. It is likely that she and George Coates were in Trafalgar Studios, Chelsea, by some date in 1905, as George joined the Chelsea Arts Club in that year.

30 Ann Galbally, *Charles Conder: The last Bohemian* (Carlton, VIC: Melbourne University Press, 1993), p. 28.

31 Letters (to Leonard Smithers), circa 4 May 1898, quoted in Galbally, p. 185.

32 *Otago Daily Times*, 18 May 1905, p. 2 (datelined London 7 April).

33 Christchurch *Press*, 8 April 1905, p. 12 (datelined 4 March), and *Otago Daily Times*, 18 May 1905, p. 2 (datelined London 7 April).

34 *The Advertiser* (Adelaide), 22 November 1905, p. 11.

35 *Otago Daily Times*, 19 May 1905, p. 6 (datelined London 15 April).

36 *Annual Report from the Council of The Royal Academy to the General Assembly of Academicians for the Year 1904, 1905* (London: William Clowes and Sons Ltd., 1905).

37 *Otago Daily Times*, 9 June 1905, p. 2 (datelined London 6 May).

38 Quoted in the *Otago Daily Times*, 4 July 1905, p. 2 (datelined 27 May). Grace exhibited *Her Child* (Ex Salon 1901, *Son enfant*).

Chapter 5

1 *Otago Daily Times*, 8 January 1906, p. 2 (datelined London 2 December).

2 Christchurch *Press*, 8 January 1906, p. 8 (datelined 2 December 1905).

3 D.H. Souter, 'Grace Joel, Painter: Some notes on her work', *Art & Architecture*, vol. 3, no. 2, March–April 1906, p. 59.

4 *Sydney Morning Herald*, 6 April 1906, p. 3.

5 Quoted in the *Evening Post*, 13 April 1909, p. 9.

6 Grace Joel, 'Australasian artists in London: A reminiscence,' *Art and Architecture*, vol. 3, no. 3, May 1906, pp. 99–103.

7 'The portrait may not have eventuated; in any case there is no hard evidence that a visit took place at that time.' Ruth E. Zubans, *E. Phillips Fox: His life and art* (Carlton, VIC: Melbourne University Press, 1995), p. 159.

8 Several years later, in 1910, Grace Joel again became a resident of the famous Cheyne Walk. She remained there for the rest of her life.

9 Susanna de Vries, *Ethel Carrick Fox: Travels and triumphs of a post-impressionist* (Brisbane, QLD: Pandanus Press, 1997), p. 93.

10 *The Age* (Melbourne), 14 July 1906, p. 10; *The Argus*, 11 July 1906, p. 4.

11 *Otago Witness*, 4 October 1905, p. 36.

12 *Evening Star*, 13 September 1906, p. 3.

13 *Otago Daily Times*, 11 October 1906, p. 9.

14 Ibid.; *Evening Star*, 9 October 1906, p. 4.

15 In the 1980 Dunedin Public Art Gallery catalogue, Dickinson suggested that a possible candidate for Image 5.2 was *A French Beggar Boy*. Subsequently, in his *Addenda & Errata* (Dunedin Public Art Gallery), he retracted this suggestion, stating that 'Dr R.D.J. Collins has traced "A French Beggar Boy" in a photograph of the Otago Art Society annual exhibition, 1905, in *Otago Witness Pictures*, November 29, 1905, p. 50. It is clearly a head and shoulders study and not the present work.' (That is, not the study of the boy nude to the waist, our Image 5.2, and featured as No. 20 in the catalogue.)

16 *Otago Daily Times*, 25 October 1906, p. 6.

17 *Otago Daily Times*, 10 November 1906, p. 5; *Otago Witness*, 14 November 1906, p. 84.

18 *Otago Witness*, 21 November 1906.

19 *Otago Witness*, 27 March 1907, p. 32. The reporter visited Joel's studio on 25 March, two days before her departure from Dunedin for London.

20 *Ashburton Guardian*, 1 June 1910, p. 2. Also reprinted in the *The Mercury*, Hobart, Tasmania, 21 May 1910.

21 From *Song of Myself* by Walt Whitman (1819–1892).

22 Zubans, *E. Phillips Fox*, p. 104.

Chapter 6

1 Annual exhibition, Canterbury Society of Arts, Christchurch, and annual exhibition, New Zealand Academy of Fine Arts, Wellington, respectively.

2 'Deceased persons' estates', *Evening Post*, 31 August 1908, p. 8.

3 *Evening Star*, 2 June 1908, p. 2.

4 *Evening Post*, 27 May 1908, p. 2.

5 Ibid.; *Evening Post*, 17 May 1911, p. 2; *Feilding Star*, 17 May 1911, p. 4; *Evening Post*, 26 May 1913, p. 7. The first reference mentioned that 'she [Rollo Fisher] is in New Zealand now.' The latter two references explicitly stated that Jean had sent a painting to Grace Joel (1911 and 1913, respectively).

6 *Otautau Standard* and *Wallace County Chronicle*, 22 December 1908, p. 7. The report goes on to state:

'Very few outsiders indeed have managed to get into the S.P.P. show this year, and Miss Joel is naturally much gratified at her success.'

7 *The Studio*, vol. 46, no. 193, April 1909, p. 231.

8 Grace Joel, 'Australasian artists in London: A reminiscence,' *Art and Architecture*, vol. 3, no. 3, May 1906, p. 100.

9 Jack Zipes, *The Oxford Companion to Fairy Tales* (Oxford: Oxford University Press, 2005).

10 In addition there is Image 6.16. Another pink gown adorns *Woman in Pink*, but it is not off the shoulders.

11 Grace is known to have made at least one other trip to Étaples in 1909, but this was too late for *Le grandpère*.

12 *The Argus*, 27 June 1908, p. 6.

13 'British picture framers, 1630–1950', National Portrait Gallery: www.npg.org.uk/research/conservation/directory-of-british- framemakers/b.php/

14 As quoted in the Doré Gallery catalogue, 1909. A translation reads: 'Miss GRACE J. JOEL's two paintings "The grandfather of Étaples" and "Motherless Children" show she has put her whole soul as an artist and a woman into them; the second of these paintings especially conveys strong emotion.'

15 Frances Hodgkins to Rachel Hodgkins. In Linda Gill (ed.), *Letters of Frances Hodgkins* (Auckland: Auckland University Press, 1993), Letter 182, 8 November 1908, p. 239.

16 *Otago Daily Times*, 27 October 1908, p. 2 (datelined London 18 September 1908). The Walker Art Gallery, Liverpool, is one of the national galleries administered by the British government. The Walker possesses one of the largest art collections in England, outside of London.

17 *Otago Witness*, 6 January 1909 (datelined 9 October 1908), p. 38.

18 *Otautau Standard* and *Wallace County Chronicle*, 23 February 1909, p. 2 (datelined London 8 January 1909); *Feilding Star*, 23 February 1909, p. 4 (datelined London 15 January 1909); *Wanganui Chronicle*, 26 February 1909, p. 3 (datelined London 15 January 1909).

19 *Otago Daily Times*, 15 May 1909, p. 14 (datelined London 2 April 1909).

20 *Otago Daily Times*, 14 January 1905, p. 10 (datelined London 10 December 1904).

21 A Dutch informant (Jannie Allen) told me that her grandparents had a coffee pot just like the one in the painting.

22 'Australian art: The two salons', *The Argus*, 27 June 1908, p. 6. *Le grandpère d'Étaples* was also mentioned: 'It is the portrait of an old peasant. Its modest size and low brown tones ...'

23 *The Studio*, vol. 46, 1909, p. 231.

24 Stamp imprints on the reverse side read: 'Doré 1909' and 'Société des Artists Français 1914'. This makes the identification conclusive because only *Une madonne moderne* was exhibited at the Paris Salon in 1914. Furthermore, it was exhibited at the Doré in 1909.

25 Roger Collins, in his article 'Grace J. Joel and France', reproduced an early twentieth-century postcard of shrimp gathers at Étaples, making for a picturesque site and a temptation for any artist. The article appeared in *Bulletin of New Zealand Art History*, vol. 21, 2000, pp. 9–25.

26 Quoted in the *Evening Post*, 28 May 1909, p. 9 (datelined London 16 April 1909).

27 Nancy Mowll Mathews, *Mary Cassatt: A life* (New York: Villard Books, 1994), p. 327.

28 Albert Ten Eyck Gardner, 'A century of women', *Metropolitan Museum Bulletin*, December 1948, p. 118, as cited in Mowll Mathews, *Mary Cassatt*, p. 327.

29 Ruth E. Zubans, *E. Phillips Fox: His life and art* (Carlton, VIC: Melbourne University Press, 1995), p. 134.

30 Honoré Daumier's *The Kiss* (c. 1848), Jean François Millet's *First Steps* (1858/59), Edgar Degas' *La Place de la Concorde* (1875) are among a handful of exceptions.

31 Zubans, *E. Phillips Fox*, p. 135.

32 'One could not forgive oneself if one overlooked Miss Joel's "Présage" in the Aquarelle section. It has the same qualities as her large oil, she being equally at home in both mediums.' From *The Argus*, 12 June 1909, p. 4. Joel's 'large oil' being *Veuvage* again confirms its large size.

33 *The Argus*, 12 June 1909, p. 4.

34 Frances Hodgkins writing from Montreuil to Rachel Hodgkins. In Gill, *Letters*, Letter 191, 25 May 1909, p. 250.

35 *Evening Post*, 28 May 1909, p. 9 (datelined 16 April).

36 *Otago Daily Times*, 9 December 1909, p. 4 (datelined London 29 October 1908).

37 In the list of principal works in Dora Meeson Coates's 1937 biography of her husband (*George Coates: His life and art*, London, J.M. Dent & Sons), one work bears the title, 'GRACE (three-quarter

length)', and is listed as being at the Ballarat Art Gallery, Victoria. The portrait is still there, but a photograph of it that the gallery sent to me clearly shows that it is not of Grace Joel.

38 Notes at the Dunedin Public Art Gallery by Peter Entwisle regarding the sitter in Image 6.9 read: 'The subject may be Grace Joel's housekeeper's daughter. This was suggested to me by Mrs Hartley Joel 26/4/86 while she was examining the work. Mrs Joel began making some kind of study of the artist's life – the notes for which still exist. She discovered not only that Grace Joel had a housekeeper at Cheyne Walk, London, but that the housekeeper had a daughter, who posed as a model for the artist on a number of occasions. Mrs Joel seemed to form the opinion that the woman in *Reclining Nude* was the housekeeper's daughter while she was examining the work. Perhaps she has seen other likenesses of the housekeeper's daughter and so formed the opinion that this is the same person.'

39 Kathleen Jones, *Katherine Mansfield: The story-teller* (Auckland: Viking Penguin, 2010), p. 130.

40 Little Lottie was a fictional folktale character who wandered the world in the then recently serialised French novel *Le fantôme de l'opéra*, by Gaston Leroux. She rose again from obscurity in Andrew Lloyd Weber's 1986 musical, *Phantom of the Opera*.

41 Raymond McIntyre, *Raymond McIntyre: A New Zealand painter* (Auckland: Heinemann and Auckland City Art Gallery, 1984) p. 40.

42 Joel, 'Australasian artists in London', 1906, p. 100.

43 *Architectural Review*, vol. LVI, p. 114.

44 McIntyre, *Raymond McIntyre*, p. 97.

45 A letter from Richard Pankhurst (Sylvia's son) to Roger Collins, 30 September 1986, stated that he knew of no connection between Sylvia Pankhurst and Grace Joel. The letter resides in the Hocken Library Collections in Dunedin.

46 'Her life was almost completely bounded by her art and her many friends in the literary and artistic circles of Paris and London – although she did emerge from it to take an interest in the suffragette movement': Gil Docking, *Two Hundred Years of New Zealand Painters* (3rd ed., Auckland, Bateman, 1990), p. 102.

47 This compendium provided up-to-date biographical information on 692 of the women most active in the suffrage movement.

48 An oral communication from a Joel relative is consistent with this view.

49 *Evening Post*, 26 July 1910, p. 3.

50 Dora de Beer diary, London, 7 July 1910, held in the Hocken Library Collections, Dunedin.

51 *Feilding Star*, 28 December 1910, p. 4.

52 Fry could also count himself among the many lovers of Lady Ottoline Morrell, along with Augustus John and Bertrand Russell.

53 Virginia Wolf, *Roger Fry: A biography* (New York: Harcourt Brace & Co., 1940), p. 156.

54 Quoted in Woolf's biography of Roger Fry, p. 153. She also wrote: 'They went from Cézanne to Gauguin, and from Gauguin to van Gogh, they went from Picasso to Signac, and from Derain to Friesz, and they were infuriated. The pictures were a joke, and a joke at their expense.'

55 Woolf, *Roger Fry*, p. 154.

56 Jones, *Katherine Mansfield*, p. 132. The author continued: 'Just as the painter [van Gogh] has distorted perspective and representation to be true to colour and emotion, taking the images towards abstraction, so his technique can be applied to literature.'

57 *Evening Post*, 23 May 1911, p. 3.

58 Ibid.

59 *The Argus*, 17 June 1911, p. 7. The *Evening Post* of 17 May 1911, p. 2, described the work as follows: 'A young girl amid a bower of flowers; the canvas is rather a large one.' Where this painting resides today is uncertain.

60 *Feilding Star*, 17 May 1911, p. 4.

61 Dora de Beer diary, London, 18 June 1911.

62 *Feilding Star*, 22 May 1912, p. 1.

63 *Evening Post*, 11 June 1912, p. 3. Another reference to this painting in *The Argus*, 8 June 1912, p. 7, states: 'Miss Grace Joel's previous successes are confirmed by her canvas, "L'amour Maternel". The silhouette and arrangement catch the eye only to retain it.'

64 *Evening Post*, 10 December 1912 p. 7.

65 *Evening Post*, 26 May 1913, p. 7.

66 *Auckland Star*, 23 August 1913, p. 14.

67 *Evening Post*, 30 July 1927, p. 25.

68 *Evening Post*, 1 July 1914, p. 4.

69 *Ashburton Guardian*, 2 August 1918, p. 2.

70 *Sydney Morning Herald*, 7 July 1914, p. 7.

71 Meeson Coates, *George Coates*, p. 95.

72 Ibid., p. 89.

73 *The Singleton Argus* (NSW), 2 October 1915, p. 5, and other papers.

74 'The war and art', *Evening Post*, 22 June 1915, p. 8.

75 Edith M. Fry, 'Australasian artists in Europe', *The British-Australasian*, September 1921, p. 48.

76 Anne Kirker, *New Zealand Women Artists* (Auckland: Reed Methuen, 1986), p. 33.
77 Peter Entwisle, *William Mathew Hodgkins & His Circle* (Dunedin: Dunedin Public Art Gallery, 1984), p. 123.
78 Also cited later where the full quote is given: *21e année*, no. 17, 15 Septembre 1921, p. 6.
79 *The Argus* (Melbourne), 1 May 1915, p. 7 (datelined London 19 March).
80 If *Divine Love* happens to be the same work as *Sacred Love*, exhibited at the London Salon in 1920 for £150, then this statement is no longer valid. Also showing at the same venue was *Her Babe* for £100. Could this latter be *Son enfant* redux that was variously offered over the years at £84, £100, £150 and £125, but never previously at the London Salon? Although we have no descriptions of *Sacred Love* and *Her Babe*, we could argue that because the portrayal of the mother in Image 6.15 is virtually that of Grace Joel, there would have been a strong personal connection with the painting. It is therefore more likely that Grace would have not offered it for sale; hence another nod towards Image 6.15 being *Divine Love*.
81 *Evening Post*, 26 May 1913, p. 7.
82 *Evening Post*, 17 April 1916, p. 9.
83 *Auckland Star*, 24 May 1916, p. 8. At one time, Max Hayman was the New Zealand manager of the import merchant company, P. Hayman & Co.
84 As quoted in Justin Paton, *How to Look at a Painting* (2nd ed., Wellington: Awa Press, 2008) p. 117.
85 Laura Brandon, *Art and War* (London: I.B. Tauris & Co., 2007), p. 49.
86 Fry, 'Australasian artists in Europe', p. 48.
87 *The Register* (Adelaide), 12 April 1920, p. 9, and *The Daily News* (Perth), 18 June 1920, p. 3, as well as others.
88 The lack of punctuation in the will was and still is the custom.
89 The introduction to the rules of the scholarship reads: 'National Gallery of Victoria: The Grace Joel Scholarship. Whereas Grace Jane Joel bequeathed to the Trustees of the National Gallery, Melbourne, the sum of £500 to found a scholarship for the painting of the nude, to be called "The Grace Joel Scholarship", and the income thereof to be awarded every two years alternately with the travelling scholarship, and desired that the principal qualities of this study of the nude should be artistic feeling and beauty of colour and line, and not technical exactness, the Trustees of the Public Library, Museums and National Gallery of Victoria make the following Rules and Regulations with regard to the said scholarship:–'
90 Herbert Alexander, *John William North, ARA, RWS* (London: The Old Water-Colour Society's Club, vol. 5, 1928), p. 48.
91 *Auckland Star*, 22 November 1916, p. 8.
92 The handwritten card reads, 'Portrait of a musician', with her name printed at the bottom: 'Miss Grace J. Joel'.
93 *21e année*, no. 17, 15 Septembre 1921, p. 6, translated from the French.
94 *Evening Post*, 24 August 1921, p. 8 (datelined 16 June 1921). Jenny was listed in the news report as 'Miss I. Wimperis'.
95 *Auckland Star*, 16 October 1920, p. 20.
96 *Otago Witness*, 17 October 1922, p. 47 (datelined 17 August).
97 Refer to Clausen letter of 14 March 1922 in Appendix B of this book.
98 Refer to Clausen letter of 17 December 1922 in Appendix B.
99 *Evening Post*, 28 July 1923, p. 10 (datelined 8 June).
100 From the obituary in the *Evening Post*, 21 April 1924, p. 9.
101 *NZ Truth*, 25 October 1924, p. 14.
102 Archival information provided by Minal Patel of Golders Green Crematorium. Blanche's address was given as 2 Ormond Terrace [Regents Park], London NW8, fewer than 10 miles from where Grace had been living in Cheyne Walk. The same address for Blanche appeared in Grace Joel's will of 1920.
103 Joel, 'Australasian artists in London', 1906, p. 101.

Bibliography

A.J.R. (ed.), *The Suffrage Annual and Women's Who's Who* (London: Stanley Paul & Co., 1913). [The identity of the editor remains unknown]

Alexander, Herbert. *John William North, ARA, RWS* (London: The Old Water-Colour Society's Club, vol. 5, 1928).

Annual Report from the Council of The Royal Academy to the General Assembly of Academicians for the Year 1904, 1905 (London: William Clowes and Sons Ltd., 1905): www.sculpture.gla.ac.uk/view/reference.php?id=msib4_1261572826

Bashkirtseff, Marie, *The Journal of a Young Artist 1860–1884*, translated by Mary J. Serrano (New York: Cassell, 1889).

Baughen, G.A.K., 'Baeyertz, Charles Nalder', from The Dictionary of New Zealand Biography: www.teara.govt.nz/en/biographies/2b1/baeyertz-charles-nalder

Beauchamp, Annie, *Victorian Voyage: The shipboard diary of Katherine Mansfield's mother, March to May, 1898*, edited by Ian A. Gordon (Auckland: Wilson & Horton, 2000).

Brandon, Laura, *Art and War* (London and New York: I.B. Tauris, 2007).

Brown, Gordon H., and Hamish, Keith, *An Introduction to New Zealand Painting, 1839–1980* (Auckland: David Bateman and William Collins, 2nd ed., 1982).

Chesterman, Sandra, *Figure Work: The nude and life modelling in New Zealand art* (Dunedin: University of Otago Press, 2002).

Coates, Dora Meeson, *George Coates: His art and his life* (London: J.M. Dent & Sons, 1937).

Collins, Roger, 'Dunedin in the eighteen-nineties', *Art New Zealand*, vol. 2, October/November, 1976, 28–32.

Collins, Roger, 'Grace J. Joel and Australia', *Bulletin of New Zealand Art History*, vol. 14, 1993, 29–40.

Collins, Roger, 'Grace J. Joel and France', *Bulletin of New Zealand Art History*, vol. 21, 2000, 9–25.

Dickinson, Frank, *Grace Joel, Paintings and Drawings* (Dunedin: Dunedin Public Art Gallery, 1980). Also *Addenda & Errata* by the same author.

Docking, Gil, *Two Hundred Years of New Zealand Painting, with Additions by Michael Dunn Covering 1970–90* (Auckland: David Bateman, 3rd ed., 1990).

Drayton, Joanne, 'The haunting: Frances Hodgkins & Jenny Wimperis', *Art New Zealand*, vol. 110, Autumn, 2004, 78–81.

Drayton, Joanne, *Frances Hodgkins: A private viewing* (Auckland: Random House, 2005).

Dunn, Michael, *Nerli: An Italian painter in the South Pacific* (Auckland: Auckland University Press, 2005).

Entwisle, Peter, *Interview with Irene Searle, Dunedin Public Art Gallery, 22 December, 1998* (Dunedin: Dunedin Public Art Gallery, 1998).

Entwisle, Peter, *William Mathew Hodgkins & His Circle* (Dunedin: Dunedin Public Art Gallery, 1984).

Exhibition Commissioners, *New Zealand and South Seas Exhibition, Dunedin, 1889–90* (official catalogue of the exhibits; Dunedin: Evening Star Jobbing Printing Works and G.R. Smith, Otago Daily Times Office, 1889).

Fergusson, Kirsten, 'Grace Joel (1865–1924): A reassessment', *Art New Zealand*, vol. 70, Autumn 1994, 86–89.

Fergusson, Kirsten, 'Grace Joel: Portraits and figure studies', Master's thesis, University of Canterbury, Christchurch, New Zealand, 1993.

Fox, Len, *E. Phillips Fox: Some recollections and reminiscences* (Potts Point, NSW: Author, 1969).

Fox, Len, *E. Phillips Fox and his Family* (Sydney, NSW: Author, 1985).

Fry, Edith, M., 'Australasian artists in Europe', *The British-Australasian*, September 1921, 46–48.
Galbally, Ann, *Charles Conder: The last Bohemian* (Carlton, VIC: Melbourne University Press, 2002).
Gill, Linda (ed.), *Letters of Frances Hodgkins* (Auckland: Auckland University Press, 1993).
Hammond, Victoria, and Peers, Juliet, *Completing the Picture: Women artists and the Heidelberg era* (Hawthorn East, VIC: Artmoves, 1992).
Hearnshaw, Victoria, *James McLauchlan Nairn: A catalogue of works* (Dunedin: Hocken Library, 1997).
Holland, Clive, 'Student life in the Quartier Latin, Paris', *The Studio*, vol. 27, no. 115, 1902, 33–40.
Jebb, Reginald, and Jebb, Eleanor, *Testimony to Hilaire Belloc* (London: Methuen, 1956).
Joel, Grace, 'Australasian Artists in London: A reminiscence', *Art and Architecture*, vol. 3, no. 3, 1906, 99–103.
Johnson, Jane, and Greutzner, A., *The Dictionary of British Artists 1880–1940* (Clopton, UK: Antique Collectors' Club, 1976).
Jones, Kathleen, *Katherine Mansfield : The story-teller* (Auckland: Viking and Penguin, 2010).
Kirker, Anne, *New Zealand Women Artists* (Auckland: Reed Methuen, 1986).
Macnaughtan, Jacqueline, *From Life: Works by early generations of students at the National Gallery Art School* (North Melbourne, VIC: Victoria College of the Arts, 2004).
Marshall, Owen, *The Larnachs* (Auckland: Random House, 2011).
Mathews, Nancy Mowll, *Mary Cassatt: A life* (New York: Villard Books, 1994).
McCahon, Colin, *Six New Zealand Expatriates: Grace Joel, Rhona Haszard, Frances Hodgkins, Francis McCracken, Raymond McIntyre, Owen Merton* (Auckland: Auckland City Art Gallery and Pelorus Press, 1962).
McCormick, Eric H., *The Expatriate: A study of Frances Hodgkins* (Wellington: New Zealand University Press, 1954).
McIntyre, Raymond, *Raymond McIntyre: A New Zealand painter* (Auckland: Heinemann and Auckland City Art Gallery, 1984).
Milner, John, *The Studios of Paris: The capital of art in the late nineteenth century*, (New Haven, CT: Yale University Press, 1989).
Moore, William, *The Story of Australian Art* (Sydney, NSW: Angus & Robertson, vol. 1, 1934).
Official Record of the Otago Jubilee Industrial Exhibition Held in Dunedin, New Zealand, from March 22nd to June 4th, 1898, to Celebrate the Completion of the First Fifty Years of the Province of Otago (Dunedin: Mills, Dick and Co., 1898).
O'Keeffe, A.H., 'Art in retrospect, early Dunedin days: Paint and personality' (first printed in *Otago Daily Times*, 23 February 1935, p. 5), *Art in New Zealand*, vol. 12, no. 3, 1940.
Paton, Justin, *How to Look at a Painting* (Wellington: Awa Press, 2nd ed., 2008).
Pearce, Georgia, 'Miss Grace Joel and her pictures', *The Woman Worker*, 10 March 1909, 229.
Pitts, Pricilla, 'Evelyn Page: Reflecting the human presence', *Art New Zealand*, vol. 26, Autumn 1983, 22–27.
Platts, Una, *Nineteenth Century New Zealand Artists: A guide & handbook* (Christchurch: Avon Fine Prints, 1980).
Scott, Myra, *How Australia Led the Way: Dora Meeson Coates and British suffrage* (Canberra, ACT: Commonwealth Office of the Status of Women, 2003).
Sealy, H.P., 'L'Académie Julian in Paris', *The New Zealand Illustrated Magazine*, vol. 5, no. 1, 1 October 1901, 17–22.
Souter, D.H., 'Grace Joel, painter: Some notes on her work', *Art and Architecture: The Journal of the Institute of Architects of New South Wales*, vol. 3, no. 2, March–April, 1906, 54–55 & 57–59.
Speaight, Robert, *The Life of Hilaire Belloc* (London: Farrar, Straus & Cudahy, 1957).
Twain, Mark, *Following the Equator: A journey around the world* (Hartford, CN: American Publishing Company, 1897).
Vogel, Julius, *Anno Domini 2000 or Woman's Destiny* (London: Hutchinson & Co., 1889; reissued by the University of Hawaii Press, Honolulu, 2002).
Vries, Susanna de, *Ethel Carrick Fox: Travels and triumphs of a post-impressionist* (Brisbane, QLD: Pandanus Press, 1997).
Weisberg, Gabriel P., and Becker, Jane R. (eds.), *Overcoming all Obstacles: The women of the Académie Julian* (New York and New Brunswick, NJ: Dahesh Museum and Rutgers University Press, 1999).
Woods, Joanna, *Facing the Music: Charles Baeyertz and the Triad*, (Dunedin: Otago University Press, 2008).
Woolf, Virginia, *Roger Fry: A biography* (New York: Harcourt Brace & Co., 1940).
Zipes, Jack, *The Oxford Companion to Fairy Tales* (Oxford: Oxford University Press, 2005).
Zola, Émile, 'A New Manner in Painting: Édouard Manet', *Revue du XX siècle*, January 1867, p. 91.
Zubans, Ruth, *E. Phillips Fox: His life and art* (Carlton, VIC: Melbourne University Press, 1995).

Acknowledgements

There are a great many people who gave all manner of assistance in order to make this book possible. First and foremost is my wife Christine who graciously allowed me to live day and night with another woman for the past few years. She also contributed many useful suggestions and rendered many appreciated judgments. Secondly, the comprehensive notes on Grace Joel from Dunedin art historian, Roger Collins, have been absolutely invaluable, and form the basis for much of what has been written here. I owe Roger the deepest sense of gratitude for these notes and his many useful insights. Another Dunedin art scholar I am indebted to is Peter Entwisle, whose monograph on William Mathew Hodgkins proved not only an indispensable source of information on the artistic landscape of nineteenth-century Dunedin, but also provided an exemplary standard of prose. We had many fruitful discussions, and it was Peter who put me onto the naval expert Ian Church with whom it was possible to untangle the convoluted travels pertaining to Grace Joel's paintings of Venice. Another art historian, Gabriel P. Weisberg, provided the critical documentary evidence of the enrolment of Grace Joel at the Académie Julian. As well, G.P. Nerli's biographer, Michael Dunn, gave me further insights into the individual who played such a singular role in Grace Joel's life.

Numerous people associated with various galleries and museums provided many of the images as well as technical information. In no particular order I wish to thank Lindsay Hazley of the Southland Museum & Art Gallery, Helene Phillips of Ferner Galleries, Jonathan Gooderham of Jonathan Grant Galleries & ARTIS Gallery, Richard Thomson of the International Art Centre, John Gow of Gow Langsford Gallery, Doreen Whiston (who miraculously located the 1998 Entwisle interview with Irene Ross) and Genevieve Webb of the Dunedin Public Art Gallery, Lydia Baxendell and Erin Kimber of the University of Canterbury, William McAloon and Rebecca Loud of the Museum of New Zealand Te Papa Tongarewa, Ron Brownson of the Auckland Art Gallery Toi o Tamaki, Christine Palmer of Dunbar Sloane, Catherine Hammond of the E.H. McCormick Research Library, Tim Jones of the Christchurch Art Gallery Te Puna o Waiwhetu, Judy Halswell of the Auckland University Library, Joy Pearson of Olveston, Linda McGregor of the Alexander Turnbull Library, Maggie Skelton of Webbs Auction House, Jill Haley of the Toitū Otago Settlers Museum, as well as Natalie Poland, Anna Petersen, Kate Guthrie and Anne Jackman of The Hocken Collections. Further assistance was provided by Ralph Body who furnished me with a copy of his excellent Master's thesis on A.H. O'Keeffe, Pauline La Rooy of New Zealand

Micrographic Services, South Canterbury expert, Dave Emery, artists Dorothy Norton and Margherita Muller, as well as Dr Paul Hafner, who made useful comments concerning the narrative.

I was indeed fortunate to have also had the assistance of the many members of the Joel whānau (extended family) both in New Zealand and England. In particular, I must single out David Joel, Grace Joel's great nephew, who made unstinting efforts in assisting me through all stages of the book. His daughter Louise Joel was my right-hand woman and helpful in countless ways.

Special thanks go to Minal Patel of Golders Green Crematorium in London for helping resolve another Grace Joel mystery – that of her final resting place.

And to those individuals who supplied various images of Grace Joel paintings or allowed a photographer to come into their home for such a purpose, I am most grateful. Which brings me finally to thank professional photographers Emily Canaan (Dunedin), Delphine Ducaruge (Christchurch), Joe Low (Winchester) and Jocelyn Horsfall (London) for doing the book proud with their superb images.

Finally, I would like to thank Rachel Scott, the publisher of Otago University Press, for her unwavering support in bringing this project to fruition; my editor, Paula Wagemaker, whose formidable editing skills substantially improved every aspect of the manuscript; and Imogen Coxhead for her sharp-eyed proofreading.

Index

Page numbers in **bold** refer to illustrations.